EIGHTH EDITION

Human Resources Administration in Education

A Management Approach

Ronald W. Rebore
Saint Louis University

PEARSON

Boston • New York • San Francisco
Mexico City • Montreal • Toronto • London • Madrid • Munich • Paris
Hong Kong • Singapore • Tokyo • Cape Town • Sydney

Senior Editor: Arnis E. Burvikovs
Editorial Assistant: Erin Reilly
Marketing Manager: Tara Kelly
Editorial Production Service: Omegatype Typography, Inc.
Composition Buyer: Linda Cox
Manufacturing Buyer: Linda Morris
Electronic Composition: Omegatype Typography, Inc.
Cover Administrator: Kristina Mose-Libon

For related titles and support materials, visit our online catalog at www.ablongman.com.

Between the time website information is gathered and then published, it is not unusual for some sites to have closed. Also, the transcription of URLs can result in typographical errors. The publisher would appreciate notification where these errors occur so that they may be corrected in subsequent editions.

Library of Congress Cataloging-in-Publication Data

Rebore, Ronald W.
    Human resources administration in education : A management approach / Ronald W. Rebore. — 8th ed.
        p.   cm.
    Includes bibliographical references and index.
    ISBN 0-205-48507-3 (casebound)
    1. School personnel management—United States.   I. Title.

LB2831.58.R43 2007
371.2'010973—dc22

                                                                2005058608

Printed in the United States of America

10   9   8   7   6   5   4   3   2   RRD-VA   11   10   09   08   07   06

As a service-rendering institution, the school will be successful in direct proportion to the quality of its employees.

To Sandy, Ron, and Lisa

Contents

3 *Recruitment*   **98**

4 *Selection*   **123**

10 *Legal, Ethical, and Policy Issues in the Administration of Human Resources*   **331**

Preface

The evolving culture of our contemporary society continues to have an ongoing and profound effect on the practice of school human resources management. Several aspects of this effect are reflected in this eighth edition of *Human Resources Administration in Education*: *A Management Approach*.

A significant example of this evolving culture is set forth in the section on the use of technology in human resources administration. This type of management strategy has enriched private business and industry for a number of years. The tenets of this strategy are now appearing in school district administration offices and, in this book, are explicated in relation to the human resources management function.

Legislation continues to have an impact on human resources management. The U.S. Congress enacted the Americans with Disabilities Act of 1990, which is the most comprehensive legislation ever passed protecting the rights of individuals with disabilities. Furthermore, the Civil Rights Act of 1991 has the potential of costing violators punitive damages through the decisions of jury trials. In 1993, Congress also passed the Family and Medical Leave Act, which gives eligible employees the right to leave employment under certain circumstances. Testing for alcohol and controlled substances is now mandated for particular occupations, such as school bus drivers, by the Omnibus Transportation Employee Testing Act of 1991. The Health Insurance Portability and Accountability Act of 1996 assured employees that they, their spouses, and their dependents, cannot be denied health insurance coverage because of an illness. In 2002, the No Child Left Behind Act ushered in the most extensive changes in federal law concerning public school education in forty years.

Beginning in 2001, military reserves and National Guard units have been mobilized into active duty as a consequence of the September 11th terrorist attacks on the United States and the wars in Afghanistan and Iraq. This has prompted most school human resources managers to investigate the responsibilities that school districts have toward those employees called up for duty in the armed services.

Sexual harassment in the workplace has gained the attention of school district personnel across the nation as the media have presented coverage of the consequences of this inappropriate and illegal behavior. The issues of human immunodeficiency virus (HIV), acquired immune deficiency syndrome (AIDS), and AIDS-related complex (ARC) challenge the ability of school human resources administrators to meet the humane needs and legal requirements of those staff members so infected while addressing the concerns of coworkers, parents, and the public at large.

The phenomenon of collaborative bargaining as an alternative to the traditional model of negotiations has also become more prevalent in school districts.

Health risks in the workplace, an issue that is related to the ever-increasing cost of workers' compensation, are seriously affecting school district budgets. Likewise, the costs of fringe benefits continue to rise, prompting managed health care as an alternative to traditional medical and hospital insurance programs.

The ethical responsibilities of human resources administrators has become a national concern over the honesty of employees in all levels of business, government, religion, and public education.

The underlying root cause of the "reform" movement is the level of accountability or lack thereof in public schools. Taxpayers in general and parents in particular believe that they are not receiving their proper entitlement. A large number of tax levy elections continue to fail because of this perception. The problem of accountability is a "people" problem and, thus, is a human resources administration problem.

It is evident that school district administration parallels that of corporations and other organizations in U.S. society. Fiscal management, curriculum development, physical plant management, employee supervision, and human resources administration have become specialties that require educationally sophisticated administrators.

The eighth edition of *Human Resources Administration in Education: A Management Approach* continues to set forth information relative to human resources administration that has surfaced since the publication of the seventh edition.

Among other updated material, the eighth edition contains information on how the following influence human resources administration: predicting enrollment increases; the No Child Left Behind Act; organizational change; professional learning communities; the Interstate New Teacher Assessment and Support Consortium (INTASC) standards; and transcendental leadership theory.

Also new with this eighth edition are PowerPoint presentations for each chapter and a test bank of questions. These are available to adopters online by contacting your local Allyn and Bacon representative.

Human Resources Administration in Education should be of interest to three categories of individuals: first, professors of educational administration who have the instructional responsibility of teaching courses in school human resources administration; second, practicing central-office administrators and building principals who want to become more familiar with the field of human resources management; and last, school board members and superintendents who may be searching for a model in order to establish a central-office, human resources administrative position.

Chapter 1 establishes the rationale and organizational structure that support effective human resource administration. Chapters 2 through 5 are concerned with the acquisition of personnel, and Chapters 6 through 9 deal with personnel retention. Each of these chapters addresses a major dimension of the entire human resources management function and identifies the processes, procedures, and techniques necessary to carry out these dimensions. This orientation to human resources administration is the reason for the subtitle of the book, *A Management Approach.* Finally, Chapter 10 considers the legal, ethical, and policy implications of human resources administration.

At this point, I would like to sincerely thank my colleagues teaching at universities and their students who reviewed *Human Resources Administration in Education* and made valuable suggestions for its improvement. I continue to incorporate as many of their suggestions as possible. I particularly want to thank the reviewers of this edition: Max Skidmore, University of Georgia, and Travis W. Twiford, Virginia Tech.

Finally, I am most grateful to my research assistant, Susan Jacobsmeyer, who provided me with invaluable help in the preparation of the eighth edition.

R. W. R.

Organizational Dimensions

The Structural Framework of Public Education

The system of free and universal elementary and secondary education in the United States is one of our nation's unique and distinguishing characteristics. It is generally considered to be our greatest safeguard of freedom and the best guarantee for the economic and social welfare of our citizens.

The school as an institution receives its mandate from the society it serves. It is, however, only one of many institutions. The government, family, and church also play a role in our society, and these institutions have complementary purposes. Each provides for the advancement of society in general and the individual citizen in particular. The educational programs of the school would be ineffective without the support of government, the family, and the church. A hallmark, however, of modern-day society and these institutions is change. This was dramatically pointed out by the National School Public Relations Association over 20 years ago and is still relevant today.

Calculators, cable television, microcomputers, video discs, satellites, teleconferencing—the list of new technologies arriving on the scene almost daily is growing and becoming more important to our lives. Only a decade ago, the idea of computers being as common in the home as the television was looked upon as an idea as far-fetched as man walking on the moon was in the middle of this century.

No one will deny that the . . . (present) is the age of technology, an age as dramatic as the industrial revolution in its capacity to change the way we live. Students today will have their future, and much of their present, dominated by electronic wizardry. And unless they have an understanding of and the ability to use the new technology, they will be as illiterate as persons who cannot read or write.[1]

---

[1]National School Public Relations Association, "New Challenge for Schools: Age of Information," *Education USA,* 24, no. 19 (January 4, 1982), 141.

This statement focuses on communicative and technological advancement, but in the complexity of any given society, infinite streams of change occur simultaneously. The family, church, school, and government, with all their subcomponents are not static institutions but rather evolving entities.

Change is not only continual but also accelerative, and is further complicated by the fact that it occurs unevenly. Technology may be currently undergoing mutations faster than educational programs can make this new knowledge available, which in turn leaves students years behind in learning about new advances.

Our perception of reality and how this relates to societal and individual needs determines the content of our educational programs. Although fundamental principles, such as individual freedom, individual responsibility, and democratic government, must be continuously taught in our schools, the accelerating rate of change in areas such as technology demands that our schools be flexible enough to adjust to new developments and conditions. Education cannot be static in the dynamic milieu of reality.

Responsibilities of Federal and State Governments

Carrying out the goals of American education is the responsibility of the individual states. The U.S. Constitution is conspicuous in its omission of any provision or specific reference to education. The Tenth Amendment to the Constitution, ratified in 1791, states that "the powers not delegated to the United States by the Constitution, nor prohibited by it to the States, are reserved to the States respectively, or to the people." Thus, education has consistently been considered a state function.

Experience shows, however, that the federal government has been involved; in fact, its involvement has been extensive. Through the legislative branch, Congress provides funds that support special services and programs in local school districts. Through the U.S. Office of Education, the executive branch of the government exercises authority over educational matters. The creation of a cabinet-level Department of Education exemplifies the extent of this involvement. The many Supreme Court decisions affecting education testify to the influence of the judicial branch of the federal government on our schools.

In an ever-shrinking world and nation, the goals of U.S. education cannot be left solely to the discretion of the states. The involvement of the federal government, however, should not supplant the jurisdiction of state governments but rather should complement and enrich their efforts.

The authority of the states to create and govern public schools is embodied in the state constitutions and exercised through the state legislatures. All state legislatures have delegated certain aspects of this authority to local units, boards of education. To ensure some control over local units, state legislatures have established minimum educational program requirements and teacher certification requirements and have provided state funds to help finance education.

The administrative arm of most state legislatures is a *State Department of Education,* which is usually governed by a board and administered by a commissioner or state superintendent. Figure 1.1 gives a visualization of the relationship between the state and the local boards of education.

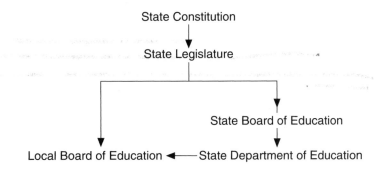

FIGURE 1.1   Jurisdictional Flow Chart

The National Council of Chief State School Officers has properly emphasized the state's educational responsibility and the state's relationship to local and federal agencies. The following quotation from the Council has historical significance because it has been invoked many times to explain the responsibility of the state.

> Our system of constitutional government makes the states responsible for the organization and administration of public education and for general supervision of nonpublic schools. Each state has in practice delegated authority to organize and operate schools to various types of local administrative units of its own creation (Boards of Education). Within its general unity, our system of education leaves room for diversified programs among states and local administrative units.
>
> Local, state and federal governments all have a vital interest in education. Each can contribute most effectively only if there is appropriate allocation of responsibility among them and only if relations among them are properly defined. Initiative and responsibility must be encouraged in the local units which operate most of the schools. The states must insure organization, financial support and effective administration of education programs of suitable quality and make certain these programs are available to every child. The federal government has an obligation to provide supplementary assistance to the states in accord with the national interest in universal education.
>
> Local school boards and other state education authorities represent the public in the administration of education. Working with their professional staffs, these authorities are responsible for carefully planned programs of education and for obtaining the participation of the people in planning the kinds of schools and education they need and want.[2]

---

[2]The National Council of Chief State School Officers, *Our System of Education* (Washington, DC: The National Council of Chief State School Officers, 1950), 5–6.

No Child Left Behind and School Reform

President Bush signed into law the *No Child Left Behind Act* (NCLB) in January 2002; this new law reauthorized the Elementary and Secondary Education Act (ESEA). NCLB ushered in the most extensive changes in federal law concerning public school education in forty years. It is the first time that federal legislation has mandated student success; all other federal legislation mandated opportunity rather than success.

The law requires all children to be proficient in reading and mathematics by 2014. Other provisions of the law mandate improved communications with parents and improved safety at school for children. While NCLB has certain provisions that apply only to Title I schools, the law clearly requires all states to develop a single system of accountability so there will be uniform standards for all children. Further, schools are required to make adequate yearly progress (AYP) toward the 2014 goal. Thus, each state must develop student testing programs that demonstrate satisfactory student improvement each year. States are also required to pay particular attention to the progress of children from minority groups, such as African Americans, Asians, and Hispanics. Children with disabilities is another identifiable group whose progress must be monitored for AYP.

The consequences of not achieving AYP vary from being designated as a school *needing improvement* to, after five years of not achieving AYP, severe repercussions, such as having school personnel replaced or having the school year extended. Further, if a student is a victim of a violent crime, that student must be allowed to transfer to another school in the district. Of course, problems with this provision arise if there is only one school in the district or if other schools are far from the student's home school.[3]

For human resources administration, the implications of these provisions require serious attention. First, the requirement to hire *highly qualified* teachers who are capable of helping students meet the proficiency requirement places a significant responsibility on all administrators, faculty, and staff members involved in the human resources function.[4] Chapter 2 of this text, "Human Resources Planning," sets forth a planning process that places a high priority on identifying the present and future goals of a school district as they relate to the current and future qualifications needed in employees. Chapter 3, "Recruitment," explains the methods that can be used to locate and attract the best possible candidates for administrative, faculty, and support positions in a school district. Chapter 4, "Selection," outlines the steps that can be used to hire the most qualified applicants.

The provision that students must demonstrate AYP has serious implications for teacher performance evaluation and staff development. Chapter 7, "Performance Evaluation," explains best practice in the evaluation of all school district employees: administrators, teachers, and support personnel. Chapter 6, "Staff Development," sets forth a critical dimension of the human resources function because a continual upgrade of knowledge and skills is required to meet the ever-changing needs of students. Further, research is constantly improving our subject matter knowledge base and pedagogical methodologies.

---

[3]Missouri Department of Elementary and Secondary Education, *Questions & Answers about No Child Left Behind—And What It Means for Missouri* (August 2003).

[4]The School Superintendent's Insider, *How Key Provisions of New Education Law May Affect Your District* (April 2002), 1–3.

Finally, the consequences for noncompliance with AYP for five years might result in the replacement of administrators, teachers, or staff members. Chapter 7, "Performance Evaluation," also contains an extended section on how to ensure due process for those administrators, teachers, and staff members who are not meeting expectations, which could lead to termination of employment.

Highlighting these particular chapters is meant to focus attention to specific processes and procedures. However, the human resources function, as laid out in this book, is a seamless function with various dimensions. It would be a mistake to think that the various provisions of NCLB only affect certain aspects of the human resources function; rather, the law affects all the interrelated dimensions of human resources administration.

NCLB is a particular manifestation of *school reform*. The reform movement is always present in education, because change and improvement are embedded in the education profession. The development of each child's potential to his or her maximum capacity is the goal of education. The culture of society is the milieu within which administrators, teachers, and staff members must carry out their responsibilities. Thus, school reform will occupy the attention of all administrators and particularly human resources administrators because people are the initiators and those who must implement all reforms.

There are certain directions that are prevalent in the present reform movements. Perhaps the most evident is the *learning community* approach that views learning as the major focus of all endeavors. Not only students but also educators are encouraged to learn from each other. This situates schools and school districts in such a manner that the organization itself, as a system and in a corporate sense, begins to learn. Thus, schools and school districts become *reframed*.

All reform begins with a vision that is formalized in individual schools through the leadership of the principal and the teachers. Evidence-based decisions must be made by the leadership team, principal and teachers, to formulate objectives and strategies to improve student performance. Today, this assessment and the formulation of objectives and strategies can be significantly enhanced through technology.

Thus, formulas for successful reform have some common elements, including

- A vision that utilizes a learning community approach and leads to organizational reform[5]
- The establishment, in each school, of a leadership team that includes teachers in consort with principals[6]
- Importance placed on making decisions based on evidence
- The beneficial utilization of technology in management and instructional strategies

All of these factors clearly recognize the importance of establishing a human resources function that will be capable of planning, recruiting, and retaining the best educators possible; all reform is dependent on the quality of the people hired to carry it out.

---

[5]David J. Ferrero, "Pathways to Reform: Start with Values," *Educational Leadership,* 62, no. 5 (February 2005), 8, 10.

[6]Barnett Berry, Dylan Johnson, and Diana Montgomery, "The Power of Teacher Leadership," *Educational Leadership,* 62, no. 5 (February 2005), 56–60.

Responsibilities of the Board of Education

School districts are perhaps the most democratically controlled of any agency of government. The citizens of a local community elect school board members, who are charged with formulating policies for the governance and administration of the schools. State departments of education exercise some regulatory authority, assuring that a minimum educational program is provided in every school district, but the citizens of the local district maintain control of the schools through locally elected boards.

As the duties and responsibilities of school boards are considered, it is essential to keep in mind that education is a state function. The courts have consistently upheld this principle. By virtue of the authority delegated to school boards from each state legislature, boards represent the state, even though the members are locally elected. Board members, as individuals, exercise no authority outside a legally constituted meeting. Policies can be agreed upon only in an official meeting, and individual members cannot commit the board to any definite action except as authorized by the board at a legal meeting.

In exercising their authority to govern schools, boards of education should carefully formulate and adopt policy statements. This very difficult task cannot be successfully accomplished without guidance from the professional educational staff and, at times, an attorney. Board policies must not conflict with the U.S. Constitution, federal law, and federal court decisions. In like manner, policies must not conflict with the appropriate state constitution, state statutes, or state court decisions. Regulations issued by a state department of education should be considered by a board in creating policies but may be ignored. However, penalties, such as loss of state aid, make it impractical for a school board to create policies in conflict with such regulations. Local traditions, opinions, and goals also should be taken into consideration because policies objectionable to the local community will weaken citizen support. There are many more influences in our contemporary society that affect board decisions today than there were even five years ago. Figure 1.2 illustrates some of these influences on policy formulation.

Some advantages for developing policies have been outlined in *The School and Community Relations* and may serve as a rationale for school boards.

- Policy facilitates the orientation of new board members regarding relations between the school and the community.

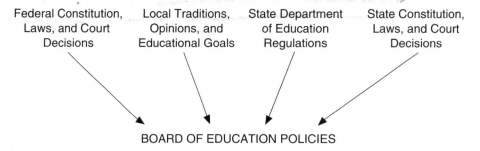

Federal Constitution,   Local Traditions,   State Department   State Constitution,
Laws, and Court   Opinions, and   of Education   Laws, and Court
Decisions   Educational Goals   Regulations   Decisions

BOARD OF EDUCATION POLICIES

FIGURE 1.2   Influences on Policy Making

- Policy facilitates a similar orientation for new employees—both professional and nonprofessional—in the school system.
- Policy acquaints the public with the position of the school and encourages citizen involvement in educational affairs.
- Policy provides a reasonable guarantee that there will be consistency and continuity in the decisions that are made under it.
- Policy informs superintendents what they may expect from the board and what the board may expect from them.
- Policy creates the need for developing a detailed program in order to implement it.
- Policy provides a legal reason for the allocation of funds and facilities in order to make the policy work.
- Policy establishes an essential division between policy making and policy administration.[7]

School board policies should not be confused with administrative rules and regulations, which constitute the detailed manner by which policies are implemented. Rules and regulations delineate who does what, when, and where. In fact, many rules and regulations may be required to implement one policy.

A properly conceived and phrased board of education policy has the following characteristics:

- It is stated in broad, general terms, but in terms that are clear enough to allow for executive direction and interpretation.
- It reveals the philosophy of the board of education as members understand the desires of the community.
- It provides purpose and rationale for the subject about which a policy is being made.
- It suggests how the matter is to be carried out.
- It is never executive in substance or tone.
- It covers situations that are likely to occur repeatedly.
- It is always subject to review by the board, with the objective of improvement in accordance with changing conditions.

Likewise, the policy should

- Provide support and authority for all school programs and activities
- Be brief, clear, concise, and complete
- Be stable, even during personnel changes
- Have adequate provisions for review and amendment[8]

After the board of education establishes its policies, the superintendent of schools and his or her staff are responsible for establishing administrative processes and procedures that

---

[7]Donald R. Gallagher, Don Bagin, Leslie W. Kindred, *The School and Community Relations,* 6th ed. (Boston: Allyn & Bacon, 1997), 37.

[8]Missouri School Board Association, *A Manual for Missouri School Board Members* (Columbia, MO: The Association, 1981), H–3.

implement the board policies. These policies are usually also incorporated into a manual that can be easily consulted by administrators, teachers, and citizens.

There are four popular formats used in writing policies. The most common format is the resolution style, on which the school board votes to take action. Equal Employment Opportunity and Affirmative Action policies are usually adopted in this resolution style. A second format sets forth the rationale for the policy and establishes broad goals. The third style incorporates an identification of who is responsible for implementing the policy. This is a common practice in formulating policies that address a specific function, such as collective bargaining. For example, the policy might identify the Director of Employee Relations as the chief negotiator for the school board and establish the confines within which he or she will function. A fourth format is used when the school board wishes to eliminate possible misunderstanding about how the policy is to be implemented. This type of style, therefore, incorporates administrative rules and regulations.

The Administrative Process

Theoretical Considerations

Administration is an indispensable component of all institutions in organized society; yet, it is often taken for granted. The need for administration has been evident whenever there was a task to be performed by two or more people. Many ancient records of significant events describe administrative activities. Building the pyramids, supervising medieval feudal domains, governing colonies in distant hemispheres—all have demanded a degree of administrative skill and understanding of the administrative process.

Our understanding of the nature of administration has evolved. The earliest concepts centered around the action model. Administrators were those who took charge of an activity and accomplished a task. The formal study of administration is a recent phenomenon that has found its most fertile climate in the business world, where much study is devoted to the effective execution of managerial leadership.

The need for the formal study of administration in public education grew out of the increased complexity of urban school districts. The illusion that anyone with a good general education could become an effective administrator was quickly shattered during the urbanization period.

Administration is the social process of managing human, financial, and material resources toward the fulfillment of a mission. The school administrator fulfills these requisites by developing and establishing administrative processes, procedures, and techniques that harness human, financial, and material energies. The importance of administrative leadership stems from its potential for converting these energies within an organization into the fulfillment of educational objectives.

This definition of administration views it as an executive activity, distinct from policy making. Administration is primarily concerned with the implementation, not the making, of policy. More specifically, the administration of a district is responsible for carrying out the policies of the board of education.

The systems approach to administration has gained steadily in popularity ever since President Johnson mandated its implementation in federal agencies, and the outcry for accountability in the public sector advanced its use. In the systems approach, the school is viewed as a network of interrelated subsystems. Emphasis is given to formulating short- and long-range objectives that can be translated into operational activities, which are implemented and evaluated.

The approach followed in this book focuses on the human resources function as a function. Thus, administration is viewed as an all-encompassing process composed of various functions. Three of the most critical functions in a school system are human resources administration, instructional programs administration, and support services administration. Support services here include transportation, food service, and financial administration. Each of these functions has goals that are implemented through administrative processes, procedures, and techniques—which are collectively referred to as *management*. This book, of course, centers on the human resources function and its management.

Functions are carried out by administrators within a given organizational framework. The remaining portion of this section delineates and clarifies the role of the superintendent of schools and major central office administrators.

The Organization of the Central Office

Historically and, in most states, by statutory mandate, school boards have delegated the responsibility for implementing policies to a chief executive officer, the superintendent of schools. The superintendent assumes full control of all operations. As school districts grow in size and complexity, it becomes necessary to develop specialized functions, and the central-office staff comes into being. However, all employees, professional and other, ultimately report to the superintendent and are subordinate to him or her. The superintendent is the only employee who deals with the board of education on a regular and direct basis.

The superintendent's role can be described in terms of the three major roles incorporated into this one position.

Chief Advisor

The superintendent is the main consultant and advisor to the school board on all matters concerning the school district. The superintendent is expected to contribute to the board's deliberations by furnishing reports, information, and recommendations, both upon request of the board and upon self-directed initiative. A list of the superintendent's duties and functions as the board's chief advisor includes the following:

1. Formulate and recommend human resources policies necessary for the efficient functioning of the school staff.
2. Provide information to the school board on vital matters pertaining to the school system.
3. Prepare and submit to the board a preliminary budget.

4. Recommend all candidates for employment. (The board may reject specific candidates recommended, but all personnel should be employed only on the superintendent's recommendation.)
5. Submit an annual report to the board on the operations of the school system.

Executive Officer

Once a policy decision has been established by the board of education, it becomes the responsibility of the executive officer of the board and the district's staff to execute that decision. The administration should implement board policies via rules and regulations. As the chief executive officer of the district, the superintendent sets the tone for the entire system. In performing this function, the duties and responsibilities of the superintendent are to

1. Carry out policies and regulations established by the board. (In matters not specifically covered by board policies, the superintendent should take appropriate action and report the action to the board no later than the next meeting.)
2. Prepare regulations and instruct school employees as may be necessary to make effective the policies of the board.
3. Direct all purchases and expenditures in accordance with the policies of the board.
4. Formulate and administer a program of supervision for the schools.
5. Develop a program of maintenance and improvement or expansion of buildings and site.

Educational Leader

The superintendent's educational leadership role should be exercised not only with other professional educators within the district but also with regional, state, and national professional educators, organizations, and agencies. As the educational leader within the community, the superintendent will be called upon to keep the public informed as to the activities, achievements, needs, and directions of the school system. The superintendent should also keep the members of the board informed of new trends in education and their implications for the local district. A leadership role must also be assumed among the staff members of the school district. Without the support and understanding of the employees, the goals and objectives set by the district cannot be achieved.[9]

An ongoing trend in school administration, particularly in the superintendency, is the administrative team approach to central office and building level management. In most districts, the administrative team is a cluster of similarly educated administrators who amplify the efforts of the superintendent.[10] Each administrator usually has the title of deputy, as-

[9]Iowa Association of School Boards, *The Iowa School Board Member: A Guide to Better Boardmanship* (Des Moines, IA, 1980), 37–40.

[10]See the American Association of School Administrators, *Profiles of the Administrative Team* (Arlington, VA: The Association, 1971), 11.

sociate, or assistant superintendent. In most school districts, personnel having the title of director or coordinator are not members of the administrative team, but rather support personnel to the team.

Formal designation of membership on the administrative team is appointment to the superintendent's cabinet, which is a strategy-planning and decision-making body. The heads of human resources administration, instructional programs administration, and support services administration are typically included in the cabinet.

This formal organization of the superintendent's cabinet is not meant to imply that the superintendent should confine the "team" effort only to the highest levels of school-district administration. Rather, the establishment of a cabinet is an attempt to share the strategy-planning process with key administrators. The issues and problems facing school districts are so far-reaching today that the superintendent must have continual and effective counsel in making decisions.

Because there is a need in all school districts to identify various echelons in the administrative organization, it is recommended that the title of director or coordinator be attached to administrative positions reporting to an assistant superintendent in charge of a particular function. Although it is in no way meant to be all-inclusive, Figure 1.3 represents a possible central-office organization that incorporates a line authority from superintendent to assistant superintendents (cabinet positions) to directors and coordinators. The number of central-office administrators listed suggests that this could be the organizational structure for a school district with a student population between fifteen and twenty thousand. Please note that the director of affirmative action and director of community relations report directly to the superintendent, which is a common practice.

Human Resources Administration

The Human Resources Function

In every school district, people must be recruited, selected, placed, evaluated, and compensated, whether by a central human resources office or various administrators within the school district.

The goals of the human resources function are basically the same in all school systems—to hire, retain, develop, and motivate personnel in order to achieve the objectives of the school district, to assist individual members of the staff to reach the highest possible levels of achievement, and to maximize the career development of personnel. These goals must be implemented through the following dimensions of the human resources function:

1. *Human resources planning.* Establishing a master plan of long- and short-range human resources requirements is a necessary ingredient in the school district's curricular and fiscal planning processes.
2. *Recruitment.* Quality personnel, of course, are essential for the delivery of effective educational services to children, youth, and adults.
3. *Selection.* The long- and short-range human resources requirements are implemented through selection techniques and processes.

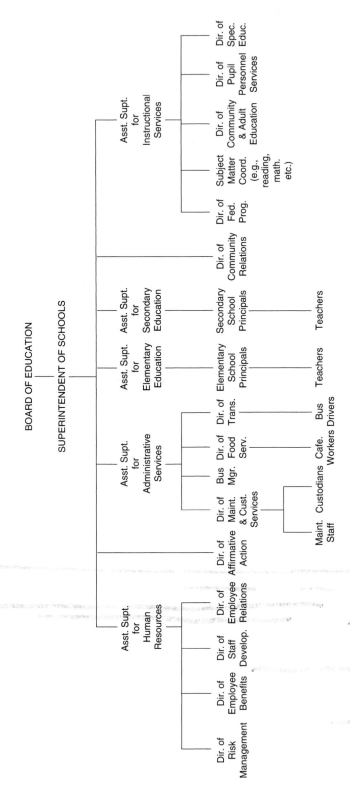

FIGURE 1.3 Possible Central-Office Organization

4. *Placement and induction.* Through appropriate planning, new personnel and the school district accommodate each other's goals.
5. *Staff development.* Development programs help personnel meet school district objectives and also provide individuals with the opportunity for personal and professional growth.
6. *Performance evaluation.* Processes and techniques for evaluation help the individual grow professionally and help the school district attain its objectives.
7. *Compensation.* Establishing programs that compensate quality performance helps to motivate personnel.
8. *Collective negotiations.* The negotiating process gives personnel an opportunity to participate in matters that affect their professional and personal welfare.

Unfortunately, many school districts still see the human resources function only as the hiring of competent teachers. These eight dimensions of the human resources function are not discrete, isolated entities, but rather, integral aspects of the same function. Each of the next eight chapters addresses one of these dimensions. Administrative processes, procedures, and techniques for accomplishing the human resources function are reviewed. Also, major issues that significantly influence the administration of human resources are addressed.

Human Resources Administrators

Many school districts have seen the need in recent times to delegate a major share of the human resources function to a specialized central-office unit. In this type of organization, an *assistant superintendent for human resources* (or *director of human resources*) administers the human resources function and aids the superintendent in solving personnel problems. Human resources administrator is usually a staff position that exists to service line administrators. Line positions include the assistant superintendents for secondary education and elementary education, administrators of certain support services, and building principals. These administrators have been granted authority to make decisions in the supervisory process as it relates to staff, faculty, and students.

The human resources function has an impact on the continual staffing of positions, which in turn directly affects the quality of educational programs, but it also has a significant effect on the budget. Approximately 80 percent of all school district expenditures are for salaries and benefits. Inefficiency in the human resources function can potentially cost the taxpayer unnecessarily large sums of money.

Boards of education and administrators are seldom fully aware of the pervasive effect their personnel decisions have on the planning process. Every position within a school system generates a series of decisions as to the type of work to be performed, the qualities needed for its proper performance, and its economic value. A variety of actions are required for the proper recruiting, selecting, inducting, developing, and evaluating of personnel. Policies and procedures also must be established regarding academic freedom, tenure, health, grievances, leaves of absences, and retirement. In all but the very smallest districts, the movement of personnel into and out of a school district requires the attention of human resources specialists.

The number of strikes by public school teachers has remained relatively constant over the last ten years. Salaries, fringe benefits, and working conditions constitute the major issues that may lead to an impasse at the table and result in a strike. Education, however, is a relative newcomer to the negotiations process.

Collective negotiation is traditionally a human resources function and correctly belongs under the jurisdiction of the assistant superintendent for human resources. Because of the magnitude of the issues involved with this process, most school districts should consider establishing the position of *director of employee relations.* The American Association of School Administrators sponsored the publication of a monograph entitled "Helping Administrators Negotiate," with the prophetic subtitle, "A Profile of the Emerging Management Position of Director of Employee Relations in the Administrative Structure of a School System."

The knowledge explosion and the constantly changing social milieu have also produced a major issue in the area of human resources administration. In the past, staff development was viewed primarily from the in-service training model, which concentrated on providing a few workshops on instructional materials. The last quarter century, however, has ushered in federal legislation and litigation that have more clearly defined the rights of racial minorities, women, students, older workers, and those with diabilities. This, coupled with the deluge of new instructional technologies, the differing attitudes of the new professionals entering teaching, and the changing values of our society as manifested by parents and students, has created a need for an ongoing staff development program for administrators and teachers alike. This function is so specialized that, like collective negotiations, it also requires the attention of a human resources specialist, the *director of staff development.*

The avalanche of federal legislation and litigation concerning human rights has made it necessary to establish a central-office administrative position, usually entitled *director of affirmative action.* Most federal legislation contains an equal opportunity clause, which in turn dictates the organization of a detailed program for carrying out the intent of the law in all phases of the human resources function. This organized program is more commonly called "affirmative action." Chapter 2 presents a complete explanation of all major civil rights legislation and the concept of affirmative action. A unique feature of this administrative position in the organizational structure of a school district is the fact that the director of affirmative action usually reports directly to the superintendent of schools. This provides integrity in the school district's compliance with civil rights legislation because the director is thus protected from the influences of other administrators.

The escalating cost of health care is an issue facing every school district that provides health care and related benefits to employees. Most school districts have undertaken drastic measures in an attempt to control costs, which has led to what is commonly referred to as "managed care." Along with the many innovations underway is the need to hire human resources staff members who not only have experience but also academic credentials in health care management. Further, the rising cost of workers' compensation reinforces the need to hire human resources staff members who also have experience with and understand of the nuances of risk management. Most school districts use the title *director of employee benefits* to designate the staff member who is responsible for managing the employee benefits and workers' compensation programs. The administrator, of course, reports to the assistant superintendent for human resources.

Contemporary society is fraught with risks to personal security and safety. This has been graphically embedded in the consciousness of all Americans because of the enormous loss of life in schools over the last decade due to student violence perpetrated against other students, teachers, staff members, and administrators. People from outside the school community have also entered school buildings and committed violent acts against students and employees. In addition, there is the ever-present risk of injury to students and employees because of accidents stemming from school facilities and equipment. Finally, there is the risk that arises from the potential breach of confidentiality in relation to student and employee records. Safety and security audits, rules, and procedures must be developed in order to ensure, as much as possible, a risk-free environment for both students and employees. This has prompted school districts to create the position of *director of risk management.*

The accompanying job descriptions for the six major human resources specialists are meant only to be a guide (see Exhibit 1.1). Each individual district must decide on the exact specifications for these positions.

EXHIBIT 1.1   Six Major Human Resources Specialists

Personal abilities and characteristics are universal for all administrators. The superintendent, assistant superintendents, directors, and building principals must have good human relations skills; they must possess good writing skills; they must work well with details; and they must be self-starters. The descriptions provided here should be seen as building on this foundation.

Job Description for the Assistant Superintendent for Human Resources

Job Summary

The assistant superintendent for human resources (or director of human resources) is responsible for managing the school district's human resources program. This includes the establishment and maintenance of effective two-way communications between the various organizational levels; and the formulation, recommendation, and administration of the school district's human resources policies.

Organizational Relationships

The assistant superintendent has a line relationship with the superintendent of schools and reports directly to him or her. He or she serves as the superintendent's chief advisor on human resources matters and has a staff relationship with other administrative personnel. The assistant superintendent for human resources has a line relationship with his or her immediate staff, which includes the director of employee relations, the director of staff development, the director of employee benefits, and the director of risk management. These administrators report directly to the assistant superintendent.

Organizational Tasks

The assistant superintendent for human resources is directly responsible for establishing administrative processes, procedures, and techniques for human resources planning, recruitment of staff, selection of personnel, the placement and induction of personnel, staff evaluation, and compensation programs. He or she is further responsible for supervising the director of employee relations, the director of staff development, the director of employee benefits, and the director of risk management.

Job Qualifications

In terms of education and experience, the assistant superintendent for human resources should possess

Continued

EXHIBIT 1.1 *Continued*

- Appropriate state administrator certification
- A doctorate in educational administration
- Formal course work in the areas of curriculum, finance, school law, human resources administration, and collective negotiations
- Classroom teaching experience and five years as a building level administrator

Job Description for the
Director of Employee Relations

Job Summary

The director of employee relations is responsible for the administration of the school district's management–employee relations program. This includes establishing and maintaining effective two-way communications between the various organizational levels; formulating, recommending, and administering the school district's management–employee relations policies; and administering the collective negotiations process.

Organizational Relationships

The director of employee relations has a line relationship with the assistant superintendent for human resources and reports directly to him or her. He or she serves as the assistant superintendent's chief advisor on employee relations. He or she has a staff relationship with other administrative personnel. The director of employee relations has a cooperative–professional relationship with nonadministrative personnel with whom he or she negotiates. Of course, the director has a line relationship with his or her immediate staff, and they report directly to the director.

Organizational Tasks

In preparing for negotiations, the director of employee relations shall

- Develop negotiations strategies for management
- Prepare proposals and counterproposals for management
- Analyze and evaluate employee proposals and advise management accordingly
- Know state laws and court decisions relevant to professional negotiations

- Secure input from all administrative personnel prior to developing management's proposals

In at-the-table negotiations, the director of employee relations shall

- Serve as the chief negotiator for the school district
- Direct the school district's negotiations team
- Keep administrative personnel informed during negotiations
- Draft negotiated agreements reached with unions
- Maintain records of proposals and counterproposals presented by all parties during negotiations

In administering the negotiated agreement, the director of employee relations shall

- Serve as the school district's chief advisor in the interpretation of adopted agreements
- Serve as the school district's chief advisor in all grievance matters
- Consult with principals and other supervisors concerning their understanding of and compliance with the adopted agreements
- Initiate management's grievances and mediation activities

Job Qualifications

In terms of education and experience, the director of employee relations should possess

- Appropriate state administrator certification
- Master's degree (minimum)
- Formal course work in the areas of educational administration with exposure to courses in curriculum, finance, school law, collective negotiations, and human resources administration
- Classroom teaching experience and at least two years as a building principal

Job Description for the
Director of Staff Development

Job Summary

The director of staff development is responsible for the management of the school district's staff development program. This includes the establishment and

EXHIBIT 1.1

maintenance of effective two-way communications between the various organizational levels; and the formulation, recommendation, and administration of the school district's staff development policies.

Organizational Relationships

The director of staff development has a line relationship with the assistant superintendent for human resources and reports directly to the assistant superintendent. He or she serves as the assistant superintendent's chief advisor on staff development matters. The director of staff development has a staff relationship with other administrative personnel and has a cooperative–professional relationship with nonadministrative personnel with whom he or she works. The director has a line relationship with his or her immediate staff, and they report directly to him or her.

Organizational Tasks

In planning and implementing a staff development program, the director shall

- Establish and implement ongoing needs-assessment techniques with all personnel
- Analyze and evaluate assessment instruments
- Secure input from administrative personnel concerning the most desirable time and place for program presentation
- Evaluate program presentations

Job Qualifications

In terms of education and experience, the director of staff development should possess

- Master's degree (minimum)
- Formal course work in the areas of testing and measurement, statistics, curriculum, and supervision
- A minimum of two years professional experience as a teacher or building administrator

Job Description for the Director of Affirmative Action

Job Summary

The director of affirmative action is responsible for administering the school district's affirmative action

program. This includes establishing and maintaining effective two-way communications between organizational levels; and formulating, recommending, and administering the school district's affirmative action policies.

Organizational Relationships

The director of affirmative action has a line relationship to the superintendent of schools and reports directly to the superintendent. He or she serves as the superintendent's chief advisor on affirmative action matters. The director of affirmative action has a staff relationship with other administrative personnel and has a cooperative–professional relationship with nonadministrative personnel with whom he or she works. Of course, the director has a line relationship with his or her immediate staff, and they report directly to the director.

Organizational Tasks

The director of affirmative action is responsible for the following tasks:

- Studying affirmative action problems and suggesting solutions to the superintendent, if possible
- Using school district data in reviewing the qualifications of all employees, with particular emphasis on minorities, women, older workers, and people with disabilities as the data relate to fair employment practices
- Developing and updating goals and timetables for correcting identifiable deficiencies
- Advising the superintendent on recruitment of minorities, women, older workers, and people with disabilities for those classified and positions in which they may be falling short of the district's affirmative action goals
- Assuming the role of compliance officer and making all contacts with state and federal agencies
- Reviewing all job announcements, job descriptions, and selection criteria to ensure compliance with affirmative action requirements
- Briefing the superintendent on the nature, purpose, and intent of all laws, executive orders,

Continued

EXHIBIT 1.1   *Continued*

policies, regulations, and reports of external agencies that affect the school district's affirmative action program

- Helping district administrators investigate formal complaints of alleged discrimination relating to fair employment practices, and recommending corrective measures to the superintendent
- Maintaining liaison with local, state, and federal agencies and with organizations concerned with promoting fair employment practices
- Representing the school district at meetings, conferences, and other gatherings pertaining to the affirmative action program
- Working with appropriate individuals and agencies in ascertaining correct population characteristic data for the district
- Compiling an annual report to the superintendent on the progress of the school district's affirmative action program

Job Qualifications

In terms of education and experience, the director of affirmative action should possess

- A master's degree (minimum)
- Formal course work in the areas of educational administration with exposure to school law, collective negotiations, and human resources administration
- Classroom teaching experience, two years as a building principal, and two years as a central office administrator

**Job Description for the
Director of Employee Benefits**

Job Summary

The director of employee benefits is responsible for the management of the school district's benefits program. This includes the establishment and maintenance of effective two-way communication between the various organizational levels; and the formulation, recommendation, and administration of the school district's employee benefits policies.

Organizational Relationships

The director of employee benefits has a line relationship with the assistant superintendent for human resources and reports directly to him or her. He or she serves as the assistant superintendent's chief advisor on employee benefits and has a staff relationship with other administrative personnel. The director of employee benefits has a cooperative–professional relationship with nonadministrative personnel with whom he or she works. Of course, the director has a line relationship with his or her immediate staff and they report directly to him or her.

Organizational Tasks

In planning and implementing the employee benefits program, the director shall

- Establish and implement ongoing monitoring techniques to evaluate the cost effectiveness and efficient management of the benefits program.
- Establish and chair the employee benefits committee which is charged with reviewing employee benefits, making suggestions for improving benefits, making suggestions for containing costs, reviewing specifications for bidding benefits insurance, reviewing the analysis of bids, and annually making recommendations to the superintendent of schools
- Collaborate with personnel from the procurement department in developing specifications for bidding benefits insurance
- Develop, implement, and evaluate an annual survey of employee perceptions concerning the scope and effectiveness of the benefits program
- Serve as the liaison between the district and those companies providing health care and related insurance
- Develop informational materials and provide presentations to employees about the district's benefits program

In planning and implementing the workers' compensation program, the director shall

EXHIBIT 1.1

- Establish and implement ongoing monitoring techniques to evaluate the cost effectiveness and efficient management of the workers compensation program
- Collaborate with personnel from the procurement department in developing specifications for bidding workers' compensation insurance
- Serve as the liaison between the district and the company providing workers' compensation insurance

Job Qualifications

In terms of education and experience, the director of employee benefits should possess

- A bachelor's degree (minimum)
- Formal course work in the areas of human resources administration, benefits management, risk management, insurance management, workers compensation
- Three years experience in at least one of the following areas: human resources administration, benefits management, insurance management, or workers' compensation management

Job Description for the Director of Risk Management

Job Summary

The director of risk management is responsible for administering the school district's risk management program. This includes establishing and maintaining effective two-way communications between organizational levels, as well as formulating, recommending, and administering the school district's risk management policies.

Organizational Relationships

The director of risk management has a line relationship to the assistant superintendent for human resources and reports directly to the assistant superintendent. He or she serves as the assistant superintendent's chief advisor on risk management matters. The director of risk management has a staff relationship with other administrative personnel and has a cooperative–professional relationship with non-administrative personnel with whom he or she works. The director has a line relationship with his or her immediate staff and they report directly to him or her.

Organizational Tasks

In planning and implementing the risk management program, the director shall

- Establish and chair the employee safety and security committee, which is charged with reviewing safety and security rules and procedures, making suggestions for improving safety and security rules and procedures, reviewing specifications for bidding risk management services and equipment, and reviewing the analysis of bids
- Develop, implement, and evaluate an annual safety and security audit
- Develop informational materials concerning safety and security on the job and providing safety and security education and training to employees
- Develop an annual safety and security report for the assistant superintendent for human resources that contains recommendations for improving the school district's safety and security program
- Investigate, assess, and manage safety and security crisis events

Job Qualifications

In terms of education and experience, the director of risk management should possess

- A bachelor's degree (minimum)
- Formal course work in the areas of risk management, human resources administration, and workers' compensation management
- Three years experience in at least one of the following areas: risk management, safety and security education and training, safety and security assessment, or workers' compensation management

Source: All six job descriptions were modeled on the job description for the Director of Employee Relations in the *American Association of School Administrators,* "Helping Administrators Negotiate" (Arlington, VA: The Association, 1974).

Leadership Theories for Human Resources Administration

There are numerous leadership theories that are currently in vogue. The most recent theories are: search for excellence, the seven habits of highly effective people, the learning organization, new science of leadership, school-based management (SBM), cultural leadership, transformational leadership, total quality management (TQM), and transcendental leadership. Only two of these theories, transcendental leadership and total quality management, will be presented here, because they appear to be the most appropriate theories for human resources administration.[11]

Transcendental Leadership

There are three major reasons why transcendental leadership[12] is an appropriate theory for human resources administrators. First, human resources administration operates within a milieu that is very complex, ambiguous, and stressful. Second, like other educational administrators, human resources administrators are required to perform their responsibilities even though they may not have job security. Finally, boards of education continue to cross the line between governance and administration.

In addition, superintendents, principals, other administrators, and human resources administrators are often criticized or blamed for the following: poor performance of students on standardized tests, substandard teacher performance, outdated curricula, student violence, and a lack of financial stewardship. Although some of these criticisms are legitimate in some schools and school districts, they do not accurately represent the general condition. In spite of such criticism and difficulties, a major influence in the lives of most administrators, including human resources administrators, is the search for meaning that goes beyond the paycheck and prestige that comes from being a superintendent, principal, or human resources administrator. This search for meaning may be identified in a very concise way as the transcendent dimension of leadership.

In this context, *transcendence* means a way of life dedicated to leadership within and on behalf of the academic community and profession rather than simply finding an administrative position in order to make a living. Obviously, making a living is an important consideration for everyone. However, without a sense of transcendence, administrators may concentrate on the performance of tasks and neglect reflecting on their overall reasons for being educational leaders.

Accepting the transcendence of leadership requires a person to undertake a lifelong process of discerning how he or she can be of service to the academic community and profession while carrying out the tasks and responsibilities of his or her leadership position within a given school or school district. This sense of service is difficult to sustain unless a person has an agenda to follow. Operating from such a theoretical base ensures that a per-

---

[11]William C. Cunningham and Paula A. Cordeiro, *Educational Administration: A Problem-Based Approach* (Boston: Allyn & Bacon, 2000), 174–187.

[12]Ronald W. Rebore, *A Human Relations Approach to the Practice of Educational Leadership,* 7th ed. (Boston: Allyn & Bacon, 2004), 75–85, 153–155.

son will develop and maintain effective job performance. In this context, such an agenda consists of the elements in a transcendental model of leadership.

Because administrators in general and human resources administrators in particular are concerned with human growth and development, they are generally more open to the cultural differences that exist between human beings and institutions. In like manner, they recognize that the values and philosophies of other people can have a profound effect upon them and the people they serve.[13] The basic premise of transcendental leadership is that a person acts from the totality of who he or she is as a human being. Most administrators are generally aware that their decisions are influenced by more that just the immediately recognizable circumstances and that the effects of their decisions can go beyond the present situation.

Transcendental leadership has two components. First, there are six elements that pertain to dispositions individual human resources administrators should possess to be centered on human growth and development. Second, there are ten focuses that establish a transcendental cultural in a school district. Such a culture is organizationally supportive of human growth and development.

The Elements of Transcendental Leadership

Operationalization is a process that includes various elements that are activated to guarantee that a theory is properly practiced. Many different theories have similar elements, but it is the combination of elements and the disposition of the person using the theory that makes it effective. There are six elements that make up transcendental leadership theory. The elements of this theory can be applied specifically to human resources administrators.

1. *Utilize reflection on practice.* The first element takes into account the importance of practice as the phenomenon upon which theory and foundational values are based. Everything begins with practice. Knowing and understanding what is occurring in human resources administration practice is the only way to evaluate effective leadership. Leadership cannot be a top-down phenomenon, but rather must begin with the processes and practices of human resources administration. This includes knowing and understanding the attitudes, emotions, and opinions of all stakeholders.

2. *Practice the principle of subsidiarity.* This element has a unique history in that it originated in social ethics and social economics. The principle of subsidiarity states that decisions should be made at the lowest possible level in a given school district. There is no question about the relevance of allowing administrators to do their jobs without interference but with monitoring from others. There is also no question about the firsthand knowledge and experience that respective administrators have, which makes them eminently more qualified than others to handle specific issues and problems. Thus, the performance evaluation process must be implemented by first-line supervisors, with support from the human resources department. The human resources function cannot be operationalized

---

[13]Carolyn Gratton, *The Art of Spiritual Guidance: A Contemporary Approach to Growing in the Spirit* (New York: The Crossroad Publishing Company, 1995), 2–3.

without input and assistance from other members of the school district community, as will be demonstrated in subsequent chapters.

3. *Act from a political base.* The third element refers to the human phenomenon whereby people try to manage the impact that their actions and decisions will have on the actions and decisions of others and on institutions. In human resources administration, the conceptualization of what constitutes a political base can be understood in a primary tension, the rights of government versus the rights of the individual. The role and function of administrators is to ensure that the rights of individual students, parents, teachers, staff members, and others are not in conflict with the rights of the local, state, and national governments. For example, there is a certain amount of tension between the right of the United States Congress to pass the Omnibus Transportation Employee Testing Act of 1991 and the right of employees to due process in the workplace.

4. *Act from a sense of duty and responsibility.* It is not easy to know one's duty and responsibility. For human resources administrators, it can be difficult and, at times, ambiguous. In the most sweeping context, people have responsibilities to themselves and their families, friends, neighbors, and colleagues in addition to their employing school district, community, state, and nation. Finally, human resources administrators have a duty and responsibility to their profession. The issue is how to balance all of their various duties and responsibilities. At times these duties and responsibilities come into conflict with each other. Reflection and common sense are the primary tools that will help administrators find the balance that is required at a given time.

5. *Advocate for social justice.* Pluralism can produce conflict; conflict can lead to injustices. Thus, there is a need to know and understand some basic notions about justice. *Justice* is that guide which regulates how people live out their lives as members of a community. In contemporary society, everyone is a member, even if he or she tries to live as a hermit. Computer and satellite technology make it possible to locate virtually every person on the planet. There are no places where a person can hide and neglect his or her obligations to society. The choice to either live in society or to retreat from it by living a solitary life no longer exists. The very fact of *being* brings with it social obligations and the need for effective human relations. Justice is one of the most important aspects of human resources administration because the actions of an administrator can have both an immediate and long-term effect on people and the person's school district. Unfairness in administering human resources policies and procedures can be masked through the details of management. Thus, a just and fair human resources administrator is critical to social justice.

6. *Formulate professional positions through discourse.* Reasoning is the basis of all discourse in that participants must agree to this rationality if it is to be effective. Participants should be free from external and internal coercion other than the force of the best argument, which supports the cooperative search for truth. Because of the limitations of time and space, it is necessary to institutionalize discourse; the topics to be discussed and the contributions of participants must be organized in terms of opening, adjournment, and resumption of discussion. Discourse can be effective only if it is applied to questions which can be dealt with through impartial judgment. This implies that the process will lead to an answer that is equally beneficial to all stakeholders. This does not mean that discourse seeks to reach consensus but, rather, to generate convictions in the participants. Further, the degree to which a society, its institutions, its political culture, its traditions, and its everyday practices permit a noncoercive and nonauthoritarian form of discourse is a hallmark of rationality. Thus, human resources administrators cannot expect to find the best solution to problems or to formulate the best policies and procedures if they carry out these tasks without discourse with those who have a stake in the problem or those who will be affected by the policies or procedures.

Focuses that Support Transcendental Culture

The following ten focuses are critical to establishing a transcendental culture[14] in a school district.

    1. *Identity focus.* The degree to which administrators, teachers, and staff members identify with the school district as a whole rather than with their job or profession. If individuals closely identify with the school district, there is a positive culture operating within that district.

    2. *Collaboration focus.* The degree to which administrators, teachers, and staff members organize their work activities around groups rather than individuals. If administrators, teachers, and staff members collaborate in developing the dimensions of the human resources function rather than relying upon a single administrator such as the superintendent to organize this responsibility, such a school district exemplifies this focus. The obvious advantage of fostering group emphasis is the empowerment experienced by individuals when the human resources function is no longer dependent only on one person who might retire or accept a position in another school district at some time in the future. In like manner, continuity is established even though the superintendent might leave the school district.

    3. *Concern for people focus.* The degree to which administrators, teachers, and staff members take into consideration the effects of their decisions on people. Of course this consideration not only applies to the decisions affecting staff but also to those decisions affecting students, parents, and members of the community. A high degree of concern is a hallmark of the humanity of the decision makers.

    4. *Coordination focus.* The degree to which divisions in the school district are encouraged to operate in a coordinated or interdependent manner. A high degree of coordination and interdependence supports and strengthens the goal attainment of a school district.

    5. *Empowerment focus.* The degree to which rules, regulations, and direct supervision are used to control the behavior of administrators, teachers, and staff members. Less control and increased levels of trust and empowerment lead to greater commitment and success.

    6. *Risk supportive focus.* The degree to which administrators, teachers, and staff members are encouraged to be aggressive, innovative, and risk seeking. A high degree of encouragement could lead to higher job satisfaction, an uplifted morale, and cutting-edge programming.

---

[14]Stephen P. Robbins, *Organizational Behavior: Concepts, Controversies, and Applications,* 6th ed. (Englewood Cliffs, New Jersey: Prentice-Hall, 1993), 602.

7. *Performance focus.* The degree to which rewards and promotions are allocated according to an administrator's, teacher's, or staff member's performance rather than seniority, favoritism, or other nonperformance factors.

8. *Criticism tolerance focus.* The degree to which administrators, teachers, and staff members are encouraged to openly express their criticisms. The educational leaders of some school districts mistakenly believe that they can squelch criticism. Heavy-handed techniques used against employees who publicly criticize will eventuate in deep-seated resentment and, in many cases, outright revolt. The mark of an effective school district is an atmosphere of openness within which everyone, including students, will be heard without reprisals. This kind of openness sends a signal to all members of the school community that people and their opinions and criticisms are valued and can make a difference in how the school district is administered.

9. *Process focus.* The degree to which administrators, teachers, and staff members focus on the strategies and processes used to achieve outcomes. Particularly in human resources administration, outcomes are not a good measure of progress or success. There are too many variables to control when dealing with people to accurately measure outcomes. Thus, a school district with a positive culture will be constantly engaged in developing, implementing, evaluating, and modifying strategies and processes.

10. *Change focus.* The degree to which a school district monitors and responds to changes in the external environment. Technology, corporate downsizing, shifts in population, violence, health issues, and all the other phenomena which constantly bombard institutions require a response from administrators, teachers, and staff members in relation to what needs to change in their school district cultures.

Total Quality Management of the Human Resources Function

In post-World War II Japan, an American named W. Edwards Deming introduced the theory and application of total quality management (TQM) to the Japanese, with outstanding results. Today, Japan occupies a prominent position among the leading industrial/business nations. It is true that the economy in Japan now suffers from the same pitfalls that plague the United States and the other industrial/business nations, but Japan's rapid rise from devastation is worthy of note and study. Deming's approach was the catalyst for this success.

In private business and industry, the first concept concerning quality management was introduced during the late 1970s. It was labelled "quality circles" and called for groups of employees to meet and discuss how improvements could be made within their areas of responsibility. Supervisors and managers were unprepared for this innovation in most companies, and the technique quickly vanished. However, a major thrust of the total quality management approach occurred in business and industry during the 1980s and is still gaining momentum.

In education, the total quality management approach is just beginning to take hold in some school districts and is certain to continue. This phenomenon is appearing not only in the management aspect of school districts but also in the instructional sphere.

This section discusses how Deming's fourteen principles can be applied to the management of human resources. These principles were elucidated in Deming's 1986 book, *Out of the Crisis.*

1. *Create constancy of purpose toward improvement of product and service.* Too often human resources administrators are so entangled in the problems of daily operations they lose sight of the overall vision that should drive the human resources function.

2. *Adopt the new philosophy.* The new philosophy is a belief that all staff members can and should contribute not only to the development of a strategic plan but also to the implementation of the plan. The assistant superintendent for human resources, along with the directors of employee relations, staff development, and affirmative action, should assume the leadership in developing the processes, procedures, and techniques for implementing the eight dimensions of the human resources function; but interviewers, direct compensation specialists, and administrative assistants along with all other staff members should also be intricately involved in this development.

3. *Cease dependence on inspection to achieve quality.* Employees must perceive that they are valued members of the school district community and, in particular, must perceive that they are appreciated as providers of service to that dimension of the human resources function for which they are responsible.

4. *End the practice of awarding business on the basis of price tag.* The application of this principle for school district employees is better understood in relation to compensation. Public recognition and compensation for outstanding performance are good ways to demonstrate that employees are valued and that their contributions to the human resources function are appreciated.

5. *Improve constantly and forever the system of production and service, to improve quality and productivity.* Improvement must be built into the design of the processes, procedures, and techniques used in the human resources function. Thus, evaluation must be a component in every dimension of human resources management.

6. *Institute training on the job.* With all the advances in technology and with the research that is constantly being conducted in the behavioral sciences, an employee can never state that he or she knows all there is to know about human resources management in general or about his or her area of responsibility in particular.

7. *Institute leadership.* This principle applies not only to the assistant superintendent for human resources and the other human resources administrators but also to all staff members who have human resources responsibilities.

8. *Drive out fear.* Quality performance occurs when staff members take a stand about ideas that they believe will enhance the human resources function. Security allows staff members to make mistakes which, in turn, will become learning experiences that will help employees to acquire new insight and more effective skills.

9. *Break down barriers between departments.* Collaboration between administrators and other staff members will produce a higher quality of service.

10. *Eliminate slogans, exhortations, and targets.* The human resources function should be driven by goals rather than slogans, exhortations, and job targets.

11. *Eliminate management by numerical quotas.* There is nothing more dehumanizing to staff members than reducing their performance to statistics.

12. *Remove barriers that prevent job managers and workers from taking pride in their workmanship.* Generally speaking, everyone wants to do a good job. Human resources administrators should strive to remove obstacles that prevent other human resources staff members from quality performance.

13. *Institute a vigorous program of education and self-improvement*. The human resources function is constantly in danger of becoming mediocre if staff members are not given the opportunity to develop their skills, learn new skills, and receive updated information.

14. *Put everybody in the company to work to accomplish the transformation*. The type of change described herein requires not only the commitment of the assistant superintendent for human resources but also commitment from every human resources staff member. It must be supported at all levels within the organization because top-level human resources administrators cannot effect this change by themselves.

The Use of Technology in Human Resources Administration

The impact of technology on the daily lives of people cannot be overestimated. It is a phenomenon that has changed the way people think and act, not only in their homes but also in the workplace. Virtually every school district in the United States is dealing with the use of technology in relation to the instructional program, and many are trying to find ways to utilize technology in central office administration.

When applied to the school district human resources function, technology has many benefits, including:

- *Cost-effectiveness*. Fewer people are required to perform certain human resources responsibilities
- *Efficiency*. Processes and procedures can be computerized
- *Engagement*. Employees themselves can access services more quickly
- *Job enhancement*. Human resources department staff members can concentrate on planning and development rather than on routine tasks
- *Assessment*. Information available in databases can be quickly and easily organized into management reports

Automating Routine Human Resources Procedures

Initial Entry and Change of Personnel Information

Most school-district employees would like to have more control over routine human resources procedures, which is easily accomplished through technology. Human resources departments have enhanced the level of service to employees by eliminating paper-intensive work through technology, which also tends to reduce errors. Self-service workflow technology also gives employees access to their ongoing status and allows them to have a quality assurance check on their status and benefits. Employees can thus have easy and reliable access to pay stub information: gross pay, deductions, year-to-date accumulations, and tax withholding data.

One of the easiest services to upgrade by using technology in school districts is benefits enrollment. Medical, dental, and life insurance plan enrollment can be accomplished through an interactive voice response telephone system commonly referred to as *IVR*. This technology utilizes a *text-to-speech* approach whereby the system voices the caller's current status and then prompts him or her to make a selection from a series of options. This type of self-service application is commonly referred to as a kiosk system, which is a stand-alone center that prompts users when data are entered. There are basically two types of kiosks: typing key words or using touch-screen technology.

This can also be accomplished through the *Internet* and an *intranet* system, which is the application of web technology to the administrative computer network of a school district. Of course, changes in status in addition to initial enrollment also can be accomplished through this same technology. A change of primary care physician, the listing of a new dependent, and a change of beneficiary are common applications of self-service technology.

Interactive voice response and Internet technology also provide a convenient way for retirees who continue to participate in district programs to make changes in their status without coming into the school district's central office or without sending in paperwork that is susceptible to keying error.

In utilizing these technologies, an employee of a school district can initiate a change in his or her home address, notify the human resources department about a newly earned degree, or initiate a change in marital status. In an automated *workflow* system, these types of changes can be programmed to activate other processes. Thus, a change in marital status might activate a request for additional information concerning name change or beneficiary election. Another example of this type of event-based processing is as follows: When a new teacher is hired and his or her human resources data file is created, event-based processing triggers the system to create a payroll file and enroll him or her in all standard employee benefits programs. The system then automatically sends a message to the staff development department, which in turn enrolls the new employee in the school district's orientation program. In the case of a newly hired administrator, the system also sends a message to the information systems department in order to set up a system security identification number. The workflow capabilities of technology are limited only by the imagination and design of human resources administrators.

The future of workflow is promising. The tremendous potential of workflow is easily seen in relation to carrying out teacher and staff member performance evaluations online. A workflow analytical system could trigger a series of considerations that a supervisor should keep in mind given the evaluation of an employee. For example, if an elementary school teacher is having difficulty teaching a newly adopted mathematics curriculum, a prompt might suggest a series of actions that the principal could consider, including asking the teacher to enroll in a workshop on the new mathematics curriculum being conducted by the publisher of the mathematics materials. The prompt could even include with the time and date that the professional development department of the school district has scheduled the workshop. Further, it is possible to design the performance evaluation online system in order to analyze the pattern that emerges in how the principal has evaluated the teachers in his or her school.

It is possible to incorporate security features into self-service programs. For example, an employee can be required to use a personal identification number to transact business, and Internet security features can be utilized to encrypt the information that employees enter and establish a secure connection to the web site.

Request and Utilization of Forms

Forms are constantly being requested by employees for personal needs and by other members of various departments within a school district to carry out ordinary human resources business. Insurance claim forms are an often-requested personal need form, while school building and department personnel are constantly in need of authorization-to-hire forms and performance evaluation documents. Requesting such forms and documents through an interactive voice response system, the Internet, or intranet saves valuable human resources personnel time. In addition, printing such forms and documents from a website saves the time and energy needed to fax or mail these items.

Task Performance

However, the most important way to save time and energy in addition to eliminating paperwork is to *perform the task* by directly using interactive voice response, Internet, or intranet technology. This is accomplished in a way that is similar to the use of these technologies for benefits enrollment.

An authorization-to-hire form, for example, can be completed by a principal or the head of a school district department by using an identification number or password along with other security methods. It is important for all employees to understand that identification numbers and passwords constitute the same authority and responsibility as a signature. Thus, the safeguarding of identification numbers and passwords is a serious professional responsibility.

Performance evaluation is another example of how the Internet or intranet can be utilized to save time and energy, and reduce paperwork. Filling out a form online and storing it in the school district's database is much more efficient than completing a form and keeping it in a file cabinet. Depending on the level of security, the performance evaluation information can be more confidential and secure in the school district's database than in a file cabinet. Of course, the employee must be given a signed hard copy of the performance evaluation. However, it can be just as effective, possibly more efficient, and ultimately more cost-effective to download the performance evaluation to a disk that can be given to the employee and utilized as an ongoing record of his or her performance. The principal or department supervisor and the employee can sign the identification sticker that is placed on the disk as an indication that the contents have been explained to the employee. An employee response can be recorded on the disk, downloaded, and a copy given to the principal who in turn can follow the ordinary procedure of response and appeal. The difference is that the district's database and a disk become the record, rather than traditional paper forms.

Posting Job Opportunities

The use of interactive voice response, the Internet, and intranet are excellent avenues for providing both employees and other people interested in working for the school district with information about available positions. These types of postings can provide the school district with more effective linkage to the best qualified people. Further, these technologies not only provide easily accessed information about job requirements and timely notification of job vacancies, but also can become the avenues for potential employees to apply for positions.

The use of these technologies can enhance the affirmative action efforts of a given school district by reaching people who do not live in the school district community or who do not have access to the daily newspapers where job vacancies are posted. This helps recruit people with disabilities, minorities, older workers, and women.

Online Recruitment and Selection

A computerized application process allows principals and department administrators to enter the competencies that are appropriate for a vacant position. The system then searches the database for a match between the competencies and available applicants' skills. Creating the applicant pool can take place through the Internet. For example, a person interested in working for a certain school district could consult the web page for that school district which, in turn, could direct the person to an online application.

If a resume is mailed by a potential candidate to a school district, it can be entered into a database and reformatted so that it will be available to principals and department directors. Optical Character Recognition (OCR) capabilities allow human resources administrators and staff members to categorize individuals according to desired competencies. In addition, background screening results can be entered online along with other candidate information, providing an ongoing status check for principals and department directors seeking to fill vacancies. Initial screen of qualifications for a position can be handled through a front-end interactive voice response system setting forth qualifications for position vacancies.

After the board of education votes to hire a candidate, a human resources data file can be created to prompt the delivery of a job description that includes expected competencies and performance criteria upon which the newly hired person's performance will be evaluated.

Online Staff Development and Training Programs

All types of staff development and training programs can be developed and provided to employees through videos and online technology. Those developed for the Internet and intranet can be interactive; an employee can be led through a series of exercises with immediate feedback concerning his or her mastering of the information or skill. Although this will not replace traditional methods of delivering staff development and training programs, many purely informational or simple skill acquisition programs are especially suited to this approach.[15]

Relational Database Reporting

The development of human resources reports once consisted of printed lists that were sorted and subtotaled according to a desired category, such as date of employment by department or job level. Human resources staff members once had to expend an enormous number of work hours taking data and reformatting them into usable information for the superintendent

---

[15]Jim LeTart, "Technology Frees HR's Time for Strategy," *HR Magazine,* 42 (December 1997), 78–93.

of schools, assistant superintendents, department heads, and principals. Software is now available that can immediately produce reports from data that have been entered into a database. For example, superintendents and other administrators can now view on-screen data in graphical formats that show turnover statistics in special education. They can also click and drag fields of information into reports or use software to create reports. In addition, reports can be extracted into word processing software and spreadsheet formats. With the advent of email in most school districts, reports can be easily transferred to the offices of numerous administrators. Exhibit 1.2 is an example of a monthly summary report that sets forth the status of those making claims as members of a self-insured school district medical insurance program. When employees, their dependent children, their spouses, or physicians send in a claim for medical services, the claim is entered into a database from which summary reports can be generated. In an actual report, the designation *employee, spouse,* and *dependent* would be accompanied by the employee's social security number or with the name of the person who made the claim.[16]

With the new technologies, human resources administrators and staff members can assume the role of internal consultants who are engaged in critical planning in order to meet the goals and objectives of a given school district. They are freed from routine tasks in order to be more involved in solving problems and addressing human resources issues.

EXHIBIT 1.2   Medical Claims Report

Claimant	Paid Year-to-Date	Diagnosis	Current Treatment
1. Dependent	$24,602.38	Broken Arm	Physical Therapy
2. Employee	$33,442.21	Heart Disease	Office Visits & Medication
3. Spouse	$28,179.17	Osteoarthritis	Lab Work, X ray, Medication
4. Employee	$27,563.02	Breast Cancer	Radiation
5. Employee	$84,253.90	Renal Failure	Dialysis—Waiting for Kidney Transplant
6. Dependent	$47,375.16	Leukemia	Office Visits
7. Dependent	$19,601.43	Nervous Disorder	Office Visits & Medication
8. Spouse	$93,610.34	Lymphomas	Chemotherapy
9. Employee	$110,592.62	AIDS	Office Visits & Medication
10. Employee	$21,237.61	Heart Disease	Lab Work & Medication
11. Dependent	$15,732.72	Intestinal Obstruction	X ray, Office Visits

[16]Joseph Wilcox, "The Evolution of Human Resources Technology," *Supplement to Management Accounting: A New Era in Human Resources Payroll,* 78 (June 1997), 3–5.

Human Resources Administration Computer Hardware and Software

Hardware and Software Selection Process

Technology accelerates processes and procedures, but it does not necessarily correct problems within a dysfunctional human resources department. Thus, there are four steps that will help human resources administrators make an appropriate selection of computer hardware and software.

First, analyze the human resources needs of the school district. If at all possible, this should be accomplished through a districtwide strategic planning process that develops a vision for the entire school district and establishes goals and objectives for each division and department of the district. The human resources function is a vital part of the operation of the entire school district, and significant changes and enhancements to the processes and procedures of the human resources department must be in consort with its overall strategic plan.

In addition to establishing goals and objectives for the human resources department, an audit of the school district's existing technology is extremely important. The hardware and software that is being used in the payroll department, the information management department, the school principals' offices, and in all other departments is important to know because, if possible, new hardware and software should interface with existing hardware and software. This is especially important because principals and department directors will use their computer terminals to access human resources information and reports.

Surveying principals and department directors to ascertain their human resources needs and ideas will help not only to select the most appropriate hardware and software but will also give human resources administrators important feedback concerning issues and problems that might be present in human resources processes and procedures. Future needs could also be identified that will be important in purchasing hardware and software that will meet needs for more than just a few years.

The growth or decline in the school district's enrollment is a key factor, because this will determine the number of teachers' and staff members' records that will be processed by the human resources department. The larger the school district, the greater the need for technology in order to contain costs and maintain effectiveness and efficiency.

Second, research the types of hardware and software that are available from vendors. Of course, the first place to search for hardware and software is in computer trade publications, which have extensive advertising. A complementary task in the identification of appropriate hardware and software is asking colleagues in other school districts about the advantages and disadvantages of the products that they are using. The Internet is also an excellent vehicle for learning about available computer products.

Third, establish a budget for the purchase of hardware and software and initiate the bidding process. The needs assessment and research into available products will help in the establishment of a budget. The cost of new technology can be prohibitive and thus, it is judicious to establish a limit beyond which costs cannot exceed for the purchase of hardware and software. At this point it is important to consider hidden costs that might be related to supporting the installation and maintenance of the products.

The development of specifications for taking bids might require the expertise of a computer consultant if a school district does not have staff members with this type of experience. The specifications must clearly set forth the needs of the school district in such a way that bidders will be able to develop a complete hardware and software package. Some vendors might be able to submit a bid for the hardware but not for the software, or vice versa. Thus, separating the bid package into these two categories is desirable. After advertising, receiving bids, and eliminating bids that exceed budget, the human resources department administrators and staff members should begin their analysis. There are ten areas to consider in the analysis phase of the bidding process:

1. The capability of the hardware and software to be integrated with existing systems
2. The degree of difficulty in entering data
3. The degree of difficulty in learning the new equipment and software
4. The scope of program functions that can be carried out
5. The type and depth of reporting possibilities
6. The expandability of the programs and upgrading capability
7. The timeline for the conversion process
8. The level and scope of technical support that the vendor will provide in the conversion process and beyond
9. The performance of the demonstration hardware and software
10. The quality of the references given by staff members from other school districts where the products are being used

The level and scope of technical support are most critical because it is possible to purchase excellent hardware and software that cannot be utilized to its full potential because of inadequate technical support. It is very desirable to have onsite support for extensive conversions, whereby staff members can be trained in small groups and coached at their workstations. The quality of the working relationship that must be established between a school district's staff and the technical support people is critical to the conversion process. The relationship can be explored through an interview and by carefully checking the references of the bidding companies.

Of course, it is typical practice to receive demonstration hardware and software from the various vendors. The staff in the human resources department can test the products for factors that could impinge upon the decision-making process. The testing should not be rushed but rather extended over a significant period of time in order to give staff members the time needed to make an accurate appraisal of the product's performance.

Fourth, make a decision based on a cost-to-benefit ranking. This ranking is established through identifying the lowest priced hardware and software that meet the human resources department's present and future requirements. In a multiple-product bidding situation, each product can be evaluated by a rating scale, and then the overall package of each vendor compared in order to identify the strengths and weaknesses. Of course, the rating would be assigned by each member of the bid evaluation committee, which could be composed of administrators and staff members from the human resources department and should include principals and other administrators if they will be using a given type of hardware or software. A weight is assigned to the ten areas considered in the analysis phase that is then matched to the cost of the products. Table 1.1 provides an example of a weighted evaluation form.

If there are three companies bidding on a payroll program that has an upgraded employee position control component and the evaluation rating system cited above is used, the bid comparisons could look like those set forth in Table 1.2. In this situation, vendor one has the highest rating but also the highest costs; vendor two has the lowest rating and the second highest cost; vendor three has the second highest rating and the lowest cost. The decision would be between vendors one and three. According to the cost-to-benefit rating approach, if the bids came in at or below budget, vendor one would be awarded the contract.

Categories of Software Applications

The amount of software that is available to human resources departments in school districts is constantly increasing, especially because the human resources function is very easily adapted to technology. More importantly, the effective use of technology can free up significant financial resources that then can be allocated to the instructional program. There are nine areas within the human resources function for which software is available:

TABLE 1.1   Analysis Rating

On a scale of 1 to 5, with 5 being the highest rating, rate each vendor's product against the following criteria:

_____ Integration with Existing Systems

_____ Degree of Difficulty in Entering Data

_____ Degree of Difficulty in Learning the New Product

_____ Scope of Program Functions

_____ Type and Depth of Reporting

_____ Expandability and Upgrading Capability of the Programs

_____ Timeline for the Conversion Process

_____ Level and Scope of Technical Support

_____ Performance of the Demonstration Product

_____ Quality of References

_____ **Total Rating (50 is the highest possible rating)**

TABLE 1.2   Bid Comparisons

Vendor	Rating	Cost
Vendor One	41	$132,000
Vendor Two	23	$105,000
Vendor Three	32	$86,000

1. *Attendance systems.* For support positions such as bus driver, cafeteria worker, and custodian, these programs eliminate the time clocks and timecards used in some large school districts. Using software for telephones, magnetic strip cards, and personal computers, the number of hours worked by employees can be electronically generated and sent to the payroll department.

2. *Compensation planning systems.* Such systems provide a structured data-based approach to planning teacher and staff member salary and benefits programs. This type of software is relatively new to school districts. However, it can provide the kind of analysis that will enhance the collective negotiations process, especially since a planning system makes it possible to identify compensation trends in large school districts.

3. *Competency management systems.* Superintendents and human resources administrators can use these kinds of programs to identify teacher and staff member educational levels, certifications, and special skills. Based on the human resources needs of the school district, such software also can help human resources staff members identify staff development needs.

4. *Decision support systems.* When an administrator needs or desires to generate data summaries and reports, these types of systems provide the analytical capability to reframe information in such a way that decision making becomes more data driven.

5. *Human resources management systems.* These programs constitute the central storage for records and for processing transactions—such as workflow—that can be initiated through self-service events.

6. *Payroll management systems.* These types of programs manage the entire payroll process including salary/benefits requirements and govermnental regulations, including tax deductions.

7. *Recruitment and selection management systems.* Through these types of software, the superintendent of schools, principals, other administrators, and human resources staff members can search databases in order to find applicants who have specific education, certification, and skills. These systems also allow an administrator to monitor the status of applicants and even to mine the Internet for potential job applicants.

8. *Retirement management systems.* Using the Internet, intranet, or interactive voice response software, retirees can transact business with the human resources department and can receive information or have their questions answered.

9. *Staff development management systems.* Such systems retain information about the specific staff development programs and activities that employees attend, and also identify the special skills acquired by teachers and staff members who attended them. Further, software is available that allows individuals to access learning and training through personal computers and through distance learning, which is very important in providing staff development in schools so that teachers and staff members do not need to travel to a central office. Also, employees can have access to expert knowledge that would not be available to large groups of teachers and staff members on a given occasion. Providing staff development via the Internet and intranet allows people to acquire new knowledge and learn new skills independent of time and location.[17]

[17]Samuel Greengard, "How to Fulfill Techology's Promise," *Workforce: HR Software Insights Supplement, 78* (1999), 12.

Legal Issues

Unfortunately, it is painfully obvious that security issues dominate the technological revolution, particularly in relation to both the Internet and the intranet.[18] Email is the primary indicator that communications are neither completely private nor completely secure. Because human resources administrators are utilizing technology to implement the various dimensions of the human resources function, it is critical to understand not only the benefits but also the liabilities of this technology.

Employee Use of Technology

First and foremost, there have been attempts by the United States Congress to prohibit certain uses of the Internet: the Communications Decency Act of 1996 and the Child Online Protection Act of 1998. These laws have been reviewed by the federal court system, and their implementation is problematic at this time. The same situation is true for the Children's Internet Protection Act of 2000, except that a provision of the law mandates school districts receiving federal funds for Internet access to develop and implement a formal Internet safety policy. The implication for human resources administration is that there should be a policy that restricts the use of school-district-owned equipment and access to the Internet for school business purposes only.

Hostile Work Environment

Title VII of the Civil Rights Act of 1964 prohibits verbal and written conduct that produces an intimidating, hostile, or offensive work environment. Further, the decision in *Burlington Industries* v. *Ellerth* (1998) clearly holds supervisors legally responsible in Title VII cases for not preventing a hostile work environment. Technology and the Internet have significantly changed the work environment so that new methods of harassment might be utilized by employees. Thus, abusive emails and Internet content is certainly a violation of Title VII. It is the responsibility of human resources administrators to develop and implement policies and reporting procedures that will help other administrators monitor the teaching environment so it is free from harassment.

Employee Privacy

The United States Supreme Court upheld in *O'Connor* v. *Ortega* (1987) the standards set forth in *New Jersey* v. *T.L.O.* (1984) concerning justified and reasonable search. In the former case, the Court held that employees have a constitutionally protected right to privacy in the workplace. However, electronic communications of public employees are considered to be discoverable in court under public records laws. The usual practice is that emails are considered private unless subpoenaed by a court.

There are many other areas of legal and security concern in relation to the use of technology and the Internet. These include student use of the Internet, student privacy, assistive technology for children with disabilities, plagiarism, copyright issues, fair use,

---

[18]David M. Quinn, "Legal Issues in Educational Technology: Implications for School Leaders," *Educational Administration Quarterly*, XXXIX, no. 2 (April 2003), 187–207.

intellectual property rights, and many other areas. The three issues listed above, however, deal specifically with human resources administration.

Future Directions

The future of technology in human resources administration will probably be centered on certain issues that are still evolving. Wireless networks may bring the workstation to every location in a school and school district building. Electronic tablets that permit handwritten note taking that can be transcribed into typewritten text, stored, and transmitted into files will revolutionize the meaning of anecdotal notes. The possibilities for conferencing between principal and teacher, and between employee and supervisor have implications for performance evaluation. Collaboration between human resources administrators, other administrators, and teachers will be possible through websites. Thus ongoing communication will require a different way of thinking and spark the need for different types of staff development. Collaboration between teachers and students through websites will also require different skills that must be incorporated into the recruiting and selection processes. Security issues will become more ominous and threatening. As more and more information about employees is electronically stored and as employees gain greater capabilities for managing their personal databases, the risk of infiltration by others becomes more possible.

More problematic than any other consideration is the threat of computer network *worms,* which are self-replicating bits of disruptive code. These electronic villains can disable entire networks and innumerable computers. To stave off these attacks, *automatic patch management* software must be used that installs the latest security patches for programs and systems. Perhaps the most promising security software applications are programs that detect unidentified viruses by recognizing viruslike patterns. However, regardless of the risks involved, there is no turning back from technology.[19]

Summary

Our system of free and universal public education is unique to U.S. society. The school as an institution receives its mandate from the society it serves. Change is an integral part of this society. The content of our educational programs must address the fundamental principles of individual freedom, individual responsibility, and democratic government, but must also retain the flexibility to meet new developments and conditions.

Implementing society's educational objectives is the responsibility of the individual states. The state's authority to create and govern public schools is embodied in the state constitution, and it exercises this authority through the state legislature. The administrative arm of the state legislature is the department of education, which is usually governed by a board and administered by a commissioner or state superintendent. The legislature also delegates authority to local units, boards of education. However, the state maintains some con-

[19]Florence Olsen, "Security: Threats Will Get Worse," *The Chronicle of Higher Education,* section B (January 30, 2004), B12.

trol over the local boards by establishing minimum educational program requirements and teacher certification requirements, and by providing funds to help finance education.

The federal government has increased its influence on education through congressional acts that provide funds for special programs, through the regulations of the U.S. Department of Education, and through Supreme Court decisions. However, the federal government's power and influence are still considerably adjunct to state authority in education.

President Bush signed into law the No Child Left Behind Act (NCLB) in January 2002. NCLB ushered in the most extensive changes in federal law concerning public school education in forty years. It is the first time that federal legislation has mandated student success; all other federal legislation mandated opportunity rather than success.

The law requires all children to be proficient in reading and mathematics by 2014. Further, schools are required to make adequate yearly progress (AYP) toward the 2014 goal. Thus, each state must develop student testing programs that demonstrate satisfactory student improvement each year. The consequences of not achieving AYP vary from being designated as a school needing improvement to severe repercussions, such as replacement of school personnel or extension of the school year after five years of not achieving AYP.

For human resources administration, the NCLB provisions require serious attention. First, there is the requirement to hire *highly qualified* teachers who are capable of helping students meet the proficiency requirements. Second, the provision that students must demonstrate AYP has serious implications for teacher performance evaluation and staff development. Finally, the consequences for noncompliance with AYP for five years might result in the replacement of administrators, teachers, or staff members.

NCLB is a particular manifestation of school reform. The reform movement is always before us in education because change and improvement are embedded in the education profession. The formulas for successful reform have some common elements: a vision that utilizes a learning community approach leading to organizational reform; the establishment of a leadership team that utilizes teacher leadership in consort with principals' responsibilities; the importance of making decisions based on evidence; and the benefits of utilizing technology in management and instructional strategies.

School districts are perhaps the most democratically controlled agencies of government. Citizens of a local community elect school board members, who adopt policies for the governance and administration of the schools. The implementation of board policies is the responsibility of the administrative staff.

Administration is the process of managing human, financial, and material resources to accomplish an educational mission formulated as policies by the board of education. Therefore, administration is an executive rather than a policy-making activity. Its various functions include human resources administration, instructional programs administration, and support services administration. Each of these functions has objectives that are implemented through administrative processes, procedures, and techniques.

Functions are performed by administrators within a given organizational structure. The superintendent, as the chief executive officer of the school board, has full control of all school operations. These operations are so complex that his or her efforts must be amplified by a central-office administrative team. This team is usually composed of assistant superintendents who administer the major functions of the school system. These assistant superintendents form a cabinet that helps the superintendent formulate strategies and shares in the decision-making process. Directors and coordinators perform administrative tasks that support the major functions of the district. They report directly to assistant superintendents.

Every school system performs a human resources function, whether accomplished by a central-office unit or assigned to various administrators within the system. The goals of the human resources function are to achieve the objectives of the school district and to help individual staff members maximize their potentials and develop their professional careers. These goals are implemented through human resource planning, recruitment, selection, placement and induction, staff development, performance evaluation, compensation, and collective negotiations.

All but the very smallest school districts should delegate the human resources function to an assistant superintendent. The complexity of this function in our schools and the great impact it has on total school operations necessitate the hiring of this personnel specialist.

Collective negotiation has also created a need in most school districts for another specialist, the director of employee relations, who reports to the assistant superintendent for human resources and who is charged with managing the negotiations process.

The knowledge explosion, increased federal legislation and litigation, and the changing attitudes of parents, students, and educators have necessitated an ongoing staff development program for administrators and teachers. Like collective negotiation, this area is so specialized that most districts should consider establishing the position of director of staff development, who also reports to the assistant superintendent for human resources.

The avalanche of federal legislation and litigation also has mandated the creation of a central-office administrative position, director of affirmative action. Each federal legislation requires that a detailed compliance program be established under the direction of an administrator who will be free from the influence of other administrators. Thus, the director of affirmative action should report directly to the superintendent of schools.

The escalating cost of health care, the need to implement managed care, and the rising cost of workers' compensation has reinforced the need for school districts to establish the position of director of employee benefits. The administrator reports to the assistant superintendent for human resources.

Like the rest of society, schools are places of potential risk to students and employees. The risks range from personal violence to accidents to loss of confidentiality. Safety and security audits, rules, and procedures must be developed in order to ensure a risk-free environment for both students and employees. Because of this need, school districts have created the position of director of risk management.

There are two leadership theories that appear most appropriate for the practice of human resources administration, transcendental leadership and total quality management.

The basic premise of transcendental leadership is that a person acts from the totality of who he or she is as a human being. Most administrators are generally aware that their decisions are influenced by more that just the immediate circumstances and that the effects of their decisions can go beyond the present situation.

Transcendental leadership has two components. First, there are six elements that pertain to dispositions individual human resources administrators should possess to be centered on human growth and development. Second, there are ten focuses that establish a transcendental culture in a school district, which will be organizationally supportive of human growth and development. The elements of transcendental leadership are: utilize reflection on practice, practice the principle of subsidiarity, act from a political base, act from a sense of duty and responsibility, advocate for social justice, and formulate professional positions through discourse. The ten focuses that support transcendental culture are: identity, collaboration, concern for people, coordination, empowerment, risk supportive, performance, criticism tolerance, process, and change.

In post-World War II Japan, an American named W. Edwards Deming introduced the theory and application of "total quality management" (TQM) to the Japanese, with outstanding positive results. Aspects of Deming's fourteen principles are being implemented in some school districts throughout the United States. These principles can be effectively applied to the human resources function in school districts.

The impact of computer technology cannot be overestimated in all aspects of educational administration. When this technology is applied to the human resources function, it produces many benefits that include cost-effectiveness, efficiency, assessment of school district operations, and engagement of employees. In human resources administration, computer technology is being used for initial entry and changes in personnel information, the request and utilization of forms, task performance, posting job opportunities, online recruitment and selection of personnel, online staff development and training, and relational database reporting. When selecting computer hardware and software, it is important to consider the human resources needs of the district; to research the types of hardware and software available from vendors; to establish a realistic budget for the bidding process; and to make decisions based on a cost-to-benefit ranking. Computer software applications are available for every dimension of the human resources function.

Security issues dominate the technological revolution, particularly in relation to the both the Internet and the intranet. The implication for human resources administration is that there should be a policy that restricts the use of school-district-owned equipment and access to the Internet for school business purposes only. In addition, abusive emails and Internet content is certainly a violation of the law. It is the responsibility of human resources administrators to develop and implement policies and reporting procedures that will help other administrators monitor the teaching environment so that it is free from harassment. Although electronic communications of public employees are considered to be discoverable in court under public records laws, the usual practice is that emails are considered private unless subpoenaed by a court.

Discussion Questions and Statements

- Describe the role of the board of education in relation to the human resources function.
- What is the human resources responsibility of the superintendent of schools?
- Describe how the dimensions of the human resources function are interrelated.
- How does the use of technology in human resources administration support data-driven decision making?
- If you were a newly appointed assistant superintendent for human resources, how would you initiate the concept of total quality management for the human resources function in a department that has had very autocratic leadership?
- Describe the link between the human resources function and both the business and instructional functions of a school district.

- Without identifying the school district, which ISLLC criteria are the most difficult to initiate in a school district that you are familiar with? Why?
- What is transcendental leadership and how is it related to effective human resources administration?
- What are the essential elements and focuses of transcendental leadership?
- How does the No Child Left Behind Act impact human resources administration?

Suggested Activities

- You have just been hired as the assistant superintendent for human resources in a school district with four elementary schools, a middle school, and one high school. There is one other assistant superintendent who is responsible for curriculum development. The human resources department consists of just yourself and a secretary. The department has been functioning only in the areas of personnel recruitment and selection. Given the fact that no additional personnel will be added to the department, create in writing an organizational chart that sets forth who in the school district will do what in order to implement all the dimensions of the human resources function.
- Develop, in writing, a job description for a director of human resources for a school district with 100 professional personnel.
- Develop, in writing, a rationale and plan for enhancing the human resources function through the use of technology in a school district with 2,000 students and minimal financial resources.

Selected Bibliography

Ashbaugh, Rowan Miranda, "Technology for Human Resources Management: Seven Questions and Answers," *Public Personnel Management,* 31, no. 1 (Spring 2002), 7–20.

Carver, John, *Boards That Make a Difference.* San Francisco: Jossey-Bass, 1990.

Drucker, Peter F., *Managing for the Future: The 1990s and Beyond.* New York: Nal-Dutton, 1992.

Finkelstein, S., "Power in Top Management Teams: Dimensions, Measurement, and Validation," *Academy of Management Journal,* 35 (1992), 505–538.

Greengard, Samuel, "How to Fulfill Technology's Promise," *Workforce,* 78, no. 2 (February 1999), 10–18.

Greengard, Samuel, "HR Technology Trends: Beyond the Millennium," *Workforce,* 78, no. 6 (June 1999), 3–8.

Johnson, James H., *Total Quality Management in Education.* Eugene, OR: Oregon School Study Council, 1993.

Jolls, Tessa, "Techology Continues to Redefine HR's Role," *Workforce,* 76, no. 7 (July 1997), 46–57.

LeTart, Jim, "Technology Frees HR's Time for Strategy," *HRMagazine,* 42, no. 12 (December 1997), 78–84.

McLeod, Willis B., Brenda A. Spencer, and Leon T. Hairston, "Towards a System of Total Quality Management: Applying the Deming Approach to the Education Setting," *Spectrum: Journal of School Research and Information,* 10, no. 2 (Spring 1992), 34–42.

Miller, Lynn, "What's New," *HRMagazine,* 43, no. 12 (December 1998), 14–15.

Plass, Jan L., "A Living-Systems Design Model for Web-based Knowledge Management Systems," *Educational Technology Research and Development,* 50, no. 1 (2002), 35–57.

Rebore, Ronald W., *Educational Administration: A Management Approach.* Englewood Cliffs, NJ: Prentice-Hall, 1985.

Schein, E. H., *Organizational Culture and Leadership,* 2nd ed. San Francisco: Jossey-Bass, 1992.

Short, Paula M., and John T. Greer, *Leadership in Empowered Schools: Themes from Innovative Efforts.* Upper Saddle River, NJ: Merrill/Prentice-Hall, 1997.

Smith, Richard E., *Human Resources Administration: A School-Based Perspective,* 2nd ed. Larchmont, NY: Eye on Education, 2001.

Wilcox, Joseph, "The Evolution of Human Resources Technology: A New Era in Human Resources/ Payroll," *Management Accounting,* 78, no. 12 (June 1997), 3–5.

Wilson, Richard B., and Mike Schmoker, "Quest for Quality," *The Executive Educator,* 14, no. 1 (January 1992), 18–23.

Witschger, Jim, "Five Easy Steps to Choosing the Right HR Software Package," *Workforce,* 77, no. 12 (December 1998), 10–11.

Yukl, Gary, *Leadership in Organizations.* Englewood Cliffs, NJ: Prentice-Hall, 1994.

Appendix
Selections from the ISLLC Standards*

The Interstate School Leaders Licensure Consortium (ISLLC) is a program sponsored by the Council of Chief State School Officers. Through this program, professionals from twenty-four state education agencies and representatives from various professional associations crafted a set of model *standards for school leaders* in 1996. The standards are compatible with the new curriculum guidelines for school administration established by the National Council for the Accreditation of Teacher Education (NCATE). Further, the ISLLC standards are being used by many states in the assessment of candidates for administrator certification and licensure.

There are six standards. Each standard is operationalized through three dimensions: knowledge, dispositions, and performances. The content of this book will help those seeking certification and licensure to understand certain ideas and concepts that are usually part of the assessment procedure. A listing of those standards follows, along with their dimensions and the chapters of this book that contain the information.

Standard 1

A school administrator is an educational leader who promotes the success of all students by facilitating the development, articulation, implementation, and stewardship of a vision of learning that is shared and supported by the school community.

Knowledge

The administrator has knowledge and understanding of:

- The principles of developing and implementing strategic plans
- Information sources, data collection, and data analysis strategies

This standard and its accompanying knowledge are treated in Chapters 1 and 2.

*Source: Council of Chief State School Officers, *Interstate School Leaders Licensure Consortium: Standards for School Leaders* (Washington, DC: The Council, 1996), 10, 12–15, 18–21.

Standard 2

A school administrator is an educational leader who promotes the success of all students by advocating, nurturing, and sustaining a school culture and instructional program conducive to learning and staff professional growth.

Knowledge
The administrator has knowledge and understanding of:

- Applied motivational theories
- Diversity and its meaning for educational programs
- Adult learning and professional development models

Dispositions
The administrator believes in, values, and is committed to:

- Life-long learning for self and others
- Professional development as an integral part of school improvement
- A safe and supportive learning environment

Performances
The administrator facilitates processes and engages in activities ensuring that:

- Professional development promotes a focus on student learning consistent with the school vision and goals.
- Life-long learning is encouraged and modeled.
- There is a culture of high expectations for self, student, and staff performance.
- Technologies are used in teaching and learning.
- A variety of supervisory and evaluation models is employed.

This standard and its accompanying knowledge, dispositions, and performances are treated in Chapters 2, 6, 7, and 8.

Standard 3

A school administrator is an educational leader who promotes the success of all students by ensuring management of the organization, operations, and resources for a safe, efficient, and effective learning environment.

Knowledge
The administrator has knowledge and understanding of:

- Theories and models of organizations and the principles of organizational development
- Operational procedures at the school and district level
- Principles and issues relating to school safety and security
- Human resources management and development

- Legal issues impacting school operations
- Current technologies that support management functions

Dispositions

The administrator believes in, values, and is committed to:

- Making management decisions to enhance learning and teaching
- High-quality standards, expectations, and performances
- Involving stakeholders in management processes
- A safe environment

Performances

The administrator facilitates processes and engages in activities ensuring that:

- Emerging trends are recognized, studied, and applied as appropriate
- Operational plans and procedures to achieve the vision and goals of the school are in place
- Collective bargaining and other contractual agreements related to the school are effectively managed
- The school plant, equipment, and support systems operate safely, efficiently, and effectively
- Financial, human, and material resources are aligned to the goals of schools
- Organizational systems are regularly monitored and modified as needed
- Responsibility is shared to maximize ownership and accountability
- There is effective use of technology to manage school operations
- Human resources functions support the attainment of school goals

This standard and its accompanying knowledge, dispositions, and performances are treated in all chapters of this book.

Standard 4

A school administrator is an educational leader who promotes the success of all students by collaborating with families and community members, responding to diverse community interests and needs, and mobilizing community resources.

Knowledge

The administrator has knowledge and understanding of:

- Emerging issues and trends that potentially impact the school community
- The conditions and dynamics of the diverse school community
- Community resources

Disposition

- The proposition that diversity enriches the school

Performances

- Available community resources are secured to help the school solve problems and achieve goals.
- Diversity is recognized and valued.
- Opportunities for staff to develop collaborative skills are provided.

This standard and its accompanying knowledge, dispositions, and performances are treated in Chapters 2, 3, 5, 6, and 8.

Standard 5

A school administrator is an educational leader who promotes the success of all students by acting with integrity, fairness, and in an ethical manner.

Knowledge
The administrator has knowledge and understanding of:

- Professional codes of ethics

Dispositions
The administrator believes in, values, and is committed to:

- The principles of the Bill of Rights
- Bringing ethical principles to the decision-making process
- Accepting the consequences for upholding one's principles and actions

Performances
The administrator:

- Demonstrates a personal and professional code of ethics
- Protects the rights and confidentiality of students and staff
- Demonstrates appreciation for and sensitivity to the diversity in the school community
- Fulfills legal and contractual obligations
- Applies laws and procedures fairly, wisely, and considerately

This standard and its accompanying knowledge, dispositions, and performances are treated in Chapters 2 and 10.

Standard 6

The school administrator is an educational leader who promotes the success of all students by understanding, responding to, and influencing the larger political, social, economic, legal, and cultural context.

Knowledge
The administrator has knowledge and understanding of:

- The importance of diversity and equity in a democratic society

Performances
The administrator facilitates processes and engages in activities ensuring that:

- Communication occurs among the school community concerning trends, issues, and potential changes in the environment in which schools operate
- The school community works within the framework of policies, laws, and regulations enacted by local, state, and federal authorities

This standard and its accompanying knowledge and performances are treated in Chapters 1, 2, and 10.

Human Resources Planning

Planning is a process common to all human experience. Before embarking on a journey an individual must understand where he or she is, know where he or she wants to go, and decide how best to get there. In an elementary form this exemplifies the essence of the process even as it is applied in educational organizations.

Through the process of human resource planning, a school district ensures that it has the right number of people, with the right skills, in the right place, and at the right time, and that these people are capable of effectively carrying out those tasks that will aid the organization in achieving its objectives. If a school district is to achieve its objectives, it needs financial resources, physical resources, and people. Too often the people are taken for granted, and yet they are the force that directly affects the main objective of a school district—to educate children. Human resources planning thus translates the organization's objectives into people requirements.

In some school districts long- and short-range objectives are couched in ambiguous language and often known only by certain central-office administrators. This makes it difficult to involve building principals in the hiring process when unexpected vacancies occur, when replacements are needed because of natural attrition, or when new programs must be staffed.

Human resources planning, as a process, ensures the smooth development of an organization. "We assess where we are; we assess where we are going; we consider the implications of these objectives on future demands and the future supply of human resources; and we attempt to match demand and supply so as to make them compatible with the achievement of the organization's future needs."[1]

Assessing Human Resources Needs

The process of assessing human resources needs has four aspects. First, human resources inventories must be developed to analyze the various tasks necessary to meet the school district's objectives; these tasks are then matched against the skills of current employees.

[1]Stephen P. Robbins, *Personnel: The Management of Human Resources,* 2nd ed. (Englewood Cliffs, NJ: Prentice-Hall, 1982), 76.

Second, enrollment projections must be developed for a five-year period. The extreme mobility of the American population has made this aspect increasingly important over the past twenty-five years. Third, the overall objectives of the school district must be reviewed within the context of changing needs. At a time when school district budgets are tight, all but the wealthiest districts must establish priorities in meeting objectives. Fourth, human resources inventories, enrollment projections, and school district's objectives must be organized into a human resources forecast, which becomes the mandate of the human resources department.

Implementing this human resource mandate becomes more complex, however, when viewed in the light of compliance with federal legislation, and in some districts when staff reductions are brought on by decreasing enrollment. Because both issues have had such a tremendous impact on the human resources function, they have been given particular emphasis in this chapter.

Human resources planning is sometimes understood only within the confines of the instructional program. However, for every two teachers there is usually one classified employee. The contemporary school district employs not only teachers and administrators but also cooks, custodians, maintenance personnel, secretaries, computer programmers, telephone switchboard operators, warehouse personnel, distribution truck drivers, and other specialists who are often considered by the average citizen to be employed only in the private business sector.

Human Resources Inventories

Human resources planning begins with the development of a profile indicating the status of current human resources. This profile is generated through forms completed by employees, verified by supervisors, and finally sent to the human resources department. This form should include name of employee, age, date employed with the school district, sex, job title, place of employment within the district, education and training along with the dates when completed, special skills, and, for instructional personnel, certification.

A human resources profile for each job classification is then developed from the forms completed by the employees. The profile lists all relevant information for each job classification.

From a planning perspective, this information is valuable not only in determining what skills are available but also in developing new instructional programs and support services. The human resources profile also helps administrators as they carry out other human resources tasks such as recruitment and staff development. For example, the length of time since an individual received his training or education helps the director of staff development plan appropriate programs.

The profile also provides crucial information for identifying weaknesses in the school district's ability to meet its objectives. For example, reviewing data under the "date employed" section will help the administration analyze such problems as staff turnover and job dissatisfaction. The "age of employee" information helps administrators formulate strategies for recruitment by identifying those individuals approaching retirement age. Accurate data are essential to every aspect of the human resources process and human resources profiles are an effective method of presenting such information.

Enrollment Prediction

Because educational institutions are service organizations, enrollment prediction is an essential aspect of human resources planning. Unless a school system makes an effort to predict declines or increases in the number of students to be served, it may unexpectedly experience half-filled classrooms and a surplus of teachers or overcrowded classrooms and a shortage of teachers.

The major question to be answered by an enrollment prediction is, How many children are expected to attend a particular school over the next five to ten years? Many methods can be used to forecast enrollments; among the most popular is the "percentage of retention" or "cohort-survival" technique. This method is predicated on birth rates and the historical retention of students (see Figure 2.1). However, there are other indicators that highlight enrollment trends before the statistical time required by the former technique has elapsed. Such indicators identify social, financial, and residential factors for critical analysis of a school and community. The following discussion of enrollment prediction and brief explanation of the most common techniques in use are taken from a handbook published by the American Association of School Administrators (AASA).[2]

The following indicators are qualitative in nature because they are based on observations rather than on statistical analysis.

- *The number of children in elementary school classes.* The use of alternative spaces as classrooms, such as the cafeteria, gymnasium, or auditorium stage, is an obvious indicator that the enrollment is increasing. A decline in student numbers in certain grade levels could indicate overall decreasing enrollments. Thus, it is important to analyze a decline of even a few children if it occurs in certain grade levels. For example, a trend may be developing when enrollments in the primary grades drop from thirty to twenty-five students, especially if this drop represents fewer students than those enrolled in grades four and five.
- *A persistent trend in elementary school enrollment over a three-year period.* Of course, there may be minor increases and decreases in enrollment over short periods of time. This may be due to outside factors such as the building of a new home subdivision or the demolition of homes because of a highway expansion project. Discounting such major factors, trends in enrollment increase or decrease must call for a larger-scale investigation.
- *Feedback from realtors.* The true insiders concerning the effects of housing on enrollments are realtors. Establishing ongoing communications with real estate firms in the community is of vital importance to enrollment prediction.

These indicators are enhanced by Exhibit 2.1 which sets forth eight normative questions. The answers to these questions, along with the other indicators, can be used by human resources administrators to ascertain if a full-scale enrollment prediction is needed such as the cohort-survival technique exemplified in Figure 2.1. Exhibit 2.2 provides information about demographic surveys, which incorporates census information into the planning process. In summary, qualitative observations, the answers to indicator questions, cohort-survival analysis, and demographic survey information constitute a multilevel approach to enrollment prediction.

---

[2]American Association of School Administrators, *Declining Enrollment: What to Do,* Vol. II, AASA Executive Handbook Series (Arlington, VA: The Association, 1974), 8, 9.

Instructions

I 1. Fill in Birth Rate
   2. Fill in 1st Grade Enrollment
   3. Do necessary calculations to find Average Ratio

II 1. Fill in Birth Rate
   2. Multiply by Average Ratio

III 1. Fill in enrollment data
    2. Do necessary calculations to find retention ratio
    3. Fill in Projected 1st Grade Enrollment from II into appropriate columns of III.
    4. Multiply enrollment for a specific year and class by the Retention Ratio for the *next* class.
       Result is the predicted enrollment for that year, next class.
    5. Complete chart

ENROLLMENT PREDICTION CHARTS
I

Birth Rate		1st Grade Enrollment		Enrollment Ratio of Birth Rate
2000		2006–07		
2001		2007–08		
2002		2008–09		
2003		2009–10		
2004		2010–11		
			Total of Ratios	
			Divide by 5	
			Average Ratio	

II

Birth Rate		× Average Ratio =	Projected 1st Grade Enrollment	For years
2005				2011–12
2006				2012–13
2007				2013–14
2008				2014–15
2009				2015–16

FIGURE 2.1 Cohort-Survival Technique

Continued

III

Year	Enrollment by Grade											
	1	2	3	4	5	6	7	8	9	10	11	12
2000–01												
2001–02												
2002–03												
2003–04												
2004–05												
Total by Grade												
Divide by 5												
Divide Grades		$\frac{2}{1}$	$\frac{3}{2}$	$\frac{4}{3}$	$\frac{5}{4}$	$\frac{6}{5}$	$\frac{7}{6}$	$\frac{8}{7}$	$\frac{9}{8}$	$\frac{10}{9}$	$\frac{11}{10}$	$\frac{12}{11}$
Retention Ratio												
P R O J E C T E D　E N R O L L M E N T　2011–12												
2012–13												
2013–14												
2014–15												
2015–16												
2016–17												
2017–18												
2018–19												
2019–20												
2020–21												

FIGURE 2.1　Continued

EXHIBIT 2.1   Enrollment Indicator Survey Questions

1. Is your community close to a metropolitan area and did your community develop and grow as a result of population expansion in that metropolitan area?

2. Is your community one with expensive houses that continue to escalate in price disproportionately to general real estate values?

3. Does your community contain a high percentage of professional people or older people whose homes fulfill their lifetime needs and whose children are now in (or have been through) the local schools?

4. Even if your community has a highly reputed school system, will that good reputation draw in young families in spite of high-priced houses?

5. Does your community have a high level of mobility, with families moving in and out? (And who's moving in—families with children or retirees?)

6. Does your community contain pockets of middle-income housing that will attract young couples and families with small children?

7. Is there still land available in your community for future residential development?

8. Have service organizations (for example, YMCA, YWCA, community clubs for children, and religious groups) been maintaining an emphasis on programs for children of elementary school age?

Source: Adapted from AASA, *Declining Enrollment,* 45–47.

EXHIBIT 2.2   Commonly Asked Questions about Demographic Survey

1. *What is a demographic survey?* A demographic survey of the school district includes a thorough census of the population determining who the people are, their living conditions, how many there are, how they intend to use the land, their length of residency, the number of children per household by ages and grades, and the various kinds of dwelling units found in the district.

2. *What are the advantages of a demographic survey?* By combining the information from a demographic survey with in-and-out migration rates, school attrition rates, and the number of live births, it is possible to make enrollment projections beyond the conventional linear model. This type of information gives the forecaster the tools with which to project more accurately by "feeling the pulse" of the district.

3. *What are the disadvantages of a demographic survey?* The two major disadvantages are costs and the time limitation on the utility of the data. The major costs will be for the personnel involved in planning, organizing, and administering the survey, processing the data and analyzing the results. Additional costs will include computer time and supplies. In regard to the time limitation on the utility of the data, unless supplemental surveys are conducted the lifetime of demographic data usually does not exceed five years. This time limitation may be considerably less in a rapidly changing community.

4. *What kind of district would benefit most from a demographic survey?* In districts where enrollments are significantly fluctuating or are changing in a nonlinear fashion, the benefits gained through a demographic survey will probably offset the cost involved.

5. *What specific outside community factors should be taken into consideration when evaluating enrollment projections?* The following are major outside community factors to be considered: transportation, movement of industry (in-out), change in zoning regulations, change in subdivisions regulations, change in government or military installations (opening or closing), urban renewal, subdivision of large land holdings (farms, estates), and highway systems.

Reviewing School District Objectives

The future objectives of a school district determine future human resources needs. The number and mix of employees are determined by the types of services called for by organizational objectives. Establishing objectives is the prerogative of the board of education. The board, however, must rely on the advice of the school administration as it establishes objectives that will best meet the educational needs of the community.

The review of current objectives in light of future educational needs is a cooperative task. In a district operating under the organizational structure presented in Chapter 1, the assistant superintendents for secondary education, elementary education, and instructional services would have the primary responsibility for determining future objectives. The assistant superintendent for human resources would develop a human resources forecast to meet the projected objectives developed by the three other assistant superintendents. The assistant superintendent for administrative services would then translate the objectives and human resources needs into a fiscal plan. The superintendent of schools is charged with prioritizing the objectives and recommending them to the school board for approval.

This review of objectives is not a one-time task but rather a continual process. The objectives, however, should be established for at least a five-year period and if the need occurs, could be revised into a new five-year plan each year. Thus a set of objectives is always in effect for a set period of time.

Human Resources Forecasting

When the objectives have been reviewed and an overall human resources forecast has been established, a more explicit projection of future human resources needs must be developed. There are five commonly accepted methods for computing future needs.[3]

1. *Expert estimate.* Those staff members in the school district most familiar with employment requirements use their experience and judgment to estimate future needs.

2. *Historical comparison.* By this method, past trends are projected into the future.

3. *Task analysis.* Each person in each type of position is studied to determine demand. This method is sometimes effective in uncovering specific quality shortages within a school system.

4. *Correlation.* Human resources requirements fluctuate in relation to such variables as decreasing enrollment, fiscal resources, and new programs. A correlation of these variables can be statistically formulated.

5. *Modeling.* This usually refers to decision-making models. However, it may be broadened to include reviewing the programs in other school systems, and how they are organized, in order to formulate a model for staffing.

Whatever method or combination of methods are used, the human resources inventories on current employees can provide data about the age, sex, education, certification, and types of positions within the school district.

---

[3]Bruce Coleman, "An Integrated System for Manpower Planning," *Business Horizons* (October 1970), 89–95.

The Supply of Human Resources

An increase in a school system's supply of human resources can come from two sources, newly hired employees and individuals returning from absences such as maternity, military, and sabbatical leaves. Both types of increases are relatively easy to incorporate into a human resources forecast because hiring is controlled and leaves are usually for set periods of time.

Decreases in a school system's supply of human resources, however, are more difficult to predict. Deaths, voluntary resignations, and dismissals are unpredictable except in the broadest sense, as through statistical averaging. However, some decreases, such as sabbatical leaves, can be controlled; and others, such as retirements, are easier to predict.

The available labor force has a significant effect on human resources forecasting. Graduates from high schools, colleges, and universities continually replenish the supply of labor necessary to carry out the mandate of public education. In recent years, however, educational organizations have experienced a decrease in the number of applicants for mathematics and science teaching positions because of the higher wages and advancement opportunities available in private business and industry.

A major source of employees other than recent graduates includes older individuals, particularly women reentering the work force and seeking full-time or part-time employment, either to supplement family income or, in many cases, to provide the primary income for the family. Divorce rates and the high cost of living are key factors contributing to the number of women reentering the labor force.

Matching Needs with Supply

A final activity in human resources forecasting is to match the school district's future human resources needs with current supply. This will pinpoint shortages, highlight areas of potential overstaffing, and identify the number of individuals who must be recruited from the labor force to satisfy future needs.

In the final analysis, human resources planning ensures that we have the right number and mix of people to meet the school district's future needs as determined by its future objectives.

Reduction in Force

Declining enrollments have particular significance in the human resources planning process and have caused the initiation in some districts of a procedure commonly referred to as reduction in force, or RIF. Excess employees are usually placed on involuntary leave according to a seniority system, which follows the principle of "last in, first out." Retained employees may be transferred within the school system to balance a particular staff or faculty. Such changes are certain to create anxiety among individuals who have become accustomed to the atmosphere and procedures of a particular school. Because many school districts have hired minorities only within the last decade, the use of seniority-based reduction procedures usually means that minority employees are among the first to go. Court-mandated desegregation and the legislative demand for affirmative action call for the introduction of alternatives to RIF whenever possible in such school districts. Exhibit 2.3 uses a question format to identify issues that must be addressed by school districts faced with reduction in force.

EXHIBIT 2.3   Commonly Asked Questions about Reduction in Force

1. *What specific steps should be used by the assistant superintendent for human resources in matters of reduction in force (RIF)?*
   - Rank employees in order of seniority.
   - Consult with legal counsel for specific wording of written notices to ensure that all the legal technicalities and notification deadlines will be met.
   - It is usually considerate to include some less formal message within the body of the letter.
   - Hold a preliminary meeting with possibly affected teachers.
   - Issue letters informing teachers that they may be excessed within the coming year (registered mail).
   - Issue letters informing teachers that they will be excessed (registered mail).

2. *What can a district do to help well-qualified, excessed teachers?* Many districts send listings of the teachers they are laying off along with their qualifications and recommendations to neighboring districts.

3. *What are alternatives to administrator RIF?* Some districts have used excessed building administrators in one- or two-year consultant positions. In one district, an excessed administrator was reassigned as a RIF coordinator.

4. *What is the role of the principal in school closings?* Elementary school principals are often the least used but probably most valuable resource of the district. Principals frequently operate on the "outer fringes" of central office, so most teachers do not regard them as "the administration"; likewise, they are not considered part of the teaching ranks by central office, so most chief administrators do not regard them as "the teachers." The unique position held is that of middle manager and, therefore, acceptable to everybody. Usually principals know and enjoy good relationships with parents and the community—frequently a much closer contact than any other person in the district. Remember, superintendents may come and go, but the elementary principal usually stays. All these factors make the elementary principal of unparalleled value in community–school relations—especially in school closings.

5. *What are suggested actions for planning for RIF?*
   - Institute a moratorium on leave policies to reduce the number of teachers returning to claim positions vacated at higher enrollment levels. Offer only one- or two-year termination contracts to new teachers (some states prohibit this policy).
   - Institute an early retirement incentive program (ERIP).
   - Institute staffing needs studies before going into contract negotiations that may call for job security items in the new contract.
   - Prepare the community and staff for possible teacher reduction.
   - Request that teachers planning to retire or leave the district file such intention at least a year in advance whenever possible.

6. *How can school districts keep job security from becoming a negotiations issue?* Keeping difficult issues off the negotiations table is the responsibility of the school district negotiator. Whether the negotiator is an outside attorney, a professional negotiator, a school administrator, or a member of the school board, the main function of the negotiator is to determine those items which are considered non-negotiable. Items dealing with control over the school system operations are essentially the domain of the school board and administration. More and more, however, any and all items that are related to the operations of schools are becoming negotiable. A firm position in this particular matter of job security, along with community understanding, is necessary.

Source: Adapted from AASA, *Declining Enrollment*, 31–34.

Alternatives to Reduction in Force

Two of the most successful alternatives to RIF have been early retirement incentive programs and retaining individuals for positions that will become vacant through attrition or will be created because of program development.

Teacher negotiations have centered in recent years on the job security issue, and many contracts now call for teachers in excess areas to be transferred to other positions, hired as permanent substitutes, or retrained for new assignments at school district expense.

The Role of the Principal

A key person in human resources planning is the building principal. He or she is usually the first to spot dwindling enrollments. The principal, of course, can provide the central-office staff with up-to-date and projected enrollment figures, with projected maintenance and capital improvement costs, and with projected staffing needs.

The principal also has front-line contact with staff members, students, and parents. Therefore, he or she should be responsible for preparing teachers with possible job loss and for easing the concerns of parents and students. To perform these tasks effectively, the principal must become an integral part of the human resources planning process—being relied upon for data and input. In like manner, he or she must be constantly kept informed of central-office decisions before such decisions are announced to the staff and public.

Federal Influences on Human Resources Planning

A hallmark of our contemporary American society is the avalanche of federal legislation and court decisions delineating and more clearly defining civil rights. The term *civil rights* is somewhat misunderstood and is most often applied to the constitutional rights of racial minority groups. However, it correctly refers to those constitutional and legislative rights that are inalienable and applicable to all citizens. The human resources forecast should provide direction for the recruitment and selection processes. In so doing, this forecast must not violate the civil rights of job applicants or lead the school district into an indefensible position.

What follows is an explanation of major federal legislation, executive orders, and court decisions that should provide direction in the implementation phase of a human resources forecast. It is not meant to be exhaustive because the legislative and judicial processes are organic in nature; therefore, modifications and change will undoubtedly occur. The underlying concept of equality, however, has timeless application.

As prelude to this information, the important concepts of *social justice* and *affirmative action* must be clearly understood because they are requirements incorporated or implied in civil rights legislation and executive orders.

Social Justice and Human Resources Administration

The notion of civil rights emanates from the concept of social justice and, thus, it is important to briefly explain how social justice is imbedded in the practice of human resources administration.[4] Justice is a guide that regulates how people live out their lives as members of various societies. The idea of justice implies that someone or a group of people can be treated fairly or unfairly. The content of justice is often referred to as entitlement and from this perspective people have claims that are properly due to them.

Because they are human beings, all people have an entitlement to be respected. Not only people but also governments and institutions must afford others this respect, which entails personal integrity, liberty, and equality of opportunity. Thus, human resources planning, recruitment, selection, placement and induction, staff development, performance evaluation, compensation, and collective negotiations policies and procedures have a foundation in social justice.

There are also various types of justice. Distributive justice refers to the responsibility of society to the individual, legal justice refers to the responsibility of each person to society, and commutative justice refers to the responsibility that exists between individuals. All three types are found in human resources administration. For example, the school district as a society has a responsibility to be racially and ethnically unbiased in the recruitment and selection of teachers. Teachers have a responsibility to provide truthful information on employment applications and human resources administrators have a responsibility to process applications for employment in a timely manner.

The notion of justice also has another dimension, restitution. It is recognized that unjustly depriving someone of an entitlement does not nullify the responsibility but rather requires the implementation of the entitlement in addition to restoring what was withheld. This is easily verified by the actions of the Equal Employment Opportunity Commission that has rendered decisions against school districts for being biased against minorities and women. Some of the decisions by EEOC required school districts to hire the people filing the complaints.

A Theory of Justice

John Rawls was an American political philosopher who had formulated a theory of justice around the notion of fairness.[5] The influence of Rawls has been extensive and he is considered to be a major defender of the social contract theory that can be found in the writings of Immanuel Kant, John Locke, and Jean-Jacques Rousseau. Rawls's basic premise is that the best principles of justice for the basic structure of any society are those that would be the object of an original agreement in the establishment of a society, which are derived by free rational persons as an initial position of equality.

In all Western societies the original agreements were initially derived through many different means, some of which were violent. In fact the murky remnants of the past are only maintained in a given society's collective consciousness. Of course, the original conflicts were eventually reduced to writing and have come down to us through time as constitutions. Nevertheless, in subsocieties there is the possibility to observe and even participate in formulating an agreement. The human resources policy formulation process

---

[4]Ronald W. Rebore, *The Ethics of Educational Leadership* (Upper Saddle River, New Jersey: Merrill/Prentice Hall, 2001), 227–238.

[5]John Rawls, *A Theory of Justice: Revised Edition* (Cambridge, Massachusetts: The Belknap Press of Harvard University Press, 1999), 10–19, 47–101.

used by boards of education and the administrative formulation of human resources procedures are examples of how original agreements live on in contemporary society. They should be the agreements of equality. Of course, it is true that state and federal laws and governmental agency regulations have established the boundaries within which policies and procedures are formulated. However, the manner in which boards of education, superintendents, and human resources administrators establish and interpret policies and procedures can violate the principle of fairness. This is seen in the human resources function particularly in regards to affirmative action and equal employment opportunity.

Further, like all other institutions, school districts go through periods of time when it is necessary to reevaluate policies and procedures for the purpose of renewal and reform. As the process of reevaluation is carried out, there arises the opportunity to examine the policies and procedures of a given school district using the notion of fairness as a criterion.

Rawls set forth two principles that he believes people should choose as a means of implementing the notion of fairness. Rawls's *first principle* states that each person is to have an equal right to a system of liberties that is compatible with a similar system of liberties available to all people. The concept of system, of course, is an essential component of this principle because it establishes that the exercise of one liberty may be, and probably is, dependent on other liberties. Further, Rawls stated that the principles of justice are to be ranked and gives the example that liberty can be restricted only for the sake of liberty. Thus, administrative internship programs that are limited to minorities and women because of their under-representation in the administrative ranks of a given school district are justifiable based on this principle.

Rawls's *second principle* asserts that social and economic inequalities must benefit not only the least advantaged but also everyone and that equal opportunity to secure offices and positions must be open to all. This principle of justice must also be ranked so that the principle of efficiency does not occupy the position of first priority. Affirmative action and equal opportunity in employment legislation and court decisions help to secure this principle along with legislation and case law that ensures equal opportunity to seek election to the board of education. The following federal laws, which are set forth later in this chapter, are examples of how this second principle has been operationalized in our American society:

- The Civil Rights Act of 1964 as amended
- Title V of the Rehabilitation Act of 1973
- The Americans with Disabilities Act of 1990

The principle of just savings must be invoked when considering how inequities can benefit the least advantaged. Therefore, a board of education that needs to raise the level of teachers' salaries because the assistant superintendent for human resources is finding it difficult to recruit and hire quality teachers, may place before the voters a tax levy referendum that will increase the amount of property taxes each property owner will pay in future years. Such an increase in taxation will benefit not only the present generation of students but also future generations.

The application of the second principle through this example demonstrates that the present generation of taxpayers will bear the burden of higher taxes in order to enhance the opportunities of other generations. If there is a lack of quality teachers, the educational programs will continue to deteriorate and ultimately the cost will be much higher in the future to bring the programs back to the appropriate level. In addition, competitive salaries will have increased to the point where it will be necessary to significantly increase the amount of taxes in order to attract the caliber of teachers required by the educational needs of the students. Consequently, future generations are saved from becoming the least advantaged through the present and immediate future generation of taxpayers.

In the United States these principles of justice are embodied in certain documents that were the cornerstones on which the nation was founded. In addition to the Constitution of the United States, the Bill of Rights and the Declaration of Independence contain the principles concerning justice that are set forth in this chapter.[6]

Affirmative Action

Definition

"There can be justice for none if there is not justice for all," captures the intent of civil rights legislation. Affirmative action programs are detailed, result-oriented programs, which, when carried out in good faith, result in compliance with the equal opportunity clauses found in most legislation and executive orders.[7] Affirmative action, therefore, is not a law within itself but rather an objective reached by following a set of guidelines that insure compliance with legislation and executive orders. Thus, an organization does not violate affirmative action; it violates the law.

Brief History of Affirmative Action

Although the term *affirmative action* is of recent origin, the concept of an employer taking specific steps to utilize fully and to treat equally minority groups can be traced to President Franklin D. Roosevelt's Executive Order 8802, issued in June 1941. This executive order, which had the force of law, established a policy of equal employment opportunity in regard to defense contracts. President Roosevelt issued a new order in 1943 extending the order to all government contractors and for the first time mandating that all contracts contain a clause specifically forbidding discrimination.

In 1953 President Dwight D. Eisenhower issued Executive Order 10479, which established the Government Contract Compliance Committee. This committee received complaints of discrimination against government contractors, but had no power to enforce its guidelines.

The period of voluntary compliance ended in 1961 when President John F. Kennedy issued Executive Order 10925. This order established the President's Committee on Equal Employment Opportunity and gave it the authority to make and enforce its own rules by imposing sanctions and penalties against noncomplying contractors. Government contrac-

---

[6]www.nara.gov/charters/constitution/amendments.html

[7]"Labor Law Reports—Employment Practices," *Office of Federal Contract Compliance Manual,* 2nd ed., Report 86, No. 580 (New York: Commerce Clearing House, July 3, 1975), foreword.

tors were required to have nondiscrimination clauses covering race, color, creed, and national origin.

In September 1965 President Lyndon B. Johnson issued the very important Executive Order 11246, which gave the secretary of labor jurisdiction over contract compliance and created the Office of Federal Contract Compliance, which replaced the Committee on Equal Employment Opportunity. Every federal contract was required to have a seven-point equal opportunity clause, by which a contractor agreed not to discriminate against anyone in hiring and during employment on the basis of race, color, creed, or national origin. Further, the contractor also had to agree in writing to take affirmative action measures in hiring. President Johnson's Executive Order 11375 in 1967 amended Executive Order 11246 by adding sex and religion to the list of protected categories.

The secretary of labor issued Chapter 60 of Title 41 of the Code of Federal Regulations for the purpose of implementing Executive Order 11375. The secretary delegated enforcement authority to the Office of Federal Contract Compliance (OFCC), which reports to the assistant secretary of the Employment Standards Administration.

The Office of Federal Contract Compliance provides leadership in the area of nondiscrimination by government contractors and also coordinates matters relating to Title VII of the 1964 Civil Rights Act, as amended, with the Equal Employment Opportunity Commission (EEOC) and the Department of Justice.

The EEOC was established by Title VII of the 1964 Civil Rights Act to investigate alleged discrimination based on race, color, religion, sex, or national origin. The EEOC was greatly strengthened in 1972 by the passage of the Equal Employment Opportunity Act. It extended coverage to all private employers of fifteen or more persons, all educational institutions, all state and local governments, public and private employment agencies, labor unions with fifteen or more members, and joint labor–management committees for apprenticeships and training. This act also gave the Commission the power to bring litigation against an organization that engages in discriminatory practices.

Equal Employment Opportunity Commission

A major failing of many school administrators is their lack of understanding about EEOC and its influence on human resources administration. From time to time this five-member commission has established affirmative action guidelines that, if adopted by school districts, can minimize liability when claims of discrimination occur. To further aid employers, on December 11, 1978, the EEOC adopted additional guidelines that can be used to avoid liability for claims of "reverse discrimination" that result from affirmative action that provides employment opportunities for women and racial and ethnic minorities. The following compilation from several sources will provide a framework for affirmative action compliance.

Eight steps have emerged from federal guidelines.[8] First, each board of education should issue a written policy covering equal employment opportunity and affirmative action to be enforced by its chief executive officer, the superintendent. Commitments that should be included in the policy are a determination to recruit, hire, and promote for all job classifications without regard to race, creed, national origins, sex, or age (except where

---

[8]The eight steps are a composite of those found in the Equal Employment Opportunity Commission's website, www.eeoc.gov.

sex or age is a bona fide occupational qualification); a determination to base decisions concerning employment solely on individual qualifications as related to the requirements of the position; and a determination to insure that all human resources matters such as compensation, benefits, transfers, layoffs, returns from layoffs, and continuing education will be administered without regard to race, creed, national origin, sex, or age.

Second, the superintendent should appoint a top level official to be directly responsible for implementing the program. This official usually has the title *Director of Affirmative Action.* He or she should be responsible for developing policy statements and affirmative action programs. In addition, he or she should initiate internal and external communications, assist other administrators in the identification of problem areas, design and implement auditing and reporting systems, serve as a liaison between the district and enforcement agencies, and keep the superintendent informed of the latest developments in the area of equal opportunities.

Third, a school district should disseminate information about its affirmative action program both internally and externally. The board policy should be publicized through all internal channels, such as at meetings and on bulletin boards. External dissemination might take the form of brochures advertising the district; written notification to recruitment sources; clauses in purchase orders, leases, contracts; and written notification to minority organizations, community agencies, and community leaders.

Step four begins with a survey and analysis of minority and female employees by school and job classification. The percentage and number of minority and female employees currently employed in each major job classification should be compared to their presence in the relevant labor market—that is, the area in which you can reasonably expect to recruit. This will determine "underutilization," defined as having fewer minorities or women in a particular job category or school than could be reasonably expected; and "concentration," defined as more of a particular group in a job category or school than would reasonably be expected. A survey also should be conducted to identify those females and minorities who have the credentials to handle other jobs. Such employees can be transferred to these positions, if necessary.

With this information, the school district's administration should proceed to step five, developing measurable and remedial goals on a timetable. Once long-range goals have been established, specific and numerical targets can be developed for the hiring, training, transferring, and promoting of personnel to reach goals within the established time frame. During this step the causes of underutilization should be identified.

Step six calls for developing and implementing specific programs to eliminate discriminatory barriers. This is the heart of an affirmative action program and must be discussed under several subheadings, which topics also will be further expanded in subsequent chapters. Everyone involved in every aspect of the hiring process must be trained to use objective standards that support affirmative action goals. Recruitment procedures for each job category must be analyzed and reviewed to identify and eliminate discriminatory barriers. Recruitment procedures should include contacting educational institutions and community action organizations that represent minorities.

Reviewing the selection process to ensure that job requirements and hiring practices contribute to the attainment of affirmative action goals is a vital part of step six. This includes making certain that job qualifications and selection standards do not screen out minorities, unless the qualifications can be significantly related to job performance and no alternate nondiscriminatory standards can be developed.

Upward-mobility systems such as promotions, transfers, and continuing education play an important role in fulfilling step six. Through careful record keeping, existing barriers may be identified and specific remedial programs initiated. These programs might include providing training for targeted minorities and women who are currently qualified for upward mobility and more extensive training for those who are not yet qualified.

Wage and salary structures, benefits, and conditions of employment are other areas of investigation. Title VII of the 1964 Civil Rights Act and the Equal Pay Act require fiscal parity for jobs of equal skill and responsibility. All fringe benefits such as medical, hospital, and life insurance must be equally applied to personnel performing similar functions. Even in instances where states had "protective laws" barring women from hard or dangerous work, the courts generally found that the equal employment requirements of Title VII superseded these state laws. Courts have also barred compulsory maternity leave and the discharge of pregnant teachers.

Under affirmative action guidelines, the criteria for deciding when a person will be terminated, demoted, disciplined, laid off, or recalled should be the same for all employees. Seemingly neutral practices should be reexamined to see if they have a disparate effect on minority groups. Special considerations, such as job transfers and career counseling, should be given to minorities who have been laid off because of legitimate seniority systems.

Step seven is to establish internal auditing and reporting systems to monitor and evaluate progress in meeting the goals of the affirmative action program. Quarterly reports based on the data already outlined should be available to all administrators, enabling them to see how the program is working and where improvement is needed. The issue of keeping records on current employees and applicants by gender, race, or national origin is a very sensitive issue. Such record keeping has been used in the past as a discriminatory device, and some states have outlawed the practice. However, in certain litigation these records have been used as evidence of discriminatory practices. The data could even be demanded by enforcement agencies, and it is necessary for affirmative action record keeping. The EEOC suggests that such information be coded and kept separate from personnel files.[9]

Developing supportive district and community programs is the last step in an affirmative action program. This may include developing support services for recruiting minority and female employees and encouraging current employees to further their education in order to qualify for promotions.

The EEOC Administrative Process

Alleged discrimination charges can be filed with any of EEOC's district offices. The following outlines the administrative process involved with an allegation of employment discrimination.[10]

[9]See Equal Employment Opportunity Commission's website.

[10]Dennis G. Collins, "Equal Employment Opportunity Act," *Journal of Missouri Bar* (October–November 1978), 467–474.

The Charge of Discrimination   A charge can be filed by any person, by others on behalf of that person, or by any of the EEOC commissioners. This charge must be filed within one hundred and eighty days from when the alleged discriminatory act occurred. In those states that have an employment discrimination law, the time may be extended to three hundred days. EEOC must first refer the charge to the appropriate state agency. The Equal Employment Opportunity Commission begins its investigation after the state agency concludes its procedures or after sixty days from the date of referral by EEOC to the state agency, whichever occurs first.

Some discriminatory practices are considered to be "continuing violations." A failure to promote because of a discriminatory system of promotions is an example of a continuing violation because it occurs each day the practice is followed. However, when an individual is denied employment because of discrimination, this constitutes a specific violation that occurred on a particular date. A continuing violation arises over a lengthy period of time. The time limit for filing a charge involving a continuing violation is one hundred eighty days after the cessation of the discriminatory practice. Therefore, as long as a practice continues, there is no time limit for filing a charge.

If an individual is subject to a collective bargaining agreement and believes that he or she has been discriminated against, he or she may follow the grievance procedures set out in the master contract. This procedure does not alter the time period during which a charge must be filed.

Investigation of the Discrimination Charge   It usually takes eighteen months after a charge is filed for an investigation to begin. The EEOC will demand broad access to an employer's records. An employer may object to the subpoena of records on the following grounds: the information is privileged, the compilation of information would be excessively burdensome, or the information sought is irrelevant to the charges.

The Determination   When the investigation has been completed, the EEOC will make a determination concerning the discrimination charges. This determination will take one of two forms: "reasonable cause," which means that the charge is meritorious and both parties (employer and charging party) are invited to conciliate the case; or "no cause," which means that the charge has no merit. If the charging party continues to believe that discrimination occurred, the court system is the next avenue of recourse.

The Process of Conciliation   This process begins when the employer or his authorized representative meets with the staff of EEOC at one of the district offices to explore methods of conciliation. The usual methods employed are listed here.

1. The employer and charging party may agree to a "conciliation agreement." The terms of this agreement are designed to eliminate the discriminatory practice and may include provisions such as back pay, reinstatement of the charging party if he or she was terminated, and establishing goals and a timetable for hiring and promoting minorities. EEOC negotiates thousands of conciliation agreements each year, recovering millions of dollars for employees who have experienced discrimination.

2. With the concurrence of EEOC, the employer may extend an offer to the charging party. If the charging party rejects the offer, EEOC issues a "right to sue" notice, which gives the charging party ninety days to bring legal action against the employer.

3. The employer and charging party may agree to a settlement for a single individual. However, if the investigation by EEOC reveals a discriminatory practice against a class of persons such as females or persons with disabilities and if the employer along with EEOC is unable to reach an agreement on a class determination, such is considered a "failure of conciliation," and the case is referred to the litigation division of the Equal Employment Opportunity Commission.

4. If the employer, charging party, and EEOC are unable to reach an agreement, this also is considered a "failure of conciliation," and referral is made to the litigation division.

The Litigation Division   When conciliation fails, the litigation division evaluates the case to determine if there is a significant legal issue involved or if the case could have a significant impact on systematic patterns of discrimination. If one or both of these conditions exist, EEOC will most likely bring a lawsuit against the alleged discriminating employer.

The vast majority of lawsuits filed in federal courts, however, are instigated by private individuals pursuing their claims of discrimination or are class action suits filed by a group of citizens. The prerequisites to filing an individual claim of discrimination in federal court are: the charge was filed first with EEOC within the required time, EEOC issues a "right to sue" letter, and the charging party filed suit within ninety days from receipt of the letter.

A "right to sue" letter is usually issued by EEOC under three circumstances: (1) when a charge of discrimination is determined to have a "no cause" status by EEOC, which allows the charging party to appeal through the courts; (2) when the litigation division of EEOC rejects a case for legal action; (3) when EEOC enters into a conciliation agreement with an employer that does not include the charging party's claim.

If a federal court rules in favor of the charging party, it may grant any award it deems equitable. Injunctive remedies, on the other hand, require an employer to do something such as modifying a promotional policy that does not follow affirmative action guidelines and discriminates against minorities. In an individual case of discrimination when back pay is involved, the court may award back pay to the discriminate for a period of up to two years prior to the date when the charge was filed with EEOC.

Bona Fide Occupational Qualification
Discrimination by sex, religion, or national origin is allowed by the Equal Employment Opportunity Act under one condition, stated in the law as follows:

> Notwithstanding any other provision of this title, (1) it shall not be an unlawful employment practice for an employer to hire and employ employees, for an employment agency to classify, or refer for employment any individual, for a labor organization to classify its membership or to classify or refer for employment any individual, or for an employer, labor organization, or joint labor management committee controlling apprenticeship or other training or retraining programs to admit or employ any individual in any such program, on the basis of his religion, sex, or national origin in those certain instances where religion, sex, or national

origin is a bona fide occupational qualification reasonably necessary to the normal operation of that particular business or enterprise, and (2) it shall not be an unlawful employment practice for a school, college, university, or other educational institution or institution of learning to hire and employ employees of a particular religion if such school, college, university, or other educational institution or institution of learning is, in whole or in substantial part, owned, supported, controlled, or managed by a particular religion or by a particular religious corporation, association, or society, or if the curriculum of such school, college, university, or other educational institution or institution of learning is directed toward the propagation of a particular religion.[11]

Therefore, a school district's personnel administrator has the right to specify a female for the position of swimming instructor when part of the job description includes supervising the locker room used by female students. In like manner, a Lutheran school official may hire only those applicants who profess the Lutheran creed because the mission of the school is to propagate that particular faith.

In certain school districts the national origin of teachers is extremely important. If in a particular school district over 30 percent of its student population has Spanish surnames, being of Hispanic origin could be a bona fide job qualification for certain teaching positions in that school system.

Judicial Review of Affirmative Action

Court decisions have further modified affirmative action regulations. Although the courts will continue to refine the interpretation of the Civil Rights Act and the Equal Employment Opportunity Act, certain basic conclusions have emerged and provide direction to school districts in their efforts to construct and implement an affirmative action program.[12]

1. Discrimination has been broadly defined, in most cases including a class of individuals rather than a single person. Where discrimination has been found by the courts to exist, remediation must be applied to all members of the class to which the individual complainant belongs.

2. It is not the intent but rather the consequences of employment practices that determine if discrimination exists.

3. Even when an employment practice is neutral in text and impartially administered, if it has a disparaging effect upon members of a protected class (those groups covered by a law) or if it perpetuates the effects of prior discriminatory practices, it constitutes unlawful discrimination.

4. Statistics that show a disproportionate number of minorities or females in a job classification relative to their presence in the work force constitutes evidence of discriminatory practices. When such statistics exist, the employer must show that this is not the result of overt or institutional discrimination.

---

[11]*The Equal Employment Opportunity Act of 1972* (Washington, DC: U.S. Government Printing Office, 1972), 4.

[12]Equal Employment Opportunity Commission.

5. For an employer to justify any practice or policy that creates a disparaging effect on a protected class, a "compelling business necessity" must be demonstrated. The courts have interpreted this in a very narrow sense to mean that no alternative nondiscriminatory practice can achieve the required result.

6. Court-ordered remedies not only open the doors to equal employment opportunity but also require employers to "make whole" and "restore the rightful economic status" of all those in the affected class. In practice, courts have ordered fundamental changes in almost every aspect of employment.

Two U.S. Supreme Court decisions from the late 1970s have had an indirect effect upon affirmative action programs in school districts. The first case, *Regents of the University of California* v. *Bakke,* was decided in 1978 and dealt with admission quotas to a medical school. The second, *United Steelworkers* v. *Brian F. Weber,* also decided in 1979, dealt with a voluntary race-conscious affirmative action plan in private industry. Both cases addressed the issue of reverse discrimination.

In June 2003, two U.S. Supreme Court rulings addressed a fundamental legal question that is at the heart of the affirmative action issue. The question concerned whether or not the United States Constitution permits affirmative action policies. The answer to the question is a resounding yes. In *Grutter* v. *Bollinger,* the Court upheld a Michigan law school's admissions policies stating that the school had a compelling interest in enrolling a racially and ethnically diverse student body because such diversity provides a significant educational benefit. However, even though the Court upheld the importance of affirmative action in *Gratz* v. *Bollinger,* it ruled that Michigan's undergraduate admissions practice placed too much emphasis on race in assessing applicants. The University used a point system that automatically gave substantial bonuses to members of certain minority groups.[13] The implications of these two rulings for human resources administrators are that affirmative action policy is constitutionally assured, but the practices that implement affirmative action must be defensible.

Exhibit 2.4 is a sample policy that has been developed to illustrate how school districts can comply with the intent of federal legislation and litigation set forth in this chapter.

Civil Rights Act, 1991

The passage of this civil rights legislation along with the Americans with Disabilities Act of 1990 set school districts on a new path during the 1990s. This has been particularly true with regards to the Civil Rights Act of 1991. The law extends punitive damages and jury trials for the first time to employees who have been discriminated against because of their race, national origin, sex, disability, or religion. School districts must be vigilant in developing and carrying out proper procedures for the selection, disciplining, and termination of employees.[14]

There have been two significant procedural changes. First, the law allows compensatory and punitive damages. Prior to passage of this law and with few exceptions, plaintiffs could

---

[13]Peter Schmidt, "Affirmative Action Survives, and So Does the Debate," *The Chronicle of Higher Education,* Special Report (July 4, 2003), S1–S7.

[14]Joann S. Lublin, "Rights Law to Spur Shifts in Promotions," *Wall Street Journal,* 30 December 1991, sec. 2, B1.

EXHIBIT 2.4   Board of Education Policy on Equal Employment Opportunity and Affirmative Action

The board of education recognizes that implementation of its responsibility to provide an effective educational program depends on the full and effective utilization of qualified employees regardless of race, age, sex, color, religion, national origin, creed, ancestry, or disability.

The board directs that its employment and human resources policies guarantee equal opportunity for everyone. Discrimination has no place in any component of this school system. Therefore, all matters relating to recruitment, selection, placement, compensation, benefits, educational opportunities, promotion, termination, and working conditions shall be free from discriminatory practices.

The board of education further initiates an affirmative action program to be in compliance with Title VII of the Civil Rights Act of 1964 and the Equal Employment Opportunity Act of 1972. This program shall insure minority and female proportional representation and participation in all employment opportunities; that civil rights will not be violated, abridged, or denied; that recruitment and selection criteria will be unbiased; that information relative to employment and promotional opportunities will be disseminated on an equal basis; and finally, that every employee has a right to file an internal or external complaint of discrimination and to obtain redress therefrom based on the finding of facts substantiating the complaint.

The following school district administrators are responsible for the effective implementation of the affirmative action program.

Superintendent of Schools. As the chief executive officer of the school system, the superintendent is directly responsible for exercising a leadership role in formulating and implementing procedures that are in keeping with this policy.

Director of Affirmative Action. Under the supervision of the superintendent, the director is responsible for the administration of the affirmative action program.

---

receive remedies limited to lost pay and benefits, reinstatement, and attorney fees. After passage, plaintiffs can receive "compensatory damages," for emotional pain, inconvenience, and mental anguish. Further, if the plaintiff can prove that the employer acted with "malice" or with "reckless indifference," he or she may be awarded punitive damages. The customary remedies of receiving lost pay and benefits, reinstatement, and attorney fees are still available in addition to compensatory and punitive damages.

The major consideration for superintendents, assistant superintendents, and school board members has been that they can be named as codefendants in an action brought against a school district under the Civil Rights Act of 1991. The reason for this is that punitive damages cannot be levied against a school district because it is a governmental agency, but punitive damages can be levied against individuals such as administrators and school board members.

Limits on the amount of compensatory and punitive damages have been established as follows:

- Plaintiffs may be awarded damages up to $50,000 if the school district has at least 15 but not more than 99 employees.
- Plaintiffs may be awarded damages up to $100,000 if the school district has between 100 and 200 employees.

- Plaintiffs may be awarded damages up to $200,000 if the school district has between 200 and 500 employees.
- Plaintiffs may be awarded damages up to $300,000 if the school district has more than 500 employees.

There are two exceptions to these limits. For age discrimination the limit is twice the amount of lost pay and benefits, and for race discrimination there is no limit. There is another liability for a school district that has not been available in the past in relation to damages. A plaintiff who prevails may also recover the cost of expert witness fees.

The second significant procedural change involves the right of a complainant to receive a jury trial in an employment discrimination case in which compensatory and/or punitive damages are being sought. Jury trials were seldom allowed in employment discrimination cases prior to this law. The major consideration concerning this issue is not only the unpredictability of juries but also the perceived bias of juries against employers.

Because of this law, there is also a significant substantive change in the way in which the school human resources function is managed. The Civil Rights Act of 1991 overruled several U.S. Supreme Court decisions that appeared to be pro employer. Under the new law, in a discrimination case, the burden of proof has been clearly placed on the school district to justify an employment practice that taken at face value is neutral but which results in discrimination against a protected class.[15]

Equality for People with Disabilities

Title V of the Rehabilitation Act of 1973 contains five sections, four relating to affirmative action for individuals with disabilities and one dealing with voluntary actions, remedial actions, and evaluation criteria for compliance with the law. The congressional intent of the Rehabilitation Act is identical to the intent of other civil rights legislation, such as the Civil Rights Act (covering discrimination based on race, sex, religion, or national origin) and Title IX of the Educational Amendments (covering discrimination based on sex). However, the U.S. Department of Health, Education and Welfare (HEW) emphasized in the Federal Register promulgating the Rehabilitation Act that it contains a fundamental difference:

> The premise of both Title VII (Civil Rights Act) and Title IX (Educational Amendments) is that there is no inherent difference of equalities between the general public and the persons protected by these statutes and, therefore, there should be no differential treatment in the administration of federal programs. Section 504 (Rehabilitation Act), on the other hand is far more complex. Handicapped persons may require different treatment in order to be afforded equal access, and identical treatment may, in fact, constitute discrimination. The problem of establishing general rules as to when different treatment is prohibited or required is compounded by the diversity of existing handicaps and the differing degree to which particular persons may be affected.[16]

[15]*Education USA,* 35, no. 18 (1993), 5.

[16]Department of Health, Education, and Welfare, "Nondiscrimination on the Basis of Handicap," *Federal Register,* 41, no. 96 (May 17, 1976).

Subpart B of Section 504 of the Rehabilitation Act specifically refers to employment practices. It prohibits recipients of federal financial assistance from discriminating against qualified individuals with disabilities in recruitment, hiring, compensation, job assignment/classification, and fringe benefits. Employers are further required to provide reasonable work environment accommodations for qualified applicants or employees with disabilities unless they can demonstrate that such accommodations would impose an undue hardship. The law applies to all state, intermediate, and local educational agencies. Finally, any agency that receives assistance under the Individuals with Disabilities Act must take positive steps to employ and promote qualified persons with disabilities into programs assisted under this act.

Reasonable Accommodation

The requirement that employers make "reasonable accommodations" in the work environment for applicants and employees with disabilities has created a great deal of confusion. Reasonable accommodations include providing employee facilities that are readily accessible to and usable by persons with disabilities; and taking action such as restructuring jobs, modifying work schedules, modifying and/or acquiring special equipment or devices, and providing readers.

In order to determine whether an accommodation imposes an undue hardship on an employer, the following factors should be considered: first, the size of the agency or company with respect to the number of employees; second, the number and type of facilities available; third, the size of the employer's budget; fourth, the composition of the work force; and finally, the nature and type of accommodation needed. If an employer believes that reasonable accommodations would impose a hardship, the burden of proof rests with the employer.

Employment Criteria

The U.S. Department of Health and Human Services (formerly HEW), in concert with the guidelines on selection procedures developed by the Equal Employment Opportunity Commission, prohibits the use of any employment test or other criteria that screens out or discriminates against persons with disabilities unless the test or selection criteria is proven to be job related. Therefore, in selecting and administering tests to an applicant or employee with a disability, the test results must accurately reflect the individual's job skills or other factors the test purports to measure rather than the person's impaired sensory, manual, or speaking skills, except when these skills are required for successful job performance.

The term *test* includes measures of general intelligence, mental ability, learning ability, specific intellectual ability, mechanical and clerical aptitudes, dexterity and coordination, knowledge, proficiency, attitudes, personality, and temperament. Formal techniques of assessing job suitability that yield qualifying criteria include specific personal history and background data, specific educational or work history, scored interviews, and scored application forms.

School district administrators must realize that they may be called on to present evidence concerning the validity and reliability of the testing procedures they use in selection and promotion processes. Casual techniques, of course, are very difficult to defend.

Preemployment Inquiries

Subpart B of Section 504 of the Rehabilitation Act specifies that recipients of federal financial assistance should take (a) remedial action to correct past discrimination, (b) voluntary action to overcome the limited participation of individuals with disabilities, (c) affirmative action to employ people with disabilities. An employer may use preemployment inquiries to determine progress in complying with the Rehabilitation Act. Subpart B also contains the following provision: An employer must state on all preemployment written questionnaires or, if no written questionnaire is used, must tell applicants that preemployment information is being requested for the purpose of implementing remedial, voluntary, or affirmative action programs; the employer must state that the information is being requested on a voluntary basis, that it will be kept confidential, and that refusal to provide such information will not subject the applicant or employee to any adverse treatment.

Nothing in Subpart B prohibits an employer from making employment conditional on the results of a medical examination prior to the assumption of duties by a person with disabilities. However, this condition can be applied only if all entering employees are required to have a medical examination and only if the results of such examinations are used in accordance with appropriate remedial, voluntary, and affirmative action programs.

The medical information collected must be maintained on separate forms from other employment data and must be accorded the same confidentiality as medical records. This information may be used by supervisors and managers to determine the restrictions in the duties of employees with disabilities and to determine necessary accommodations. First aid and safety personnel may also use this information when emergencies occur. Finally, government officials may have access to such information when investigating an employer's compliance with the Rehabilitation Act.

Organizational Action Required

Although Subpart B of Section 504 does not require school districts to develop an affirmative action program for those with disabilities, it does require three types of organizational activities: remedial action, voluntary action, and self-evaluation. The Office of Civil Rights investigates allegations of discrimination by school districts against people with disabilities and the director of the office can require remedial action if discrimination is confirmed against persons with disabilities who are currently employed, who are no longer employed in the district but were when the discrimination occurred, or who would have been employed in the district had the discrimination not occurred.

In addition, school districts may take voluntary measures to alleviate discrimination. Such measures usually begin with the construction of a self-evaluation procedure. Paragraph 87.4 of the Federal Register outlines the self-evaluation requirements as follows:

> Within one year of the effective date of publishing Section 504 regulations (May 4, 1977), local school districts must: (a) evaluate, with the assistance of handicapped individuals and organizations, current district policies and practices that do not meet Section 504 requirements, (b) modify such district policies and practices, and (c) take appropriate remedial steps to eliminate the effects of any discrimination that resulted from adherence to such policies and practices.

Furthermore,

a local school district that employs fifteen or more persons must, for at least three years following completion of the self-evaluation, maintain on file and make available for public inspection: (a) a list of the interested individuals consulted, (b) a description of areas examined and any problems identified, and (c) a description of any modifications made and of any remedial steps taken.[17]

Table 2.1 schematically presents the necessary components for planning, conducting, and analyzing a self-evaluation procedure.

The Americans with Disabilities Act, 1990

President George Bush signed into law the *Americans with Disabilities Act* (ADA) on July 26, 1990. This has been the most comprehensive legislation ever passed protecting the rights of individuals with disabilities. Within the first eleven months after its passage, the Equal Employment Opportunity Commission received 11,760 discrimination complaints which represented about 15 percent of that agency's caseload. During that same period aggrieved persons collected over $11 million in awards.[18] From a practical perspective, however, ADA is an extension of the Rehabilitation Act of 1973. This extension pertains to the private sector and to those local and state governmental agencies that receive no federal monies. Because almost every school district in the nation receives some federal financial assistance, either directly or indirectly, which is the threshold requiring adherence to the Rehabilitation Act, school districts in compliance with the Rehabilitation Act have little difficulty complying with the ADA.

There are five titles to ADA. All of them except Title IV have some impact upon school districts. Title IV pertains to telecommunications companies.

TABLE 2.1   Conceptual Components for a Self-Evaluation Model

Phase I	Develop policy statements, goals, and objectives
Phase II	Appoint a self-evaluation coordinator and define this individual's responsibilities
Phase III	Develop a self-evaluation design
Phase IV	Implement the self-evaluation design
Phase V	Analyze staffing procedures and practices
Phase VI	Modify procedures and practices
Phase VII	Monitor and evaluate these procedures and practices

Adapted from Richard Clelland, *Section 504: Civil Rights for the Handicapped* (Arlington, VA: American Association of School Administrators, 1978), 28.

[17]Dept. of HEW, *Nondiscrimination.*

[18]*Wall Street Journal,* 27 July 1993, sec. 1, A1.

Title I

This title regulates employment practices and took effect on July 26, 1992 for school districts.

Title II

All services, programs, and activities of state and local governmental agencies are subject to Title II even if they are provided by a contractor. This title took effect on January 26, 1992 and includes all activities involving all public contact as part of ongoing operations. Thus, classroom instruction and pupil transportation are affected. Even though Title II includes employment practices, the Department of Justice has decided that Equal Employment Opportunity regulations governing Title I are sufficient for Title II.

Title III

This title also took effect on January 26, 1992. It pertains to public accommodations and applies only to the private sector. School districts are not covered by Title III as such. However, if a school district contracts with a private company, for example, to provide pupil transportation or food service, the district must ensure that the private company is operating in compliance with Title III. This compliance issue is usually set forth as a section in the contract between the district and the company providing the service.

Title IV

This title took effect on July 26, 1993, and requires telecommunication companies to provide telecommunication relay services for people with hearing or speech disabilities.

Title V

This title contains a number of provisions. The most important for school districts involves the relationship of ADA to other laws. It states, for example, that the "highest standard" applies whether that standard is ADA, the Rehabilitation Act, a state law, or even a local ordinance. It also prohibits retaliation against persons seeking redress under the ADA and allows the court to award attorney fees to the prevailing parties.[19]

Jurisdiction and Scope of ADA

Under the jurisdiction of the Equal Employment Opportunity Commission, the ADA covered all school districts with 25 or more employees after July 26, 1992, and all districts with 15 or more employees after July 26, 1994. However, under the jurisdiction of the Department of Justice, discrimination is prohibited by school districts regardless of the number of employees after January 26, 1992.[20]

Because both the Department of Justice and the Equal Employment Opportunity Commission have been given jurisdiction for the enforcement of ADA, coordination between

[19]National School Boards Association, "Americans with Disabilities Act," *Updating School Board Policies,* 23, no. 4 (May 1992), 1–2.

[20]U.S. Equal Employment Opportunity Commission, *The Americans with Disabilities Act: Your Responsibilities as an Employer* (Washington, DC: The Commission, 1991), 1.

these two agencies is necessary. Further, because the Department of Labor has jurisdiction in cases involving discrimination and affirmative action under the Rehabilitation Act of 1973, coordination between this agency and the Department of Justice and the Equal Employment Opportunity Commission is not only necessary but also critical.

Under ADA it is unlawful to discriminate in all human resources functions, including:

recruitment
selection
promotion
training
staff development
rewards including direct and indirect compensation
reduction in force
termination
placement
leave
voluntary fringe benefits

Those Protected by ADA

Title I sets forth who is qualified to be protected by ADA. Essentially, under ADA a person is disabled if he or she has a physical or mental impairment that substantially limits a major life activity. ADA also protects individuals who have a record of a substantially limiting impairment, and people who are regarded as having a substantially limiting impairment.

The terms *physical or mental impairment* in this definition include cerebral palsy, muscular dystrophy, multiple sclerosis, AIDS, HIV infection, emotional illness, drug addiction, alcoholism, and dyslexia, etc. However, such conditions as a person's height, weight, or muscle tone, if these are within normal ranges, do not qualify under these terms. Further, the color of hair or eyes, being pregnant, or having served a sentence in prison are not examples of a physical or mental impairment. When determining if a person has a protected disability, the decision must be made without regard to mitigating measures such as medication and assistive or prosthetic devices.

The term *major life activity* means an activity that an average person can perform with little or no difficulty. Thus, hearing, seeing, speaking, breathing, performing manual tasks, walking, caring for oneself, learning, or working are major life activities. The Equal Employment Opportunity Commission takes into account three factors when determining if a disability substantially limits these major types of life activities: (1) the nature and severity of the impairment; (2) its duration or expected duration; (3) the actual or expected permanent long-term impact resulting from it. Thus, a broken limb, influenza, or a tonsillectomy are not disabilities.[21]

The term *record of impairment* refers to a disability for which an individual no longer receives treatment. Therefore, people who have a history of heart disease, mental illness, drug disease, or alcoholism are also protected by this law.

---

[21]Equal Employment Opportunity Commission, Final Rule, "Equal Employment Opportunity for Individuals with Disabilities," *Federal Register,* 56, no. 144 (July 26, 1991), 35735.

The term "regarded as impaired" is meant to indicate those individuals who are not physically or mentally impaired but who are regarded as impaired as a result of fear or stereotyping. This definition applies to people about whom there is unsubstantiated concern regarding productivity, safety, insurance, liability, attendance, cost of accommodation, accessibility, workers' compensation costs, or acceptance by co-workers.[22]

In March, 1995, the Equal Employment Opportunity Commission issued an interpretation of the Americans with Disabilities Act setting forth that the law protects people from employment discrimination who are healthy but who carry abnormal genes. More and more people are taking advantage of new genetic tests that can identify a person's predisposition to diseases such as Alzheimer's, heart, and certain types of cancer. This information allows individuals to access preventive measures and early treatment; it is also helpful in predicting what disease genes can be passed on to their children. If the results of these tests are known by potential employers, some of them might discriminate against those applicants who carry abnormal genes, in order to avoid future lost days from work and higher employer-paid health care premiums. Further, such information might tempt an employer to fire an employee for the same reason.[23]

The Selection Process under ADA

An applicant for a position in a school district who is also protected by ADA must otherwise qualify for the job. The term *otherwise qualify* means that the applicant can perform the essential functions of the job with or without reasonable accommodation.

Therefore, the applicant must satisfy job requirements for educational background, employment experience, skills, licenses, and other qualification standards that are job-related. Further, the person must be able to perform those tasks that are essential to the job either with or without reasonable accommodation.

The school district can still hire the best qualified applicant and it does not impose any affirmative action obligations.

Determining what are essential functions is critical to not discriminating against a qualified candidate who has a disability under ADA. This determination about essential functions must be made before carrying out certain processes of the human resources function. This is certainly true in relation to initiating the selection process which includes developing a job description and advertising the position. A number of factors should be considered in determining if the function is essential:

1. The actual work experience of present and/or past employees in the job
2. The time needed to perform a function
3. The terms of a collective bargaining agreement
4. The consequences of not requiring that an employee perform a function
5. The degree of expertise or skill required to perform the function
6. The number of other employees available to perform the function or among whom the performance of the function can be distributed
7. Whether the reason the position exists is to perform that function[24]

[22]National School Boards Association, 23, no. 4, 3.

[23]*St. Louis Post-Dispatch,* "Health Carriers of Bad Genes Protected," 9 April 1995, A8.

[24]Equal Employment Opportunity Commission, Final Rule, 35735.

Reasonable accommodation may be defined as any change or adjustment to the job or the work environment which will permit a qualified person with a disability to participate in the selection process, to perform the essential functions of a job, and to enjoy benefits and privileges of employment equal to those enjoyed by employees without disabilities. Therefore, reasonable accommodation may include:

1. Acquiring or modifying equipment or devices
2. Job restructuring
3. Part-time or modified work schedules
4. Adjusting or modifying examinations, training materials, or policies
5. Providing readers and interpreters
6. Making the workplace readily accessible to and usable to people with disabilities[25]

The reasonable accommodation requirement also applies to employees who become disabled after employment with the district. All of the above with the addition of *reassignment to another position* must be considered for the employee who becomes disabled.

In determining what accommodations may be necessary, the Equal Employment Opportunity Commission recommends the following approach. First, determine the essential functions of the job. Second, consult with the individual who has the disability in order to determine the individual's precise limitations and how they may be overcome. Third, also with the individual's assistance, identify potential accommodations and assess their effectiveness. Fourth, after considering the preferences of the individual with the disability, implement the accommodation most appropriate for the individual and the employer. It is important to understand that ADA does not require selection of the best accommodation as long as the accommodation selected provides an equal opportunity to perform the job. Examples of equipment which may be a reasonable accommodation include telecommunications devices, special computer software to enlarge or convert print documents to spoken words, telephone headsets, speaker phones, and adaptive light switches.

Undue Hardship

It is not necessary to provide a reasonable accommodation if this would cause an undue hardship on the school district. This means that the accommodation would be unduly costly, extensive, substantial, disruptive, or would fundamentally alter the nature of operation of the school district. Factors that can be considered in making this determination of undue hardship are the cost of the accommodation, the size of the school district, the financial resources of the district, and the nature or structure of the district's operations.

If a particular accommodation would be an undue hardship, the school district staff must try to identify another accommodation which will not pose a hardship. Further, if the hardship is caused by the lack of financial resources, the school district must attempt to find funding from an outside source such as a vocational rehabilitation agency. The applicant or employee must also be given the opportunity to provide the accommodation or pay for a portion of the accommodation that constitutes an undue hardship.[26]

[25]*Ibid.,* 35735–35736.

[26]U.S. Equal Employment Opportunity Commission, 5–6.

Accessibility

Title II contains the provisions of ADA relating to accessibility. ADA required school districts to conduct a self-evaluation by January 26, 1993. Most school districts have a self-evaluation on file which complied with Section 504 of the Rehabilitation Act of 1973. Thus, the school district should have included in that evaluation only those policies and practices that were not covered in the previous self-evaluation. The self-evaluation should provide an opportunity for input from interested individuals, from individuals with disabilities, and from organizations representing people with disabilities. Each school district is to maintain a file that is open to inspection by the public that includes the names of the interested persons consulted, a description of the areas examined, the problems identified, and a description of any modifications made.[27]

School districts also must maintain on file a transition plan open to inspection by the public that sets forth the structural changes to facilities that were to be undertaken in order to achieve program accessibility. This should include a time schedule for taking corrective action and the name of the school district official responsible for implementing the plan.

ADA also required school districts to appoint a staff member responsible for investigating complaints regarding noncompliance and a procedure for the prompt and equitable resolution of complaints.

Damages for Noncompliance with ADA

Hiring, reinstatement, back pay, and injunctive relief are some of the remedies that are possible under ADA. The list has been expanded by the Civil Rights Act of 1991 to include damages such as future pecuniary losses, inconvenience, mental anguish, and emotional pain subject to specific dollar limitations. Punitive damages may not be awarded against a school district under ADA.[28]

AIDS and Discrimination

There is no topic or issue that has focused the attention and concern of so many people recently as the disease of AIDS (acquired immune deficiency syndrome). Without going into a long discussion of the medical aspects of the disease, it is sufficient here to state that the disease can be transmitted to others and that it is always fatal.

The hysteria over this disease caused Dr. C. Everett Koop, the surgeon general when the syndrome was first publicized, to send an explanatory brochure to all the households in the United States. All health officials are in agreement about the manner in which the disease may be transmitted. Sexual contact with an infected person and the sharing of drug needles or syringes are the most common ways that the disease is transmitted.

Health officials are also in agreement that the disease cannot be transmitted by casual contact with an infected person. In fact, ordinary and casual contact between family members where a member had AIDS verified that the disease cannot be transmitted this way.

---

[27]National School Boards Association, "Americans with Disabilities Act," *Updating School Board Policies,* 23, no. 5 (June 1992), 3–4.

[28]National School Boards Association, 23, no. 4, 2.

The hysteria continues to exist, however, and has caused concern in the workplace, which has resulted in discriminatory practices by some individuals, companies, agencies, and organizations. A significant development occurred in 1987 that was helpful in dealing with discrimination against people infected with the AIDS virus. In *School Board of Nassau* v. *Arline,* the U.S. Supreme Court ruled that an infectious disease could constitute a disability under Section 504 of the Rehabilitation Act of 1973. In this case, the infectious disease was tuberculosis. However, in that same year a federal district circuit court of appeals in California applied the *Arline* decision to a case involving an Orange County teacher with AIDS. The court ordered the school district to reinstate the teacher to his previous duties.[29]

A further development occurred in 1988, when the U.S. Justice Department reversed its earlier position on AIDS and declared that fear of contagion by itself does not permit federal agencies and federally assisted employers to fire or discriminate against workers infected with the virus.

This legal opinion is binding on school boards, federal agencies, government contractors, managers of federally subsidized housing projects, and other organizations receiving federal contracts or financial assistance. The opinion emphasized that each situation must be determined on a case-by-case basis in order to decide if an infected person poses a direct threat to the health of others in the workplace.

The Rehabilitation Act of 1973 requires an employer to make "reasonable accommodations" for people with disabilities, which now includes AIDS. The accommodations must be made if the person with AIDS can still perform the essential requirements of his or her job. If an employer can demonstrate that making such accommodations would pose an undue hardship, then the company, agency, or organization can be excused. However, the regulations governing undue hardship are very stringent.

A situation in which the reasonable accommodation regulation probably would not apply is in the case of a school bus driver who has advanced symptoms of the disease. The effects of AIDS on the central nervous system would preclude that person from continuing to drive a school bus.

It is extremely important to protect the privacy of individuals who have AIDS. Medical information on employees is confidential. This fact is clearly set forth in *Gammel* v. *United States* (1984). In this case the U.S. government wanted to review the medical records of a federal employee, Mr. Gammel. The U.S. contended that Gammel was a potential health risk to the general public and reviewing his medical records would provide the necessary information in order to suitably assign him where he would not be a threat to the public.

Gammel's attorney argued that the Fourteenth Amendment of the United States Constitution protects the privacy rights of citizens and the release of medical information would violate this Amendment unless there was proof that a clear and present danger to public safety, in fact, existed. The U.S. government failed to establish such proof and therefore, the federal district court ruled in favor of Gammel.

Therefore, if the personnel records of public school districts contain medical information about employees, these records are confidential. The only reason for revealing the contents of such records would be the existence of a clear and present danger to public health or safety.

---

[29]Sally Banks Zakariya, "What if AIDS Comes on Staff?" *The Executive Educator,* 9, no. 4 (April 1987), 21–22.

There is also an area of concern in relation to the rights of coworkers of AIDS infected employees. This issue has been addressed in a private sector federal court case, *Whirlpool v. Marshall* (1988). The case reaffirmed that the best available medical information does not consider casual contact with an AIDS infected person to be a health risk. The contact in schools between staff members and, in fact, between staff members and students can be classified as casual and thus there is no risk of contracting AIDS. School district human resources policies and procedures must reflect this position.

In summary, case law clearly upholds the employment and privacy rights of persons with AIDS, with ARC, and with an HIV positive test. Further, case law upholds these same rights for persons suspected of being infected. It is imperative that the assistant superintendent for human resources insure that discrimination does not occur in school district practices against persons with AIDS or with the above-mentioned AIDS related conditions. A potential area for serious discrimination exists in life, medical, and hospitalization insurance programs. Exhibit 2.5 is a sample board of education policy that incorporates both the legal rights and humane treatment that should be provided to employees with HIV, AIDS, and ARC.

EXHIBIT 2.5   Sample AIDS Policy

The board of education is committed to providing a school environment free from health risks for all students and staff members. This policy has been developed utilizing information from the federal Center for Disease Control. In particular it has been written to protect the rights of school personnel who are infected with the human immunodeficiency virus (HIV) that causes acquired immune deficiency syndrome (AIDS), which, in turn, can cause AIDS related complex (ARC).

Further, the development of this policy has been guided by medical information which has documented that the HIV virus cannot be transmitted by casual person-to-person contact.

Thus, the Board of Education sets forth the following provisions.

- Each case of HIV, AIDS, or ARC will be evaluated on an individual basis.
- The administration will provide an ongoing program of education on the subject of HIV, AIDS, and ARC to students, staff, and the community.
- Employees who have been diagnosed as infected with HIV, AIDS, or ARC are encouraged to report this to the superintendent of schools accompanied by a written statement from a licensed physician which reports on the employee's medical condition and capability of continuing in his or her present position.
- This medical information will be confidential to the superintendent of schools. The superintendent will share this information with other employees only on a "need to know" basis which determination will be made in consultation with the infected employee. Those staff members so informed will also be instructed by the superintendent on the legal and policy provisions that require this information to be confidential.
- The employee shall continue in his or her position unless a deterioration in the employee's health significantly interferes with the performance of his or her job responsibilities. The employee's physician may also determine that the employee's job responsibilities pose a threat to his or her health. In either situation, a reasonable effort will be made to place the employee in another position.
- The employee is guaranteed all the protections and safeguards that other employees have according to law and board of education policy.

Vietnam Era Veterans Readjustment Assistance Act

The Vietnam Era Veterans Readjustment Assistance Act was passed by Congress in 1974. School districts receiving $10,000 or more in federal funds must take affirmative action to hire veterans with disabilities of all wars, and all veterans of the Vietnam era. This act defines a veteran with a disability as a person who has a 30 percent or more disability rating from the Veterans Administration, or who was discharged or released from active duty for a service-connected disability.

Mobilization of Military Reserves and National Guard into Active Duty

On August 22, 1990, President George Bush ordered the mobilization of U.S. military reserves and National Guard units into active duty. This was the first mobilization in twenty years. It activated approximately 40,000 troops. This mobilization, of course, was necessary in order to support the then forthcoming war in the Persian Gulf against Iraq. The war was named Desert Storm.

When the employee enters active military service, he or she is immediately covered by the military health care system. Dependents of the employee are eligible to be covered by the Civilian Health and Medical Program of the Uniformed Services (formerly CHAMPUS, now called TRICARE) under certain conditions. The most significant condition is the length of time that the employee will be on active duty. If the mobilization is for less than thirty days, dependents cannot be enrolled in TRICARE. However, if the mobilization is extended, TRICARE coverage will begin on the thirty-first day of active duty. If the mobilization is for more than thirty days at the outset, coverage begins from the first day of active duty. Dependents must receive health care from military health facilities or receive permission to go to a civilian facility.

Reservists and National Guard members are covered under the provisions of the Veteran's Reemployment Act of 1940, which also was amended in 1986. This act obliges the school district to give reservists and National Guard members time off from their civilian jobs to participate in military training and active duty. Also, the act protects them from termination and discrimination because of their military obligations. Further, the reservist or National Guard member is covered by an "escalator principle" which means that he or she will continue to accrue seniority, fringe benefits, and salary increases. Thus, if other employees in the same job category as the reservist or National Guard member received an increase in salary and/or additional fringe benefits, he or she will receive the same salary increase and/or fringe benefits when he or she returns to work. However, if there was a reduction in fringe benefits or salary for all the members of the job category, the same reductions will apply to the reservist or National Guard member upon his or her return.

Upon his or her release from military training or active duty, the reservist or National Guard member has ninety days to apply for reinstatement into his or her prior held position. If the prior held position is not available, he or she must be offered a position of like status or the job that is nearest in duties to the one he or she left.

In regard to health care benefits, the employer cannot impose a preexisting exclusion or waiting period before reinsuring the reservist or National Guard member.

The Omnibus Transportation Employee Testing Act, 1991

On October 28, 1991, President Bush signed into law the Omnibus Transportation Employee Testing Act, which required the Secretary of Transportation to promulgate regulations for alcohol and controlled substances testing for persons in safety-sensitive positions including motor carriers. Implementation for districts with 50 or more employees was done in 1994. For districts with fewer than 50 employees, implementation began in early 1995.[30]

Regulations have been established that require school bus drivers and drivers of private motor carriers of passengers to submit to controlled-substance testing.

Other regulations require school districts to conduct preemployment, postaccident, random, reasonable suspicion, and return-to-duty testing. School districts must publish the board of education policy concerning this law and must publish implementation procedures which should include the action that the school district will take if a bus driver is found to be in violation of this law.

School districts must also develop procedures for the collection, shipment, and accessioning of urine specimens. The Department of Transportation requires urine samples to be analyzed by laboratories certified by the Department of Health and Human Services' National Institute on Drug Abuse. Laboratories are required to report the analysis to a medical review officer who contacts the bus driver concerning the results of the testing and who reports the results to the school district. Of course, these reports are confidential. The school district administrator responsible for determining if a reasonable suspicion exists to require a bus driver to undergo testing must receive at least 60 minutes of training on the physical, behavioral, speech, and performance indicators of probable controlled substance abuse. Finally, a bus driver who has violated this law must receive information from the school district concerning resources that are available for helping the bus driver with his or her drug abuse problem.

Family and Medical Leave Act, 1993

President Clinton signed into law the Family and Medical Leave Act (P.L. 103–3) on February 5, 1993.[31] The fundamental purpose of this act is to provide eligible employees as defined by section 3(e) of the Fair Labor Standards Act with the right to take twelve weeks of unpaid leave per year in connection with certain circumstances.

An employee may invoke this law in conjunction with the following:

1. The birth and first-year care of a child. This includes paternity leave.
2. The adoption or foster parent placement of a child. The entitlement ends when the child reaches age one or the twelve-week period ends.
3. The illness of an employee's spouse, child, or parent. This includes a step-child, foster child, a child over eighteen years of age incapable of self care, and a step-parent.
4. The employee's own illness. This means a serious health condition that may result from not only illness but also injury, impairment, physical or mental condition. This may

---

[30]Jim Wright, "School Districts Must Plan in 1993–94 Budget Costs for Drug Testing Employees," *School Bus Fleet* (February/March 1993), 48.

[31]U.S. Congress, *Family and Medical Leave Act.* Washington, DC: U.S. Government Printing Office, 1993.

involve inpatient care or any incapacity requiring absence from work for more than three days and which involves continuing treatment by a health care provider. Also, this refers to any treatment for prenatal care.

The law became effective on August 5, 1993. However, in those school districts that have a collective bargaining agreement with one or more bargaining units, the law became effective upon the termination of the master contract or on February 5, 1994, whichever occurred earlier. Because this is a labor law, the United States Department of Labor is the federal agency responsible for the development of implementation regulations.

All employees of private elementary and secondary schools and all employees of public school districts are covered by this law. In business and industry, a company must employ fifty or more people to be subject to the mandates of the law.

Eligibility under this law means that an employee must have worked for the school district at least twelve months. The employment may have been consecutive or nonconsecutive. Also, the employee must have worked at least 1,250 hours during the year preceding the leave. Thus, many part-time employees are not eligible. There is also an exemption which could apply to the superintendent of schools and many other administrators. This exemption allows a board of education to deny the request for leave of an employee whose salary falls within the highest 10 percent category. The reason for the exclusion is that the absence of such an employee may cause substantial and grievous economic injury to the school district.

A school district may use a number of methods to calculate the twelve-month period during which twelve weeks of leave may be requested. For example, the district policy may be the calendar year, twelve months forward from the date that an employee returned from a leave, or any fixed twelve-month period. When both spouses are employees of the same school district, the combined amount of leave for birth, adoption, and family illness may be limited to twelve weeks. Obviously, this restriction does not apply to personal illness.

There are special regulations pertaining to "intermittent leave," "reduced leave schedule," and "leave near the end of an academic term." This provision applies to teachers and does not include teacher assistants and aides unless their principal job is actual teaching. Counselors, psychologists, curriculum specialists, and support staff such as cafeteria, maintenance, and transportation employees are not covered by the special regulations.

Thus, a teacher may take intermittent leave, which means a period of time from one hour to several weeks. A person being treated with chemotherapy is an example of such a situation. However, if a teacher will be absent more than 20 percent of the total number of working days during the period of the leave which is considered a reduced leave schedule, a school district may require the teacher to take leave for a particular duration which must not be longer than the duration of the treatment. An alternative approach for a school district is to transfer the teacher to a different assignment on a temporary basis. The teacher must receive equivalent pay and benefits. For example, a school district could assign the teacher to a full-time substitute teacher position.

In regards to leave near the end of an academic year, a school district may require a teacher to continue on leave until the end of the term if the leave begins more than five weeks but continues into three weeks before the end of the term. Further, the school district may require the teacher to continue leave until the end of the term unless the leave is for the teacher's own serious health condition under two circumstances: (1) if the leave begins with five or fewer weeks before the end of the semester but lasts for more than two weeks and ends during the two-week period before the end of the term; (2) if the leave begins during the three-week period before the end of the semester and will last for more than five days.

If the employee has prior knowledge about the need for a leave, he or she is required to give thirty days verbal or written notice. When the employee does not have prior knowledge about the need for a leave, notice must be given as soon as is practicable, which may be interpreted as two working days.

The school district may require the employee to first use accrued paid leave such as sick, personal, or vacation leave. The district must continue to pay health plan premiums for the employee during the period of leave and this period must be treated as continued service for purposes of vesting and eligibility to participate in retirement plans. However, the employee is not entitled to accrue additional benefits during the period of unpaid leave, such as additional paid sick leave.

The school district may require certification from the employee's health care provider or the family member's health care provider concerning the date when the condition began, its duration, the necessity for leave, and the employee's inability to perform his or her job functions. A second opinion from a health care provider can be required by the school district at its own expense; and a third opinion can be obtained on the same condition with this opinion binding.

Upon return from leave, an employee is entitled to the same position or an equivalent position as when leave commenced, with the same salary, benefits, and working conditions. The district may require a certification from the employee's health care provider stating that the employee is able to resume work. School districts must inform employees about the provisions of this act. Also, policies and procedures for invoking this act must be in writing and be provided to the employee prior to taking leave in order for the district to enforce the act.

Complaints by employees can be initiated with the U.S. Department of Labor. The Department may conduct an administrative investigation or may file suit in court. Thus, federal record keeping requirements and investigations will be consistent with the Fair Labor Standards Act. The statute of limitations is two years, except in cases where willful violation is alleged, which carries a three-year limitation. A school district that violates this law may be subject to the following damages: (1) lost wages and benefits; (2) all other costs other than wages that an employee may have incurred as a result of the violation. The other costs usually include attorney and witness fees, but could also include, as an example, reimbursement for professional nursing care up to a sum equal to twelve weeks of wages if the employee's leave was denied.

Equality for Women

The French writer Stendhal believed that granting women equality would be the surest sign of civilization and would double the intellectual power of the human race. Although he wrote over one hundred years ago, equality for women continues to be a significant issue in our society.

In educational organizations the question of equal employment opportunity for women traditionally applies to a specific job classification—administration. It is clear to all observers that women are well represented in teaching, custodial, food service, and bus driving positions. Skilled trade positions (carpenters, electricians, and plumbers) in most school districts, however, are dominated by males, as are industrial arts teaching positions. In such situations, the norms of affirmative action previously outlined in this chapter are applicable. The critical issue, however, is the need to have women better represented in administrative ranks.

Why are there so few female administrators? Many researchers have put forth various theories. One such study argues that the causes are increased salary levels for teachers, which attracted more men, who were subsequently promoted to administrative positions; entry of male veterans into education after World War II and the Korean War, which also led to their eventual entry into administration; the executive image projected for administrators in the 1950s and 1960s, which attracted more men; and myths of male superiority.[32]

The legal mandate of equal employment opportunity for women emanates primarily from two federal laws: Title IX of the Education Amendments of 1972, which prohibits sex discrimination in educational programs or activities, including employment, when the school district is receiving federal financial assistance; and, of course, Title VII of the Civil Rights Act of 1964, as amended in 1972, which prohibits discrimination on the basis of sex as well as religion, national origin, race, or color.

In February 1992 the U.S. Supreme Court issued a unanimous opinion in connection with a lawsuit, *Franklin* v. *Gwinnett County Public Schools,* which upheld unlimited punitive and compensatory damages for victims of gender discrimination under Title IX of the Education Amendments of 1972. This is a landmark decision. Prior to this a female employee who believed that she had been discriminated against could seek only back pay in addition to the injunctive and declaratory relief otherwise available.

In November 2004, the U.S. Supreme Court ruled in *Jackson* v. *Birmingham Board of Education,* No. 02-1672, that advocates and whistle blowers, along with victims may sue under Title IX of the Education Amendments of 1972. The case involved a physical education teacher in the Birmingham, Alabama, School District who also coached the high school girls' basketball team. He was fired from his coaching position after he complained that the female basketball players were being discriminated against because of their gender.

The coach sued the Board of Education in 2001. The trial court threw out the suit stating that Title IX did not apply in that case. The U.S. Court of Appeals for the Eleventh Circuit upheld that decision, but the U.S. Supreme Court overturned the lower courts' rulings.[33]

This is a significant ruling for human resources administrators because it is an extension of the prevailing attitude that retaliation for reporting violations of legal mandates will not be tolerated by the courts and federal agencies. For example, this ruling is certainly in consort with the guidelines of the United States Equal Employment Opportunity Commission (EEOC) that oppose retaliation in the administration of Title VII of the Civil Rights Act. EEOC guidelines prohibit the firing, demotion, harassment, and other forms of retaliation against individuals who file a charge of discrimination, participate in a discrimination proceeding, or otherwise oppose discrimination. The Supreme Court ruling, however, forges a new dimension in that it gives the same protection against retaliation to advocates and whistle blowers.[34]

---

[32]John and Gail McLure, "The Case of the Vanishing Woman: Implications for the Preparation of Women in Educational Administration," *UCEA Review,* XVI (September 1974), 6.

[33]Sara Lipka, "High Court Expands Protections of Title IX," *The Chronicle of Higher Education* LI, no. 31 (April 8, 2005), A1, A36.

[34]www.eeoc.gov/types/retaliation.html

Potential Areas of Employment Discrimination Concerning Women

As a general rule, school districts—and all employers—are prohibited from establishing job qualifications that are derived from female stereotyping. The courts have uniformly required employers to prove that any sex restriction is indeed a bona fide occupational qualification.

Some of the most common forms of discrimination against females in the industrial/business community are even less defensible in educational organizations. For example, females have been denied employment because of height and weight limitations. In such situations a woman who is capable of performing the job-related tasks has clearly established case law precedent to bring the employer to court. However, it still occurs that an exceptionally talented woman may not be hired for an administrative position because she is a "nice and petite" person who does not measure up to the image of a strong leader.

The Equal Employment Opportunity Commission prohibits discrimination against women for the following reasons: because of their marital status, because they are pregnant, because they are not the principal wage earner in a family, or because they have preschool age children.

The preferences of customers and clientele are not bona fide occupational qualifications. Thus, the preference of parents and even students for male principals and administrators in a given school district does not permit the district to discriminate against females seeking administrative positions.

Maternity as a Particular Form of Discrimination

On October 31, 1978, President Carter signed into law a pregnancy disability amendment (PL 95-555) to Title VII of the Civil Rights Act of 1964. The law had the effect of eliminating unequal treatment for pregnant women in all employment-related situations. The EEOC issued guidelines for implementing this law, indicating that it is discriminatory for an employer to refuse to hire, train, assign, or promote a woman solely because she is pregnant; to require maternity leave for a predetermined time period; to dismiss a woman because she is pregnant; to deny reemployment to a woman who has been on maternity leave; to deny seniority credit to a woman who has been on maternity leave; and to deny disability or medical benefits to a woman for disability or illness unrelated to but occurring during pregnancy, childbirth, or recovery from childbirth.

Recruitment and Selection

To insure that discrimination against women does not occur in employment, as a first step, the school district's leadership should review recruitment and selection procedures. The following specific actions will minimize the potential for discriminating:

1. Use women as recruiters and interviewers.
2. Develop a list of women for potential promotion from within the school district.
3. Encourage female employees to apply for available administrative positions.
4. When recruiting outside the school district, contact for referrals such organizations as the American Association of University Women (AAUW), the National Council of Administrative Women in Education (NCAWE), the National Organization for Women (NOW), and minority employment agencies.

5. Include female representatives on selection committees.

6. Remove such title designations as *Mr., Mrs., Miss,* and *Ms.* from application forms.

7. When interviewing female applicants, ask only questions that are related to the abilities needed for job performance.

8. Review and evaluate the entire selection process to assure that job descriptions, selection criteria, and data-gathering instruments (such as paper-pencil tests and job applications) are job-related and do not screen out women.

Promotion and Training

Positive steps also must be taken to overcome patterns of inequality that have become traditional in some school districts. Among the most effective procedures are the following:

1. Publicize all promotional opportunities.

2. Seek out capable women and assign them administrative tasks when possible, giving them the experience to move into administrative positions.

3. Examine procedures for promotion to eliminate all facets except those that present a fair assessment of the employee's ability and record.

4. Recommend women for administrative internship and in-service programs.

Sexual Harassment

In 1980 the Equal Employment Opportunity Commission declared sexual harassment to be a violation of Title VII of the Civil Rights Act of 1964.[35] Basically there are two types of sexual harassment, *quid pro quo* discrimination and hostile environment discrimination. The first type is obvious. *Quid pro quo* discrimination occurs when an employment or personnel decision is based upon an applicant's or employee's submission to or rejection of unwelcome sexual conduct. Thus, a *quid pro quo* personnel decision occurs when employment opportunities or fringe benefits are granted because of an employee's submission to the employer's or supervisor's sexual advances.

Hostile environment discrimination occurs when unwelcome sexual conduct interferes with the employee's job performance. The standard for deciding environmental discrimination is if the sexual conduct substantially affected the job performance of a reasonable person. Factors to consider in investigating hostile environment discrimination are: was the conduct physical, verbal, or both; the frequency of the conduct; the position of the harasser, coworker, or supervisors; if other employees were involved in the conduct; if there was more than one person against whom the conduct was directed; and was the conduct hostile or patently hostile.

It is also important to investigate if the sexual conduct was unwelcome. Did the person alleging sexual harassment indicate by his or her conduct that the sexual advances were unwelcome? In making this determination, the timing of the protest and whether a prior consensual relationship existed with the alleged harasser are significant factors.

---

[35]Equal Employment Opportunity Commission, *Guidelines on Sexual Harassment in the Workplace.* (Washington, DC: U.S. Government Printing Office, 1991).

School districts are liable for the actions of their administrators and supervisors when these individuals act as the "agent" for the school district at the time of the harassment. For *quid pro quo* discrimination, the administrator or supervisor is always acting as the agent of the school district. For hostile environment discrimination, the school district is liable if the district knew or should have known of the sexual harassment of the supervisor.

For coworkers who sexually harass their colleagues, the school district is liable if the agents, administrators and supervisors, knew or should have known about the harassment. When sexual conduct becomes known, the appropriate administrator or supervisor must act to remedy the situation.

It is also the responsibility of the administrators and supervisors to take appropriate action to protect employees in the workplace against sexual harassment by non-employees. This responsibility is present when school district agents knew or should have known about the harassment.

In order for a school district to demonstrate to employees and the general public that sexual harassment will not be tolerated, the board of education should adopt a policy prohibiting such conduct and administrative procedures should be developed to effectively deal with allegations. Further, all employees should be required to participate in a staff development program about the issue of sexual harassment.

The board of education policy should set forth the commitment of the school district to deal with sexual harassment in an expeditious and effective manner. Administrative procedures to implement the policy should set forth the complaint process and should include the filling out of a complaint form which must be signed by the complainant. The appropriate human resources administrator should inform all the parties of their rights. Both the complaint and the investigation should be kept confidential. The procedures also should contain a timeline for completion of the investigation. The policy and procedures must be communicated to all staff members.

A staff development program about sexual harassment for all employees should contain the following components: an explanation of the board policy and administrative procedures; specific examples of sexual harassment; myths about sexual harassment; the distinction between welcome, consensual, and illegal sexual harassment. Administrator and supervisor staff development should include the above but also should stress the importance of protecting the complainant against retaliation. Exhibit 2.6 is a sample board of education policy on sexual harassment.

Policy of Nondiscrimination on the Basis of Sex

Good intentions by school administrators to remedy past practices of discrimination against women and to prevent future practices are not sufficient. The only defensible course of action is for the superintendent of schools to recommend a policy for adoption by the board of education. This would complement the school district's affirmative action policy and would provide the assurance required by law. The American Association of School Administrators has published a sample policy which is intended to be a guide for local boards of education in their policy formulation efforts. The entire sample policy includes sections dealing with educational programs, facilities, and services; the part reprinted here deals only with employment activities (see Exhibit 2.7).

EXHIBIT 2.6   Sample Sexual Harassment Policy

The board of education is committed to providing a work environment free from sexual harassment by administrators, supervisors, coworkers, and nonemployees.

It is a violation of this policy for the above-named categories of employees and nonemployees to engage in sexual harassment by making unwelcome sexual advances, unwelcome requests for sexual favors, and by other unwelcome verbal or physical conduct of a sexual nature.

It is a violation of this policy for an administrator or supervisor to make a decision affecting the employment of an individual on the basis of that person's submission to or rejection of sexual conduct. If an administrator or supervisor offers an opportunity or fringe benefit to an employee on the basis of that person's submission to or rejection of sexual conduct, it also is a violation of this policy.

Conduct of a sexual nature that unreasonably interferes with a person's job performance will be considered sexual harassment.

It is the duty of each administrator and supervisor to monitor his or her area of responsibility for the purpose of maintaining an environment free from sexual harassment. Further, it is the duty of each administrator and supervisor to protect an employee who files a complaint of sexual harassment from retaliation.

An employee or former applicant for employment who believes that he or she has been a victim of sexual harassment should file a complaint with the director of affirmative action as soon as possible after the incident. If the director of affirmative action is the alleged harasser, the complaint should be filed with the superintendent of schools. If the superintendent is the alleged harasser, the board of education should receive the complaint.

When the complaint is received, the director of affirmative action should initiate an investigation as soon as possible. If the complainant requests an investigator of the same sex and if the director of affirmative action is not of the same sex, another person of the same sex as the complainant will be appointed by the director to conduct the investigation. After the investigation, a report of the findings will be presented to the complainant, the alleged harasser, and the superintendent of schools. Both the investigation and the report are to be considered confidential. An employee who is found to be in violation of this policy will be subject to disciplinary action up to and including termination of employment with the school district.

It is the responsibility of the superintendent of schools to cause the development of administrative procedures to implement this policy; to cause the initiation of a staff development program concerning sexual harassment in the workplace, this policy, and administrative procedures. This program must be offered to every employee.

The Equal Pay Act

The U.S. Congress enacted in 1963 the Equal Pay Act, which requires employers to pay males and females the same salary or wage for equal work. This act is part of the Fair Labor Standards Act and protects employees who work for an employer engaged in an enterprise affected by interstate commerce. The interpretation of interstate commerce was broadly defined by the court in *Usery* v. *Columbia University,* 568 F. 2d 953 (2d Cir. 1977). In addition, the interpretation of equal work has been broadly defined to mean *substantially* equal and thus, strict equality of jobs is not required. Thus, this act requires equal pay for jobs that demand equal skill, effort, and responsibility, and that are carried out under similar working conditions. However, if salaries or wages are contingent upon a seniority system, a merit system, a system that measures pay by production quantity or quality, or factors other than sex, this act does not apply.

EXHIBIT 2.7 District Employment Activities

This policy applies to all aspects of the district's employment programs, including but not limited to recruitment, advertising, the process of application for employment, promotion, granting of tenure, termination, layoffs, wages, job assignments, leaves of absence of all types, fringe benefits, training programs, employer-sponsored programs, social or recreational programs, and any other term, condition, or privilege of employment. Specifically, the following personnel employment practices are prohibited:

a. *Tests.* Administration of any test or other criteria that has a disproportionately adverse effect on persons on the basis of sex unless it is a valid predictor of job success and alternative tests or criteria are unavailable.
b. *Recruitment.* Recruitment of employees from entities that furnish as applicants only or predominantly members of one sex, if such action has the effect of discriminating on the basis of sex.
c. *Compensation.* Establishment of rates of pay on the basis of sex.
d. *Job Classification.* Classification of jobs as being for males or females.
e. *Fringe Benefits.* Provision of fringe benefits on the basis of sex; all fringe benefit plans must treat males and females equally.
f. *Marital and Parental Status.* Any action based on marital or parental status; pregnancies are considered temporary disabilities for all job-related purposes and shall be accorded the same treatment by the district as are all other temporary disabilities. No inquiry shall be made by the district in job applications as to the marriage status of an applicant, including whether such applicant is "Miss or Mrs." But, inquiry may be made as to the sex of a job applicant for employment if it is made of all applicants and is not a basis for discrimination.
g. *Employment Advertising.* Any expression of preference, limitation, or specification based on sex, unless sex is a bona fide occupa-

tional qualification for the particular job in question.

Policy enforcement To ensure compliance with this policy, the superintendent shall

1. Designate a member of the administrative staff
   a. to coordinate efforts of the district to comply with this policy;
   b. to develop and ensure the maintenance of a filing system to keep all records required under this policy;
   c. to investigate all complaints of this policy;
   d. to administer the grievance procedure established in this policy; and
   e. to develop affirmative action programs, as appropriate.
2. Provide for the publication of this policy on an ongoing basis to students, parents, employees, prospective employees, and district employee unions or organizations, such publication to include the name, office address, and telephone number of the compliance administrator designated pursuant to this policy.

Grievance procedure Any employee of this district who believes he or she has been discriminated against, denied a benefit, or excluded from participation in any district activity, on the basis of sex in violation of this policy, may file a written complaint with the compliance administrator designated by this policy. The compliance administrator shall cause the review of the written complaint to be conducted and the written response mailed to the complainant within ten working days after receipt of the written complaint. A copy of the written complaint and the compliance administrator's response shall be provided each member of the Board of Education. If the complainant is not satisfied with such response, he or she may submit a written appeal to the Board of Education, indicating with particularity the nature of disagreement with the response and his or her reasons underlying such disagreement.

Continued

EXHIBIT 2.7   *Continued*

The Board of Education shall consider the appeal at its next regularly scheduled Board meeting following receipt of the appeal.

The Board of Education shall permit the complainant to address the Board in public or closed session, as appropriate and lawful, concerning his or her complaint and shall provide the complainant with its written decision in the matter as expeditiously as possible following completion of the meeting.

Evaluation   The Superintendent shall present a report to the Board of Education in a public meeting on or about July 21, 1976, and in a public meeting to be held on or about the anniversary of that date each year thereafter, describing the district's compliance with this policy during the previous year, which report can be the basis of an evaluation of the effectiveness of this policy by the Board of Education and a determination as to whether or not additional affirmative action is necessary in light of all the facts.

Source: Sample Policy for the Sex Equality in Education (Arlington, VA: American Association of School Administrators, 1977), modified for this chapter.

An example of a court case involving the Equal Pay Act is *EEOC* v. *Madison Community Unit School District Number 12,* 818 F. 2d 577 (7th Cir. 1987). In this case, a female who coached girls' track and tennis was paid substantially less than the males who coached the boys' track and tennis at the same school. In addition, a female assistant coach of the girls' basketball team was paid less than a male assistant coach of the boys' track team; still another female coach was paid less for coaching girls' basketball, softball, and volleyball than a male coaching boys' basketball, baseball, and soccer. Finally, an assistant coach of the girls' track team was paid less than the assistant coach of the boys' track team.

The Equal Employment Opportunity Commission filed a lawsuit against the school district, stating that the inequities violated the Equal Pay Act. The U.S. District Court ruled in favor of the EEOC but the school district appealed to the U.S. Court of Appeals, Seventh Circuit. This Court affirmed the district court's decision in the following situations: boys' and girls' track, boys' and girls' tennis, boys' baseball and girls' softball. However, the Court of Appeals reversed the district court's decision in comparing boys' soccer to girls' volleyball, boys' soccer to girls' basketball, and boys' track to girls' basketball. The Court stated that these situations did not require equal skill, effort, and responsibility.[36]

There is another aspect to the equal pay issue. When a school district has a performance-based evaluation system that is used to determine the salaries and wages of employees, the Equal Pay Act does not apply. However, in all organizations employees tend to compare their salaries and wages with those of coworkers and to compare how productive these coworkers are in comparison with themselves. The effects of this situation for school administration can be serious. It is a situation that will only fester if it is ignored. The best approach is to reemphasize the relationship between performance and reward; it is also important to reiterate that the performance-based evaluation process is the vehicle for determining the level of performance and the amount of reward.

[36]Data Research, Inc., *Deskbook Encyclopedia of American School Law* (Rosemount, Minnesota: Data Research, 1989), 216–218.

Obviously, if a school district does not have an effective evaluation process, a merit-based reward program cannot be initiated. Performance and reward are two aspects of the same process—They go hand in hand![37]

Equality by Age

The Age Discrimination in Employment Act of 1967, as amended, is taking on ever-increasing importance for human resources administrators. This act was passed by Congress to promote the employment of the older worker based on ability rather than age by prohibiting arbitrary discrimination. Also, under this act the Department of Labor has consistently sponsored informational and educational programs on the needs and abilities of the older worker. The "Statement of Findings and Purpose" in the Age Discrimination in Employment Act sets forth a rationale for its passage that is a true reflection of current societal trends towards older workers:

> Sec. 2.(a) The Congress hereby finds and declares that
>
> (1) in the face of rising productivity and affluence, older workers find themselves disadvantaged in their efforts to retain employment, and especially to regain employment when displaced from jobs;
> (2) the setting of arbitrary age limits regardless of potential for job performance has become a common practice, and certain otherwise desirable practices may work to the disadvantage of older persons;
> (3) the incidence of unemployment, especially long-term unemployment with resultant deterioration of skill, morale, and employer acceptability is, relative to the younger ages, high among older workers; their numbers are great and growing; and their employment problems grave;
> (4) the existence in industries affecting commerce of arbitrary discrimination in employment burdens commerce and the free flow of goods in commerce.

Provisions of the Age Discrimination in Employment Act

The law protects individuals who are at least forty years of age but less than seventy. It applies to private employers of twenty or more persons. The law also applies to employment agencies and labor organizations having twenty-five or more members in an industry affecting interstate commerce. The law does not apply to elected officials or their appointees.

In January 2000 by a five-to-four decision, the U.S. Supreme Court held that Congress did not have the authority under the Fourteenth Amendment to the U.S. Constitution to extend this act to states and their political subdivision. Thus, at this writing it appears that public school districts cannot be sued in federal court under the Age Discrimination in Employment Act. However, there are age discrimination statutes in almost every state in the nation that can be invoked by job applicants and employees of school districts who believe that they have been discriminated against because of age. Thus, state compliance agencies and the state courts can provide remedies to age discrimination.

---

[37]"Incentive Pay Plans Full of Problems . . . ," *Education USA,* 28, no. 32 (April 7, 1986), 248.

It is against the law for an employer to refuse to hire or otherwise discriminate against any person as to compensation, terms, conditions, or privileges of employment because of age; to limit, segregate, or classify employees so as to deprive any individual of employment opportunities or adversely affect that individual's status as an employee because of age. It is against the law for an employment agency to refuse to refer for employment or otherwise discriminate against an individual because of age, or to classify and refer anyone for employment on the basis of age. It is against the law for a labor union to discriminate against anyone because of age by excluding or expelling that person from membership; to limit, segregate, or classify its members on the basis of age; to refuse to refer anyone for employment so as to result in a deprivation or limitation of employment opportunity or otherwise adversely affect an individual's status as an employee because of age; or to cause or attempt to cause an employer to discriminate against an individual because of age.

Furthermore, the provisions of the Age Discrimination in Employment Act prohibit an employer, employment agency, or labor union from discriminating against a person for opposing a practice that is unlawful because of this act, discriminating against a person making a charge, assisting or participating in any investigation, proceeding, or litigation under this act; publishing a notice of an employment vacancy that indicates a preference, limitation, or specification based on age.

Exceptions to the Age Discrimination in Employment Act

The prohibitions of this act do not apply if age is a bona fide occupational qualification reasonably necessary to the normal performance of a given task. Therefore, test pilot positions might be filled with individuals no older than forty-five, because accurate and quick reflexes are necessary to the safe flying of experimental aircraft. However, it would be difficult to justify age as a bona fide occupational qualification in education institutions.

The prohibitions of the Age Discrimination in Employment Act do not apply when an individual is discharged or disciplined for good cause, and when the terms of a new or existing employee seniority or benefits program differentiates by reason of age. However, no employee benefits plan can be used as an excuse for failing to hire an individual because of age.

Enforcement of the Age Discrimination in Employment Act

The administration of this act passed from the Department of Labor to the Equal Employment Opportunity Commission on July 1, 1979. At that time the average number of complaints had reached five thousand annually. The EEOC can conduct investigations, issue rules and regulations to administer the law, and enforce the provisions of the law through the courts when voluntary compliance cannot be obtained.

Conclusion

This section has dealt with four major federal influences on the human resources planning process. Although affirmative action and the legislation on equality for people with disabilities, women, and individuals by age represent central trends in human resources administration, these are by no means the only federal considerations that affect human resources processes.

The following laws enacted by Congress constitute a significant part of the national public employment policy that directly and indirectly affects the employment policies of public and private educational institutions. They should be studied by all human resources administrators.

1883 Pendleton Act (Civil Service Commission)
1931 Davis–Bacon Act
1932 Anti-Injunction Act
1935 National Labor Relations Act
1935 Social Security Act
1936 Walsh-Healey Public Contracts Act
1938 Fair Labor Standards Act
1947 Labor–Management Relations Act
1959 Labor–Management Reporting and Disclosure Act
1962 Work House Act
1967 Reemployment of Veterans Act
1968 Garnishment Provisions, Consumer Credit Protection Act
1974 Employee Retirement Income Security Act
1986 Immigration Reform and Control Act
1990 Immigration Act

In addition, it must be kept in mind that various states and cities have enacted statutes and ordinances that also exert significant influence on human resources administration.

Finally, Chapter 2 includes three appendices: (A) Steps in Developing an Affirmative Action Program; (B) Summary Facts Concerning Job Discrimination; and (C) Steps in Filing a Charge of Job Discrimination. These provide summary data that further clarify how federal legislation impinges on human resources management.

Summary

Planning is a process common to all human experience. It encompasses an understanding of the present condition, future objectives, and methods for reaching these objectives.

Human resources planning as a process in human resources management is undertaken to ensure that a school district has the right number of people, with the right skills, in the right place, and at the right time.

The first step in the human resources planning process is to assess human resources needs, which includes the following four aspects: developing human resources inventories, developing a five-year enrollment projection, developing school district objectives, and developing a human resources forecast.

Two of the most pressing problems facing school districts are human resources planning and increasing and decreasing pupil enrollments. Two of the most successful alternatives to reduction in a workforce have been early retirement incentive programs and the retraining of individuals for positions that become vacant through attrition or are created through program development.

A hallmark of our contemporary American society is the avalanche of federal legislation and court decisions, which in turn has had a definite influence on the human resources planning process. Incorporated or implied in all civil rights legislation are the important concepts of social justice and affirmative action.

Justice is a guide that regulates how people live out their lives as members of a given society. The substance of justice is entitlement that refers to those rights to which individuals and groups of people have a claim. The responsibility of society to the individual is called distributive justice. The responsibility of each person to society is termed legal justice. Commutative justice involves the responsibility that exists between individuals. Justice also involves restitution that is the right of a person to have an entitlement restored.

John Rawls was a contemporary political philosopher who described his theory of justice in terms of fairness. His basic premise is that the best principles of justice for the basic structure of any society are those that would be the object of an original agreement in the establishment of a society. Rawls elucidated two principles that he believes people should choose to implement the notion of fairness. The first principle asserts that each person is to have an equal right to a system of liberties that is compatible with a similar system of liberties available to all people. The second principle asserts that social and economic inequalities must benefit the least advantaged and that equal opportunity to secure offices and position must be open to all. In explaining how present inequities may benefit the least advantaged, he developed the principle of just savings.

Affirmative action is not a law within itself but rather an objective reached by following a set of guidelines that ensure compliance with legislation and executive orders. The Equal Employment Opportunity Commission was established by Title VII of the Civil Rights Act to investigate alleged discrimination in employment practices based on race, color, religion, sex, or national origin. This five-member commission has also established, from time to time, affirmative action guidelines. Alleged discrimination charges can be filed with any of EEOC's district offices. The administrative process includes an individual's filing of a charge, investigation of the charge, determination of the charge, and the process of conciliation.

Limited discrimination is allowed by the Equal Employment Opportunity Act under one condition: when there is a bona fide occupational qualification mandating the employing of an individual of a particular sex, religious affiliation, or national origin. Therefore, a school district human resources administrator has the right to employ a female rather than a male for the position of swimming instructor when the job description includes supervising the locker room used by female students.

The Civil Rights Act of 1991 is landmark legislation because it extends punitive damages and jury trials for the first time to employees who have been discriminated against because of their race, national origin, gender, disability, or religion.

The Rehabilitation Act of 1973 prohibits recipients of federal financial assistance from discriminating against qualified individuals with disabilities in recruitment, hiring, compensation, job assignment/classification, and in those fringe benefits provided. Employers are further required to provide reasonable accommodations for qualified employees with disabilities. The Vietnam Era Veterans Readjustment Assistance Act of 1974 requires affirmative action to hire veterans with disabilities of all wars and all veterans of the Vietnam era.

The Americans with Disabilities Act of 1990 is also landmark legislation because it is the most comprehensive legislation ever passed protecting the rights of individuals with disabilities. There are five titles to ADA, and all of them except Title IV have some impact upon school districts.

On August 22, 1990, President George Bush ordered the mobilization of U.S. military reserves and National Guard units into active duty. This triggered several issues concerning the health care of dependents and the reentry of reservists and members of the national guard into the workplace.

On October 28, 1991, President Bush signed into law the Omnibus Transportation Employee Testing Act, which required the Secretary of Transportation to promulgate regulations for alcohol and controlled substances testing for persons in safety-sensitive positions including school bus drivers.

President Clinton signed into law the Family and Medical Leave Act on February 5, 1993. The fundamental purpose of this act is to provide eligible employees with the right to take unpaid leave in connection with certain circumstances.

Equality in employment opportunity for women is a central issue in human resources management. The legal mandate of equal opportunity for women emanates primarily from two federal laws: Title IX of the Education Amendments of 1972, which prohibits sex discrimination in educational programs or activities, including employment, when the school district is receiving federal financial assistance; and, of course, Title VII of the Civil Rights Act of 1964, as amended in 1972. In addition, President Carter in 1978 signed into law a pregnancy disability amendment to the Civil Rights Act. This law had the effect of eliminating unequal treatment of pregnant women in all employment-related situations.

Since 1980 the Equal Employment Opportunity Commission has considered sexual harassment to be a violation of Title VII of the Civil Rights Act of 1964. The issue of sexual harassment in the workplace has gained national attention and will continue to be a concern in school districts across the nation.

The Equal Pay Act of 1963 requires employers to pay males and females the same salary or wage for equal work.

The Age Discrimination in Employment Act of 1967, as amended, promotes the employment of the older worker by prohibiting arbitrary discrimination based on age.

Because of their importance, only major federal influences in the human resources planning process have been presented in this chapter in detail. However, human resources administrators must also become familiar with all legislation that protects employment opportunity rights.

Discussion Questions and Statements

- Why is the assessment of human resources needs so important for a school district?
- Compare and contrast the various methods of human resources forecasting.
- Define *affirmative action* and explain its significance in establishing accountability in the human resources department.
- What is the relationship of John Rawls's principles of social justice to human resources administration?
- Explain the role and function of the Equal Employment Opportunity Commission.
- What conclusions can be drawn from the judicial review of affirmative action?

Suggested Activities

- As the Assistant Superintendent for Human Resources in a school district with three central office administrators and eleven building level administrators, develop, in writing, an outline of a presentation on sexual harassment intended to make administrators more aware of potential violations of the school district's sexual harassment policy. Assume that the district's policy is the same as the one in this chapter.
- In order to become familiar with the cohort-survival technique, simulate an enrollment projection for your school district.
- Obtain the board of education policies from a school district concerning equal employment opportunity and affirmative action. Write a comparison of these policies with those in this chapter.
- Develop, in writing, a *quick reference guide* setting forth the important aspects of the federal laws explained in this chapter.

Selected Bibliography

Americans with Disabilities Act. (1990), P. L. 101–336, 42 U.S.C., 12101 et seq.

Arnold, Jean B., "Family Leave: It's the Law," *The American School Board Journal,* 180, no. 10 (October 1993), 31–34.

Breck, William, "Suit Yourself with Strategic Planning," *The School Administrator,* 8, no. 46 (September 1989), 14–16.

Buckingham, Marcus, and Richard M. Vosburgh, "The 21st Century Human Resources Function: It's the Talent, Stupid!" *Human Resources Planning,* 24.4 (2001), 17–23.

Clay, Katherine, Sara Lake, and Karen Tremain, *How to Build a Strategic Plan: A Step-by-Step Guide for School Managers.* San Carlos, CA: Ventures for Public Awareness, 1989.

Cohan, Audrey, Mary Ann Hergenrother, Yolanda M. Johnson, Laurie S. Mandel, and Janice Sawyer, *Sexual Harassment and Sexual Abuse: A Handbook for Teachers and Administrators.* Thousand Oaks, CA: Corwin Press, 1996.

Collier, Beverly H., "Halting Sexual Harassment," *The Executive Educator,* 11, no. 11 (November 1989), 28–33.

Equal Employment Opportunities Commission and the U.S. Department of Justice, *Americans with Disabilities Act Handbook.* (EEOC Publication No. BK-19.) Washington, DC: U.S. Government Printing Office, 1991.

Gittins, Naomi E., and Jim Walsh, *Sexual Harassment in the Schools: Preventing and Defending Against Claims.* Alexandria, VA: National School Boards Association, 1991.

Gupton, Sandra Lee, and Gloria Appelt Slick, *Highly Successful Women Administrators: The Inside Stories of How They Got There.* Thousand Oaks, CA: Corwin Press, 1996.

Hu-DeHart, Evelyn, "To Treat People Equally, We Must Treat Them Differently," *College Board Review,* no. 183 (Winter 1997–1998), 24–31.

Lavelle, Marianne, "Defiance Can Backfire in Sexual Harassment Cases," *The National Law Journal* (June 17, 1996), B1, B2.

Leonard, Bill, "On a Mission: Cari M. Dominquez Discusses Her Plans for EEOC," *HR Magazine,* 47, no. 5 (May 2002), 38–44.

Lewis, John F., Susan C. Hastings, and Anne C. Morgan, *Sexual Harassment in Education.* Topeka, KS: National Organization on Legal Problems in Education, 1993.

McDowell, Douglas S., Jeffrey A. Norris, and Lorence L. Kessler, eds., *Basic EEO Resource Manual: Practical Guidance for EEO Professionals and Attorneys.* Washington, DC: National Foundation for the Study of Employment Policy, 1988.

Meisinger, Susan, "Challenges and Opportunities for HR," *HR Magazine,* 50, no. 5 (May 2005), 10.

Miron, Louis F., *Resisting Discrimination: Affirmative Strategies for Principals and Teachers.* Thousand Oaks, CA: Corwin Press, 1996.

Polansky, Harvey B., "Early Retirement Incentive Plans," *School Business Affairs,* 56, no. 12 (December 1990), 26–30.

Rawls, John, *A Theory of Justice: Revised Edition.* Cambridge: The Belnap Press of Harvard University Press, 1999.

Robinson, Robert K., Neal P. Mero, David L. Nichols, "More Than Just Semantics: Court Rulings Clarify Effective Anti-harassment Policies," *Human Resource Planning,* 24.4 (2001), 36–47.

Shopp, Robert J., "How to Investiagate a Sexual Harassment Complaint," *School Business Affairs,* 63, no. 5 (May 1997), 16–20.

U.S. Congress, Senate Committee on Labor and Public Welfare, *The Equal Employment Opportunity Act of 1972,* 3. Committee Report, 92nd Congress, 2nd session, March 1972. Washington, DC: U.S. Government Printing Office, 1972.

U.S. Equal Employment Opportunity Commission, *Affirmative Action and Equal Employment,* Vols. I & II. Washington, DC: U.S. Government Printing Office, 1974.

Vickers, Mark R., "Business Ethics and the HR Role: Past, Present, and Future," *Human Resource Planning,* 28, no. 1 (2005), 26–32.

Weast, Jerry D., "Strategic Planning Based on Comprehensive Data," *Spectrum: Journal of School Research and Information,* 7, no. 3 (Summer 1989), 3–7.

Wilson, William Julius, "The New Social Inequality and Affirmative Opportunity," *WorkingUSA,* 1, no. 6 (March–April 1998), 74–87.

Wirtz, Thomas J., and Anne Kiefer, "Community-Based Strategic Planning," *Spectrum: Journal of School Research and Information,* 6, no. 3 (Summer 1988), 3–9.

Wright, Jim, "Ready to Meet New Drug Test Requirements?" *School and College* (March 1994), 13–19.

Zakariya, Sally Banks, "What to Do If Someone on Your Staff Has AIDS," *The Executive Educator,* 9, no. 4 (April 1987), 19–21.

Appendix A
Steps in Developing an Affirmative Action Program*

- Establish a strong company policy and commitment.
- Assign responsibility and authority for the program to a top company official.
- Analyze present work force to identify jobs, departments, and units where minorities and females are underutilized.
- Set specific, measurable, attainable hiring and promotion goals, with target dates, in each area of underutilization.
- Make every manager and supervisor responsible and accountable for helping to meet these goals.
- Reevaluate job descriptions and hiring criteria to assure that they reflect actual job needs.

*Source: U.S. Equal Employment Opportunity Commission, *Affirmative Action and Equal Employment* (Washington, DC: U.S. Government Printing Office, 1974), 3.

- Find minorities and females who qualify or who can become qualified to fulfill goals.
- Review and revise all employment procedures to assure that they do not have a discriminatory effect and that they help attain the goals.
- Focus on getting minorities and females into upward mobility and relevant training pipelines especially where they have not had previous access.
- Develop systems to monitor and measure progress on a continued basis. If results are not satisfactory in meeting goals, find out why, and make necessary changes.

Appendix B
Summary Facts Concerning Job Discrimination

Title VII of the 1964 Civil Rights Act, as amended, provides that an individual cannot be denied a job or fair treatment on a job because of

- Race
- Color
- Religion
- Sex
- National origin

The act established the Equal Employment Opportunity Commission (EEOC) to insure that these rights are protected. If an individual believes that he or she has been discriminated against in the workplace by any of the groups listed here, he or she may file a charge of discrimination with the EEOC.

- Private employer of fifteen or more persons
- State and local government
- Public and private educational institutions
- Public and private employment agencies
- Labor unions with fifteen or more members
- Joint labor-management committees for apprenticeship and training programs

Also a charge may be filed by another person or by a group if the person alleging the discrimination gives his or her permission to these other parties.

The EEOC does not cover discrimination because of

- Citizenship
- Political affiliation
- Sexual orientation

It also does not cover job discrimination by federal government agencies, government-owned corporations, Native American tribes, or by small private employers with fewer than fifteen workers.

If a person wishes to file a charge of job discrimination, he or she must do so promptly—within 180 days from the time the discrimination took place.

An employer is prohibited by law from harassing or bothering an individual in any un-fair manner because he or she filed a charge, assisted in an investigation, or opposed un-lawful employment practices.

Appendix C
Steps in Filing a Charge of Job Discrimination

To file a charge of job discrimination, an individual must

- Visit the nearest EEOC District Office or mail in a "Charge of Discrimination" form. If a form cannot be obtained, a written statement may be sent identifying all parties and clearly describing what act(s) of discrimination took place.
- Be interviewed by an intake officer of the commission at the district office or be in-terviewed by telephone if an in-person interview is impossible.
- Provide information, including records and names of witnesses to the discrimination.
- Swear or affirm, under oath, to the charge of discrimination, or make a declaration under penalty of perjury.

As the charging party, an individual must

- Cooperate with the commission
- Attend fact-finding conferences and other meetings when scheduled
- Inform the commission of changes in his or her address, telephone number, and other such information
- Contact the commission if he or she wishes to withdraw the charge

After a charge is filed

- The employer, union, employment agency, or labor-management committee named in the charge will be notified.
- In many states, the charge may be referred for remedy to a state or local fair employ-ment practices agency for 60 days (120 days if the agency is new).
- The commission may require the person making the charge to attend a fact-finding conference in order to establish facts, define issues, and determine a basis for negoti-ating a settlement.
- If settlement efforts are unsuccessful, the commission may investigate to determine the merits of the charge.
- After the investigation, the commission will issue a letter of determination on the mer-its of the charge.

Recruitment

After the human resources planning process identifies current and future staffing needs, the next step is to recruit personnel. In the 1970s many school districts experienced a rather dramatic decrease in pupil enrollment. This phenomenon forced districts to lay off large numbers of teachers, which affected the number of college students entering schools of education. Young people interested in teaching anticipated a rather dismal job market upon completion of their education and thus changed their career goals. This situation was compounded by the large number of teachers who retired in the 1980s and by the many teacher defections to the business community.

Now, school districts across the country are suffering the effects of the past decade. There is a shortage of teachers, particularly in large metropolitan school districts. In fact, the National Center for Educational Statistics has predicted a significant shortage of teachers reaching far into the 2000s.

There is a particular concern in urban school districts where African American and Hispanic student populations continue to grow yearly. Demographers predict that this trend will continue to gain momentum. Hispanic student growth will eventually overtake the growth in African American students. There is no corresponding increase in the percent of African American and Hispanic teachers and administrators.[1]

However, for human resources administrators, the issue of diversity is a much broader issue. The United States continues to be a nation of immigrants, but the immigrants no longer come from Western Europe. Although there is a definite influx of immigrants from Eastern Europe, the most significant number of immigrants comes from Asia and the Americas. Of course this has changed the composition of the population in the United States, not only ethnically but also religiously. Although the United States is still a nation of Christians and Jews, it is also a nation of Muslims, Hindus, and Confucians. In fact the United States is now the most diverse country on earth.

Obviously, the population is also composed of citizens from the traditional categories of age, disability, gender, illness, and lifestyles. Thus one of the most important issues fac-

[1]Sarah Lubman, "Efforts to Hire Minority Educators Aim to Narrow Student-Teacher Ethnic Gap," *Wall Street Journal,* 7 September 1993, sec. B, B1, B9.

ing many human resources administrators is recruiting teachers, staff members, and administrators from underrepresented categories. This is a necessity for two reasons. First, it is crucial to have teachers, staff members, and administrators who are ethnically representative of the community in which the schools are located. Second, all children should be exposed to teachers, staff members, and administrators who are representative of the larger population in the United States.[2]

Obviously this situation places an immediate and long-term responsibility on human resources administrators to develop strategies for recruiting minority employees.[3] Therefore, the recruitment process has never been more important to school districts as they search for the best people available to help achieve the mission of each district, educating children and young people. This is the major thrust of every recruitment program—not to hire just to fill a position, but rather to acquire the number and type of people necessary for the present and future success of the school district. Affirmative action requirements, future staffing needs, and dual certification are issues that impinge on recruitment programs. It is a mistake to assume that the correct mix of people will be available to fill vacancies without making a concerted effort to find the most qualified individuals to fill specific human resource needs.

Recruitment as a process also entails discovering potential applicants for anticipated vacancies. This perspective on the recruitment process depends to a great extent on the size of the school district. An urban or metropolitan school district engages, of course, in recruiting potential applicants more often than smaller suburban districts. Many other variables influence the extent of recruiting activities. First, the employment conditions in a community where the school district is located affect recruitment. For example, the existence of a university with a school of education located near the district often ensures sufficient applicants for entry-level teaching positions. In like manner, the labor pool in a metropolitan area has many skilled carpenters, electricians, and plumbers.

A second set of variables affecting recruitment include working conditions, salary levels, and fringe benefits provided by a school district. These affect employee turnover and, therefore, the need to engage in recruitment activities. Districts experiencing a rapid increase in pupil population, and hence a need for increased staff, look upon recruitment as a major human resources priority.

Finally, even school districts experiencing decreasing enrollment and reduction in the workforce may need to engage in recruitment activities from time to time, because certain vacancies require special skills that current employees lack. Industrial arts is a case in point. A school district may find that teachers who are already employed and scheduled to be placed on involuntary leave cannot be transferred to fill a vacancy in industrial arts because they lack the required certification.

Recruitment, therefore, should be common to all school districts. The idea of "stealing" proven employees from another company has become an acceptable practice, considered perfectly legitimate if no coercion or illegal pressures are brought to bear on a potential employee. Talent and skills are scarce commodities. School districts are ethically

---

[2]Kathryn H. Au and Karen M. Blake, "Cultural Identity and Learning to Teach in a Diverse Community: Findings from a Collective Case Study," *Journal of Teacher Education,* 54, no. 3 (May/June 2003), 192–205.

[3]Donald J. Fielder, "Wanted, Minority Teachers," *The Executive Educator,* 15, no. 5 (May 1993), 33–34.

bound to find the most talented and skilled people available to achieve their mandate of educating children. In practice, this requires them to develop employment conditions, salary levels, and benefits that will attract the best applicants while remaining within the fiscal constraints of the school district.

The practice of overtly contacting and recruiting individuals who meet a given set of job requirements and encouraging them to become applicants should be emulated by school districts. It is recruitment in its purest form.

Many state departments of elementary and secondary education have recognized the need to assist school districts that are having difficulties finding and hiring qualified teachers. Thus, the phenomenon of *alternative certification programs* has emerged in many states. Usually these are programs at colleges and universities that provide individuals who have bachelor's degrees the opportunity to obtain certification as teachers in a relatively short period of time. Of course, the curriculum varies in the different colleges and universities. However, the emphasis is on the essentials of pedagogy and adapting a person's life skills and academic knowledge to the instructional process.

For example, such programs would help a retired accountant adapt his or her knowledge into lesson plans to teach high school accounting. Of course, considerable attention would also be afforded to understanding adolescent and educational psychology. Obviously, the target populations for these programs are retired people and those seeking a second or third career.

Constraints on Recruitment

Affirmative Action

Many school districts make a practice of promoting already hired employees into supervisory or administrative positions. A school bus driver could advance to dispatcher and on from there to route supervisor and eventually become director of transportation. A classroom teacher may become a department chairperson and, if certificated as an administrator, an assistant principal, with eventual promotion into the principalship. This is, of course, a legitimate practice with many advantages for building morale within the school district.

Employees who recognize that the district provides them with an opportunity to advance their careers through promotion to positions of greater responsibility are more likely to make a long-term commitment to the school district. In like manner, employees should also be made aware of the link between job performance and promotion. This places a responsibility on the administration to develop procedures that ensure promotion opportunities for those who have demonstrated on the job that they are capable of handling higher-level tasks. The appraisal process is the vehicle for documenting the quality of such performance.

Chapter 2 presented in detail the affirmative action and equal employment opportunity requirements mandated by various civil rights legislation. This legislation basically prohibits discrimination in recruitment because of race, age, disability, military service, color, religion, sex, pregnancy, and national origin. The concept of equality in opportunity, however, must eventuate in a set of recruitment procedures.

Internal promotion as a practice does not nullify affirmative action requirements. The only exceptions to such requirements are those situations in which sex, not being disabled, etc., constitute bona fide occupational qualifications. Thus, a school district may discriminate against a teacher's aide who has an orthopedic disability by promoting another aide to a gymnastics teaching position when the ability to demonstrate routines is part of the job description.

Except for bona fide occupational qualifications, a district must establish promotion procedures that clearly do not discriminate against minorities and protected groups of employees. A district can demonstrate equal opportunity by advertising promotional opportunities, establishing promotion criteria, and offering equal access to career advancement training programs. No position should be filled without giving all qualified employees an opportunity to apply. This may be accomplished by publishing promotion opportunities on bulletin boards or in a district publication such as a newsletter. Whatever the method, it must be clear that all qualified employees have been informed of the opening and have been given an opportunity to apply.

Promotion criteria should include the level of current job performance, qualifications and skills, and job knowledge. Affirmative action does not require the promoting of unqualified employees; it does require that all qualified individuals be given an equal opportunity. Finally, minority employees, those with disabilities, and other employees should be encouraged to participate in educational and training programs that will enhance their knowledge and skills, thus providing them with the qualifications necessary to apply for promotions.

The size of a school district usually determines not only the extent of internal recruitment for promotion but also the extent of external recruitment. In a small school district it may happen that no one currently employed is qualified for an administrative or supervisory opening. Thus, external recruitment is the only available avenue for filling the vacancy.

Affirmative action and equal employment opportunity must be a major consideration in developing and implementing recruitment practices and procedures. The days should be gone when a person can be hired simply because he or she is someone's friend or relative. Physical appearance and the interviewer's hunch are also no longer acceptable criteria for hiring or promoting an individual.

The Reputation and Policies of the School District

A second possible constraint on recruiting candidates for a position emanates from the school district itself. Prospective candidates may not be interested in pursuing a job opportunity in a particular school district because of that district's image in the community. For example, a district that offers an inferior curriculum, that is understaffed, or that lacks support services will find it difficult to attract the best people in education.

The policies of the board of education and the administrative processes and procedures of the district are also important considerations to most candidates. These are the criteria by which the quality of the work environment may be measured. If, for example, a school district lacks a well-defined and effective appraisal process, the prospective candidate will have little confidence in the district's ability to evaluate adequately his or her future performance, which in turn may affect his or her salary increases.

The Position to Be Filled

A third constraint in recruiting for a position centers around the attractiveness of the job itself. A position that is viewed as anxiety laden or that lacks promotion potential may not interest the best people.

The most common situation that falls within this category is the succession problem. Following either a very successful person or a person who was a failure will be difficult. If the person who previously held the position was exceptionally capable, a successor may find the expectations of the school board, parents, students, and even colleagues to be beyond anyone's capabilities. Following someone who failed in a position will probably be easier. However, the responsibilities of the job may have been neglected to the point where chaos and disorganization reign. A person brought in to restore order may make other employees anxious if they have become accustomed to a lack of supervision.

Salary and Fringe Benefits

The best people for a job will become candidates only if the financial compensation is in keeping with the responsibilities of the position. Education is a service enterprise and, as such, the major priority must be attracting highly qualified employees. Recruiters may need to negotiate compensation with candidates. This practice helps to attract highly qualified individuals for less desirable positions. In school districts the salary for a position is usually fixed on a salary schedule, and the fringe benefits are universally applied to all employees in a certain category. This makes the recruitment of highly skilled candidates a very difficult task, particularly if the job is undesirable or if the district has a poor image.

The exceptions to this rule are the central-office administrative positions at the superintendent and assistant superintendent levels. In recruiting candidates for such positions, both salary and fringe benefits are usually negotiable.

A Theory of Occupational Choice

Although the focus of human resources administration is on the theory and practice of this function from an organizational perspective, in recruitment it is important to understand those factors that influence the career choices of prospective candidates. Further, recruitment as a practice is more effective if it is based on a vocational development theory.

Many theories of vocational development have become classics and are widely applied in the practice of vocational guidance. Eli Ginzberg, Donald Super, Anne Roe, and David Tiedeman are only a few of the researchers who have helped to advance the field of vocational guidance. This section will not do justice to the intricacies of these and other theories but will provide an overview that may be used in formulating recruitment strategies.

First, people have different interests, abilities, and personalities that, nevertheless, will qualify each person for many different occupations. In fact, experience verifies that an individual will probably change his or her entire occupational field at least three times during his or her working lifetime. When recruiting people for a particular position, the recruiter should understand how ability, interest, and personality interface in various occupations. For example, the successful high school journalism teacher may be a good candidate for the position of public relations director. Both occupations require the ability to communicate ideas, both require an interest in writing, and both require a person capable of relating to other people on a professional level. There are also links between guidance counseling and human resources administration, between the principalship and central-office administration. The essence of this observation is that the recruitment of candidates for a particular position must not be limited only to individuals who already perform similar tasks.

Second, occupational preferences, competencies, and the self-image of people will change with time and experience, making personal adjustment a continuous process. It is therefore unwise to assume that current employees are probably not interested in changing occupations within the organization. An internal search for potential applicants often reveals that many employees are interested in alternative positions.

Third, both life and work satisfaction depend on how well an individual can utilize his or her abilities and find adequate outlets for his or her interests, personality traits, and values. A high turnover of people in a certain position should clue a human resources administrator to reevaluate the responsibilities of the position to ascertain the accuracy of the job description. This reevaluation should then provide a clearer profile of the type of individual who will be successful in the job. It is obviously important to link the interest, abilities, and personality traits of potential candidates to how such individual characteristics will be challenged in the position. For example, a particular middle school principalship located in an urban ghetto may require a self-motivated individual who feels comfortable in an environment laced with a constant demand to handle students who are chronic behavioral problems, while at the same time supervising a highly unionized teaching staff. Not every applicant will have the personal characteristics necessary to be successful in this situation.

Fourth, the process of occupational choice is influenced by employment variables such as salary, fringe benefits, location, opportunity for advancement, and the nature of the work to be performed.[4] The importance of these variables will differ from one applicant to the next. In recruitment it is important from the very start to present this information to every candidate in an extremely clear format. Sometimes, people are so intent on finding an alternative to their present employment that they initially tend to overlook these variables. However, when an employment offer is made, these factors become very apparent, which may result in a refusal by the candidate after a search that has cost the school district considerable time and money.

Finally, vocational development is essentially a compromise between personal characteristics, such as interests and abilities, and external factors, such as the type of work to be performed. The effectiveness of this compromise is tested out through role playing, whether this be in fantasy, simulation, or in the actual work environment. The emergence of assessment centers gives testimony to this principle. Assessment centers set up career paths for already-hired employees. At such a center the capabilities of an employee are matched with the requirements of various positions within the school district. A career path is then planned that will allow the employee to experience various levels of responsibility in different locations. As he or she demonstrates success at each level, the employee is

[4]See Stephen P. Robbins, *Personnel: The Management of Human Resources,* 2nd ed. (Englewood Cliffs, NJ: Prentice-Hall, 1982), 98–99.

advanced to a higher level along the path. Thus, an individual who has been hired as a maintenance supervisor may be promoted, after an assessment, to assistant director of maintenance, then eventually promoted to director.

The implication is that job success is the only true measure of how effective the recruitment process has been. This implication is often overlooked, and many school districts never evaluate their recruitment procedures through a follow-up study on the success of those who were hired.

Methods of Recruitment

It can be demonstrated from experience that certain recruiting methods produce the best candidates for particular job vacancies. Consequently, before initiating the recruitment process, each job vacancy should be analyzed to ascertain what method will be most effective. For example, an advertisement for a business manager's position appearing in the classified section of *School Business Affairs* will most likely reach individuals with the required qualifications. An advertisement in a local newspaper will probably produce few, if any, qualified candidates. In like manner, a recruiter who visits students at a four-year teacher education college in search of candidates for a high school principal's position requiring a minimum of a master's degree in educational administration is looking in the wrong place.

Internal Search

Some school districts find it advantageous to train their own employees for all positions beyond the lowest level. As mentioned, promotion from within has definite advantages, particularly in creating high morale among employees. The second and most obvious benefit to promoting from within is that supervisors have greater knowledge about a person already on the payroll than about an unknown applicant. The selection process discussed in the following chapter helps to minimize the danger of making the wrong choice. However, firsthand information about an employee's performance is the best basis on which that person can be promoted.

Many school districts have not traditionally promoted from within because of the minimal number of job categories found in most school districts. Classroom teachers, principals, cooks, custodians, bus drivers, and a superintendent of schools continue to constitute the breadth of differentiation in staffing in rural and very small suburban school districts.

School districts located in metropolitan areas offer such a multitude of services that promotion from within is a possibility even for teaching positions. Teacher aides and substitute teachers can be promoted into full-time teaching positions when vacancies occur. Similarly, most large school districts have some classroom teachers who are qualified to become principals. The same situation occurs in support areas such as transportation, food service, and maintenance. Theoretically, a cook can be promoted into a commodities purchasing position and on to director of food services.

There are a few disadvantages to rigidly following a system of promoting from within. First, mediocre personnel in the school district may be promoted while excellent individuals in the community are not considered. Second, affirmative action requirements may dictate searching for personnel outside the organization. Finally, there is the possible danger of inbreeding. New ideas and methods are not only a welcomed change; they are absolutely necessary when the personnel in a school district appear content with the status quo.

The observations and performance evaluations of supervisors and principals are sources of information available to human resources administrators as they analyze a promotion-from-within policy.

It is a standard operating procedure in many school districts to post job vacancies on bulletin boards, in newsletters, or in special publications issued from the human resources office. This allows current employees to apply for positions or to notify friends, relatives, and associates about vacancies. The assumption here is that current employees should not be overlooked, but that a policy limiting all promotions to those presently employed is not the most beneficial approach for a school district.

Large urban school districts are using an approach unique to school districts. Many of these districts are having difficulty recruiting teachers particularly in science and mathematics. They are offering to pay a portion of the costs for staff members to acquire a college degree in order to hire them to fill teacher vacancies. Teacher assistants have been targeted as a group of staff members who are more likely to take advantage of this kind of program.

Referrals

Current employees are perhaps the best source of referrals when a vacancy occurs. There are a number of reasons for this observation. The most significant reason is that employees will not usually recommend someone unless they believe that the referred person will do a good job, since their reputations as recommenders are at stake.

A quality control on referrals from current employees is the job performance of the recommender and his or her satisfaction with the school district as a whole. A recommendation from an employee with inferior performance or from an employee who is constantly complaining about the policies and procedures of the district should be carefully reviewed.

The employee recommending a friend may also confuse friendship with potential job success. It is not uncommon for people to want friends in the workplace, both for social and economic reasons. An employee, for example, may want to share a ride to work with a friend who lives in the same neighborhood.

Referrals from teachers and principals, however, often reflect professional rather than social contact. Membership in professional organizations such as the National Association of Secondary School Principals or the National Education Association is one way in which people become acquainted with the competencies of colleagues. Consequently, such referrals may be more credible than referrals based only on social contact.

A school district should establish a policy and procedures that encourage employees to recommend people for job vacancies. A common practice is for the employee to provide the human resources department with the name or names of potential candidates. The human resources department can then send letters to the referred individuals, stating that they have been recommended to become candidates and inviting them to submit an application for the job. It should be noted that the invitation is extended to become a *candidate;* a human resources administrator must be very careful not to give the referred person the impression that the job is being offered.

Employment Agencies

Employment agencies fall into two categories; public or state agencies and private agencies. For all practical purposes, teachers and administrators have made limited use of employment agencies in their searching for professional positions. This is not the case for support personnel such as custodians, bus drivers, and cafeteria workers.

A public employment service was established in 1933 as a federal–state partnership. It was created not only to help individuals find suitable employment but also to help employers find qualified workers. All fifty states have a state employment service agency, with branch offices strategically located throughout each state. The U.S. Training and Employment Service supervises these agencies. The agencies provide services to those receiving unemployment benefits; benefits are available only to people who are registered with the state employment agency. Although state employment agencies are happy to list individuals with extensive training and highly developed skills, most people with such qualifications go to private agencies. Nevertheless, it is foolish for a school district not to list all vacancies with the appropriate state employment service agency because of the possibility that the right employee may be registered. The financial outlay for such a listing is negligible, requiring nothing more than the cost of postage.

Private employment agencies, of course, charge a fee for their services. This fee may be charged to either the employer or employee, or shared by both. The fee arrangement is usually dictated by the supply-and-demand principle. When applicants are abundant, potential employees are usually required to absorb the fee. When applicants are scarce, the employers pay the fee.

Another major difference between public and private employment agencies is in the scope of services provided. Private agencies not only advertise and screen applicants for a job but also provide a guarantee against unsatisfactory performance for a specified period of time, usually six to twelve months. If a particular employee does not work out, the agency will place him elsewhere and find the company another without a fee.

Some private employment agencies specialize in helping to fill executive positions, a practice commonly referred to as head-hunting. Through nationwide contacts and through extensive investigation of each potential executive's credentials, these agencies are able to recommend candidates for executive management positions, usually in private business and industry. They charge a rather high fee for this service, usually a percentage of the executive's first-year salary; 30 percent of a salary in excess of $100,000 is not uncommon.

Although most school districts do not engage the services of private employment agencies in searching for potential candidates to fill school executive positions, a growing trend in this direction can be seen, particularly in relation to the position of superintendent of schools. This trend is reflected in the consulting services offered by the American School Board Association and such state organizations as the Illinois Association of School Boards. These associations offer basically the same type of services as the private employment agencies in searching for school superintendents. The fee, however, is not as high as that charged by the private agencies, usually ranging between $5,000 and $25,000, depending on the time and expenses incurred during the search.

Further, in recent years private consulting firms have begun to specialize in the recruitment of potential candidates for vacant superintendencies. Like other private agencies, they have nationwide contacts, advertise the position, and screen potential candidates.

This is certainly a healthy trend in education, but it carries with it a potential danger. Associations and private consulting agencies may develop a list of favored candidates who are continually recommended for positions; in turn, it could become difficult for even qualified individuals to "break into" the inner circle of favored candidates.

Colleges and Universities

Most colleges and universities offer placement services not only to recent graduates but also to former graduates. The most important service available in these placement departments is the maintaining of a personal file containing references, transcripts, and other pertinent documents. Thus, each time an individual leaves a position, he or she may request his or her supervisor and other colleagues to send letters of reference to his or her placement service. This, in turn, will alleviate the burden of requesting former employers and colleagues to write reference letters each time an application is made for a different job. The placement service simply duplicates the references and sends them to prospective employers on the request of the graduate.

In terms of recruiting, listing vacancies with college and university placement services will not only reach recent graduates but also individuals with extensive experience who still use the service as a receptacle for employment references. Because teachers and administrators seeking jobs in school districts seldom use private or public employment agencies, college and university placement services are the best sources for finding potential candidates for professional positions.

Most college and university placement services also sponsor job fairs at which human resources administrators can meet potential teachers. It is an opportunity for recruiters to highlight the positive aspects of their school districts in order to attract quality applicants. Some school districts that are having a difficult time recruiting teachers, may be given the authority by their respective boards of education to make a job offer to qualified candidates at these events.

Professional Organizations

Many professional organizations and labor unions provide limited placement services for their members. These organizations either publish a roster of job vacancies or notify individual members concerning potential jobs. They usually list job vacancies in the classified section of their publications. However, having a classified section advertising jobs in a professional publication is common only to those organizations representing a specialty in educational administration. Professional education administration organizations include the American Association of School Personnel Administrators (AASPA), Association for Supervision and Curriculum Development (ASCD), Association of School Business Officials (ASBO), Council of Educational Facility Planners International (CEFPI), National Association of Elementary School Principals (NAESP), National Association of Pupil Personnel Administrators (NAPPA), National Association of Secondary School Principals (NASSP), National School Boards Association (NSBA), and National School Public Relations Association (NSPRA).

The American Association of School Administrators (AASA) is an exception. It publishes a listing of vacancies nationwide covering the following categories: the superintendency, the assistant superintendency, central-office positions, administrative positions in higher education, and professorships of educational administration.

Recruiting on the Internet

Both job seekers and human resources departments in school districts have discovered the benefits of *online* recruiting. It has transformed the recruiting process.

School districts are designing *home pages* that provide potential employees access to information about school districts, such as salary and fringe benefits information, student–teacher ratios, financial solvency, employee turnover, student discipline, and so on. A potential employee can also access information about the application process and even send a resume via email directly to a school district.

Of course, there are school districts experiencing difficulties that will prevent them from recruiting through the Internet. For example, a district with substandard salaries and fringe benefits probably will not provide such information which, in turn, will discourage seasoned job seekers from considering school districts that neglect to include such information.

When a school district has a unexpected vacancy, recruiting on the Internet could provide a pool of applicants in the shortest period of time. In addition, there are companies and organizations that provide their members with a job-posting site on the Internet. This allows a job seeker to post copy of his or her resume on the site and allows school district recruiters the ability to search the resume bank on a daily or weekly basis in order to find suitable candidates for job vacancies. This is a compelling reason to use this recruitment tool. The greatest advantage, however, to recruiting through the Internet is the ability to reach as many potential applicants as possible in the most cost-effective manner. If this method gains acceptance among job seekers, it could reduce postage costs and may even eventuate in a reduction in the number of staff members needed to manage the recruitment process in school districts.

There is a relatively new approach that is being used by companies and is commonly referred to as *social network recruiting,* which could be utilized by school districts. It is a modification of the long-standing *networking* approach that has always existed in some form or fashion. People make social contacts with other people in order to form a network that will be supportive when they are searching for a different place to work. Now there are companies that provide networking services. An interested person registers with a networking company, supplying his or her name, location, and employment status. Networking companies provide privacy and usually pledge not to sell personal information to a third party.

Thus, an individual adds his or her name to an enormous list that can be accessed to find contacts by ZIP code, job, and even place of employment. The objective is to find other people who live and work in places and organizations that interest you. Some companies allow human resources administrators to place job postings on the network, and even to transmit applications and other job-related information through email. The people who are networked can also direct employment information to each other. The effectiveness of this type of recruiting and job searching is not conclusive. However, no one disputes the large number of people who are members of Internet-based social networks that function for other purposes, such as finding a compatible significant other. It is a trend that all human resources administrators should be cautiously investigating.

Other Sources for Recruitment

There are two other avenues for obtaining potential job applicants: unsolicited or walk-in applicants and minority media resources. Although affirmative action requirements usually dictate advertising most positions, the walk-in applicant can be a good candidate. Most unsolicited applicants contact the school district either by mail, by telephone, or in person. It is important to inform such individuals of the potential for employment with the district and to present them with an application to be filled out. If a vacancy occurs that fits an applicant's qualifications, that individual should then be contacted and invited to activate his or her application by written notification.

Every metropolitan area has minority populations that are serviced by media resources that can be used in recruiting minorities. For example, in the southwestern United States, there are many local radio stations that are directed to the Mexican American population. Advertising vacancies on these radio stations can be a valuable method of recruiting.

Advertising Position Vacancies

When a school district wishes to communicate that it has a vacancy, it usually develops a formal advertisement. This advertisement can be used to implement the various methods of recruitment.

The Content and Style of an Advertisement

The content of an advertisement is determined by the job description and criteria that will be used in selecting the most qualified candidate for the position. The procedures used in determining and writing job descriptions along with the method of developing selection criteria will be addressed in Chapter 4.

To be effective, an advertisement must accurately reflect the major responsibilities of the position and the minimum qualifications to become a candidate. This is no easy task, because the advertisement must also be brief if it is to appear in a newspaper, newsletter, or professional publication. Appendix A contains sample advertisements that may be used as models in writing vacancy notices and that reflect some factors that should be taken into consideration.

The sample ads are modeled after those found in newspapers. The first two advertise vacancies in educational organizations, a school district and a college of education at a state university. The following five advertise vacancies in private business and industry. The most striking difference between the two types of advertisements is usually the format. Educational organizations traditionally begin by giving the name of the organization, then the title of the position, along with very specific and quantitative requirements.

For example, the first advertisement in Appendix A states:

GOODVILLE SCHOOL DISTRICT
SPECIAL EDUCATION POSITIONS AVAILABLE
Instructor for students with severe disabilities.

Further, it states that the positions require a B.S. degree in special education, certification (licensing) to work with students who have severe disabilities, with preference given to applicants who have teaching experience.

Advertisements for positions in private business and industry usually begin by giving the title of the job and then information about the company, along with detailed and subjective requirements. The advertisement for "Training Executive" in Appendix A states that the desired candidate should be a high-powered and seasoned professional with seven years experience in professional training. Only two of the advertisements for the private sector, "Direct Compensation Specialist" and "Human Resources Planning & Research Senior Specialist," do not emphasize subjective qualifications. However, it is interesting to note that these two are also the only ones for positions in the private sector that are not blind ads. A blind ad is one with no identification of the company; interested persons are asked to reply to a newspaper box number or a post office box number. These two ads place greater emphasis on the company and the responsibilities of the position. Large corporations with a national reputation seldom use blind advertisements when they are seeking to fill a position that is currently unoccupied.

School districts usually identify their districts and list objective rather than subjective requirements. These are desirable practices. Candidates should know the name and location of the educational organization, since this may determine the level of interest they have in the position and, in turn, may limit the number of applicants to those who are seriously interested in the job. Subjective requirements for a job are better evaluated through the selection process. Individuals are seldom good judges of their subjective qualifications, and many could be falsely encouraged or discouraged from applying for a position if subjective qualifications are listed in the advertisement. The practice of giving information about the organization and listing the job title first effectively attracts the attention of those individuals who are most qualified for the position.

A final note about the advertisements for educational organizations in Appendix A: These two models illustrate a very common but sometimes misleading technique. Each ad contains a number of vacancies, which might imply that the organization has a high turnover of employees and, further, might suggest that selection will not be a very discriminating process because of the number of applicants for numerous positions. It might be more appropriate for a school district to place fewer vacancies in any one advertisement and, when possible, to advertise each position by itself.

Recruitment Brochures

Appendix B contains samples of a special type of advertisement, the recruitment brochure. These brochures are usually mailed to individuals who have indicated an interest in an advertised position. The brochure provides potential candidates with extensive information, enabling them to better ascertain if they wish to apply for the job and also if they possess the minimum requirements. The recruitment brochure is obviously much more extensive in content and scope than the normal advertisement.

The format for such brochures will vary, but certain information is usually provided. The most important information to communicate includes the announcement of the vacancy, the procedure for applying, a description of the qualifications that the successful candidate must possess, information about the community served by the school or school district, and data about the school and/or school district, which normally includes financial, personnel, and curriculum information.

Appendix B contains two models of recruitment brochures for the positions of superintendent of schools and high school principal. Such brochures are normally used when recruiting candidates for school executive positions.

Brochures are certainly a valuable recruitment tool and should be used as much as possible for all vacancies in a school district. A general information brochure containing data about the community and school district could be used when recruiting for teachers and support personnel. The tailored, special-position brochure could be reserved for executive educational positions. This approach would help to hold down the cost of printing a special brochure for the more commonly occurring vacancies in a school district.

Summary

After the human resources planning process identifies current and future staffing needs, the next step is to recruit qualified personnel. However, certain constraints on recruitment must be taken into consideration. Affirmative action requirements, the reputation and policies of a school district, the enormous responsibilities of positions in education, the salary and fringe benefits offered in certain school districts—all have an influence on how a district will implement the recruitment process.

To carry out a recruitment program effectively, human resources administrators must have a good understanding of vocational development theory. The following principles are common to many theories and can be used to formulate recruitment strategies. First, people have different interests, abilities, and personalities, which will qualify them for a number of occupations. Second, the occupational preferences, competencies, and the self-image of people will change with time and experience, making personal adjustment a continuous process. Third, both life and work satisfaction depend on how well individuals can utilize their abilities and find outlets for their interests, personality traits, and values. Fourth, the process of occupational choice is influenced by employment variables such as salary, fringe benefits, location, the opportunity for advancement, and the nature of the work to be performed. Finally, vocational development is essentially a compromise between personal characteristics such as interests and abilities, and external factors such as the type of work to be performed.

Experience shows that certain recruiting methods produce the best applicants for particular job vacancies. Therefore, before initiating the recruitment process, administrators should analyze each job vacancy to ascertain what method will be most effective. The most common methods include internal search, referrals, contacting employment agencies, advertising vacancies with college and university placement services or job fairs, advertising on the Internet, advertising in newspapers and in the publications of professional organizations, following up on unsolicited applications, and contacting community organizations that promote the interests of minority groups.

When a school district wishes to communicate that it has a vacancy, it usually produces a formal advertisement. The content of an advertisement is dictated by the job description and criteria to be used in selecting the most qualified candidate for the position. An effective advertisement must accurately reflect the major responsibilities of the position and the minimum qualifications an individual must possess to become a candidate for the job.

In terms of content and style, the most effective advertisement will include the title of the position, information about the school district, information on how to apply, and desired qualifications for candidates. Listing subjective qualifications and using "blind ads" are generally not appropriate. It is also more effective for a school district to place only a few vacancies in a given advertisement and, when possible, to advertise each position by itself.

A special type of advertisement is the recruitment brochure. Its purpose is to provide potential candidates with enough information to allow them to determine if they wish to apply for the job and if they possess the necessary requirements. The brochure should include the announcement of the vacancy, the procedure for applying, a description of the qualifications that the successful candidate must possess, information about the community served by the school or school district, and financial, personnel, and curricular data about the school and/or school district.

General information brochures containing data about the community and school district could be used when recruiting teachers and support personnel. The more extensive brochure is commonly reserved for recruiting school executives. The cost of printing such brochures for each vacancy would be prohibitive.

Discussion Questions and Statements

- Given the teacher shortage, what strategies do you think are the most effective in recruiting teachers?
- Describe the factors that influence people to become applicants in certain school districts.
- How do the theories of occupational choice affect the recruitment process?
- Describe the elements that make up an effective newspaper advertisement for position vacancies.
- What is the advantage of using recruitment brochures in place of newspaper-type advertisements for certain positions?

Suggested Activities

- You are the Assistant Superintendent for Human Resources in a school district that is experiencing a shortage of qualified teacher and other employee applicants. You have scheduled a meeting with the administrative staff, the teacher organization leaders, and the support staff organization leaders in order to elicit their assistance in recruiting applicants. Outline, in writing, your presentation and develop five discussion questions that will help you interact with them about this issue.
- Obtain a copy of the advertisements for administrative, teaching, and support services positions in local newspapers and write a comparison of them with the advertisements in this chapter.
- Obtain a copy of a recruitment brochure for an administrative position that has been used in a school district in your geographic area and write a comparison of it with the brochures in this chapter.

- Review the recruitment policies of a school district and write an analysis concerning its potential effectiveness.
- In person or on the telephone, interview a human resources administrator from a school district that is having difficulty in recruiting administrators, teachers, or other employees in order to ascertain his or her opinion about the reasons why the district is not being successful in the recruitment process.
- Visit college or university placement offices and talk with career counselors in order to gain a better understanding of their services. Also, ask career counselors about the effectiveness of job fairs and about the emerging pool of future teachers and administrators.

Selected Bibliography

A Quality Work Force: America's Key to the Next Century. Denver, CO: Education Commission of the States, 1989.

Au, Kathryn H., and Karen M. Blake, "Cultural Identity and Learning to Teach in a Diverse Community: Findings from a Collective Case Study," *Journal of Teacher Education,* 54, no. 3 (May/June 2003), 192–205.

Barker, Sandra L., "Is Your Successor in Your Schoolhouse? Finding Principal Candidates," *NASSP Bulletin,* 81, no. 592 (November 1997), 85–91.

Fielder, Donald J., "Wanted: Minority Teachers," *The Executive Educator,* 15, no. 5 (May 1993), 33–34.

Goldstein, William, *Recruiting Superior Teachers: The Interview Process.* Bloomington, IN: Phi Delta Kappa Education Foundation, 1986.

Gordon, June A., "Why Students of Color Are Not Entering Teaching: Reflections from Minority Teachers," *Journal of Teacher Education,* 45, no. 53 (November–December 1994), 346–353.

Grogan, Sonetta, and Barbara Eshelman, "Staffing Strategies for a More Diverse Workforce: Case Examples from Cornell Cooperative Extension," *Journal of Extension,* 36, no. 1 (February 1998), 36–42.

Hammond, Doug, and Gary Blakey, "School Bus Drivers: Recruitment & Training," *School Business Affairs,* 57, no. 4 (April 1991), 26–30.

Hubbard, Joan C., Alexa B. North, and H. Lari Arjomand "Making the Right Connections: Perceptions of Human Resource/Personnel Directors Concerning Electronic Job-Search Methods," *Journal of Employment Counseling,* 34, no. 1 (March 1997), 29–39.

Ingersoll, Richard M., "The Teacher Shortage: A Case of Wrong Diagnosis," *Bulletin,* 86, no. 631 (June 2002), 16–30.

Liu, Edward, Susan Moore Johnson, and Heather G. Peske, "New Teachers and the Massachusetts Signing Bonus: The Limits of Inducements," *Educational Evaluation and Policy Analysis,* 26, no. 3 (Fall 2004), 217–236.

U.S. Department of Education, *Teacher Attrition and Migration.* Washington, DC: OERI/Education Information Branch, 1993.

Varma, Gale, "Attracting the Right Talent: Prerecruiting Ideas for New Recruiters," *Journal of Career Planning & Employment,* 58, no. 1 (Fall 1997), 45–48.

Winston, Mark, "The Role of Recruitment in Achieving Goals Related to Diversity," *College & Research Libraries,* 59, no. 3 (May 1998), 240–247.

Winter, Paul A., and Jayne R. Morgenthal, "Principal Recruitment in a Reform Environment: Effects of School Achievement and School Level on Applicant Attraction to the Job" *Educational Administration Quarterly,* XXXVIII, no. 3 (August 2002), 319–340.

Witty, Elaine P., *Teacher Recruitment and Retention.* West Haven, CT: NEA Professional Library, 1990.

Appendix A
Model Newspaper Advertisements

GOODVILLE SCHOOL DISTRICT
SPECIAL EDUCATION POSITIONS AVAILABLE

Instructor for children with severe disabilities. Requirements are B.S. degree in Special Education and certification in SD; teaching experience is preferred.

Educational examiner. Requires MA degree and certification in one or more special education areas. Knowledge of and/or experience in psychometric administration and interpretation are desirable. Expertise in assessment of functional abilities, social adaptation, and perceptual and language skills is mandatory. Previous experience in either diagnostics or educational programming would be highly beneficial.

Speech/language/hearing pathologists. Openings include Language classroom instructors; Speech/Language pathologists. Requirements are MA degree, eligibility for state certification; Certificate of Clinical Competence from the American Speech-Language-Hearing Association; classroom experience preferred. Part-time positions are also available requiring MA degree and state certification in Speech Correction. Hours are 4–6, Monday through Thursday.

Interpreter for the hearing impaired. Requires a minimum of 64 college hours, Expressive Interpreter certificate, knowledge of different sign systems, and experience with students who have disabilities.

Excellent fringe benefits. For application call or write

Goodville School District
Director of Human Resources

An Equal Opportunity and Affirmative Action Employer

GOODVILLE STATE UNIVERSITY

Goodville State University is a regional multipurpose institution enrolling 9,000 students. It is located in Goodville, a community with a population of 37,000 located 120 miles south of a major metropolitan area.

Educational administration and foundation. Associate or Assistant Professor to coordinate Ed.D. Degree Program, teach graduate and undergraduate courses, including Methods of Research and one or more of the following: Educational Finance, Secondary School Administration, and Foundations of Education. Experience withstate financial accounting systems and familiarity with schools in or similar to the Southeast state region desired. Doctorate in educational administration or educational leadership required. Five years' experience including district-level administration required.

Educational administration and foundations. Assistant Professor to teach graduate and undergraduate courses, including Methods of Research and one or more of the following: Educational Finance, Secondary School Administration, Secondary School Supervision, and Foundations of Education. Advise graduate and undergraduate students. Doctorate in educational administration or educational leadership desired; doctorate in directly related field considered. Five years' experience in educational administration required. Experience in urban school administration, multicultural programs, or secondary administration desired.

Reading education. Assistant Professor or Instructor to teach undergraduate and graduate courses including developmental, secondary, and remedial reading, and graduate reading practicum. Competency in assessment techniques required. Advise graduate and undergraduate students. Doctorate in reading preferred; active doctoral candidate in reading considered. Five years' experience including elementary or secondary classroom teaching required. College teaching preferred.

University school faculty positions. The University School is a K–12 instructional program for 340 students that functions as an integral part of the Department of Education and the teacher education program. All positions require strong classroom skills and a special interest in working with teacher education programs.

Applications. Applicants are required to have their placement file forwarded immediately. Completed application, current resume, and transcripts should be mailed by February 1 to

Dean
School of Education
Goodville University

HUMAN RESOURCES DIRECTOR

A large well-established company that is a leader in its field, with its corporate offices conveniently located in the Midwest, is seeking a Human Resources Director. This individual will have the complete responsibility for directing the human resources function involving such activities as benefits administration, wage and salary administration, staff development, selection, employee relations, and EEOC.

The ideal candidate will have 4–6 years experience, be degreed (preferably in human resources administration) with previous supervisory experience. Good planning and organizing skills are essential, as well as the ability to communicate effectively.

This highly visible position on our corporate staff offers an excellent compensationand benefits package in addition to professional and personal growth opportunities.

Apply in complete confidence by sending resume and salary requirements to

Metro Daily Newspaper
Box 325

Equal Opportunity and Affirmative Action Employer

DIRECT COMPENSATION SPECIALIST

We're Chemomax, the pace-setting, $4-billion energy-based company that's increasing America's energy options. Our activities are diverse—natural gas, LNG, propane, coal and petrochemicals. Our operations extend from Alaska to the Gulf of Mexico, in Canada and in the continental United States, on-shore and off-shore. Our operations range from transmission and exploration to managing large petro-chemical complexes. Rapid expansion of our alternative energy programs has generated superlative career opportunities.

As our Direct Compensation Specialist, you will be responsible for developing annual proposals for structure increases in the corporation's basic exempt salary schedule and the schedule covering corporate executives. You will be working with our operating companies regarding the design of base salary and incentive plans as well as recommending new and/or innovative forms of compensation.

You will need at least two years experience in salary plan design and administration. Some experience in foreign and executive compensation is desirable. You should possess a good knowledge of job evaluation, salary survey techniques, and salary structure design along with government wage laws and related regulations.

To explore this excellent opportunity, please send your resume, including salary history, in complete confidence to

Director of Human Resources
Chemomax Corporation

An Equal Opportunity and Affirmative Action Employer

HUMAN RESOURCES PLANNING & RESEARCH SENIOR SPECIALIST

As part of our company's commitment to effectively selecting and developing its employees, the company has launched an extensive approach to selection, career path planning, and employee development. Due to the success of the initial work in this area, an experienced Human Resources Planning and Research Specialist is needed to join a team of talented professionals to assist in development and imple-mentation of these processes.

The successful candidate will have had significant experience with test valida-tion; design and administration of assessment centers; design, administration, and interpretation of organizational diagnostic instruments; career path planning; and succession planning. Experience in the design and development of courses would be a plus. This is a unique opportunity to design and install selection and development systems for an industry leader whose senior management fully supports the effort. The successful candidate will have a master's degree in the behavioral sciences, preferably a Ph.D., and experience in the industrial application of selection/development programs.

We offer an excellent salary and complete company-paid fringe benefits, including a dental plan. Interested and qualified applicants should send a resume, including education and income history, in confidence to

Director of Human Resources
Windstorm Industries

An Equal Opportunity and Affirmative Action Employer

Training Executive
WHAT HAVE YOU DONE
FOR YOURSELF LATELY?

Your time and energy are being spent on training other managers for successful careers. You do it well. You've seen others succeed because of your efforts and talents. Now ask yourself a few questions. Within your present organizational structure, are there opportunities for your own career success? Are you being taken for granted? Are you with a corporation that's totally committed to the training function? If you're uncomfortable with your answers, it's time to do something for yourself. Think about joining a multibillion dollar corporation that is structured for personal growth and individual recognition. We believe we are such a corporation.

```
          /\
         /  \
        / SELF \
     ACTUALIZATION
      / EGO-STATUS \
     / BELONGINGNESS \
    /     SAFETY      \
   /      BASIC        \
  /_____\
   A HIERARCHY OF NEEDS
```

The individual we're looking for is a high-powered, seasoned professional who currently holds a responsible managment position within the Training function of a large corporation. Candidate's responsibilities must have included the design, implementation, and presentation of effective Management Development and/or Sales Management Training programs. A minimum of 7 years of professional training experience is preferred, ideally with emphasis in middle to upper management training programs.

Our training complex is located in the Midwest and is considered one of the most sophisticated in the country. Along with the opportunity for personal career development, we offer an excellent compensation plan, plus complete benefits including relocation expenses. For prompt and confidential consideration, send a letter or resume, including salary history, to:

Daily Newspaper
Box 530

An Equal Opportunity and
Affirmative Action Employer

LABOR RELATIONS

A Goodville Corporation is seeking a Manager of Labor Relations. We are a world leader in the institutional furniture industry, with a major commitment in open office systems furniture, entertainment, and transportation seating.

This is an outstanding opportunity for a human resources generalist who enjoys labor relations and wishes to concentrate in that field. Must have minimum five years' experience, including contract interpretation. The successful candidate should be aggressive and yet objective; creative, mature, well-organized, and a person of integrity. Communication skills are a must as is some experience in safety and training. We offer a professional atmosphere and a secure future.

This highly valuable position offers an attractive salary, equitable relocation assistance, and excellent benefits. Qualified candidates should submit resume and salary history in confidence to

Metro Daily Newspaper
Box 645

An Equal Opportunity and Affirmative Action Employer

Appendix B
Model Recruitment Brochures for the Positions of
Superintendent of Schools and High School Principal

POSITION AVAILABLE

SUPERINTENDENT OF SCHOOLS
GOODVILLE SCHOOL DISTRICT

An Equal Opportunity and
Affirmative Action Employer

ANNOUNCEMENT OF VACANCY

The Board of Education of Goodville School District is seeking a superintendent of schools. The salary of the superintendent selected will be determined by his or her professional preparation and by his or her successful experience in educational administration, as well as by other qualifications.

Professional assistance for the initial screening of applicants has been secured, which is a special consultant committee consisting of

- A superintendent from a neighboring school district
- Dean of the School of Education, Goodville University

All letters of application, nominations, inquiries, credentials, and copies of legal proof of administrative qualifications should be mailed to the President of the Goodville School Board.

To receive consideration, applicants must do the following by January 1:

1. Submit a formal letter of application indicating a desire to be a candidate for the position
2. Send up-to-date confidential credentials from his or her university, up-to-date resume, and a listing of educational accomplishments by title
3. Provide legal proof or other evidence showing qualification to be a superintendent

THE PERSON NEEDED

The Board of Education of the Goodville School District and the community it serves are committed to the continuing development of quality schools. They are seeking a person who has had successful administrative experience as a superintendent, or in a central-office position with comparable responsibilities. The superintendent they are seeking should have a thorough understanding of and interest in public school education; a concern for the welfare and motivation of students is of prime importance. By his or her experience, knowledge, and stature, he or she must reflect credit upon himself or herself and the district he or she serves.

The superintendent selected must be skilled in providing educational leadership; he or she must be a goals-oriented educator with proven success in the continuing development of teamwork among the administrative/teaching staff, board of education, and community.

Although no candidate can be expected to meet all qualifications fully, preference will be given to candidates with capabilities and/or potential as follows:

- Successful experience in financial management, budgeting, and fiscal responsibility, with the ability to evaluate the financial status of the district and establish a management plan based on projected revenues and future curriculum programs
- In the area of human relations, the ability to work with the public, students, and staff, thus leading to good school human resources management; this aspect also includes evaluation of and in-service training for staff
- An "educational manager" who delegates responsibility, yet maintains accountability through the management–team concept
- Ability to exercise leadership and decision making in selection and implementation of educational priorities—a person with a realistic and responsible educational philosophy
- The ability to objectively select, evaluate, assign, and realign staff
- Willingness to help formulate, review, and effectively carry out board policies and to communicate and relate openly and honestly with the board of education, keeping members informed on issues, proposals, and developments within the district
- Ability to maintain desired student behavioral patterns
- Successful administrative experience in a comparable district
- A strong academic background in curriculum planning and an ability to evaluate and plan curriculum and programs while constantly keeping in mind the present and future financial status of the district
- Skillful educational leadership in the development of long- and short-range district goals and objectives—a "management type" educational leader

THE COMMUNITY

The Goodville School District is currently serving the educational needs of nearly 20,000 residents in a geographic area of great growth potential. It covers 80 square miles—one of the largest school districts in the state.

Continued

The district is highly diverse and is rich in cultural background and life styles. Approximately 30 percent of the residents live in a rural setting, with the remaining 70 percent located in suburban communities. Our district is enriched by a broad range of ethnic and racial compositions. As Goodville is located 25 miles south of a major metropolitan area, many of our residents can conveniently commute to work to and from the city. Local employment continues to be enhanced with the growth of many industrial parks. As a microcosm of lifestyles and cultures, the school district encourages unique opportunities in community living and education. It is a district of parks, forest preserves, churches, schools, shopping centers, and excellent recreational facilities. We are served by three local newspapers, in addition to a large daily newspaper and a local radio station. Goodville State University is located in our district, and many other colleges and universities are within an hour's drive.

THE SCHOOLS

The Goodville School District enrolls more than 5,600 pupils in K–12. Additionally, the district offers services in preschool education, special education, and adult education. Currently there are six K–5 elementary schools; two middle schools, 6–8; and one high school fully accredited and recognized. The school system is supported by approximately 361 certificated staff members and 171 support personnel.

Concern and support for the teaching of basic skills has been equally recognized by the school board and administrative staff. However, many innovative services and programs are provided to teachers, parents, and students. An alternative education program for secondary students is recognized as the finest in the county. Additionally, great steps have been taken toward identification of pupils' learning styles and the proper mode of instruction to enhance these styles. Bilingual programs, special education, teacher staff development, and parent workshops have led state trends. Extracurricular activities have always been a vital part of the educational program. The district prides itself on its athletic programs and band/orchestra activities for both boys and girls.

PHILOSOPHY OF THE BOARD OF EDUCATION

Policy-Making Body

The Board of Education is primarily a policy-making body and shall maintain an administration to operate the schools efficiently with the funds available, shall constantly strive to improve all aspects of the school system, and shall keep the public well informed about educational issues.

Education of the Child

The Board believes that the education of each child in the district is the heart of the entire school operation and that administration, business management, building management, and all other services should be appraised in terms of their contributions to the progress of instruction. It shall be the goal of the Board to offer each child the opportunity to develop his or her educational potentialities to the maximum. It shall be the intention of the Board of Education to provide for equality of educational opportunity for all children regardless of sex, race, color, creed, national origin, or disability.

STAFF

Administration:		
	1	Superintendent
	2	Assistant Superintendents
	5	Directors
	9	Principals
	7	Assistant Principals
	6	Curriculum Coordinators
	1	Business Manager
Staff:	314	Classroom Teachers
	14	Guidance Counselors
	12	Learning Resource Specialists
	16	Special Education Teachers
	8	Nurses
	5	Speech and Language Professionals
	30	Paraprofessionals
	43	Secretarial/Clerical Personnel
	40	Custodial/Maintenance Personnel
	30	Bus Drivers
	20	Cafeteria Workers
Student Composition:	730	African Americans
	152	Hispanic Americans
	32	Asian Americans
	9	Native Americans
	4,677	European Americans
	5,600	Total Enrollment

FINANCIAL DATA

Assessed Value	$280,000,000.00
TAX RATE	4.50
Bonded Indebtedness	10,000,000.00
BUDGET EXPENDITURES	40,000,000.00

Announcing a Vacancy

PRINCIPAL OF THOMAS JEFFERSON HIGH SCHOOL

THE COMMUNITY

Goodville is primarily a suburban residential community with easy access to the metropolitan area, as well as to all major shopping centers. Parochial schools, both elementary and secondary, are located within the school district's boundaries. There are many active parent organizations working on behalf of the students, all of which foster a close relationship between the schools and the parents in the community. The Chamber of Commerce functions as a viable catalyst for the business community. The Goodville School District has one of the highest tax bases in the county.

Continued

THE PRINCIPAL

The Goodville School District is seeking qualified applicants for the position of principal for Thomas Jefferson High School. The following qualifications and leadership abilities will be taken into consideration in the selection process:

- Good interpersonal relations skills
- Skill in all types of communications
- Ability to generate support and enthusiasm among students, faculty, and the community for the total educational program, including extracurricular activities
- Proven ability to formulate and implement both short- and long-range objectives
- Experience in the evaluation process of both staff and programs
- Certification as a secondary school administrator
- Classroom teaching experience for five years
- Educational administrative experience for three years

THE SCHOOL DISTRICT

The Goodville School District was organized in 1875. Education in Goodville encompasses the entire community. Starting with the preschooler, aged 3–5, there are tuition-sponsored programs in early childhood education. Evening courses are offered to adults in a continuing education program.

The total district enrollment is about 5,500 students. There are four elementary schools, one middle school, and one high school. The district employs approximately 300 professional educators and 100 support employees.

The Board of Education is composed of six members, each elected for a three-year term. The district's budget is $40 million and the average per pupil expenditure is approximately $7,000.

THE HIGH SCHOOL

Thomas Jefferson High School has an enrollment of 2,000 students and a staff of 98 full- and part-time certificated professionals. The school is fully accredited by the North Central Association of Colleges and Secondary Schools.

Approximately 68 percent of the graduating class goes on to college. This requires a comprehensive offering of courses, which currently numbers approximately 150.

The High School campus is located on a twenty-four acre site. Built in several stages, the school was completed in 1972, when a major addition provided much-needed classrooms and expanded physical education and drama facilities.

THE STAFF

"Experienced and highly qualified" best describes the high school faculty. Approximately 65 percent have more than fifteen years teaching experience; 60 percent have taught fifteen years or more in the high school; 75 percent of the faculty members have a master's degree or better.

Salaries are paid according to placement on an adopted schedule that recognizes experience and education. Fringe benefits include a unique plan for staff sick leave, personal leave, major medical insurance, dental insurance, term life insurance, and excellent retirement benefits. Administrators with a twelve- month contract receive one month's vacation.

Contact the Human Resources Department of the Goodville School District for an application package.

4

Selection

The objective of the selection process is to hire individuals who will be successful on the job. Self-evident as this purpose may appear, its implementation requires a rather thorough process. The cost of selecting employees is a major expenditure for most school districts. If the process does not produce effective employees, the cost to the district is often incalculable because of inadequate performance, the expense connected with the termination process, and the expense involved in hiring new employees.

The minimum cost in hiring any new employee has been calculated at $1,000; it can cost more than $25,000 to hire a superintendent of schools. In selecting an individual for most positions in a school district, the costs include advertising the position; printing and mailing applications; and personnel time required to review applications, to interview candidates, and to check references. This presupposes that many routine tasks, such as writing job descriptions and establishing proper selection criteria, have already been accomplished. Training and orienting new employees are additional costs directly related to the hiring process but often overlooked. Therefore, selecting individuals who will be successful and will remain with the school district for a reasonable period of time is an extremely important human resources process, not only significant in fulfilling the district's mandate to educate children but also affecting the financial condition of the school district.

Chapter 2 established the necessity of human resources planning because it is impossible for school districts, and all other organizations, to achieve their goals and objectives without having the right number of people, with the right skills, in the right place, and at the right time. Adequate human, financial, and physical resources constitute the three requisites for organizational success. However, organizational success is synonymous with *organizational change*. School districts must meet the ever-changing educational needs and expectations of parents and students in order to be successful. In Chapter 6, the concept of organizational change will be molded into the notion of the *professional learning community*.

It is important for human resources administrators to understand the current research on organizational change that has proven to be helpful not only to schools and school districts but also to many business enterprises. School districts have much in common with other organizations, and many of the principles concerning change are applicable across all organizations. For example, two fundamental principles apply to school districts and all other organizations: stakeholders and vision.

First, all internal stakeholders constitute the organization. Thus, the board of education, superintendent, central-office administrators, principals, and all other employees are, in the aggregate, the school district. Buildings and financial and other material resources are not the school district. Rather, the board, administrators, teachers, and staff members use these resources to fulfill their responsibilities and the mission of education.

Second, all organizations are driven by a vision. The board of education, superintendent, other administrators, teachers, and staff members usually operationalize the vision through the establishment of goals and objectives. The vision of a school district will certainly revolve around the intellectual, emotional, physical, and ethical development of students. Of course all stakeholders must have a voice in the establishment of a school district's vision, which means that parents, students, and other members of the community, along with the board and staff, must be engaged in public discourse.

The implications for human resources administration are obvious. The planning process, as set forth in Chapter 2, requires the school district to be focused on a vision that addresses the *signs of the times* along with operational goals and objectives. All the other elements of the human resources function must be constantly monitored so they are in consort with the *directives* of vision, goals, and objectives.[1]

The steps in the selection process that follow must support these directives. This is particularly important in relation to the *selection criteria*, which must incorporate indicators that reflect the vision, goals, and objectives of the school district. Such an approach will ensure the hiring of administrators, teachers, and staff members who are capable and willing to implement the directives. Appendix B contains selection criteria indicators that model such directives.

A selection decision may result in four possible outcomes: two are correct decisions and two are errors. The correct decisions occur when the individual hired proves to be successful on the job or when a rejected applicant would have performed inadequately if hired. In both instances the selection process has met the objective of hiring the most appropriate candidate. The process has failed when a rejected candidate could have performed successfully on the job or when the individual hired performs inadequately.[2]

The selection process, therefore, should be implemented through a series of activities that will minimize the chances of hiring individuals who are inadequate performers. Exhibit 4.1 sets forth these activities in a sequence that will serve as a model throughout this chapter.

[1]Lee G. Bolman and Terrence E. Deal, *Reframing Organizations: Artistry, Choice, and Leadership* (San Francisco: Jossey-Bass, 1997, 101–103.

[2]See Stephen P. Robbins, *Personnel: The Management of Human Resources,* 2nd ed. (Englewood Cliffs, NJ: Prentice-Hall, 1982), 122.

EXHIBIT 4.1   Steps in the Selection Process

1. Write the job description
2. Establish the selection criteria
3. Write the vacancy announcement and advertise the position
4. Receive applications
5. Select the candidates to be interviewed

6. Interview candidates
7. Check references and credentials
8. Select the best candidate
9. Implement the job offer and acceptance
10. Notify unsuccessful candidates

Steps in the Selection Process

Writing the Job Description

A written job description is the end product of a process that is commonly referred to as "job analysis." This process gathers information about the position: what an employee does; why he or she performs certain tasks; how he or she does the job; what skills, education, or training are required to perform the job; the relationship the job has to other jobs; what physical demands and environmental conditions affect the job. This information also is relevant to human resources forecasting, to creating job evaluation instruments, and in determining compensation programs.[3]

A number of recognized techniques can be used in job analysis. These include:

1. *Observation.* The person conducting the analysis directly observes the employee as he or she is performing his or her job.
2. *Individual interviews.* Certain employees are extensively interviewed and the analyzed results from a number of these interviews are combined into the job analysis.
3. *Group interviews.* This technique is similar to individual interviews except that a number of employees are interviewed at the same time.
4. *Job questionnaire.* Employees check or rate tasks which they perform from a pre-established list of possible job tasks.
5. *Consulting.* Expert consultants are employed to describe specific tasks that should be performed by a certain category of employees.
6. *Supervisor analysis.* Those who supervise certain categories of employees are consulted on the tasks which are appropriate to the job classification under study.
7. *Diary method.* Certain employees are required to maintain a diary of their daily activities for a given period of time.[4]

The seven methods described above are not meant to be used in isolation from each other. They are complementary techniques that will result in a superior job analysis if used

---

[3]George B. Redfern, "Using Job Descriptions as an Administrative Tool," *Spectrum,* Winter 1984, 21.

[4]Robbins, *Personnel,* 79.

in combination with each other. Of course, not all techniques are required for each analysis. However, certain techniques are more appropriate to particular classifications of jobs. The first three methods would probably be more effective in analyzing the jobs of classified employees. Techniques four, five, and seven would be beneficial in analyzing the tasks common to professional positions. Number six would always be helpful in analyzing both professional and classified jobs.

The job analysis is, as previously mentioned, the vehicle for obtaining the necessary data to write a job description. The job description is an outline providing specific details concerning a job and the minimum qualifications necessary to perform it successfully.

No one format for writing a job description can be universally acclaimed as most effective in each and every circumstance. However, certain elements should be common to most job descriptions. These include the title of the job, duties that must be performed, the authority and responsibilities accompanying the job, and specific qualifications necessary to successful performance of the job.

Appendix A provides two sample job descriptions that are models of a particular style appropriate for school district positions. Note that the titles for these two positions are very specific. The first is a job description for a middle school principal; and the second, for a high school biology teacher.

Each description begins with a summary of the job, outlining the overall responsibilities of the position. This is followed by a detailed explanation of specific job tasks and the relationship of the job to other positions in the organizational structure of the school district. At a time when legal rights and responsibilities are being emphasized by parents and employees, organizational relationships are extremely important and must be clearly explained to prospective employees. Finally, minimum job qualifications are listed as an integral part of the job description.

Job descriptions should be updated from time to time because working conditions change with advances in technology and education. But it is absolutely critical to perform a job analysis and to revise the job description for a position each time it becomes vacant. This will affect the establishment of the selection criteria and will ensure that the individual being hired properly understands the responsibilities and duties of the job.

Establishing the Selection Criteria

The second step in the selection procedure is to establish the criteria against which the candidates will be evaluated to determine who will be offered the job. Selection criteria are very different from the job description, in that the selection criteria delineate those ideal characteristics that, if possessed by an individual to the fullest extent possible, would ensure the successful performance of the job. Obviously, no one person will possess all the characteristics to their fullest extent, and not all characteristics have equal importance in determining who is the best candidate.

The use of selection criteria also can become a method for quantifying the expert opinions of those who will interview candidates. Without criteria, each interviewer is left to his or her own discretion in determining if an individual will be able to perform the job.

Quantifying the opinions of interviewers also provides data to show that the best candidate was offered the position, thus demonstrating that the school district is an affirmative action and equal opportunity employer. The candidate with the highest score should be offered the position first; if he or she does not accept, then the candidate receiving the next highest score should be offered the position, and so on.

It is a generally accepted practice for the human resources department to assume the responsibilities for organizing and conducting job analyses, for writing job descriptions, and for establishing the selection criteria used in filling a vacancy.

The timing for writing the job description and for developing the selection criteria is extremely important. Both tasks should be performed before a job vacancy is advertised and before applications are received, not only because the advertisement should be based on the description but also because it will demonstrate that the criteria were not prepared to favor a particular applicant.

Appendix B presents a sample of three sets of selection criteria, one for a high school English teacher and a second for a sixth-grade elementary school teacher; the third presents general criteria for an elementary school teacher in a self-contained classroom. Each criteria instrument has been constructed in such a way that particular characteristics may be rated and a final score obtained. The significant difference between the first two instruments and the third is the weighting that is designated on the general criteria instrument. The compatibility of an applicant's educational philosophy with the school district's policies and curriculum is of primary importance, as indicated on this third instrument. Professional preparation is second, personal characteristics third, and experience the least important. The assumption underlying this third selection instrument is that an individual will best meet the needs of the school district if he or she has the proper attitude and philosophy. Experience will enrich an individual's performance, but philosophy is necessary to direct the benefits obtained by the experience. In like manner, an individual will grow in the job if his or her educational values are in harmony with those of the school district.

Note too that this third instrument is less specific in describing desirable characteristics and leaves the interviewer with more discretion in making a judgment about the candidate's qualifications. For example, an individual with a Ph.D. in early childhood education may not be the most desirable candidate for a first-grade self-contained classroom position. That applicant would be overqualified for such a position, but would be an appropriate candidate for a position in a laboratory school attached to a university in which aspiring teachers observe instructional techniques. In this latter situation, the candidate with a Ph.D. would likely receive the maximum number of points in the "professional preparation" category.

The first two criteria instruments, for a high school English teacher and sixth-grade teacher, are rather detailed and more traditional in style and content. Each is divided into categories, delineating academic, personal, and experiential qualifications.

This method of evaluating candidates places a responsibility on each interviewer to make a discriminatory judgment concerning the qualifications of each individual. The interview itself will not be the only source of information used to fill out the selection criteria instrument. The application, placement papers, transcripts, and letters of reference also will be used by the interviewers in determining an individual's qualifications for the job.

Each interviewer will sign and return to the human resources department a selection criteria instrument for each person interviewed. The human resources department is then responsible for compiling the results.

Writing the Job Vacancy Announcement and Advertising the Position

Chapter 3 describes in detail the nuances of writing a job vacancy advertisement. The advertisement should be viewed as an integral part of the selection process. It is based on the job description and should provide potential candidates with sufficient information to make a decision on whether to apply for the position. Consequently, an advertisement must clearly identify the job title, major responsibilities of the job, the name and location of the school district, how to apply for the job, and the minimum qualifications to become a candidate.

It is the responsibility of the human resources department to write the advertisement and to publish it according to the recruitment policy of the school district. In providing information about how to apply for a position, the advertisement should include a deadline for receiving applications. It is a common practice to allow a two-week period for receiving applications for classified and teaching jobs. A month is the usual time period allotted to receiving applications for school executive positions. Of course, each individual situation will dictate the length of time allotted for the receiving of applications and may deviate from these usual time periods.

A common mistake made by some school administrators and inexperienced human resources administrators is not providing sufficient time to effectively implement the selection process. A hurried process may place the school district in an indefensible position in terms of affirmative action requirements and, in addition, may result in the hiring of the wrong person. In an average-size school district, with a human resources department or at least one central-office human resources administrator, two months will be a comfortable time period to carry out the selection process. This period begins with the publication of an advertisement and extends through to the time when a job offer is made.

Receiving Applications

A central-office staff member, usually a secretary, should be assigned to receive all the applications for a given job vacancy. As the applications are received, they should be dated and placed in a designated file folder. This will provide integrity to the process, and also will provide a method of monitoring the incoming applications for a particular vacancy.

Many applicants will request their college or university placement offices to send their transcripts and letters of reference to the school district. These documents must also be dated and attached to the appropriate applications.

After the deadline for receiving applications has been reached, a master list should be compiled with the names, addresses, and telephone numbers of those who have applied. The master list also should include by title the other documents that have been received in support of each application, such as transcripts and letters of reference. The entire folder of applications, support documents, and the master list can then be assigned and given to a human resources administrator, who will perform the initial screening of the applications.

Keeping applicants informed during the selection process will help to cut down on the number of inquiries that are normally received in the human resources department. One very effective method is to send a postcard to each applicant stating that his or her application has been received and listing a date by which individuals will be selected for interviews.

It is also important to notify immediately those who sent in applications after the deadline that they will not be considered for the position. A common practice is to accept those applications postmarked on the day of the deadline.

Some school districts and many colleges and universities have initiated the practice of receiving applications *until the position is filled.* Under this procedure individuals who sent their applications to the school district by the deadline are given first consideration. If a suitable candidate is not identified, then those individuals who sent their applications to the district before a later designated date are considered, and so on until a suitable candidate is offered and accepts the position. This is an acceptable practice which can encourage qualified individuals to apply for positions even though they did not know about the positions in a timely manner.

At this point a procedure can be initiated that will help in evaluating the effectiveness of the school district's affirmative action program. The master list of applicants should be given to the administrator responsible for monitoring the affirmative action program. He or she can then send a letter to all those who have made application, asking them to identify if they belong to one or more minority groups listed on an enclosed form, and requesting them to mail the form back to the school district. Because the purpose of the selection process is to hire the best candidate, it is important to state in this letter that filling out the form will have no bearing on who is hired for the position. Consequently, the form should not be signed by the applicant and should not be sent to the human resources department but rather to the affirmative action officer.

Selecting the Candidates to Be Interviewed

Screening the applications is the fifth step in the selection process. It is initiated to identify those applicants who are to be interviewed for the position.

The application form should contain a statement requesting the applicant to have his placement papers, transcripts, and letters of reference sent to the human resources department. These documents along with the application form will provide the human resources administrator with sufficient information to evaluate each person against the selection criteria and against the minimum education and certification requirements.

The number of applicants to be interviewed will depend on the number of people who apply and on the nature of the position to be filled. If only five people apply for a vacancy and if each person meets the minimum qualifications, all five can be interviewed. This, of course, is not the norm except for those very few job classifications in which there is a shortage of qualified individuals, such as the field of special education. On the average, between three and five applicants are selected to be interviewed for classified and teaching positions. For school executive positions, the average number interviewed is between five and ten applicants.

Interviewing the Candidates

Interviewing candidates is a responsibility shared between the human resources department and other school district employees. The individuals who will participate in the interviewing process will be determined by the position to be filled. It is important to include not only those who will supervise the new employee but also others who have expert knowledge about the duties to be performed by the successful candidate. For example, candidates for a high school biology teaching position should be interviewed by the high school principal, the chairperson of the biology department, a biology teacher, a human resources administrator, and the assistant superintendent for secondary education. In like manner, candidates for an elementary principal position should be interviewed by the superintendent of schools, the assistant superintendent for elementary education, an elementary school principal, and a human resources administrator.

This same process is also useful in hiring classified employees. Applicants for a custodial position can be interviewed by the head custodian in a building, the director of maintenance and custodial services, a custodian, and a human resources administrator. However, the importance of involving employees with experience and expert knowledge in the hiring of employees for lower-level positions is seldom recognized in most school districts.

Members of the interviewing committee will need assistance in learning the strategies of credentials evaluation and interviewing. A method that will hold down expenses and make maximum use of the skills learned through a staff development program is to select a group of teachers, department chairpersons, classified employees, and building principals who will participate in the selection process for a year's time. Each year a different group of employees can be selected and trained to participate in evaluating credentials and interviewing applicants.

How these individuals are selected to participate in the hiring process will depend on the size of the school district. Seniority in the school district, of course, in one of the most defensible methods for selecting participants, but it is also imperative to have individuals who represent all job categories and teaching disciplines. Thus, a maintenance staff member, bus driver, cafeteria worker, elementary school art teacher, mathematics teacher, science teacher, social studies teacher, and so on, will be needed and should be available.

Released time from work is the most effective way to involve staff members. Substitute teachers and temporary classified employees will be needed to fill in for individuals who will be interviewing candidates and evaluating credentials during the working day. The average turnover of employees during a year's period of time is usually between 5 and 10 percent. This means that a given employee will participate in the selection process only on particular occasions, probably no more than ten working days a year.

Some school executives, such as assistant superintendents, will be more involved in the process because of their line authority to so many categories of employees. The assistant superintendent for elementary education, for example, will interview candidates for all elementary teaching and administrative vacancies. Of course, the immediate supervisor for the position to be filled is always a member of the committee.

Definition of an Interview

Essentially, an interview is a conversation between two individuals set up to generate information about the person being interviewed or other matters that are familiar to the respondent.[5] However, there are four characteristics of an interview that distinguish it from an ordinary conversation. First, an interview is a structured conversation with direction and

[5]See Henry S. Dyer, *The Interview as a Measuring Device in Education* (Princeton, New Jersey: ERIC Clearing House on Tests, Measurements, and Evaluations, 1976), 2.

a format; it has a beginning, middle, and conclusion. Second, the interview is conducted by an individual who is prepared to move it in a direction dictated by the occasion. Third, both parties to the interview understand its purpose, which can be accomplished only through cooperation. Finally, the nature of the interview is clearly defined and specified.[6]

Types of Interviews

There are two basic types of interviews, the standardized interview and the open-ended interview. The standardized interview is conducted by asking a set of questions established to help insure that the responses of the candidates can be readily compared. It is most effective in the initial interviewing of all candidates.

The open-ended interview encourages the candidate to talk freely and at length about topics introduced by the interviewer to suit the occasion. It is very helpful in the follow-up sessions with the finalists for the job.[7]

In both types of interviews, the objectives are basically the same. The interviewer is attempting to gather facts from the respondent; to learn about the respondent's opinions, beliefs, and attitudes; and to experience the respondent as a person.[8]

The Role of the Interviewer

The interviewer has extremely important responsibilities. Not only does he or she direct the interview by asking questions, but also he or she must record the respondent's answers and present the respondent with a favorable image of the school district. Through the interview process, the interviewer must evaluate and come to a conclusion about the suitability of each candidate. A selection criteria instrument will be used to quantify the observations of the interviewer, but ultimately the observations are subjective interpretations.

All interviews are more effective if they are conducted in a pleasant environment. This will help put the candidate at ease and will facilitate the kind of verbal exchange that gives the interviewer the most information about each candidate. The interviewer should find a room that allows the interview to be conducted without interruptions and should arrange the furniture in the room so as to have eye contact with the candidate during the session.

Legal Implications of Interviewing

Federal legislation and court decisions have had a significant impact on the types of questions that legally may be asked in an interview. For example, it was once common practice to ask a candidate if he or she had ever been arrested or spent time in jail. Because of a court case, *Gregory* v. *Litton Systems, Inc.,* school districts are now permitted to ask only about a candidate's record of criminal conviction.[9] Further, questions about sexual preference are prohibited under antidiscrimination laws.[10]

---

[6]See Auren Uris, *The Executive Interviewer's Handbook* (Houston, TX: Gulf, 1978), 2.

[7]Dyer, *The Interview,* 2.

[8]See Uris, *Interviewer's Handbook,* 4.

[9]See "New Rules for Interviewing Job Applicants: Schools Ignore Them at Their Peril," *American School Board Journal,* 164 (1977), 28.

[10]Junda Woo, "Job Interviews Pose Rising Risk to Employers," *Wall Street Journal,* 1994.

Below is a list of the more common inquiries that have legal implications:

1. *Name.* It is lawful to inquire if an applicant has worked under a different name or nickname in order to verify work or educational records; it is unlawful to ask questions in an attempt to discover the applicant's ancestry, lineage, or national origin.
2. *Age.* For a minor, requiring proof of age in the form of a work permit or certificate of age is lawful; it is unlawful to require adults to present a birth certificate or baptismal record to the district.
3. *Race.* To request information about distinguishing physical characteristics is legal; to ask the color of the applicant's skin, eyes, and so on, is illegal if this indicates directly or indirectly race or color.
4. *Religion.* All inquiries are illegal.
5. *Sex.* Inquiries regarding sex are permissible only when a bona fide occupational qualification exists.
6. *Ethnic background.* It is legal to ask which languages the applicant reads, writes, or speaks fluently; inquiries about the applicant's national origin are illegal.
7. *Marital and family status.* Questions to determine if a man or woman can meet specific work schedules are lawful; inquiries about being married, single, divorced, and so on, are unlawful.
8. *Credit rating.* All questions about charge accounts or credit rating are unlawful.
9. *Work experience.* It is lawful to ask why an applicant wants to work for a particular company or institution; asking what kind of supervisor the applicant prefers is unlawful.
10. *Life style.* Asking about future career plans is lawful; asking an applicant if he or she drinks alcoholic beverages or takes drugs is unlawful.[11]

The Art of Questioning

The success of the entire interviewing process rests on the interviewer's skill in asking questions. It is a skill that is acquired through experience. However, a well-planned interview with a pre-established set of questions can be extremely useful to even the most experienced interviewer, and it is a necessity in the standardized interview.

Group Interviewing

Some school districts prefer group interviewing, in which a number of staff members who are scheduled to interview a candidate jointly perform this task. Group interviewing can be very effective, and it certainly cuts down on the amount of time spent on this process. The dynamics described in this chapter are also applicable to the group interviewing method. However, to be effective, one staff member must serve as the group leader and take responsibility for directing the interview.

---

[11]Anna Nemesh, "The Interviewing Process," *Business Education Forum,* 33 (1979), 19–20.

Checking References and Credentials

Credentials

Checking references and credentials, the seventh step in the selection process, has profound implications. A candidate's "credentials" include such items as a college or university transcript, administrator or teacher certification document, and a physician's verification of health. Transcripts and health verifications should not be accepted if they are presented to the human resources department by the applicant; rather, they should be mailed directly to the school district by the respective college or university and physician. It is important to inform a candidate that his or her file is not complete until these documents are received.

It is common and accepted practice to request the health verification from a candidate only if he or she is chosen for the position. However, a contract or formal employment should not be initiated until the health verification has been received in the human resources department. It is best to state on the application form that a health examination will be required as a condition of employment if a job offer is made.

An administrator or teacher certification document is usually issued by a state department of education and given directly to the individual. Although the candidate presents the certification document to the human resources department, it is still necessary to contact the issuing state in order to ascertain if the certification remains valid. When a certification is revoked, the actual document is not always returned by the individual to the state department of education.

If a person is applying for a teaching or administrative position in a state where he or she is not currently certificated, he or she is responsible for obtaining written verification from the state department of education that he or she has the qualifications to receive certification. For such positions, a contract should never be offered to a candidate in the absence of a certification document or verification letter.

Letters of Reference

Letters of reference are the most vulnerable part of this process. A human resources administrator must write, telephone, or contact in person those individuals who have sent in reference letters supporting an applicant. The application form should state that a minimum of three reference letters are required; they should be mailed directly to the human resources department; and they must include a reference letter from the applicant's current or last immediate supervisor.

Evaluating reference letters is a very difficult task. There are three basic types of references. First is the glowing letter, affirming in detail that the candidate is an excellent employee with tremendous potential. Second is the letter indicating that the applicant's performance has been inferior and that he or she would be the wrong person for the job. Third is the reference letter telling very little about the applicant and couched in vague language. However, reference letters often have hidden messages, and understanding the significance of these references requires the talent of a human resources administrator who is skilled in detecting discrepancies between the candidate's credentials, his or her interview performance, and the reference letters. Consider, for example, the candidate who performs rather poorly in the interview and has unimpressive credentials, but who has an excellent letter of reference from his immediate supervisor. This could be an individual who is not performing satisfactorily in his or her present position and whose supervisor would be happy to see him or her find another job.

Obviously, it is the responsibility of a human resources administrator to verify the reference letters of the candidates who have been interviewed. It is impossible and unnecessary to check every reference for each candidate. However, it would be very difficult to choose the best candidate from those interviewed without reference verification.

Criminal-Background Investigation

The risk of hiring a person who has a criminal record has created much concern for human resources administrators. School districts have been sensitized to this possibility because of the news media notoriety given to educators who have been convicted of child molestation. This is probably the ultimate nightmare of every school administrator.

Criminal-background investigations are time-consuming and expensive, in addition to being controversial. The National Education Association has taken a position in opposition to fingerprinting as a condition of employment. The often heard criticism is that fingerprinting is an insult to teachers and their profession. However, many school districts require the fingerprinting of potential employees as part of a background investigation conducted through law enforcement agencies.

Conducting criminal-background investigations and the extent of such investigations is usually dependent upon a mix of school district policy, state statutes, and the discretion of the interviewing human resources administrator.[12] The extent of the investigation is usually limited in most school districts to checking with the local and state police in order to ascertain if the potential employee has been convicted of a crime. If he or she is a teacher, it is also possible to check with the Teacher Identification Clearinghouse, which is maintained by the National Association of State Directors of Teacher Education and Certification (NASDTEC). This nationwide clearinghouse has a database of all teachers who have been denied certification and whose certification has been revoked or suspended for moral reasons. The data are available only to states that have joined the Clearinghouse. Individual school districts can neither join the Clearinghouse nor directly obtain information from it. Only states may join.

Those states that are members agree to list, by name, any known alias, date of birth, and social security number of those persons from whom certification has been withdrawn or withheld over the past fifteen years. The individual state certification officials are responsible for finding out why the action was taken. This can easily be accomplished by contacting the certification official in the state where this occurred.[13]

A school district wishing to check the fingerprints of an applicant against the files of the FBI can do this only if the state in which the school district is located has passed legislation authorizing this type of investigation. This legislation must also have the approval of the U.S. Attorney General's Office. Even then, the request must be processed by a law

---

[12]Sally Banks Zakariya, "How You Can Identify People Who Shouldn't Work with Kids," *The Executive Educator,* 10, no. 8 (August 1988), 17.

[13]"Check Here for Help on Background Checks," *The Executive Educator,* 10, no. 8 (August 1988), 21.

enforcement agency such as the state police, which then acts as the conduit through which the information is channeled to the school district.[14]

As a final note to this issue, it is good human resources administration practice to conduct criminal-background investigations. In fact, if the wrong person is hired because a criminal-background investigation was not conducted, the liability of the school district for the wrongs committed by this person could be staggering.

Unlawful Employment of Aliens

In 1986 the U.S. Congress passed the Immigration Reform and Control Act, which makes it unlawful to knowingly hire an unauthorized alien, to continue the employment of one who becomes an unauthorized alien, or to hire any individual without first verifying his or her employability and identity.

Selecting the Best Candidate

The human resources administrator responsible for implementing the selection process for a particular vacancy must organize all relevant data in such a manner that a choice may be made by the superintendent of schools. The data should include the rank ordering by scores against the selection criteria of those candidates who were interviewed, verified credentials and reference letters, and the application forms.

The superintendent then selects the candidate who appears best qualified. If this selection process is utilized, this will usually be the candidate who scored the highest against the selection criteria.

Implementing the Job Offer and Acceptance

Professional Positions

The superintendent of schools may wish to interview the candidate he or she selects for a position or may wish to interview the top two, three, or five candidates before making a final choice. When the final decision has been made, the selected candidate must be offered the job in a formal manner. If this individual accepts the offer, a contract must be approved by the board of education and signed by the finalist. Usually, a board of education will require the superintendent to make a recommendation of employment and will want an explanation of why this particular person was selected.

Classified Positions

The superintendent also may want to interview candidates for classified positions, but in most cases will accept the recommendation of the human resources department to hire the candidate with the highest score in relation to the selection criteria. The superintendent may make the job offer himself or delegate this to a human resources administrator. Once the candidate accepts the offer, employment may commence at a mutually acceptable time.

---

[14]Zakariya, "How You Can Identify People Who Shouldn't Work with Kids," 17.

Notifying the Unsuccessful Candidates

The final step in the selection process is to notify all applicants that the position has been filled. This is initiated only after the offer of employment has been accepted by the selected candidate, since there may be a need to offer the position to another candidate if the first refuses the offer. Good public relations also dictates that all applicants be notified when the job has been filled; they have expended some time and money in applying for the position.

Principles of Constructing Application Forms

The first task in applying for a position is filling out an application form, an often tedious task enjoyed by very few people. There are two major reasons why most people dislike these forms. First, some forms require information that seems irrelevant, and second, some forms allot too little space for filling in the required information.

Application forms are constructed in one of two basic formats. The first style emphasizes detailed and extensive factual information about the individual; little or no attention is given to the person's attitudes, opinions, and values. Conversely, the second style emphasizes the applicant's attitudes, opinions, and values and asks for less factual information.

Appendix C provides examples of both styles. The application for a teaching position and the one for a classified job are samples of the factual information style. A third application form, one for a high school principal's position, is a sample of the second, less factual, style.

These samples also demonstrate the types of style commonly used for particular positions. The style is dictated by the kind of information the district needs to elicit from the applicants. For teaching and classified positions, factual information about the applicants' personal characteristics, their work experience, their professional preparation, and supportive data such as references help the personnel department determine who should be interviewed.

For school executive positions, the minimum requirements are highly specialized and thus can be requested on an application in a relatively limited space. Applicants to be interviewed are best selected by evaluating a set of responses that give some indication of each person's attitudes, opinions, and values.

Contents of the Application Form

The basic principle in constructing application forms is to only ask for information you need to know. Most information requested on applications falls under one of the following headings: personal data, education and professional preparation, experience, and references. Exhibit 4.2 lists information that is inappropriate on an application form either because it is irrelevant or because it is illegal under civil rights and labor legislation.

The physical layout of the application form should give an individual sufficient space to answer the questions and to provide the requested information. The kinds of information requested should also be grouped under headings to provide continuity. This helps the human resources department in analyzing the applications, and helps the individual providing the data.

**EXHIBIT 4.2   Information that Is Irrelevant or Inappropriate for
Application Forms**

Maiden name

Marital status

Name of spouse

Occupation of spouse

Number and age of children

Physical handicaps

Arrest record ("Convictions" is appropriate)

Height and weight (unless these are bona
   fide occupational qualifications)

If applicant owns a home or rents

If applicant has relatives employed by the
   school district (A policy against hiring

relatives of present employees is questionable.)

If the applicant has an automobile and a
   driver's license (unless this is a bona fide
   occupational qualification)

Where the applicant attended elementary and
   high school (irrelevant on professional
   applications)

Religion

National origin

Race

A Final Note

Employment Tests

Intelligence, aptitude, ability, and interest tests can provide valuable data when selecting classified employees. Legal rulings, however, have significantly limited their use because tests must be clearly job related to justify their administration.

Aptitude and ability tests are easiest to justify and can be used successfully for most classified jobs. In fact, it would be inappropriate to hire a person to train as a school bus mechanic who did not possess mechanical aptitude. In like manner, an applicant for a secretarial position must be administered a keyboard test to measure the person's skill in this necessary secretarial area. It should be remembered that testing has definite limitations and the results must be interpreted in relation to the interview, references, and other employment documents.

Assessment Centers

Assessment centers are places where supervisors have an opportunity to observe candidates for a particular job. Assessment centers are used primarily for management positions. The candidates are taken through a series of simulations dealing with administrative problems of the type that will probably be encountered on the job. The simulations usually take the form of case evaluations or decision-making exercises.

Although the expense in establishing an assessment center will make it prohibitive in most school districts, large metropolitan districts could find the use of an assessment center extremely beneficial in selecting teachers to be promoted into the principalship and other administrative positions.

Summary

The objective of the selection process is to hire individuals who will be successful on the job. Individual success is measured against organizational success, which is synonymous with "organizational change." Because of the evolutionary nature of human needs, school districts must continually involve stakeholders in crafting their vision. Further, the cost of the selection process is a major expenditure for most school districts, which includes advertising the position, printing and mailing applications, and human resources costs for interviewing candidates and checking references. The selection process should be implemented through a series of steps that will minimize the chances of hiring individuals who are inadequate performers. These steps are as follows:

1. *Writing the job description.* The job description is the end product of another process known as the "job analysis." This process gathers information about each job through observations, interviews, questionnaires, consulting, and the diary method. The job description outlines specific details of a position and establishes the minimum qualifications needed to perform the job successfully.

2. *Establishing the selection criteria.* Criteria instruments delineate those ideal characteristics that, if possessed by an individual to the fullest extent possible, will ensure the successful performance of the job. The selection criteria instrument can be used also to quantify the expert opinion of those who will be interviewing candidates.

3. *Writing the job vacancy announcement and advertising the position.* The advertisement is based on the job description and provides interested individuals with sufficient information to decide if they wish to apply for the position. The advertisement must clearly identify the job title, major responsibilities, name and location of the school district, application procedure, and the minimum job qualifications.

4. *Receiving applications.* A central-office staff member should be assigned to receive all applications for a given vacancy. As the applications are received, they should be dated and filed in a designated folder. This will provide integrity to the process and will establish a method of monitoring the progress toward filling the vacancy.

5. *Selecting the candidates to be interviewed.* The application form should contain a statement requesting the applicants to have their placement papers, transcripts, and letters of reference sent to the human resources department. The application should provide sufficient information to evaluate each person against the selection criteria and against the minimum requirements for the job. A selected group of applicants are then interviewed for the position.

6. *Interviewing the candidates.* Interviewing candidates is a responsibility shared by the human resources department and other school district employees. It is important to include not only those who will supervise the new employee but also others who have expert knowledge about the duties which will be performed by the successful candidate. An interview is essentially a conversation between two or more individuals conducted to generate information about the candidate. Interviewing is a learned skill; it also has profound legal implications.

7. *Checking references and credentials.* "Credentials" refers to such items as a college or university transcript, teaching certification, and a physician's verification of health. These credentials along with letters of reference, whenever possible, should be sent directly to the human resources department by the issuing source.

8. *Selecting the best candidate.* The human resources administrator who is responsible for implementing the selection process for a particular vacancy must organize all relevant data in such a manner that a choice may be made by the superintendent of schools.

9. *Implementing the job offer and acceptance.* For professional positions, a contract must be approved by the board of education and signed by the finalist before this step is completed. For classified positions, once the candidate affirms that he will accept the offer, employment may commence at a mutually acceptable time.

10. *Notifying the unsuccessful candidates.* This step is initiated only after the offer of employment has been accepted by the candidate because there may be a need to offer the position to another individual if the first selected candidate refuses the offer.

The risk of hiring a person who has a criminal record has created much concern for human resources administrators over the past five years. Conducting criminal-background investigations and the extent of such investigations are usually dependent upon a mix of school district policy, state statutes, and the discretion of the interviewing human resources administrator. The extent of an investigation is usually limited in most school districts to checking with the local and state police in order to ascertain if the potential employee has been convicted of a crime. When the potential employee is a teacher, it is also possible to check with the Teacher Identification Clearinghouse if the school district is in a state that is a member of this organization. A school district wishing to check the fingerprints of an applicant against the files of the FBI can only do this if the state in which the district is located has passed legislation authorizing this type of investigation.

The first task in applying for a position is filling out the application form. There are two basic formats used in constructing applications. The first format emphasizes detailed factual information; the second emphasizes the applicant's attitudes, opinions, and values.

The basic principle in constructing application forms is to only ask for information you need to know. The information requested on most applications falls under one of the following headings: personal data, education and professional preparation, experience, and references. The physical layout of the form should allot sufficient space for answering the questions and providing the requested information.

Aptitude and ability testing can be used successfully as part of the selection process for most classified jobs in school districts. In fact, they are necessary for some positions. Assessment centers are places where supervisors have an opportunity to observe candidates for a particular job. Candidates are taken through a series of simulations dealing with administrative problems, the kind of which will probably be encountered on the job. Large metropolitan school districts could find the use of an assessment center beneficial in selecting teachers to be promoted into the principalship and other administrative positions.

Discussion Questions and Statements

- Identify the steps in the selection process and explain how they are interrelated.
- Why is the *sequence of steps* so important in the selection process?
- Describe the most common methods of performing a job analysis.
- How is the job description related to the selection criteria?

Suggested Activities

- Your school district has been investigated by the Equal Employment Opportunity Commission because of complaints from a number of people who are members of minority groups protected by federal laws concerning the interview process. In your position as the Assistant Superintendent for Human Resources, you are meeting with the administrators, teachers, and support staff members who will be involved in the interview process to fill a number of vacancies. Write a brief explanation of the interview process setting forth its objectives and format. Also, identify the types of questions that are appropriate and those that are not.
- Obtain a copy of the policies from a school district concerning the selection process and write a comparison of them with the process set forth in this chapter.
- Review the job descriptions from a school district for a teaching and an administrative position. Write a comparison of them with those found in this chapter.
- Review the application forms used in a school district and evaluate them in relation to the principles for application construction found in this chapter.
- Develop, in writing, a list of interview questions that you think will help identify the most qualified applicant.
- Interview a human resources administrator in person or on the telephone in order to find out how his or her school district conducts background checks.

Selected Bibliography

Al-Rubaiy, Kathleen, "Five Steps to Better Hiring," *The Executive Educator,* 15, no. 8 (August 1993), 21–23.

Arvonio, L., I. Cull, and I. Marini, "Employment Interview Perceptions of Persons with Visible Disabilities," *International Journal of Rehabilitation Research,* 20, no. 4 (December 1997), 413–416.

Bolman, Lee G., and Terrence E. Deal, *Reframing Organizations: Artistry, Choice, and Leadership,* 2nd ed. San Francisco: Jossey-Bass, 1997.

Boody, Robert L., and Carmen Montecinos, "Hiring a New Teacher? Ask for a Portfolio," *Principal,* 77, no. 1 (September 1997), 34–35.

Davis, Beverly Irby, and Genevieve Brown, "Your Interview Image," *The Executive Educator,* 14, no. 6 (June 1992), 22–24.

Ficklen, Ellen, "Inflated Resume, Deflated Career," *The Executive Educator,* 10, no. 6 (June 1988), 22–23.

Finn, Jr., Chester E., "Pick Principals With Promise," *The Executive Educator,* 10, no. 6 (June 1988), 20–22.

Fullan, Michael, *Change Forces: The Sequel.* Philadelphia: Falmer Press, 1999.

Gokey, William, "Hiring? Consider Expanded Interviews," *The Executive Educator,* 11, no. 3 (March 1989), 27–28.

Hollwitz, John C., and Donna R. Pawlowski, "The Development of a Structured Ethical Integrity Interview for Pre-Employment Screening," *Journal of Business Communication,* 34, no. 2 (April 1997), 203–219.

Kowalski, Theodore J., Phillip McDaniel, Andrew W. Place, and Ulrich C. Reitzug, "Factors that Principals Consider Most Important in Selecting New Teachers," *Spectrum: Journal of School Research and Information,* 10, no. 3 (Summer 1992), 34–39.

Maurer, Steven D., "A Practitioner-based Analysis of Interviewer Job Expertise and Scale Format as Contextual Factors in Situational Interviews," *Personnel Psychology,* 55, no. 2 (Summer 2002), 267–306.

Mixon, Stewart, "Decentralizing Hiring via an Electronic Information System," *CUPA Journal,* 48, no. 1–2 (Spring–Summer 1997), 21–29.

Norris, Gary, and Robert W. Richburg, "Hiring the Best," *American School Board Journal,* 184, no. 11 (November 1997), 46, 48, 55.

Posthuma, Richard A., Frederick P. Morgeson, and Michael A. Campion, "Beyond Employment Interview Validity: A Comprehensive Narrative Review of Recent Research and Trends over Time," *Personnel Psychology,* 55, no. 1 (Spring 2002), 1–81.

Principal Selection Guide. Washington, DC: Superintendent of Documents, U.S. Government Printing Office, 1988.

Steller, Arthur W., "Chart a Course for Selecting New Principals," *Updating School Board Policies,* 15, no. 5 (May 1994), 1–3.

VanWagenen, Linda, and Michael K. Hibbard, "Building Teacher Portfolios," *Educational Leadership,* 55, no. 5 (February 1998), 26–29.

Zakariya, Sally Banks, "Wanted: Criminal Background Checks," *The Executive Educator,* 10, no. 8 (August 1988), 17–19.

Appendix A
Job Descriptions

JOB DESCRIPTION FOR A
MIDDLE SCHOOL PRINCIPAL

Job Summary

The middle school principal is responsible for the maintenance and continuation of a sound instructional program within his or her school building. This includes using leadership and communication skills in dealing with teachers, counselors, and other professional staff members, and with classified personnel, in order to develop a climate that promotes quality educational practices.

Organizational Relationships

The middle school principal has a line relationship with the assistant superintendent for secondary education. He or she is directly responsible to the assistant superintendent for secondary education. The middle school principal also has a line relationship with the building staff, which includes the assistant principal, teachers, counselors, librarian, and all other certificated and classified personnel within the building complex.

Organizational Tasks

The middle school principal is responsible for establishing administrative processes and procedures in the middle school for the following areas: staff development, curriculum planning, scheduling and grading, budget development, building and grounds maintenance, classroom instruction, consulting with individual pupils, parents, and staff members. He or she is also responsible for other duties assigned by the assistant superintendent for secondary education and is directly responsible for supervising and evaluating the assistant principal, teachers, counselors, librarian, educational specialists, secretaries, and custodians within the building complex.

Job Qualifications

The middle school principal should possess the following educational and professional qualifications:

- A master's degree in educational administration
- A state middle school principal's certificate
- Minimum of five years experience as a classroom teacher
- Minimum of two years experience as an assistant principal

JOB DESCRIPTION FOR A HIGH SCHOOL BIOLOGY TEACHER

Job Summary

The high school biology teacher is responsible for teaching five periods of Biology I per school day with one noninstructional period for planning, grading papers, and individual conferences with parents and students. Teaching biology includes following the general curricular program established by the science department and approved by the building principal. The biology teacher accepts responsibility for the academic success of students when he or she is given reasonable control over those factors that contribute to such outcomes. He or she is responsible directly to the building principal.

Instructional Tasks

The high school biology teacher is responsible for promoting an effective instructional program in the classroom. This can be accomplished as follows: by evaluating the strengths and weaknesses of the curricular program and instructional materials; helping develop, implement, and evaluate new ideas, methods, and techniques for teaching biology; assisting in departmental budget preparation to ensure the appropriateness of instructional supplies; recognizing that each student is an individual with different needs and abilities; utilizing a variety of instructional techniques; serving on textbook committees; maintaining effective discipline and high academic standards; accepting constructive criticism; and recognizing the need for continuous self-evaluation.

General Professional Duties

In addition to specific instructional tasks, the high school biology teacher is also expected to maintain professional standards, including keeping up-to-date on biology research findings; serving on committees to advise on such nonacademic affairs as school discipline, honors awards, assemblies, etc.; serving on science curriculum committees; advising guidance personnel on matters relating to the science program; showing concern for the totality of the science program; and participating in local and national science, teaching, and civic associations.

Job Qualifications

The high school biology teacher should possess the following minimum educational and professional qualifications:

- A bachelor's degree with a major or minor in biological science
- A State Secondary School Teaching Certificate in high school biology

Appendix B
Selection Criteria

SELECTION CRITERIA FOR A HIGH SCHOOL ENGLISH TEACHER

Applicant's Name _____ Date _____

A check on the scale is an indication of initial judgment. It is assumed that other sources of information may alter the interviewer's judgment as to the applicant's suitability. 1= Inferior; 5 = Superior

SELECTION CRITERIA

A. *Personal Characteristics and Qualifications*

	1	2	3	4	5
1. Personal appearance—neat, clean, etc.					
2. Poise/stability—knows self					
3. Ability to present ideas					
4. Voice projection					
5. Use of English language/speech					
6. Pleasant personality—not irritating					
7. Exemplifies leadership traits					
8. Demonstrates good judgment					
9. Interacts well in a group					
10. Shows signs of creativity					
11. Flexible—evidence of cooperation					

Subtotal _____

B. *Professional Characteristics and Qualifications*

	1	2	3	4	5
1. Knowledge of subject matter					
2. Educational philosophy compatible with district's philosophy					
3. Concern for student differences					
4. Enthusiasm for teaching					
5. Teaching methodology—shows variety					
6. Pupil control techniques					
7. Professional attitude					
8. Knowledgeable about English curriculum					
9. Willingness to sponsor extracurricular activities					
10. Undergraduate and/or graduate grades in English					

Continued

11. Classroom management techniques
12. Job-related hobbies and/or special talents
13. Overall undergraduate and/or graduate
    grade-point average
14. Knowledge of teaching/learning process

1	2	3	4	5

Subtotal _____

C. *Experience and Training*
   1. Relevance of previous teaching experience
   2. Scope of previous teaching experience
   3. Relevance of student teaching
   4. Appropriateness of participation in professional
      organizations
   5. Relevance of nonprofessional work experience

1	2	3	4	5

Subtotal _____

Total Score _____

The following is a general appraisal of this individual's promise for future success as an English teacher in our school district.

Should not be considered; poor applicant	Endorse with reservations; inferior applicant	Should be considered; average applicant	Good first impression; strong applicant	Exceptional potential; outstanding applicant

Additional comments:

Interview began _____ **Interview ended** _____

_____
Interviewer

SELECTION CRITERIA FOR A SIXTH-GRADE TEACHING POSITION

ACADEMIC CRITERIA

1. Has appropriate college or university course work and degree(s)
2. Has earned a grade point average in undergraduate and/or graduate courses that meets the acceptable standards of the district
3. Demonstrates through an appropriate interview a working knowledge of the English language in verbal and written context
4. Demonstrates an understanding and working knowledge of elementary mathematics skills that are compatible with the district's mathematics curriculum guide

5. Demonstrates the skills necessary to teach reading in a manner compatible with the district's reading curriculum guide
6. Has had some formal or informal education in music and has developed the skill to perform with a musical instrument
7. Has completed courses in drama or participated in extracurricular dramatic performances, plays, or musical presentations during high school or college

PERSONAL CRITERIA

8. Indicates a willingness to interact and communicate in a constructive fashion with district staff and community constituents
9. Exhibits healthy, considerate, mature attitudes that would promote positive intrastaff and community relationships
10. Dresses in a manner meeting the expectations of the school district and meets socially acceptable standards of hygiene and health care
11. Is capable of actively participating with minimum proficiency in a sixth-grade outdoor experience that includes repelling, canoeing, spelunking, and ropes course participation
12. Expresses a willingness to abide by and implement the district's policies as prescribed by the board of education

EXPERIENTIAL CRITERIA

13. Has relevant past teaching experience
14. Has relevant student teaching experience
15. Has a record of participating in extracurricular activities during high school and/or college (extracurricular being defined as any organized school-approved activity)
16. If applicant has had teaching experience, has demonstrated an interest in ongoing self-improvement by participating in professional workshops, seminars, college/university courses, or other professional programs

---

SELECTION CRITERIA GRID FOR A SIXTH-GRADE TEACHING POSITION

Name of Applicant _____ Date of Interview _____

	Academic Criteria							Personal Criteria					Experiential Criteria				Total Points
	1	2	3	4	5	6	7	8	9	10	11	12	13	14	15	16	
3																	

Continued

	Academic Criteria							Personal Criteria					Experiential Criteria				Total Points
	1	2	3	4	5	6	7	8	9	10	11	12	13	14	15	16	
2																	
1																	

3 is the highest possible score   **Grand Total** _____

Additional comments:

_____

Interviewer

SELECTION CRITERIA FOR AN ELEMENTARY SCHOOL TEACHER, SELF-CONTAINED CLASSROOM

Applicant _____ Date of Interview _____ Interviewer _____

	Possible Points	Designated Points
1. *Professional preparation.* Does the applicant hold the necessary and desired college preparation and state certification?	25	
2. *Experience.* Was the applicant's past teaching experience or student teaching experience successful?	10	

3. *Personal characteristics.* Are the applicant's mannerism and dress appropriate to the standards of the school district?	15	
4. *Educational philosophy.* Are the educational ideas and values of the applicant compatible with the school district's policies and curriculum?	50	

Comments:

Appendix C
Job Applications

TEACHER'S APPLICATION
Goodville School District

For Office Use Only

Interview Date _____

Interviewer _____   Date _____

Position _____   Soc. Sec. No. _____

I. Personal Information:

Name _____

         Last   First   Middle

Date of birth _____   Age _____

Present Address _____   Phone _____

             Street   City   State   Zip

Permanent Address _____   Phone _____

             Street   City   State   Zip

General conditions of health _____

Are you willing to take a physical exam? _____

II. Professional Information:

List in order of preference, the subjects or grades you are prepared to teach:

1. _____   2. _____   3. _____

List the Teaching Certificates held: State Retirement No. _____

_____

List Teaching Certificates held (other States):

_____

Continued

Membership in professional organizations: _____

What co-curricular activities are you prepared to sponsor (secondary level)? _____

_____

III. Teaching Experience:

List experience in chronological order (starting with first position held), and account for each school year since you began teaching.

No. Yrs Exp.	Inclusive Dates		Name of School	Location City or County, State	Grades, Sub. or Position	Annual Salary	Name of Prin.	Present Address of Principal
	From	To						

Kindergarten _____ Years   Middle School _____ Years

Elementary _____ Years   High School _____ Years   Other _____ Years

Total Teaching Exp. _____ Years

Name of superintendent under whom you last taught _____

IV. Educational and Professional Education:

Total Number of Hours to Date _____ Undergraduate _____ Graduate _____

Major _____ Number of Major Hrs. _____ Minor _____ Number of Minor

Hrs. _____

	Name of Instit. Attended	State	Dates Attended		Time in Yrs. and Fractions of Yrs.	Graduation		Subjects	
			From	To		Date	Degree	Major	Minor
A. **Undergraduate** **Work**									
B. **Graduate** **Work**									
C. **Additional** **Education**									

D. For both secondary and elementary majors

Hours of Student Teaching	
Place of Student Teaching	
Name of Coop. Teacher	
Subject or Grade Level of Student Teaching	

V. Professional References:

Location of confidential placement file _____

It is the responsibility of the applicant to have his/her placement file and college/university transcripts sent to the school district.

Please list three people who have firsthand knowledge of your work performance. Have these individuals send letters of reference to the human resources department if references are not included in your placement file. One of the three reference letters must be from your current or last immediate supervisor.

Name	Official Position	Present Address

Signature: _____

Goodville School District

For Office Use Only

Date Received _____

Interview Date _____

Starting Date _____

Position _____

School _____

Salary _____

Termination Date _____

Continued

CLASSIFIED APPLICATION FOR EMPLOYMENT

Position _____

PLEASE PRINT OR TYPE

Today's Date _____

PERSONAL INFORMATION

Name _____
        Last   First   Middle

Present address _____
                Street   City   State   Zip code

Phone _____   Social Security No. _____

Date of birth _____   Place _____

General condition of health _____

Are you willing to take a physical exam? _____

EDUCATION INFORMATION

Circle Highest Grade
Completed: 1 2 3 4 5 6 7 8 9 10 11 12 13 14 15 16

Name of school and location:	Dates of Attendance	Day or Night	Full- or Part-time	Type of Course(s)
Elem:	from ____ to ____	_____	_____	_____
Jr. High	from ____ to ____	_____	_____	_____
Sr. High	from ____ to ____	_____	_____	_____
College	from ____ to ____	_____	_____	_____

MILITARY SERVICE

Branch _____ From _____ To _____ Present Status _____

Highest rank _____ Duties _____

List any special training received in service _____

Type of discharge _____

EMPLOYMENT RECORD

List the most recent employment first and work back consecutively

From	To	Firm Name & Supervisor	Firm Address	Salary Beg.	Last	Position, Duties, and Reason for Termination

List any experience, skills, or qualifications that you feel would especially fit you for work in our district: _____

Are you a member of the Non-Teacher Retirement System? _____
If Yes, give Retirement No. _____

GENERAL INFORMATION

When can you start work? _____ What wage or salary do you expect? _____

List civic organizations to which you belong and office(s) held within last three years:
_____

Have you ever been convicted of any violation of law other than a traffic violation? _____
If yes, give particulars of each conviction and state what disposition was made of each:
_____

Have three people with firsthand knowledge of your work performance send letters of reference to the human resources department. One of the three reference letters must be from your current or last immediate supervisor.

_____
Signature

APPLICATION FOR HIGH SCHOOL PRINCIPAL

PERSONAL INFORMATION

Date _____

_____
Last Name   First   Middle
Business Address _____ Telephone_____
City _____ State _____ Zip Code _____
Home Address _____ Telephone _____
City _____ State _____ Zip Code _____
PRESENT POSITION _____
School's student enrollment _____ School's annual budget _____
Salary during current school year _____

PROFESSIONAL PREPARATION: Highest degree earned _____

Institution and Location	Major/Minor	Degree	Date Received
_____	_____	_____	_____
_____	_____	_____	_____

My confidential file can be acquired from:
            Name of Institution: _____
            Address: _____
            _____

Continued

SUMMARY OF EXPERIENCE: List all experience in reverse chronological order. Please include both school and nonschool experience.

Institution and Location	Position	From/To	Years	Size/Unit	Highest Salary
_____	____	____	___	____	____
_____	____	____	___	____	____
_____	____	____	___	____	____
_____	____	____	___	____	____

Type of administrator certificate held _____

In which state(s) _____

QUESTIONS

The following questions are designed to help the interviewers know you as a person and as a professional. Your concise and candid responses are very important.

1. Why do you or did you want to become a high school principal?

2. What do you or would you consider to be your major strengths as an administrator?

3. In your previous experience, in what ways have you most influenced a school?

4. What basic problem-solving approaches do you or would you use to deal with school issues?

5. What methods or approaches do you or would you use to bring about change in a school?

6. How do you or would you delegate responsibilities to others?

7. As a principal, what communication approaches are or would be most effective for you?

8. How do you or will you, as a principal, work most effectively with central-office administrators?

9. What about being a high school principal has been or will be most rewarding to you?

_____
Signature

Placement and Induction

After a person has been hired, the next two processes involve placing that individual in an assignment and orientating him or her to the school community. Both of these processes are covered in this chapter because they are interrelated; both also are continual processes because some staff members will be reassigned each year and thus will require a certain amount of induction. Placement and induction, therefore, should not be viewed as a one-time task but rather as an ongoing concern of the human resources department.

Placement

In all but the very smallest districts, a new employee should not be told that he or she has been hired only for a particular job in a specific school building. The selection process explicated in the previous chapter will result in the employment of an individual for a certain position. However, the employee must understand from the outset that the assignment can be changed, even immediately, if the administration deems such to be in the best interest of the school district.

Placement Policy

The following sample placement policy specifies how placement could be handled by a school district:

> The placement of employees within the school system is the responsibility of the superintendent of schools. The superintendent may delegate the implementation of the placement process to other appropriate administrators, but he or she ultimately retains the responsibility for placement. In determining assignments, the wishes of the employee are taken into consideration if these do not conflict with the requirements of the district's programming, staff balancing, and the welfare of students. Other factors that will be taken into consideration in making

assignments are educational preparation and training, certification, experience, working relationships, and seniority with the school system.

A staffing survey form will be secured from each employee annually in February to assist in making assignment plans for the forthcoming school year.

Professional staffing assignments will be announced by April 1. Administrators affected by an assignment change will be notified of the change by the superintendent of schools. Teachers affected by a change in grade or subject assignment will be notified of the change by their respective building principals. Teachers affected by a building transfer will be notified of the transfer by an administrator from the human resources department.

Classified staffing assignments will be announced by May 1 and will become effective on July 1. Supervisors and managers affected by an assignment change will be notified of the change by the superintendent of schools or his designated representative. Other employees affected by a change in assignment will be notified by their immediate supervisors.

This sample board of education placement policy clearly specifies the role of the superintendent in assigning all staff members to particular positions within the school system. The planning required in making assignments is very complicated, demanding the full-time attention of at least one human resources administrator in most metropolitan school districts. The human resources planning inventories described in Chapter 2 could provide the human resources department with valuable information for making assignments. Of course, it is to the advantage of the school district to make assignments that are in harmony with the wishes of the employees. A significant cause of low morale, particularly among teachers, is the assigning of individuals to schools, grade levels, and subject areas that they find undesirable. Using the staffing survey is one method of minimizing discontent over reassignments. The survey instrument can be very simple in construction and very easy to fill out. Exhibit 5.1 is an example of an instrument that would provide the human resources department with information concerning the placement preferences of staff members.

The human resources department must also consider a number of circumstances in trying to fulfill the wishes of employees in making reassignments. Some of these circumstances include maternity leave, resignations, retirements, deaths, and terminations. In addition, the following variables must be taken into consideration: staff balancing, affirmative action requirements, the certification of professional employees, experience in an assignment, and working relationships.

For example, a teacher who is having difficulty accepting a certain principal's philosophy about how to handle children with behavioral problems might request reassignment to another school. The human resources department then would determine if another position is or will become available that requires the certification qualifications of the teacher. Further, an analysis must be made to determine if such a reassignment would upset the balance in either school between experienced and inexperienced teachers, male and female teachers, and minority representation.

The welfare of students and implementation of the school district's instructional program are other important considerations in making reassignments. A biology teacher who is certificated also as a physical education teacher might be denied reassignment to the

---

EXHIBIT 5.1   Staffing Survey

Name _____

Present Job Position Assignment _____
_____

Present Building Assignment _____
_____

I wish to be considered for reassignment as follows:

Requested Job Position Assignment _____
_____

Requested Building Assignment _____
_____

    I understand that reassignment requests will be reviewed but are not guaranteed and that all decisions will be based on seniority and availability, and will be made in accordance with the best interests of the school district.

                                              _____

                                              Signature

---

physical education department because of the scarcity in applicants for biology positions or because he has taught only biology throughout his fifteen-year career as a teacher.

    When there are a number of requests for reassignment, seniority is a defensible criterion in making decisions only after the other variables have been considered. Those employees with the most seniority in the school district should be given the first choices in assignments; involuntary reassignments should be given to those employees with the least seniority. Involuntary reassignments are sometimes necessary because of unexpected vacancies.

Placement Grievance Procedure

    If an employee has a concern regarding a permanent or temporary change in assignment, the following procedure must be observed: (1) The employee should initiate an interview with the administrator who processed the assignment change. (2) If agreement is not reached at this point, the employee may initiate an interview with the superintendent of schools and formally request a review of the reassignment; should the employee continue to be dissatisfied, he may resign his position with the school district.

    The due process presented in this grievance procedure identifies the superintendent of schools as the ultimate authority in reviewing assignments within the school district. A grievance procedure is necessary to effectively operate the district and highlights the fact that an individual is employed in the district and not in a particular school or position. Exhibit 5.2 is an example of a form that can be used when reviewing an assignment that an employee finds undesirable.

EXHIBIT 5.2   Request for Assignment Review

Name _____

Present Job Assignment _____
_____

Present Building Assignment _____
_____

Job Reassignment _____
_____

Building Reassignment _____
_____

Please state in detail why you would like to have your assignment reviewed:
_____
_____
_____
_____
_____
_____
_____
_____
_____
_____
_____

_____
Signature

Induction

Induction is the process designed to acquaint newly employed individuals with the community, the school district, and with their colleagues. Reassigned employees need to be acquainted with their new school, program, and colleagues. Much of what this section covers is equally applicable to both newly employed and reassigned individuals. It is an administrative responsibility that is often neglected or loosely organized in many school districts. The industrial and business communities place a high priority on induction; they have recognized for many years the cause-and-effect relationship of this process to employee retention and job performance.

An effective induction program must have well-defined objectives that reflect the needs of new employees and the specific philosophy of the school system. Although the objectives of an induction program will vary among individual school districts, some universal objectives should be common to all programs:

1. To make the employee feel welcome and secure
2. To help the employee become a member of the "team"
3. To inspire the employee towards excellence in performance
4. To help the employee adjust to the work environment

5. To provide information about the community, school systems, school building, faculty, and students

6. To acquaint the individual with other employees with whom he or she will be associated

7. To facilitate the opening of school each year

These objectives support the ultimate purpose of an induction program, to promote quality education for children. The employee who is able to adjust in a reasonable period of time to a new position helps to accomplish this purpose.

Once the overall purpose and specific objectives are defined, the subsequent steps include deciding on the most effective method of implementation and the content of the program. Some school districts consider a one- or two-day orientation at the beginning of each school year to be sufficient. Other districts provide an ongoing induction program to orient new employees and reassigned employees. Certainly, an ongoing program is better able to meet the concerns of reassigned individuals in large school districts who will need information about their new school building, the faculty, the students, and the community it serves. The fallacy, as previously mentioned, is assuming that induction is a one-time task, only for new employees.

Induction programs fall into one of two major categories: informational and personal adjustment programs. Informational programs, in turn, are concerned with either initial material or updating information. Initial data consist primarily of information about the school system, the community it serves, and the particular school in which the employee will work. New employees, of course, are targeted for this type of program. Updating informational programs are geared to the employee who is reassigned; they concentrate on the particular school and community to which he or she has been reassigned.

Personal adjustment programs aim at helping the newly hired or reassigned employee interact with the principal, faculty, students, and parents of a particular school. With a classified employee, the emphasis should be on helping the individual interact with his or her supervisor and coworkers as well as those administrators, faculty members, students, and parents with whom he or she will come into contact.

The following four sections deal with the content and methods of four induction programs. The first is most effective in orienting individuals to the school system; the second helps orient individuals to the community served by the school system or particular school. The third is designed to orient employees to the school to which they are assigned; the fourth is geared to orienting the employees to the people with whom they must establish a relationship.

The School District

The human resources department is responsible for implementing this part of the induction program. The main thrust of this program is to convey an understanding of the school system's policies and services and to identify system wide personnel such as assistant superintendents, program directors, and coordinators.

All employees should receive a copy of the school board policies and a copy of the employee manuals that pertain to their specific job. They should be allowed time during the orientation sessions to become familiar with these policies and manuals. To be truly effective, the program should also give the employees the opportunity to ask clarifying questions about policies and procedures.

Of course the policies of the school district should set forth the vision and mission of the district. It is always a good idea to begin an orientation session with the vision and mission statements. Because schools are service-rendering institutions, the vision and mission are people driven. Thus, most statements are focused on providing the children with an opportunity to develop all dimensions of their potentiality to the fullest extent possible. Such development includes the intellectual, emotional, physical, ethical, and cultural aspects of education. Teachers, staff members, and administrators are usually interested in this type of presentation; it is why they chose education as their career. Such an approach adds significance to the more mundane aspects of employment orientation.

The employee benefits provided by the school district must be carefully explained to new employees. Major medical and hospitalization insurance applications, retirement forms, government payroll withholding forms, and other enrollment documents are generally explained to new employees at the earliest possible time during the orientation process. Most insurance programs require a new employee to enroll a spouse and dependents within thirty days after commencing employment. If a spouse or dependent is enrolled after that time, he or she is usually required to take a physical examination, and the insurance company may deny coverage because of a medical condition. For example, a newly employed female teacher who does not enroll her husband in a medical insurance program within the thirty-day grace period may be denied coverage for him because he has a heart condition. The most effective vehicle for conveying an understanding of policies, procedures, and services is the small-group seminar. In this format, five to ten employees are assigned to a human resources administrator who presents the material and instructs them about how to fill out all necessary forms. This is usually done within the first few days of employment. A meeting, breakfast, or luncheon could be held each year, during which the superintendent of schools, board members, and other central-office administrators and staff members are introduced to new employees. Such a special event is very effective in conveying to new employees their importance to the district.

The Community

Orientation to the community is also the responsibility of the human resources department. Employees should be presented with information about the economic, social, racial, cultural, ethnic, and religious makeup of the community. Specific topics to be covered should include occupations, customs, clubs and organizations, church denominations, museums, libraries, colleges or universities, and social services.

Orientation to the community usually begins during the selection process, particularly during the interview. Candidates are told about the community and questioned about how they would respond to its various publics if they were employed with the district.

A very effective way to begin the orientation process after selection is with a tour of the community conducted by the human resources department or, perhaps, the Chamber of Commerce. Other methods include introducing new employees at club or organization meetings and inviting representatives from community resource services, such as libraries or museums, to address the new employees about their programs.

Orientation to the community does not end with the initial program; rather, a continuous updating should be provided by the human resources department. For example, as community service resources are improved or changed, this information should be brought to the attention of school staff members.

The School Building and Program

The building principal has the responsibility for orienting new teachers to a particular school. First and most important is introducing new teachers to all other employees, both professional and classified, who work in the building. Classified employees should be introduced by their immediate supervisors to both professional and other classified employees.

New employees must know, in detail, the layout of the building in which they will work. This is best accomplished by giving new employees a tour of the facility and, if it is a large school, presenting each person with a map.

Explaining administrative procedures is also the responsibility of the building principal. It is essential for new teachers to know how to complete attendance forms, where to obtain supplies and materials, how to requisition audiovisual equipment, and how the school schedule operates. An initial conference with the building principal, an assistant principal, or a department chairperson is one method of explaining these procedures to new staff members.

Orienting the new teacher to the instructional program is the responsibility of the building principal. Like administrative procedures, this may be delegated to an assistant principal or a department chairperson. At times explaining the instructional program might be a central-office task, especially when the school district has subject matter coordinators and a uniform curriculum in all the schools.

In some school districts a new teacher is assigned to an experienced teacher during the first year of employment. The new teacher will then have a definite person to call on when questions arise about the curriculum or building procedures. This has proven to be a successful technique because the experienced teacher does not pose a threat to the new teacher, whereas an administrator might.

Personal Adjustment

In line with the current research on the effectiveness of participatory decision making, establishing good working relationships among colleagues is viewed as most important if an organization is to achieve its objectives. In a service-rendering organization, such as a school district, that is even more crucial because good human relations is the basis for the effective delivery of services. Forming relationships with other staff members helps an employee to achieve satisfaction in his or her work. Nothing is less satisfying than being alienated from colleagues in an organization.

The responsibility for helping a new employee form meaningful relationships with other staff members rests with the individual's immediate supervisor or, if the new employee is a teacher, with the building principal.

A highly effective orientation method for new employees is to organize activities that give them the opportunity to socialize with other staff members. Many schools make a practice of serving refreshments and allotting a certain amount of time for personal interaction either before or after meetings. Holiday parties or dinners are also an effective means of enabling employees to meet each other on a social level, which can provide staff members with new insights about each other.

Service on faculty, school, and district committees is another way for employees to become acquainted with each other while providing the district with valuable assistance in carrying out projects. Textbook selection committees, energy conservation committees, and principals' advisory committees are common in many school districts and have proven to be very successful.

Finally, it is important for professional staff members to become affiliated with local, state, and national teacher and administrator organizations. These organizations not only provide an avenue for exchanging ideas but also are a source of current professional information. Their social activities certainly help the individual form relationships with professionals in other school districts.

A Final Note

Many new employees come from other states or, at least, have lived beyond the immediate vicinity of the school district. Although not a part of the formal induction program, helping the new employee relocate is a valuable service that the human resources department can provide. Relocation can be facilitated by making initial contacts with real estate agents for new employees and by chauffeuring them around the area, pointing out aspects of neighborhoods reasonably close to their school and the district.

Evaluating the effectiveness of induction programs is an extremely important part of the induction process. Evaluation of the programs for professional employees is best accomplished by establishing an induction committee chaired by a human resources administrator and composed of teachers, principals, and supervisors. This committee should gather input from new teachers that can be used to make changes in the programs. This same procedure can be initiated to evaluate programs for classified employees, that is, by establishing a committee composed of classified staff members and supervisors to react to the suggestions and insights of new employees after their first year with the district.

The Induction of First-Year Teachers

Although other professions provide transitional assistance for new members (e.g., residents in medicine, interns in architecture, and associates in law), historically the education profession has ignored the support needs of its new recruits.[1]

Statistical information on the plight of new teachers indicates that nearly one-fourth of them will leave the profession after two years of service, and a staggering one-third will leave after three years. These data clearly indicate that the needs of new teachers are not being met by school districts. Possible remedies for this situation fall within the following categories:

- A school level systemic approach to mentoring
- Assistance in knowing and understanding the teacher's role and function

[1]Linda Molner Kelley, "Why Induction Matters," *Journal of Teacher Education*, 55, no. 5 (November/December 2004), 438.

- Assistance in knowing and understanding school and school district policies and procedures
- Collegial encouragement and support[2]

School district and school building administrative policies can have a significant effect on the induction of beginning teachers. The scope and sequence of such policies are most effective if they call for a multiple year approach to the mentoring of new teachers. From this perspective, the administrators of school districts and individual schools assume the role of teacher educators.[3]

The National Association of Secondary Principals (NASSP) initiated a project to study the induction of first-year teachers. The committee also developed a four-phase time period during which induction should occur. Phase I would begin during the summer months and would concentrate on orienting the new teachers to the school, school district, and community. Phase II, scheduled for the week before school opens, would emphasize procedures and identify support personnel. Phase III, during the first semester, would include daily meetings between a beginning teacher and a cooperating master teacher. They would review practical aspects of teaching, such as lesson planning, testing, grading, and disciplinary techniques. During the second semester, the final phase would emphasize a more theoretical approach to teaching. The new teacher would be encouraged to begin evaluating his or her performance and verbalizing his or her philosophy of education.

Mentoring as an Induction Strategy for Beginning Teachers

The education reform movement, which formally began with the publication of *A Nation at Risk,* has resulted in the enacting in over sixteen states of legislation calling for the inclusion of *mentoring* as an induction strategy for newly hired teachers. These states have mentoring programs that differ one from the other to some degree. However, the basic concept is the same in all of the programs, which is the pairing of an experienced teacher with a beginning teacher in order to provide the beginning teacher with support and encouragement.

The experienced teacher can act as a role model for the beginning teacher and through coaching help the teacher develop his or her competencies, self-esteem, and sense of professionalism. In some school districts, the beginning teacher attends traditional orientation and induction programs. A mentor is assigned to each teacher, who then provides support throughout the entire year. In other school districts, beginning teachers are assigned to a group comprising other beginning teachers, the interaction of which is facilitated by a mentor.

It is important to clarify the role of the mentor to building principals and to the beginning teachers. This is especially true in relation to the issue of teacher evaluation. The mentor should not be an evaluator, but rather someone who assists. Teacher evaluation should be the responsibility only of administrators.

[2]Synthia Simon Millinger, "Helping New Teachers Cope," *Educational Leadership,* 61, no. 8 (May 2004), 66–69.

[3]Pamela Grossman and Clarissa Thompson, "District Policy and Beginning Teachers: A Lens on Teacher Learning," *Educational Evaluation and Policy Analysis,* 26, no. 4 (Winter 2004), 298.

The criteria for selecting mentors and the process for matching such mentors with beginning teachers are also important considerations. Research indicates that mentors are successful when they are older than the beginning teachers and when they are of the same gender.[4]

Other research sets forth the issues that confront beginning teachers and therefore reveals the kinds of competencies that mentors must possess. This is extremely helpful information in the mentor selection process. Beginning teachers need assistance from mentors in handling discipline problems, classroom management, lesson planning, understanding the written and unwritten rules of the school, developing socialization skills, and developing techniques for handling parent conferences.[5]

Newly selected mentors usually require some type of staff development in order to acquire or enhance certain skills. For example, programs to enhance supervision and coaching techniques or programs that update the mentors on instructional strategies can be most helpful.

Mentoring as an Induction Strategy for Beginning Administrators

Whereas mentoring programs for beginning teachers are becoming commonplace, mentoring programs for beginning administrators are rare. Ohio is an exception. This state plan mandates the following:

Participation of currently employed, experienced administrators in the planning of the entry-year program.

Provision of initial orientation for the new staff member, including an introduction to: the pupils and community; school policies, procedures and routines; courses of study; competency-based education programs; the layout and facilities of the assigned building(s); the nature of the entry-year program; and "additional information an entry-year person may need to be adequately prepared for a specific assignment."

Provision of ongoing assistance for the entry-year person differentiated to provide for professional needs related to his or her specific assignment.

Ongoing assistance in acquiring knowledge of the district curriculum, responsibilities for implementing that curriculum, and the instructional resources available for such implementation.

Assistance with management tasks identified as especially difficult.

Provision of a mentor for the entry-year administrator. The mentor must hold an administrative personnel certificate similar to that of the entry-year person.[6]

The Dayton City School District in Ohio expanded the state's requirements for mentors. The volunteer mentors must have between two to ten years of effective experience in

---

[4]C. Galvey-Hjornevik, "Mentoring Among Teachers: A Review of the Literature," *Journal of Teacher Education,* 37, (1986), 6–11.

[5]T. Brzoska, *Mentor Teacher Handbook* (Vancouver, WA: Evergreen School District, 1987), 288.

[6]William R. Drury, "Entry-Year Administrator Induction: A State and Local School District Model," *Spectrum: Journal of School Research and Information,* 6, no. 1 (Winter 1988), 8.

their current positions or roles with Dayton Public Schools; be interested in working with relatively inexperienced administrators to assist them with their personal and professional improvement; be willing to share vulnerabilities, as well as experiences and strengths; serve as "friendly critics"; and make time in hectic schedules to serve as a helper.[7]

An evaluation of the program in Dayton after the initial year of the mandate brought forth the following conclusion:

> In summary, the experience with this program for school administrators has been very positive from the perspective of both the school district and the participating administrators. The program has done much to alleviate the natural feelings of anxiety that accompany the entry year for district school administrative personnel. For school districts that recognize the value of new administrative staff getting started on the right foot, such a program deserves consideration.[8]

Administrators who were mentors have indicated receiving many benefits as a result of their participation. Among these benefits are exposure to ideas from other school districts, learning about research, satisfaction from being a teacher again, and affirmation of their professional competence.[9]

An Induction Model

The approach exemplified in Appendix A, Orientation Checklist for Newly Assigned Teachers, is based on induction models used in business and industry. This model attempts to deal with the major problems associated with induction through a series of one-on-one interviews, explanations, observations, and evaluative discussions. This model constitutes an expansion of the mentoring approach.

The new teacher encounters key staff members who can offer assistance in becoming acclimated to the total school community. This approach applies the "team management" concept to the induction process. Eight to ten people are selected to serve on the induction team based on their position, experience, and professional expertise. The most appropriate team in a high school would include the principal, an assistant principal, the new teacher's department chairperson, a guidance counselor, an audiovisual coordinator, the activities director, the athletic director, a student council advisor, a librarian, and a senior faculty member.

Each of these individuals will meet with the new teacher on at least two scheduled occasions during the academic year. The principal, assistant principal, and department chairperson individually will observe a class taught by the new teacher during the first semester. A conference is held one week prior to each observation in order to discuss the content of the lesson and the teaching techniques that will be used by the teacher. A post-observation conference between the teacher and observer is then held to review the teacher's performance.

[7]Drury, "Entry-Year Administrator Induction," 9.

[8]Drury, "Entry-Year Administrator Induction," 10.

[9]Marsha A. Playko and John C. Daresh, "Mentoring Programs for Aspiring Administrators: An Analysis of Benefits to Mentors," *Spectrum: Journal of School Research and Information,* 11, no. 3 (Summer 1993), 14–15.

The observer prepares a written critique of the class, including a mutually agreed on action plan for improving the teacher's performance. This report may describe points on which the teacher and observer disagree. The teacher receives a copy of the critique, which is filed with the building principal.

The guidance counselor, audiovisual coordinator, activities director, athletic director, student council advisor, librarian, and senior faculty member are selected to provide support to the new teacher. These professionals are valuable resource persons who are associated with different aspects of the school. Through discussions with these staff members, the new teacher is given the opportunity to seek advice and help in dealing with student-related problems and instructional concerns.

Summary

After a person has been hired, the next two processes involve placing that individual in an assignment and orienting him to the school community.

The placement of employees within the school system is the responsibility of the superintendent of schools. The planning required in making assignments is a very complicated task, demanding the full-time attention of at least one human resources administrator in most metropolitan-area school districts. It is to the advantage of the school district to make assignments that are in harmony with the wishes of the employees. A staffing survey is one method of systematically gathering information on the placement preferences of employees.

Other variables that the human resources department must take into consideration in making assignments include staff balancing, certification requirements, experience, and working relationships. However, the welfare of students and implementation of the school district's instructional program are the most important considerations. When there are a number of requests for reassignment, seniority is a defensible criteria after these other variables are considered. A due process should be established to give employees the opportunity to have an assignment reviewed by the appropriate administrator.

Induction is the process designed to acquaint newly employed individuals with the school system and with other staff members. It is also the process for acquainting reassigned employees with their new school, program, and colleagues. An effective induction program must have well-defined objectives that will help the employee to feel welcome and secure, to become a member of the "team," to be inspired towards excellence in performance, to adjust to the work environment, and to become familiar with the school community.

Induction programs fall into one of two major categories: informational and personal adjustment programs. Informational programs are concerned with providing either initial material or updated information. Initial data consist primarily of information about the school system, the community it serves, and the school where the new employee will work. Updated informational programs are geared to the employee who is reassigned; they concentrate on a particular school and community. Personal adjustment programs are designed to help the newly hired or reassigned employee interact with the other people for whom and with whom he or she will work.

To orient new employees effectively to the school district, policies and services must be thoroughly explained and systemwide personnel identified. Orientation to the community must convey to employees a knowledge of the economic, social, cultural, ethnic, racial, and religious makeup of the community. The occupations, customs, clubs and organizations, church denominations, museums, libraries, colleges and universities, and social services are also topics that should be covered in this program.

Orienting a new employee to a particular school begins with an introduction to the other staff members. A tour of the facility and an explanation of administrative procedures along with an orientation to the instructional program are also important aspects of this induction.

Personal adjustment orientation centers on encouraging new employees to establish working relationships with their colleagues. Organized activities such as faculty meetings, holiday parties or dinners, faculty and district committees, and membership in professional organizations provide new employees with the opportunity to establish desired relationships with other professionals.

Evaluating the effectiveness of the induction process is extremely important and will provide the necessary data for improving the programs.

An area of special concern centers on the induction of first-year teachers. Many potentially excellent teachers are lost to the education profession because they were not properly inducted. A number of suggestions and models have been developed. They all recognize the importance of giving first-year teachers time to consult with colleagues and providing them with feedback concerning their performance. Many school districts have developed mentoring programs not only for beginning teachers but also for entry-year administrators.

Discussion Questions and Statements

- When placing employees in certain job positions, what variable should be taken into consideration?
- What is the rationale for having an assignment grievance procedure?
- What are the most common objectives for developing an induction program?
- Identify the reasons why the induction of first-year teachers is so important.
- Describe mentoring and explain why it is such an effective method of induction.
- What are the elements of mentoring programs for both first-year teachers and administrators? Who (by job position) does what and at what time in the programs?

Suggested Activities

- As the Director of Staff Development, you are preparing an induction program for newly hired employees. Identify, in writing, the elements of the program that you have created and further identify how the program will differ for teachers and support personnel.
- Obtain a copy of a school district's placement policies and write a comparison of them with the policy and grievance procedures in this chapter.
- Obtain a copy of a school district's induction policies and write a comparison of them with the principles of induction set forth in this chapter.
- Interview a human resources administrator in person or on the telephone in order to elicit his or her opinion about the difficulties and positive aspects of the induction process.

Selected Bibliography

Barry, Carol Kuhl, and Jan Kaneko, "Mentoring Matters!" *Leadership,* 31, no. 3 (January/February 2002), 26–29.

Bey, T. M., C. F. Holmer, eds., *Mentoring: Developing Successful Teachers.* Reston, VA: Association of Teacher Educators, 1990.

Brock, B. L., "Profile of the Beginning Teacher," *Momentum* (1990), 54–57.

Brock, Barbara L., and Marilyn L. Grady, "Beginning Teacher Induction Programs: The Role of the Principal," *Clearing House,* 71, no. 3 (January–February 1998), 179–183.

Carver, Cynthia L., and Daniel S. Katz, "Teaching at the Boundary of Acceptable Practice: What Is a New Teacher Mentor to Do?" *Journal of Teacher Education,* 55, no. 5 (November/December 2004), 449–462.

Chester, Mitchell D., and Barbara Q. Beaudin, "Efficacy Beliefs of Newly Hired Teachers in Urban Schools," *American Educational Research Journal,* 33, no. 1 (Spring 1996), 233–257.

Cohn, Kathleen C., "Mentor Principals to Ensure Success," *The School Administrator,* 48, no. 3 (March 1991), 40–43.

DeBolt, G. P., ed., *Teacher Induction and Mentoring: School-Based Collaborative Programs.* New York: State University of New York, 1991.

Drummond, R. J., M. L. Grimes, and M. S. Terrell, "Beginning Teacher Program: Perceptions of Policy," *Education,* 111, no. 2 (1990), 187–189.

Drury, William R., "Entry-Year Administrator Induction: A State and Local School District Model," *Spectrum: Journal of School Research and Information,* 6, no. 1 (Winter 1988), 8–10.

Fox, Suzy, and Paul E. Spector, "Emotions in the Workplace: The Neglected Side of Organizational Life Introduction," *Human Resource Management Review,* 12, no. 2 (2002), 167–172.

Gratch, Amy, "Beginning Teacher and Mentor Relationship," *Journal of Teacher Education,* 49, no. 3 (May–June 1998), 220–227.

Grossman, Pamela, and Clarissa Thompson, "District Policy and Beginning Teachers: A Lens on Teacher Learning," *Educational Evaluation and Policy Analysis,* 26, no. 4 (Winter 2004), 281–301.

Holdaway, Edward A., Neil A. Johnson, and Eugene W. Ratsoy, "The Value of an Internship Program for Beginning Teachers," *Educational Evaluation and Policy Analysis,* 16, no. 2 (Summer 1994), 205–221.

Johnson, Nancy C., and J. Kenneth Orso, "Teacher Induction Programs," *Spectrum: Journal of School Research and Information,* 6, no. 3 (Summer 1988), 22–24.

Kelley, Linda Molner, "Why Induction Matters," *Journal of Teacher Education,* 55, no. 5 (November/December 2004), 438–448.

McKenna, Georgiann, "Mentor Training: The Key to Effective Staff Development," *Principal,* 77, no. 3 (January 1998), 47–49.

Metropolitan Life Survey of the American Teacher, *The Second Year: New Teachers' Expectations and Ideals.* New York: Metropolitan Life, 1992.

Millinger, Synthia Simon, "Helping New Teachers Cope," *Educational Leadership,* 61, no. 8 (May 2004), 66–69.

Odell, Sandra J., *Mentor Teacher Programs.* West Haven, CT: NEA Professional Library, 1990.

Pence, Jean L., "Mentorship Programs for Aspiring and New School Administrators," *Oregon School Study Council Bulletin,* 32, no. 7 (1989).

Perez, Katherine, et al., "An Analysis of Practices Used to Support New Teachers," *Teacher Education Quarterly,* 24, no. 2 (Spring 1997), 41–52.

Playko, Marsha A., and John C. Daresh, "Mentoring Programs for Aspiring Administrators: An Analysis of Benefits to Mentors," *Spectrum: Journal of School Research and Information,* 11, no. 3 (Summer 1993), 12–17.

Reinhartz, Judy, ed., *Teacher Induction.* West Haven, CT: NEA Professional Library, 1990.

Sindelar, Nancy W., "Development of a Teacher Mentorship Program: High Professionalism and Low Cost," *Spectrum: Journal of School Research and Information,* 10, no. 2 (Spring 1992), 13–18.

Strusinski, Marianne, "The Professional Orientation Program in the Dade County Schools," *Spectrum: Journal of School Research and Information,* 11, no. 2 (Spring 1993), 10–16.

Tomlin, Michael E., "The Evolution of a New Teacher," *The Executive Educator,* 15, no. 3 (March 1993), 39–41.

Tranter, William H., "The New Principal," *The Executive Educator,* 14, no. 2 (February 1992), 29–32.

Vienne, Dorothy T., "Mentors with a Mission," *The Executive Educator,* 13, no. 8 (August 1991), 32–34.

Appendix
Orientation Checklist for Newly Assigned Teachers

ORIENTATION CHECKLIST FOR NEWLY ASSIGNED TEACHERS

School building: Questions concerning this
                                                             should be directed to:

NAME	POSITION	DEGREES	DEPT.	DATE OF EMPLOYMENT

The majority of new teachers begin their careers with an enthusiastic, sincere desire to be successful. Each looks not only to the principal but also to various professional coworkers for information and instruction concerning his or her specific position, equipment, materials, and numerous regulations that apply to the teaching profession. Coupled with professional preparation, personal drive, and creativity, success or failure of a new member of the staff rests in large part on his or her interaction and cooperation with supervisors and fellow workers.

The checklist that follows has been devised as a minimum measure of the responsibilities that professional staff members have to newly hired teachers in their orientation and induction into the teaching profession in a specific system and locale.

TO BE DONE

WHO	WHEN	ACTION TO BE TAKEN	NOTES
Superintendent or Assistant Superintendent for Human Resources	Date contract signed	1. Welcome to school district. 2. Discuss district regulations concerning length of school day, pay periods, job assignment. 3. Give out district handbook, which includes available information about fringe benefits, retirement, payroll deductions, etc. 4. Present signed copy of contract and related information concerning Teachers Association Agreement.	
NAME	DATE		
Principal	Preservice interview	1. Welcome to the school. 2. Give out and discuss a copy of school philosophy, faculty handbook, student handbook (some topics, e.g., discipline).	
NAME	DATE		

Continued

TO BE DONE

WHO	WHEN	ACTION TO BE TAKEN	NOTES
		3. Discuss newly contracted teacher's resume and the manner in which the information in this document can help the teacher with students. 4. Present and explain the school orientation-induction calendar (assistance offered, observations and critique discussions, interviews). 5. Introduce to assistant principal.	
Assistant Principal _____ NAME	Preservice Interview _____ DATE	1. Welcome to staff. 2. Discuss special administration procedures: reporting teacher or student absenteeism, policies on leaves of absence, workshops, instructional needs, etc. 3. Introduce the teacher to department chairperson, librarian, guidance counselor, student activities director, AV coordinator, student council advisor, athletic director (all members of induction team).	
Department Chairperson _____ NAME	Inservice day through first week _____ DATE	1. Welcome the teacher to the department. 2. Introduce the teacher to other members of the department. 3. Discuss and explore topics of concern: departmental objectives, classroom methods, text(s) and workbook(s), experiences of person (travel, clubs, hobbies, etc.) 4. Review school/district policies concerning guest speakers, field trips, films and other materials, assignments of students. 5. Discuss lesson planning: what the teacher is going to do, or how it will be done; what the department chairperson expects to be done. 6. Discuss grading system and entire philosophy for evaluation of student progress within school system. 7. Discuss association memberships that are recommended for professional growth and development.	
Guidance Counselor _____ NAME	By end of second week _____ DATE	1. Reintroduce yourself and welcome the teacher. 2. Discuss general characteristics of the student body. 3. Explore services provided to students and the role that the teacher may play in directing students to counselors.	

TO BE DONE

WHO	WHEN	ACTION TO BE TAKEN	NOTES
		4. Explain academic advisement program and the role of the teacher.	
		5. Discuss the discipline/communication problems the teacher may be having with students.	
AV Coordinator NAME	By end of second week DATE	1. Reintroduce yourself and explain the role of AV coordinator. 2. Explain procedures for acquiring various pieces of equipment (usage, forms involved, time factors, etc.) along with how to set up and operate equipment; indicate common problems, appropriate action to correct, etc.; detail methods for obtaining required locations for use of hardware and equipment when applicable.	
Activities Director, Student Council Advisor, Athletic Director NAMES	By end of second week DATE	1. Reintroduce yourselves and explain areas of responsibility. 2. Explain the various types of activities currently available to the student body. 3. Discuss the procedures for organizing activities: district rules, State Athletic Association rules, etc. 4. Explain the financing of activities, how faculty members are compensated, and limits that exist concerning money. 5. Discuss the various rules established for use of school facilities outside the normal school day and explain the procedures that must be followed for club activities, fund raising, etc.	
Librarian NAME	By end of second week DATE	1. Reintroduce yourself and explain the role of the librarian. 2. Explain library procedures and services available to the teacher and students.	
Department Chairperson NAME	By end of second week DATE	1. Meet with the new teacher and discuss problems that may have occurred. 2. Establish observation date for following week. a. What will teacher be covering? b. What methods will be used? c. What particular item(s) would the teacher like the chairperson to pay special attention to during the class?	Observation Date _____ Period _____ Class _____ Level _____ Room _____

Continued

TO BE DONE

WHO	WHEN	ACTION TO BE TAKEN	NOTES
		3. By talking with the teacher, try to alleviate any fears he or she may have regarding the observation. 4. Inform principal of the date and period of the observation if a substitute teacher is needed to fill in for the chairperson.	

Department Chairperson
 	
_____
NAME
	After observation, during next planning period of new teacher
	
	_____
	DATE
		1. Meet with the teacher and discuss observation.
		  a. Very important to emphasize positive items, especially those the teacher might not be aware of.
		  b. Carefully discuss item(s) about which the teacher wanted feedback.
		  c. Be certain to call attention to any negative items and suggest ways teacher might improve. Discuss thoroughly and try to work out an action plan on one or more items with the teacher.
		2. Write a report summarizing both the good and bad points, points of disagreement, and the action plan agreed on to remedy any weakness.
		3. Give a copy of the report to the teacher and to the principal.
		4. Discuss with the principal the need for further observation.	

Senior Faculty Member _____ NAME	By end of third week _____ DATE	1. Reintroduce yourself and reidentify your role for teacher. 2. Find out how the teacher is faring. Discuss experiences you have had that might help the teacher to identify with you. 3. Answer those questions/problems you can and direct the teacher to particular people for more detailed answers to questions you are not able to answer.	

Principal
 	
_____
NAME
	By end of fourth week
	
	_____
	DATE
		1. Meet with the teacher and discuss problems mentioned in department chairperson's report. Also, explore the success or failure the teacher has experienced in carrying out the action plan.
		2. Establish observation date for following week.
		  a. What will teacher be covering?
		  b. What methods will be used?
		  c. What particular item(s) would the teacher like the principal to pay special attention to during the class?
			Observation
			Date _____
			
			Period _____
			(different from first)
			
			Class_____
			Level _____
			Room _____

TO BE DONE

WHO	WHEN	ACTION TO BE TAKEN	NOTES
		3. Make certain that you will not be observing the same period as during the first observation.	
AV Coordinator _____ NAME	By end of fourth week _____ DATE	1. Meet with the teacher, reintroduce yourself if necessary; talk further with the teacher about equipment and if necessary, demonstrate use of equipment. 2. Suggest some equipment (if teacher has not yet used any equipment) that might facilitate his or her teaching. 3. Review procedure for getting and using equipment. Encourage the teacher to incorporate audiovisual techniques into classroom instruction.	

Principal _____ NAME	After obser- vation, during next plan- ning period of teacher _____ DATE	1. Meet with the teacher and discuss observation.
		   a. Emphasize the teacher's positive points.
		   b. Carefully review your observations on items that the teacher wanted feedback about.
		   c. Discuss items mentioned by department chairperson. Carefully explore weak points of instruction and suggest further ways to improve.
		   d. Update the action plan.
		 2. It is very important to avoid too authoritarian an approach in your discussion with the teacher. The teacher must be encouraged to develop his or her best style.
		 3. Write a report summarizing improvements shown and areas still in need of improvement; include any points of disagreement and the updated action plan.
		 4. Give a copy of the report to the teacher and place a copy in his or her file.
		 5. Discuss your observation with department chairperson and jointly decide if chairperson should set up a future observation for seventh week.	

Librarian _____ NAME	By end of sixth week _____ DATE	1. Meet with the teacher in library, reintroduce yourself if necessary, and further explain available resources to the teacher. 2. Offer to suggest library assignments that he or she might use with his or her class.	

Continued

TO BE DONE

WHO	WHEN	ACTION TO BE TAKEN	NOTES
Guidance Counselor _____ NAME	By end of eighth week _____ DATE	1. Reintroduce yourself, if necessary, to the teacher when you meet and discuss problems that the teacher may be having with students. 2. Review the school's grading system with the teacher and listen to the teacher's views on grading. Give your views on how realistic or unrealistic you consider his or her ideas to be. 3. Discuss any problem situations the teacher may have encountered and how he or she handled or might have handled the situations. 4. Review available services that might help the teacher and his or her students.	

Activities Director, Student Council Advisor, Athletic Director
 	
_____
NAMES
	Tenth week
	
	_____
	DATE
		1. Explore what interest the new teacher has in sponsoring extracurricular activity.
		2. Review rules of the school concerning supervision of students participating in extracurricular activities and building usage by clubs.
		3. Offer the necessary help to the teacher if he or she wants to sponsor an extracurricular activity.
		   a. Explain how to request P.A. announcements.
		   b. Point out what bulletin boards may be used for the posting of meeting notices.
		   c. Introduce the teacher to available books and materials on sponsorship that might be of help.
		4. Discuss the interest of the teacher in coaching sports.	

Department Chairperson _____ NAME	Eleventh week _____ DATE	1. Check on progress the teacher is making with action plan by talking with him or her during a planning period. Make other suggestions that might help the teacher. 2. Review the teacher's grading of students. Discuss student reactions to grades. If any problems surfaced, try to help the teacher plan a course of action to avoid future problems.	

TO BE DONE

WHO	WHEN	ACTION TO BE TAKEN	NOTES
		3. Discuss the assignments, projects, and other work performed by students. Is too much or too little being demanded of pupils?	
Assistant Principal	Twelfth week	1. It is your function at this time to review with the teacher problems or concerns that you have as a member of the administration. a. Teacher arriving at school on time?	Last Observation Date _____
NAME _____	DATE _____	b. Showing up for assigned duties on time? c. Administrative duties performed in a satisfactory manner? Any deadlines missed? Other problems? Any complaints against the teacher should be given to him or her in writing, and he or she should be given the opportunity to clarify and write a response to the complaints. It must be remembered that teachers and administrators can make mistakes. Education is a joint effort; sometimes new and experienced teachers forget this. 2. The next step is to set up with the teacher an observation date for the coming week. a. What material will be covered? b. What particular items of the teacher's action plan are most in need of observation? c. What new teaching techniques has the teacher tried? What success has he or she experienced with them? d. Have the other three observations, discussions, and action planning been of much help? Why? Why not?	Period _____ (different from first, second, and third) Class _____ Level _____ Room _____
Assistant Principal	After observation, during next planning period of teacher	1. Meet with teacher to discuss the observation. a. Stress positive aspects of his or her teaching. b. Review improvements noted from earlier observation reports. c. Have teacher self-evaluate the lesson before you give your observations.	
NAME _____	DATE _____	d. Add any additional prescriptive items to action plan. 2. Write up a report summarizing both the good and bad points observed, points of disagreement, and additional items added to the action plan by agreement of the teacher.	

Continued

TO BE DONE

WHO	WHEN	ACTION TO BE TAKEN	NOTES
		3. Give a copy of the report to the teacher and a copy to the principal. 4. Discuss the observation with the principal. 5. Include negative reactions of the teacher to your critique.	
Principal —————— NAME	Before holiday break —————— DATE	1. Call a meeting of the team members who have been working with the new teacher. 2. Discuss the observed strengths and weaknesses of the new teacher and how well he or she has taken advice, improved teaching, and carried out aspects of the action plan. 3. Begin to create a staff development program for the teacher to be implemented during the second semester.	
Principal —————— NAME	January —————— DATE	1. Hold a conference with the teacher to discuss his or her progress, particularly in relation to the action plan. 2. Discuss the recommended staff development program. 3. Discuss the various ways in which the staff development program may be implemented: literature, teacher center workshops, additional college courses, etc. 4. Try to finalize plans for the staff development program. 5. Review administrative problems that may have occurred during the first semester.	
Senior Faculty Member —————— NAME	January —————— DATE	1. Sit down with the teacher and discuss how he or she is getting along. 2. Let the teacher know that you are concerned. Be a good listener. Again, offer suggestions if sought by the teacher.	
Librarian —————— NAME	February —————— DATE	1. Reoffer services if not already used. 2. Help set up a library project or assignment with the teacher for his or her class. 3. Discuss new acquisitions that might be of value to the teacher.	

TO BE DONE

WHO	WHEN	ACTION TO BE TAKEN	NOTES
AV Coordinator	February	1. Review usage of AV materials by the teacher. 2. Make suggestions for second-semester use of AV equipment. 3. Discuss new acquisitions that might be of use to the teacher. 4. Help the teacher arrange for classroom use of materials and equipment.	
_____ NAME	_____ DATE		

Principal	March	1. Meet with the teacher to discuss extension of his or her contract.
		2. Discuss teacher's first-year experiences.
		  a. How he or she feels about
		    i. Teaching as a career.
		    ii. This school, faculty, students, rules, etc.
		    iii. Subjects taught.
		  b. How he or she would evaluate the induction program:
		    i. What was most helpful?
		    ii. What was least helpful?
		    iii. Was anything disliked?
		    iv. What was most liked?
		    v. Was there something that might have helped more?
		    vi. Suggestions for improving the program.
		3. Review other areas of concern.
		  a. Areas in which the teacher is still weak.
		  b. Remind the teacher of school policies.
		  c. Encourage the teacher to keep striving for excellence and thank the teacher for past efforts.
		4. If contract will not be extended, explain why, orally and in writing.	

_____ NAME	_____ DATE		

Source: Adapted from Ronald Gagnepain, M. A., "Induction Schedule." (Unpublished research paper, St. Louis University, 1978.)

6

Staff Development

Change is a constant occurrence in contemporary society. Instant communication channels, produced by technological advances, present students and educators with changes in politics, economics, science, and social status from every corner of the world. The mandate of public schools, of course, is to educate the children, adolescents, and young adults of our country in order to help them meet the challenges that tomorrow will bring because of these changes.

As an organization, a school district needs well-qualified administrators, teachers, and support personnel to fulfill this mandate. As the positions and job requirements within a school district become more complex, the importance of staff development programs increases.

Staff development practices have undergone considerable change over the last two decades. Three trends that have contributed to this metamorphosis are: results-driven education, the systems approach to school and school district organization, and constructivism. As a practice, results-driven staff development is concerned with changing the behavior and attitudes of teachers, administrators, and staff members rather than being concerned with the number of participants in such programs. The systems approach to administration recognizes the interrelatedness of all components in a given school and ultimately in a school district. Thus, an innovation in elementary school instructional techniques could have ramifications for the counseling program and for the curriculum committee in a school. Across the district, an innovation in an elementary school could affect the program in that district's middle school and eventually, the high school instructional program.

Finally, constructivism sets forth the premise that learners build knowledge structures in their minds rather than having the knowledge received and imprinted in their minds by a teacher. The implication for staff development is that teachers, administrators, and staff members could be engaged in such activities as action research and mentoring programs in addition to the more traditional milieu through which programs are delivered.[1]

It is literally impossible today for any individual to take on a job or enter a profession and remain in it for forty or so years with his or her skills basically unchanged. Therefore,

[1]Dennis Sparks, "A Paradigm Shift in Staff Development," *Education Week,* 16 (March 1994), 42.

staff development is not only desirable but also an activity to which each school system must commit human and fiscal resources if it is to maintain a skilled and knowledgeable staff.

Professional Learning Communities as the Foundation for Staff Development

As a dimension of the human resources function, staff development can be organized according to various structures. Currently, the most effective structure is probably the *professional learning community*. Such a structure has four major focuses:

1. Learning rather than teaching
2. Collaboration
3. Viewing all members of the community as learners
4. Self-accountability

The first focus is a departure from the traditional approach to educating students, which centers on the responsibility of schools and school districts to ensure effective teaching. When the focus is placed on *learning,* teachers, administrators, and staff members tend to see their responsibilities in a different light. They begin to analyze the cultures of the school and school district in order to ascertain whether it supports student learning. Further, teachers, administrators, and staff members begin to understand that effective school and school district cultures are founded on a commitment to learning that must be articulated to all stakeholders, which includes students and parents. It is important to keep in mind that the term *staff members* refers to guidance counselors, media specialists, special education teachers, assistant superintendents for instruction, human resources administrators, and all other professional and support members of the school and school district community.

Of course this focus on learning that can be investigated through cultural analyses and commitment leads to the second focus, which is collaboration. Teachers, administrators, and staff members must collaboratively discourse and investigate what students need to learn, how to assess what students have learned, and how to help students who are having difficulty learning.

Collaboration also means that teachers, administrators, and staff members will recognize that every aspect of the learning process is subject to team efforts. For example, if a certain student is having difficulty learning, assisting the student is not the responsibility of only his or her classroom teacher. All members of the community who have related expertise will formulate a timely and required intervention plan to help the student. The usual format for collaboration is teaming, whereby a number of different teams of teachers, administrators, and staff members come together based on the expertise of the individual members in order to address common professional issues. Once formed, a given team may meet on a continual basis or only when necessary.

The third focus of professional learning communities empowers all members of the school and school district communities, not just students, to become learners. Of course, the most fundamental reality of this focus is that everything in life continually changes. Thus, it is impossible for anyone to know all that he or she needs to know for all times in order to effectively carry out his or her responsibilities. Consequently, parents, teachers, administrators, and staff members are constantly in need of acquiring new information, knowledge, skills, and attitudes. It is impossible to remain static in the dynamic environments of schools and school districts. This, of course, is the domain of staff development.

The final focus centers on self-accountability. The notion of *professional learning communities* rests on the ability of all members to self-actualize in a manner that contributes to the mission of their respective schools and school districts. For the human resources function, this means not only that professional staff development programs need to be organized and carried out in relation to the four focuses of the professional learning community but also that the other human resources functions need to be geared towards these same focuses. The recruitment, selection, and performance evaluation functions are the most affected by the professional learning community approach. Thus the concepts and processes set forth in this chapter constitute a professional learning community approach to human resources administration and, particularly, to professional staff development.[2]

Adult Learning

Adult learning usually consists of two processes, training and education. Training is the process of learning a sequence of programmed behaviors.[3] Keyboarders, custodians, cooks, and maintenance personnel thus can be trained because their job-related activities are capable of being broken down and analyzed in order to determine the best way to perform certain tasks. In this connotation training is the application of knowledge that provides employees with a set of procedures that will guide their work-related behaviors.

The emphasis in the training component of a staff development program is on the acquisition of motor skills and on producing simple conditioning methods that will improve an employee's ability to perform his or her job.

Education is the process of helping an individual understand and interpret knowledge.[4] Education emphasizes acquiring sound reasoning processes rather than learning a body of serial facts. Education helps an employee develop a rational approach towards analyzing the relationship between variables and consequently understanding phenomena.

Teachers and administrators have job responsibilities that, in most respects, require education rather than training. Teachers and administrators usually do not perform programmed work. For example, an administrator can be trained in management techniques and procedures. However, an administrator cannot be trained to manage. Speaking about managers in the private sector, Stephen Robbins summarizes the differences between training and education:

> Successful managers have analytical, human, conceptual, and specialized skills. They are able to think and understand. Training, per se, cannot overcome the inabil-

---

[2]Richard DuFour, "What Is Professional Learning Community?", *Educational Leadership,* 61, no. 8 (May 2004), 6–11.

[3]Stephen P. Robbins, *Personnel: The Management of Human Resources,* 2nd ed. (Englewood Cliffs, NJ: Prentice-Hall, 1982), 220.

[4]Robbins, *Personnel, ibid.*

ity of a manager or potential manager to understand cause-and-effect relations, to synthesize from experience, to visualize relationships, or to think logically. As a result, we suggest that management development must be predominantly an education process rather than a training process![5]

In discussing the distinction between training and education, care must be taken not to assume that all job-related activities of a particular position are either trainable or educable. Teachers and administrators perform some activities that can be enhanced by training because these activities are capable of being programmed. Both teachers and administrators need good listening skills and interviewing skills; in today's automated society, they also need skills in using the computer. However, understanding the instructional-learning process and being able to create a learning environment conducive to teaching goes beyond the scope of training and requires education.

This same distinction must also be applied to support personnel. An administrative assistant needs to develop and upgrade skills in using word-processing programs and in carrying out routine office procedures; these are trainable skills. However, this person is often called on to make decisions about setting up and prioritizing appointments for an administrator; this requires an understanding of the importance of each appointment relative to the responsibilities of that administrator. An effective administrative assistant should also have the ability to analyze inquiries and to refer them to the appropriate staff member. Acquiring such abilities goes beyond the scope of training and requires education.

To some, this distinction between training and education may seem to be only an academic exercise; however, it has very practical application. As will be demonstrated later in this chapter, it is extremely important to categorize and analyze the needs of employees in order to establish objectives for the various components of a staff development program. Understanding the type of learning required to meet these needs is essential to an effective program.

The Conditions of Learning

A staff development program centers around creating instructional-learning situations. Consequently, those charged with organizing such a program must have a profound understanding of the psychology and conditions required for effective learning. Numerous theories have been proposed about how learning occurs. This chapter will not elucidate all the principles described by these theories, but rather will present those aspects of learning common to the major theories.

Learning is a change in human capability that can be retained and that is not simply ascribable to the process of growth. The manifestation of change as described in this definition is the behavior of the learner. The extent to which learning has occurred is measured by comparing those behaviors that were present before the individual was placed in the instructional-learning situation against those behaviors that can be demonstrated after the experience. The desired change is usually an increased skill or capability of more than momentary significance.

[5]Robbins, *Personnel, ibid.*

Changes in behavior are brought about by four basic learning conditions: stimulus, response, reinforcement, and motivation. A *stimulus* is someone or something that initiates an action. An instructor will stimulate a learner by asking a question. The learner answering the question makes a *response*. If the instructor responds to the learner with, "that is a correct and appropriate answer," the learner is receiving *reinforcement*. Finally, if the learner perceives completion of the course of instruction as a means of obtaining a job, a promotion, a raise in salary, or some other desired goal, the learner is said to have *motivation*. Although this explanation of the four basic components of learning is rather simplistic, it does present the necessary conditions for learning to take place.

Considerations that impinge on these conditions of learning should be mentioned here for the sake of completeness, but they will not be elaborated on to any great extent. First, a certain amount of planning must precede the instructional learning situation to determine the most appropriate learning structure for the subject matter that will be taught. In learning, every new capability builds on a foundation established by previously learned capabilities. Planning specifies and orders these prerequisite capabilities in order that a learning objective can be reached. For example, a staff development workshop designed to help teachers construct metric system materials for classroom use should be preceded by a seminar explaining the metric system to teachers who are not proficient with the system.

Second, the environment of learning must be effectively managed. Those responsible for planning should ask themselves what is the most appropriate time and setting to carry out instruction. A comfortable and stimulating environment certainly enhances learning; and especially for adult learners, the instruction should take place at a time of day when they are not fatigued. This suggests that certain staff development seminars, workshops, or courses for teachers should be scheduled on days when school is not in session. This also implies that an effective staff development program should provide employees with released time from their regular duties so they can attend during the working day.

Third, instruction must have some practical application for the adult learner. Adults generally can learn more material in less time than children, but they must see that the material can help them in their work. A school bus driver who attends a workshop on managing student behavior must be shown techniques that he or she can actually use with disruptive students.

Fourth, learning rarely takes place at a constant rate; rather, it fluctuates according to the difficulty of the subject matter or skill to be learned and the ability of the learner. Developing keyboarding skills is a good example. During the first three months of instruction, the learner becomes familiar with the keyboard and basic techniques. During the next three months, the individual develops speed, and learning accelerates. After six months of instruction, learning normally slows down because the individual has progressed to the point of technique refinement.

Creating a Staff Development Program

Experience has taught human resources administrators the folly of approaching staff development merely from the "Let's have a workshop" model. This traditional concept of what was and is still referred to in some school districts as "inservice training" has severe limitations, not only in scope but also in effectiveness. Rather, the concept of "staff development" addresses the real needs of educational organizations. The evolution of this approach is mirrored in all of our societal institutions. In the past, changes were thrust upon the schools without giving teachers and administrators an opportunity to prepare for such changes. With the decline in pupil enrollments, there was a greater need for developing existing personnel resources to assume different positions created by change. Also, both the Elementary and Secondary Education Act of 1965 and the Education Professions Development Act of 1968 provided funding for staff development projects. These funds helped to forward the current interest in staff development.

During the last decade, there has been a myriad of research on staff development. Most of this research has centered on identifying those variables that produce effective staff development programs. As a consequence of this research, many models have been created. Some of the most often proposed in staff development literature are PET (Program for Effective Teaching); RPTIM (Readiness, Planning, Training, Implementation, Maintenance); CBAM (Concern-Based Adoption Model); and SDSI (Staff Development for School Improvement). A common thread connecting all these models is the goal of producing effective instruction through clinical supervision. As principals evaluate and supervise teachers in order to improve instruction, staff development programs become a vehicle through which teachers can enhance skills and remedy deficiencies.

Some employees perceive staff development activities as ineffective because they receive little support for implementing newly acquired skills and ideas. Other conditions that affect the success of a staff development program include lack of appropriate program organization and lack of supervision during implementation. Clearly, these conditions are symptomatic of a more fundamental problem, the lack of commitment. In any organization this commitment must emanate from the highest level of responsibility down through the various levels of administration to the employees. In order to be effective, the board of education must support the program; the administration must organize and supervise the program; and the employees must participate in program planning.

In delineating the tasks to be performed by the various components of a school district, the board of education must set the stage by creating a positive climate for the program and by providing the necessary fiscal funding and appropriate policies for implementation. The central-office administration, through the director of staff development, is responsible for creating a master plan and for overall management and supervision of the program. Building principals and supervisors are responsible for identifying the knowledge, skills, and abilities that are needed to carry out the goals and objectives of the school district. Teachers and staff members are responsible for participating not only in program planning but also in the programs. Consequently, the success of a staff development program depends on the commitment of each individual within each level of the school district.

Georgea Sparks confirms the importance of commitment as follows:

> . . . the major factor affecting success of the program was administrative support from both principals and superintendents. . . . Simply put, in schools where staff development had the greatest influence on teaching, teachers shared their ideas

about instruction and tried out new techniques in their classrooms . . . the major responsibility for planning and implementation is given to the local school staff . . . the most commonly mentioned strength of the program was the opportunity to have responsibility for the staff development and the improved school climate.[6]

Sparks also promotes the concept of *site specific* staff development, an approach that places the responsibility for program development at the local school level. Although this concept has merit, the contemporary school faculty is already so burdened with tasks and responsibilities that the idea is very difficult to implement.

Figure 6.1, a model for a staff development program, is a summary of the steps necessary for designing an effective program, which is elucidated in the following pages.

School District Goals and Objectives

Educational goals and objectives, taken in the broadest sense, are similar across the country. Schools are concerned about educating children in the basic skills and developing in our children those cultural values that will perpetuate our American heritage. How the var-

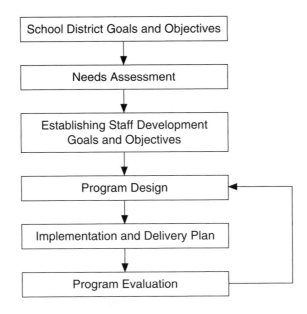

**FIGURE 6.1   A Model for a Staff
Development Program**

[6]Georgea Sparks, "Synthesis of Research on Staff Development for Effective Teaching," *Educational Leadership* (November 1983), 66.

ious school districts adjust these goals and objectives to their particular situation accounts for the fact that no two staff development programs are exactly the same.[7]

The genesis of a staff development program, therefore, originates from educational goals and objectives. When these goals and objectives are formulated into written policies of the board of education, a staff development program has the guidance necessary for integrating the individual goals of employees with those of the school district.

Needs Assessment

The primary purpose of a staff development program is to increase the knowledge and skills of employees and thereby increase the potential of the school district to attain its goals and objectives. The process of assessing employee needs is essentially the process of determining the discrepancy between the existing and the needed competencies of the staff. This analysis also must consider projected human resource needs. Thus, a staff development program must be concerned not only with the abilities of individuals currently occupying positions but also with the abilities individuals need to qualify for promotion to positions of more responsibility. The data obtained from the human resources inventories used in the human resources planning process along with the data obtained from needs assessment techniques provide the framework within which program goals and objectives can be established.

Establishing Staff Development Goals and Objectives

Staff development goals and objectives continually change to meet the continually changing needs of individual staff members and the school district. A predominantly European American suburban school district that begins to get an influx of African American families might consider creating a program for the administrative, teaching, and support staffs on the impact that the mingling of these two distinctive American cultures will have on the functioning of the school district. The purchase of new computer equipment will create a need to instruct the office staff on its most effective use.

These examples of changes that affect the operations of a school district should be more broadly formulated into goals and objectives. For example, a staff development goal involving integration might be stated as follows: to prepare the administration, teachers, and staff to effectively address the integration of African American students into the school community. Objectives specifying this goal could be formulated as follows:

1. To develop a sense of appreciation for cultural differences on the part of teachers, administrators, and staff members
2. To develop strategies that will help students acquire an understanding of different cultural heritages

Such a goal with accompanying objectives provides direction to the next phase in creating a staff development program—designing the program.

---

[7]See D. R. Davies and C. D. Armistead, *Inservice Education: Current Trends in School Policies and Programs* (Arlington, VA: National School Public Relations Association, 1975), 10.

Program Design

Designing a program involves more than simply finding a university professor who is interested in giving a workshop on a particular topic. Broadly conceived, program design is a process of matching needs with available resources through an effective delivery method. Therefore, it is obviously unproductive to assign or endorse an activity without considering how this activity helps to meet goals and objectives.

Also, it is unproductive to consider only one method of delivering a staff development program. The National Education Association's Research Division lists nineteen methods used in program delivery:

1. Classes and courses
2. Institutes
3. Conferences
4. Workshops
5. Staff meetings
6. Committee work
7. Professional reading
8. Individual conferences
9. Field trips
10. Travel
11. Camping
12. Work experience
13. Teacher exchanges
14. Research
15. Professional writing
16. Professional association work
17. Cultural experiences
18. Visits and demonstrations
19. Community organization work

This is certainly not a listing of all the possibilities for designing a staff development program, and it is important to recognize that no one technique will satisfy all individuals, but that different techniques will meet different needs.[8]

A variety of resource people will also enhance a staff development program. Among the most available and knowledgeable persons are teachers, senior staff members, college and university professors, professional consultants, journal authors, teacher organization representatives, and administrators.

Group-oriented design has proven to be an effective method for delivering staff development programs. In Omaha, Nebraska, this method was used to adapt new mathematics materials to individual student needs. After group meetings were held to identify areas of study, the staff was then divided into teams that specialized in single problem areas. Upon completion of the study, the various teams reported to the entire group, providing suggestions and techniques for individual application of the materials.[9]

Another group-oriented program, implemented in Mamaroneck, New York, centered around behavior modification techniques in the instructional-learning environment. Traditional workshops and seminars were employed to explain the theory of behavior modification and to analyze those behaviors amenable to each technique. Two teams of teachers

[8]See Jay E. Greene, *School Personnel Administration* (Philadelphia: Chilton Book Co., 1971), 275.

[9]See D. R. Davies and C. D. Armistead, *Inservice Education: Current Trends in School Policies and Programs* (Arlington, VA: National School Public Relations Association, 1975), 25.

were then selected to observe groups of children. After the observations were made, these two groups met to present and discuss the results of the observations.

Individualized programs are another alternative to the traditional program design model. Such programs allow the individual maximum creativity in matching personal interests and needs to the goals and objectives of the school district. Teachers who engage in personalized activities usually improve their teaching skills. Selma, Alabama, has implemented an individualized development program that gives teachers an opportunity to contract in writing each year to carry out certain self-selected activities. These activities include the following:

1. Long-range activities, which could include serving on curriculum research and improvement committees
2. The development of curriculum materials
3. Professional writing for journals and conducting research
4. Professional reading, which must include three books and at least ten articles
5. Attending conferences and conventions
6. Professional development through travel
7. Engaging in community relations activities that include conducting parent discussion groups and initiating community projects
8. Sponsoring uncompensated student activities
9. Other activities that have a demonstrated effect on implementing school district goals and objectives[10]

Program design is an organic process that will continually change to meet the needs of individual staff members and the needs of the school district.

Implementation and Delivery Plan

A critical aspect in all staff development programs is the implementation and delivery phase. The very best of intentions and planning may fail unless attention is paid to providing employees with appropriate incentives to participate, satisfactory time arrangements are made, and ordinary organizational problems are properly handled.

A common practice is to reimburse employees for tuition and fees incurred in attending workshops or taking courses. Many school districts also pay for substitutes in order to facilitate program arrangements.[11] The research on staff development programs generally agrees that incentives should be provided. For example, one study identified the following incentives in order of preference: credit for certificate renewal; reimbursement for expenses incurred for attendance at meetings, workshops, and other qualified programs; college or university credit; and advancement on the salary schedule.[12] Although direct payment in

---

[10]Davies and Armistead, *Inservice Education,* 21–23.

[11]See Davies and Armistead, *Inservice Education,* 36.

[12]See Darrell Jenson, Loren Betz, and Patricia Zignarmi, "Organizing Inservice for Teachers," *NASSP Bulletin,* LXII (April 1978), 13.

the form of salary increments is a proven incentive, this study indicates that indirect financial aid is more influential in promoting participation in staff development programs.

Time is a valuable commodity to all employees and, thus, it is a key factor in organizing and encouraging employee participation in development programs. There is a growing trend to incorporate staff development programs as part of the working day or, at least, as an extension of the day. Some school districts set aside a number of afternoons each month for development programs; others bring courses and lectures directly to the schools.

In Providence, Rhode Island, every school has thirty days of early dismissal each year for staff development programming. A variation of this approach is to release students by subject area so that the teachers in a given discipline can meet for an entire day.

Whatever the arrangement for delivering a staff development program, experience indicates that the least effective time is after a full day of teaching or work. No teacher, administrator, or employee will be able to assimilate new ideas when fatigued. The common practice in business and industry should be established in school districts—namely, that staff development programs should be conducted on "company time."[13]

A final consideration in administering a staff development program is providing the administrative mechanism to handle the ordinary problems that occur in all human interaction. Some specific problems that tend to hinder employee participation include the following:

1. Participants being unclear about what they hope to achieve
2. Participants considering past programs a waste of time
3. Programs being so highly structured as to hinder creativity
4. Individuals employed to conduct a given program not being the best available
5. A given program having no orderly plan
6. Group involvement with a specific program being so large as to hinder participation
7. Programs having no acceptable method of evaluation[14]

When administrators do their best to deal with such problems effectively, employees will more readily participate and will be more satisfied with the development programs.

Program Evaluation

Effective evaluation is the final phase in a staff development program. Some school districts see this as a rather complicated task involving multiple applications of statistics; others neglect it entirely. For most programs, a perception-based approach is both appropriate and effective. Participants are asked to rate the instructor or individual conducting the program, the content of the program, how the program was organized, and the time and place of the program presentation.

---

[13]See Davies and Armstead, *Inservice Education,* 36.

[14]John Clinton Moffitt, *In-Service Education for Teachers* (New York: The Center for Applied Research in Education, 1963), 53–54.

When a particular program centers on skill or technique acquisition, it is appropriate to conduct a follow-up evaluation after the participants have had the opportunity to implement the techniques or use their new skills. The evaluations are then used in future program planning and also should provide the necessary data to improve the entire staff development program. The controlling effects of program evaluation are as follows:

1. The evaluation of staff development programs should attempt to ascertain if the participants acquired the intended knowledge and skills.
2. The evaluation should attempt to ascertain if the participants utilize their newly acquired knowledge and skills in fulfilling their responsibilities.
3. The evaluation should address the impact that the new knowledge and skills has had on student learning outcomes.[15]

Also, the director of staff development should evaluate the program to ascertain if the program is helping to achieve the mandate of the school district as outlined in its goals and objectives. This is a much more complicated process than evaluating a specific course or workshop and must involve the perceptions of the board of education, superintendent of schools, other central-office administrators, and building administrators.

Staff Development for the Instructional Staff

During the first few decades of this century, boards of education were concerned about encouraging teachers to earn a baccalaureate degree. This orientation changed in the 1970s to one that emphasized the remediation of teacher deficiencies. The current thrust is to provide teachers with the opportunity to maintain a favorable outlook on teaching and to improve their effectiveness in the classroom. At times it is necessary for principals to recommend certain staff development programs to teachers who are not performing at the level established by the board of education. Therefore, performance appraisal and staff development are complementary aspects of effective supervision. A staff development program can offer the teacher opportunities to:

1. *Update skills and knowledge in a subject area.* The knowledge explosion has created the need to reinterpret and restructure former knowledge. A teacher can no longer assume on the basis of past learning that he or she understands the nuances of a subject area.
2. *Keep abreast of societal demands.* Our society is continually changing. This has presented the teacher with a need to understand and interpret the new demands society is placing on all its institutions and on the school in particular.
3. *Become acquainted with research on the instructional process and on new methods of teaching.* Like other professionals, teachers generally have good intentions of keeping up with the advances that are being made in their field. A shortage of available time often prevents them from carrying out this intention, and a staff development program can meet this need.

---

[15]Thomas R. Guskey, "Does it Make a Difference? Evaluating Professional Development," *Educational Leadership,* 59, no. 6 (March 2002), 45–51.

4. *Become acquainted with the advances in instructional materials and equipment.* Cable TV and computer-assisted instruction are only a few of the many new innovations that have potential for improving the quality of classroom instruction.

In the process of assessing teacher needs, the following sources of information can be of considerable help in designing a staff development program. First, the teacher needs assessment survey has been a very effective technique. Most surveys take the form of a checklist containing many areas of possible needs and interests (see Appendix).

A second source of information is the community survey, which is administered to parents, usually through a school-based organization such as the Parent–Teacher Association. This survey may reveal parental concerns about a wide range of issues such as grading, student groupings, discipline, and drug use by students.

Third, certification requirements vary from state to state and occasionally change. The director of staff development needs to keep all teachers and other certificated employees informed about requirements and should plan appropriate credit courses on both an off-campus and on-campus basis. The human resources master plan also will provide the director with information about the future needs of the district in relation to certain categories of certificated employees.

The final source of information is curricular research. Staff development programs can be planned to correlate with future curriculum changes. Research points to future skills and competencies that can be acquired and gradually introduced to insure an even transition.

The historic report, *A Nation At Risk,* published by the National Commission on Excellence in Education, was the impetus for many states to pass legislation centered on improving the quality of education. Much of this legislation calls for the establishment of professional development committees composed of teachers and other staff members who are responsible for assisting the administration in identifying the staff development needs of teachers. Along with the administration, these committees are also involved in the creation of staff development delivery systems.

Staff Development for School Principals

All administrators wonder from time to time about how they will be able to continue meeting the multiple challenges of their job, but school principals are particularly vulnerable because they are on the front line. James L. Olivero, a member of the Association of California School Administrators, wrote an article for the *Bulletin of the American Association of School Administrators* entitled "Reducing Battle Fatigue—or: Staff Development for School Principals," which significantly addresses this problem. Much of the material in this section was gleaned from this article.

Types of Staff Development Programs

Many studies concerning the ever-changing role of the school principal have been conducted over the last fifteen years. These studies have identified the following major areas as appropriate for development programs:

1. *Instructional skills.* To effectively evaluate and supervise the instructional process, which includes providing curriculum leadership and securing instructional resources.

2. *Management skills.* To establish job objectives and be able to assess the needs of the staff. To be able to identify problem areas and to plan towards an effective solution. To be capable of unit budgeting and reviewing priorities in the efficient use of scarce resources.

3. *Human relations abilities.* To establish an open, two-way system of communication between students, parents, teachers, and other members of the community. To develop a method of involving parents, students, and teachers in the school-based decision-making process. To create an atmosphere of trust in the school that encourages the staff and students to perform to the best of their abilities.

4. *Political and cultural awareness.* To have the ability to identify the leaders within the community and to involve them in school-level decision making. To address with positive techniques the resolution of conflicts between the school and community. To work towards meeting the needs of all clients of the school through school programs.

5. *Leadership skills.* Through a plan of self-development, to keep current with advances in the field of education. To share leadership skills with other professionals and with parents and other publics.

6. *Self-understanding.* To develop a plan of self-improvement through evaluation by school-based publics.

Staff Development Programming for Principals

Two types of programming can meet the development needs of principals. The first is the traditional vehicle, which includes workshops, conferences, and seminars that usually focus on a single topic and attempt to transmit a given body of information on such issues as new legislation or drug abuse.

A growing number of school districts are taking a more personalized approach to staff development for principals. This second type of program emphasizes acquiring skills that either help principals with their job or enhance their personal development.

Programs that emphasize the principal's job could include budget preparation, developing performance objectives, and initiating procedures to improve building maintenance. Programs that emphasize personal growth might address techniques for working with advisory groups, methods of communicating verbally and in writing, stress management, or time management.

Whatever an individual principal identifies as the area of personal need, a prerequisite for success is commitment. Therefore, it is advantageous to write down such personalized programs in a document that includes a personal needs assessment and a plan of action.

Future Directions for the Principal and Staff Development

Dramatic changes have occurred in our society over the last ten years, and they in turn have created a new set of competencies that principals need to acquire. A great many principals were educated before the emergence of such current trends as cultural pluralism, community involvement, program assessment, instruction-assisted technology, and the inclusion of students with disabilities. These trends, of course, are by no means the end but rather just the beginning of even more dramatic changes taking place at an accelerated pace. We must be prepared to meet this ongoing challenge in staff development. Effective staff development for principals can be enhanced if the development programs are

1. Systematic, concrete, and relevant to the principal's job, including not only what the job is but what the job should be
2. Ongoing and personalized
3. Flexible and adaptable to change as the need arises
4. Carried out when the participant is not fatigued because of work
5. An integral part of the school district's policies and supported by adequate funds

Staff Development for Classified Employees

Employee development programs in some school districts are limited to teachers and administrators. Development programs for classified employees have just recently taken hold on a large scale throughout the United States.

Three methods of development are commonly used for classified employees: on-the-job, off-the-job, and apprenticeship training. Because of the nature of their job responsibilities, classified employee development programs are aimed more at training than education. Nevertheless, there is a growing awareness that administrative assistants, custodians, bus drivers, and cafeteria workers will perform more efficiently if they are given the opportunity to participate in personal growth activities. Time management and human relations skills are important abilities for all school district employees, particularly with the current emphasis on community involvement in the schools.

Staff development has a definite orientation for classified employees. It is used not only to update skills but also to introduce new employees to the requirements and tasks they will be responsible for performing. Classified employees who are promoted to supervisory positions, in most cases, will learn how to handle their new responsibilities through a staff development program. This is also a nuance of development programs for classified employees.

On-the-Job Training

Most training takes place on the job, and in all probability this method is an effective means of training.[16] Besides being the easiest form of training to organize, it is also least costly to operate. Employees are placed in the actual work situation, which makes them feel immediately productive. They learn by doing, which is the most suitable training method for jobs that are difficult to simulate or that can be learned quickly by performance. A significant drawback to on-the-job training is the possibility of future low productivity, because in this setting an individual may never fully develop needed work-related skills when left to work alone.

A modification of on-the-job training is job-instruction training, a more systematic approach to training. This highly effective method consists of the following steps: (1) prepar-

[16]See Robbins, *Personnel,* 207, 208.

ing trainees by telling them about the job, (2) presenting information essential to performing the job, (3) having trainees demonstrate their understanding of the job, and (4) placing trainees in the job on their own and assigning a resource person to assist the trainees if they need help.

Off-the-Job Training

The term *off-the-job* training refers to various kinds of programs, such as lectures, seminars, workshops, case studies, programmed instruction, and simulations.[17] The lecture method is best suited to conveying information such as procedures, methods, and rules. Contrary to common assumptions, lectures can be either highly structured or fairly informal, allowing for a considerable amount of two-way communication.

In the last two decades there has been an increase in the use of case studies, programmed instruction, and simulation exercises in training programs. The case study allows the employee to study a particular problem in depth. After analyzing the problem, the individual evaluates alternative courses of action and finally selects one that appears to provide the best potential for solving the problem.

Programmed instruction is a method that can be carried out through manuals and textbooks as well as teaching equipment. This approach condenses the material to be learned into a highly organized and logical sequence. The trainee responds to a question or set of circumstances and is provided with immediate feedback, telling the trainee if the response was right or wrong.

Simulations are the most expensive but also most effective method of training. The trainee is placed in an environment that nearly duplicates the actual work situation. This method has been widely used by airlines to train pilots and by schools in driver education classes. By using computer-enhanced instruction, it is possible to simulate a wide variety of job dimensions without risking mistakes in a real-life situation, which might be dangerous or very costly.

Apprenticeship Training

The oldest form of training is the apprenticeship.[18] By this method, a trainee understudies a master worker for a given period of time or until the trainee acquires the necessary skills. Apprenticeships are common in the skilled trades but have seldom been used in staff development programs. However, the concept is applicable and is gaining in popularity.

Teacher Centers and Staff Development

In the early 1980s, there were ninety teacher centers operating in the United States under the U.S. Department of Education's Teacher Center Program (Public Law 94–482). This

[17]See Robbins, *Personnel,* 208, 209.
[18]See Robbins, *Personnel,* 207–208.

legislation was a direct outgrowth of the strategy employed by the National Education Association in its efforts to help teachers gain more control over curricular innovations. Teacher centers had long existed throughout the world before their emergence in the United States. Although the orientation of such centers varied considerably, many had evolved as a mechanism to help teachers deal with change. In the early fifties, the Japanese Education Centers were founded to help implement post-World War II curricular emphasis on the sciences. These centers are in direct contrast to the Japanese "study circles," which receive little official sanction and no government funds but provide places where teachers can address common interests and problems.

The British teacher centers, which are the most renowned, were developed in the early sixties to help implement the Nuffield Mathematics Program and have governing boards composed predominantly of teachers. These centers now number over five hundred, and have evolved into places where teachers plan and implement their own in-service education.

With the proliferation of teacher-center literature during the last two decades, many different center models have been initiated in the United States. Many were cooperative endeavors that included centers established by local school districts along with universities. Some state-funded teacher centers also emerged, along with federally funded centers established under Title III of the Elementary and Secondary Education Act.

The U.S. Congress, through the provisions of the Education Amendments of 1976 (PL 94–482, Section 153), funded the establishment of local teacher centers that operated in-service programs aimed at improving the classroom skills and techniques of teachers.

Essentially, a teacher center program is concerned with curriculum development and/or in-service education for elementary and secondary teachers carried out in one or more local education agencies. The Teacher Center Policy Board (TCPB) should be composed primarily of practicing elementary and secondary teachers from the area served. Other membership on a policy board may include administrators, board members, or representatives from institutions of higher education—all from the local area to be served.[19]

Teacher centers were founded on the premise that teachers are self-motivating professionals who are capable of determining their own needs and who, through the policies of the governing board, can best deliver a staff development program to meet these needs. Although the premise is undeniably true, there remain a number of concerns that must be outlined. First, federal funding for teacher centers no longer exists. Second, staff development is a need not only for teachers but also for all employees of a school district. Therefore, a board of education should assume the initial responsibility in providing fiscal resources to develop and administer such programs. Third, teacher centers are essentially delivery systems and should be funded with local and state funds if this is determined to be the most effective way to conduct a staff development program. Teachers, like all employees, must be involved in the entire staff development planning process if such programs are going to meet their needs. This is a normal procedure in all effective staff development programs.

---

[19]See "Congress Enacts NEA Teacher Center Bill," *Today's Education,* LXVI (March–April 1977), 74.

Teacher centers have been a worthwhile innovation for those school districts that lacked an effective staff development program, but they should not be considered a panacea for all school districts. With commitment and proper local and state funding, most school districts are capable of providing adequate programs utilizing a more traditional model administered by a director of staff development.

Summary

Change is a constant condition of our American way of life. Improved communications place before students and educators changes in politics, economics, and science almost as soon as they occur.

School districts have a mandate to educate the youth of our country. To do so successfully, schools need well-qualified teachers, administrators, and support personnel. No employee will remain qualified in the face of accelerating change without some form of ongoing education and training. This is the impetus behind the recent emphasis on staff development programs.

As a dimension of the human resources function, staff development can be organized according to various structures. Currently, the most effective structure is probably the *professional learning community*. Such a structure has four major focuses: learning rather than teaching, collaboration, viewing all members of the community as learners, and self-accountability.

Adult learning usually consists of two processes, training and education. Training is designed to teach a sequence of programmed behaviors; education seeks to impart understanding and an ability to interpret knowledge. Both types of learning can occur in a staff development program depending on the objectives to be reached.

In all learning environments four basic components must be present to ensure success: stimulus, response, reinforcement, and motivation.

Creating a staff development program consists of six separate but sequential processes: (1) establishing school district goals and objectives, which become the foundation of the program; (2) assessing the needs of the school district employees to determine if there is a discrepancy between the competencies of the staff and the requirements of the organization; (3) establishing staff development goals and objectives; (4) designing a program that will meet the staff development requirements; (5) implementing the designed plan in such a way that effective learning may occur; and (6) evaluating the program to ascertain if it is meeting its objectives, which in turn will affect future program designs.

A staff development program for the instructional staff focuses on updating subject area skills and knowledge in order to improve instruction; outlining societal demands and changes; presenting the findings of research on teaching methods and practices; and updating teachers on the advances in instructional materials and equipment.

In assessing the needs of teachers, four sources of information may be helpful: (1) the teacher needs assessment survey, (2) community surveys, (3) certification information coupled with the human resource master plan, and (4) research and curricular studies.

In the last decade the school principalship has experienced multiple challenges brought on by such trends as cultural pluralism, community involvement, program assessment, instruction-assisted technology, and the inclusion of students with disabilities. A study conducted in California identified the following areas as appropriate for principal development programs: instructional skills, management skills, human relations abilities, political and cultural awareness, leadership skills, and self-understanding.

Besides the traditional models of staff development for principals, which include workshops and seminars, many school districts are taking a more personalized approach directed at helping principals acquire skills that relate simultaneously to their job and their personal development.

Staff development programs have been limited to the professional staff in many school districts. However, all employees can profit from development programs, and classified employees should have the opportunity to increase their skills and to participate in personal growth activities. Newly hired and promoted classified employees can be inducted into the responsibilities of their positions through a staff development program. The three most commonly used methods are on-the-job training, off-the-job training, and apprenticeship training.

An innovation in staff development programming was the emergence of teacher centers, which was a direct result of Public Law 94–482, Section 153. These federally funded centers were locally governed and operated. They aimed at improving the instructional techniques of teachers.

Discussion Questions and Statements

- Explain how staff development is related to the performance evaluation of employees.
- Discuss the benefits of effective staff development programs.
- What are some strategies that can be used to motivate employees to participate in staff development programs?
- How might the principles of adult learning influence the creation of staff development programs?
- What types of staff development programs are best suited for employees in classified positions?
- Identify and describe staff development programs that are most beneficial for building administrators.

Suggested Activities

- You are the Director of Staff Development for a school district with 250 teachers and nine administrators. The state legislature has just mandated that 1 percent of the state aid that a school district receives must be used for teacher staff development. Thus, you have approximately $150,000 to spend on staff development. Describe, in writing, the aspects of a staff development program that you would develop with the money. Begin by stating the program goals and objectives.
- Obtain the policies of a school district on staff development. Write a comparison of the policies with the principles set forth in this chapter.

- Obtain needs assessment surveys that are being used in a school district to create staff development programs for administrators, teachers, and classified employees. Using the principles in this chapter, write an analysis of the surveys.
- Interview a director of staff development in person or on the telephone concerning the strategies that can be used to create and deliver effective staff development programs.

Selected Bibliography

Black, Susan, "Evaluating Professional Development Programs: The Elmira School District Model," *Spectrum: Journal of School Research and Information,* 7, no. 1 (Winter 1989), 34–40.

Caldwell, Sarah DeJarnette, ed., *Staff Development: A Handbook of Effective Practices.* Oxford, OH: National Staff Development Council, 1989.

DeFigio, Nicholas F., Naomi Zigmond, and Paul LeMahieu, "Educators' Views of Educational Problems: Changes Related to a Staff Development Initiative, 1990–1996," *Spectrum: Journal of School Research and Information,* 8, no. 1 (Winter 1990), 39–47.

DuFour, Richard, "What Is a Professional Learning Community?", *Educational Leadership,* 61, no. 8 (May 2004), 6–11.

Edwards, Sara A., and Susan Barnes, "A Research-Based Staff Development Model that Works," *Educational Leadership,* 42, no. 7 (April 1985), 54–57.

Glatthorn, Allan A., and Linda E. Fox, *Quality Teaching through Professional Development.* Thousand Oaks, CA: Corwin Press, 1995.

Goldstein, I. L., *Training and Development in Organizations.* Monterey, CA: Brooks-Cole, 1992.

Ingvarson, Lawrence, "Professional Development as the Pursuit of Professional Standards: The Standards-Based Professional Development System," *Teaching & Teacher Education,* 14, no. 1 (January 1998), 127–140.

Jaramillo, Ann, "Professional Development from the Inside Out," *Tesol Journal,* 7, no. 5 (Autumn 1998), 12–18.

Joyce, Bruce, ed., *Changing School Culture Through Staff Development.* Alexandria, VA: Association for Supervision and Curriculum Development, 1990.

Lieberman, Ann, and Lynne Miller, eds., *Staff Development for Education in the '90s: New Demands, New Realities, New Perspectives.* New York: Teachers College Press, Columbia University, 1991.

Marczely, Bernadette, *Personalizing Professional Growth: Staff Development That Works.* Thousand Oaks, CA: Corwin Press, 1996.

Marx, Ronald W., Phyllis C. Blumenfeld, and Joseph S. Krajcik, "New Technologies for Teacher Professional Development," *Teaching and Teacher Education,* 14, no. 1 (January 1998), 33–52.

Noe, R. A., "Mentoring Relationships for Employee Development," *Applied Psychology in Business: The Manager's Handbook.* Lexington, MA: Lexington Press, 1991, 475–482.

Ondrovich, Peggy Chnupa, "Staff Development: Meeting Teachers' Psychological and Professional Needs," *Spectrum: Journal of School Research and Information,* 7, no. 4. (Fall 1989), 22–26.

Peterson, Kent, "The Professional Development of Principals: Innovations and Opportunities," *Educational Administration Quarterly,* XXXVIII, no. 2 (April 2002), 213–232.

Richardson, Virginia, ed., *Teacher Change and the Staff Development Process: A Case in Reading Instruction.* New York: Teachers College Press, 1994.

Senge, Peter, Nelda Cambron-McCabe, Timothy Lucas, Bryan Smith, Janis Dutton, and Art Kleiner, *Schools that Learn: A Fifth Discipline Fieldbook for Educators, Parents, and Everyone Who Cares about Education.* New York: Doubleday, 2000.

Showers, Beverly, "Teachers Coaching Teachers," *Educational Leadership,* 42, no. 7 (April 1985), 43–49.

Strong, Richard W., Harvey R. Silver, J. Robert Hanson, Robert J. Marzano, Pat Wolfe, Tom Dewing, and Wende Brock, "Thoughtful Education: Staff Development for the 1990s," *Educational Leadership,* 47, no. 5 (February 1990), 25–30.

Tessmer, M., D. McCann, and M. Ludvigsen, "Reassessing Training Programs: A Model for Identifying Training Excess and Discrepancies," *Educational Technology Research and Design,* 47, no. 2 (1999), 86–99.

VanNote Chism, Nancy, "How Faculty Development Programs Evaluate Their Services," *Journal of Staff, Program & Organizational Development,* 15, no. 2 (1997–1998), 55–62.

Wexley, K. N., and G. P. Latham, *Developing and Training Human Resources in Organizations.* Glenview, IL: Scott Foresman, 1991.

Wideen, Marvin F., and Ian Andrews, *Staff Development for School Improvement: A Focus on the Teacher.* New York: The Falmer Press, 1987.

Zepeda, Sally J., *Staff Development: Practices that Promote Leadership in Learning Communities.* Larchmont, NY: Eye on Education, 1999.

Appendix
Needs Assessment Survey

NEEDS ASSESSMENT SURVEY FOR THE INSTRUCTIONAL STAFF

**(Directions: Please check all items according to your degree of interest.
Return this completed form to the administration office.)**

Degree of Interest

	None	Some	Much
1. Methods of Motivating Students	___	___	___
2. Behavioral Objectives	___	___	___
3. Dealing with Individual Differences	___	___	___
4. New Grouping Patterns (Nongraded school team-teaching)	___	___	___
5. Teaching Critical Thinking Skills	___	___	___
6. Programmed Learning	___	___	___
7. Designing Independent Projects	___	___	___
8. Work–Study Programs	___	___	___
9. Career Education	___	___	___
10. Using Performance Objectives	___	___	___
11. Advanced Placement	___	___	___
12. Linguistics	___	___	___
13. Teacher-Made Tests and Mechanical Scoring	___	___	___
14. Modern Math Workshop	___	___	___
15. Elementary School Science (Experiment & demonstration)	___	___	___
16. Seminar on Literature	___	___	___
17. Computer Programming (Course of study)	___	___	___
18. Oral Communication	___	___	___
19. Education for Economic Competencies	___	___	___
20. Developmental Reading	___	___	___
21. English for Junior and Senior High Teachers (Develop a course of study)	___	___	___
22. Audiovisual Aids Workshop (Teachers)	___	___	___
23. Audiovisual Aids Workshops (Teachers' aides)	___	___	___

Degree of Interest

	None	Some	Much
24. African American History Workshop	____	____	____
25. Consumer Education in the Secondary Curriculum	____	____	____
26. New Directions in Social Studies	____	____	____
27. Outdoor Education Workshop	____	____	____
28. Ecology Workshop	____	____	____
29. Minicourses (In your field)	____	____	____
30. Music for Elementary School Teachers	____	____	____
31. Seasonal Art Projects for Elementary Classrooms	____	____	____
32. Public Library Resources	____	____	____
33. Selection and Evaluation of Audiovisual and other Instructional Media	____	____	____
34. Spanish for Teachers	____	____	____
35. Math for 1st- and 2nd-grade Teachers	____	____	____
36. Learning Disabilities (Identification and remediation)	____	____	____
37. Social Studies for 5th- and 6th-grade Teachers	____	____	____
38. Art Workshop	____	____	____
39. Field Trips	____	____	____
40. Physical Education Specialists	____	____	____
41. School Library	____	____	____
42. Industrial Arts (All-purpose)	____	____	____
43. Pupil Services	____	____	____
44. Speech Therapy	____	____	____
45. Driver Training (Rap sessions)	____	____	____
46. Learning Center (Elementary)	____	____	____
47. Teaching English Composition	____	____	____
48. Modern Economics	____	____	____
49. Medical Seminar (Nurses)	____	____	____
50. Math Enrichment (Elementary)	____	____	____
51. Retirement and Social Security (Teachers of retirement age)	____	____	____
52. New Elementary Math Adoptions (Primary)	____	____	____
53. New Elementary Math Adoptions (Intermediate)	____	____	____
54. Early Childhood (Kindergarten curriculum)	____	____	____
55. Teachers' Legal Limitations and Liabilities in the School	____	____	____
56. Learning and Behavior	____	____	____
57. Behavior and Discipline in the Elementary School	____	____	____
58. The Open Space School	____	____	____
59. Language Arts (Elementary)	____	____	____
60. Elementary Library Facilities	____	____	____
61. Parent–Teacher Relations	____	____	____
62. Involving the Child in Social Studies (Elementary)	____	____	____
63. Involving the Child in Science (Elementary)	____	____	____
64. Personalizing Math (Elementary)	____	____	____
65. Music for Secondary School Teachers	____	____	____
66. Orientations for New Teachers	____	____	____
67. The Psychology of the Disadvantaged Child	____	____	____
68. Classroom Management	____	____	____
69. Behavior Modification	____	____	____
70. Parliamentary Procedure	____	____	____
71. Home Economics	____	____	____
72. Special Education on Elementary Level	____	____	____
73. Special Education on Secondary Level	____	____	____

Continued

Degree of Interest

	None	Some	Much
74. Guidance Workshop	____	____	____
75. Seminar in Your Subject Area	____	____	____
76. Adolescent Psychology in the Modern World	____	____	____
77. General Trends in Education	____	____	____
78. Newspaper in the Classroom	____	____	____
79. Data Processing Seminar (Student attendance and grade reporting)	____	____	____
80. Teacher-Made Training Aids	____	____	____
81. Rap Sessions in Your Subject Area	____	____	____
82. Creative Classroom (Display and bulletin boards)	____	____	____
83. Individualized Reading	____	____	____
84. Techniques of Teaching Slow Children	____	____	____
85. Instruction Materials	____	____	____
86. Instructional Games	____	____	____
87. Physical Education (Elementary)	____	____	____
88. Constructive Seat Work	____	____	____
89. Individualized Teaching and Learning (Elementary)	____	____	____
90. Involving the Child in Language Arts (Elementary)	____	____	____
91. Updating Courses of Study (In your field)	____	____	____
92. Community Resources	____	____	____
93. Effective Questioning	____	____	____
94. Interaction Analysis	____	____	____
95. Metric Measurement (International system)	____	____	____
96. Communications and Drug Abuse Seminar	____	____	____
97. Other Suggestions	____	____	____

Source: Adapted from Lincoln Intermediate Unit No. 12, New Oxford, Pennsylvania.

CHAPTER 7

Performance Evaluation

The evaluation of teachers' performance is as old as the education profession. However, for the most part, only three stages of historical development in American education during this century were concerned with the formal evaluation of teachers. During the 1920s, the efforts were primarily centered around analyzing if a given teaching style correlated with the philosophy and psychology of William James or John Dewey. The second stage was more concerned with ascribing certain personality traits as being related to excellence in teaching. The final stage, which appeared in the 1960s and persisted through the 1970s, emphasized generic teaching behaviors that would be effective in all instructional settings. The research in this area coined such catch words as *structured* and *task-oriented* when speaking about the types of teacher behavior that produced effective student outcomes.

In 1976 the National Institute of Education, in a request for proposals, called for a new approach to the definition of effective teacher training. This signaled the growth of a movement to license teachers on the basis of competencies and performance rather than on the completion of a teacher education program at an accredited college or university. Obviously, such an approach is predicated on a preconceived notion of what constitutes effective teaching.

The last decade has ushered in a dramatic change in the entire concept of quality teaching that is centered on the relationship between teacher qualifications, teacher preparation, teaching performance, and educational outcomes.[1] In addition, an ongoing trend requires more accountability at all levels of performance. School board members are also subject to this trend towards accountability, which has developed to the point that school employees, parents, and even organizations support specific candidates in school board elections because of their dissatisfaction with the policies of particular board members.

The "systems" approach to management, which has been used extensively by industry and received a big boost in the early 1960s when Robert S. McNamara advocated its

---

[1]Marilyn Cochran-Smith, "Teaching Quality Matters," *Journal of Teacher Education: The Journal of Policy, Practice, and Research in Teacher Education,* 54, no. 2 (March/April 2003), 95.

use in the U.S. Department of Defense, shifted the emphasis away from the traditional concept of teacher evaluation to the broader concept of employee evaluation management. Evaluation by objectives has become a touchstone. This implies that an employee can be effectively evaluated only within the context of attaining certain preestablished objectives. Establishing these objectives is part of the overall process of determining the organizational objectives of the school district.

Because of the integral relationship between all employees and because one employee's performance can affect the performance of other employees, all personnel should be evaluated. This begins with the evaluation of the superintendent of schools by the board of education and proceeds down through the chain of command, with each administrator evaluating those employees reporting to her or him. This process applies not only to the professional staff but also to classified employees, whose performance should be evaluated by their immediate supervisors.

It is important for all employees to recognize the positive nature of performance evaluation. Of the six reasons for evaluation given here, only number five could be interpreted as being negative. However, it is a positive reason because students are entitled to the best services possible. Thus, it is not the reasons that make performance evaluation a negative experience, but rather, in some school districts, it is the manner in which it is carried out. Procedural due process is an important element because it ensures fairness and the positive effects of performance evaluation.

This is the role that is played by teacher and labor unions; it is also the role of negotiated master contracts. Performance evaluation is always considered to be a *management prerogative* process. However, a master contract negotiated by a teacher or labor union will certainly include a clause on procedural due process that helps to protect employees' rights to fairness.

1. Evaluation fosters the self-development of each employee.
2. Evaluation helps to identify a variety of tasks that an employee is capable of performing.
3. Evaluation helps to identify staff development needs.
4. Evaluation helps to improve performance.
5. Evaluation helps to determine if an employee should be retained in the school district and how large a salary increase he or she should be given.
6. Evaluation helps to determine the placement, transfer, or promotion of an employee.

Parents and taxpayers are demanding increased accountability in employee performance; employees also are demanding accountability in the evaluation methods and techniques used in their evaluations. Administrators and supervisors are being asked to defend their evaluations and the procedures they used in making them. Consequently, it is extremely important to develop a consistent benchmark in establishing an evaluation process.

The benchmark is the "job description" under which an individual was employed. Thus, employees are evaluated in relation to their job descriptions, which is the only defensible criterion against which performance should be measured.[2] Although this does not

---

[2]See Stephen P. Robbins, *Personnel: The Management of Human Resources,* 2nd ed. (Englewood Cliffs, NJ: Prentice-Hall, 1982), 318–319.

mean that a given job position will remain unchanged, it does imply that a revised job description may be needed if a job has undergone considerable modification.

A significant distinction must be made at this point to avoid confusion. This chapter is addressing the evaluation process from a central-office perspective with emphasis on the development of procedures, on the use of instruments and methods, and on the legal considerations of the process. It is not concerned with supervision as a task of the principal and other administrators. Supervision addresses the human interaction between teachers and administrators, an interaction that is required of the principal in fulfilling his or her role as the instructional leader within a particular school.

Developing a Performance Evaluation Process

The ultimate goal of all school districts is to educate children and adolescents. How this is accomplished depends upon a multitude of subordinate goals and objectives. It is not only organizationally appropriate but also legally wise for a school board to establish a policy statement on employee appraisal that will serve as one of these supportive goals. Such a policy gives direction to the various administrative divisions of the school district in their development of organizational objectives. A policy statement might read:

> Recognizing that quality education for the children and adolescents of this school district depends on the level of teacher, administrator, and staff member performance, the board of education directs the superintendent of schools to develop and implement a process for employee evaluation.
>
> This process must address as its first priority the impartial and objective evaluation of individual employees, in relation to the requirements of their positions within the school district. A second priority is to analyze how these positions help to actualize and support the instructional goals and objectives of this school board.

Thus, organizational context is critical to the development and attainment of school and school district goals.[3] The three major divisions in most school districts are human resources, instruction, and support services. Following the organizational structure outlined in Chapter 1, the assistant superintendents for human resources, administrative services, secondary education, elementary education, and instructional services must develop divisional objectives. In the human resources division, objectives might center on improving recruitment techniques, human resource planning methods, or interviewing procedures.

The administrative services division could establish objectives in business management aimed at constructing a more effective investment schedule. The transportation component of this division might work on fuel-efficient bus routing, which would free up funds to improve other areas in the organization.

It is certainly obvious that this procedure of developing objectives may reach a level of refinement within a division that would reach down to component objectives developed

---

[3]Carolyn J. Kelley and Kara Finnigan, "The Effects of Organizational Context on Teacher Expectancy," *Educational Administration Quarterly,* XXXIX, no. 5 (December 2003), 618–620.

by directors (director of federal programs, director of special education, director of pupil personnel services, and so on). This is a procedure that is followed in some school districts. However, individual school districts may not need this level of refinement and divisional objectives could be sufficient—the assumption being employed in this chapter.

After divisional objectives have been established by the appropriate assistant superintendents, all employees in that division are responsible for developing personal objectives that support the divisional objectives. An assistant superintendent for secondary education might see a need to be present more often in the schools to observe operations firsthand. This would constitute a personal objective to be accomplished over a given period of time. A high school teacher of U.S. history might develop an objective aimed at using more audiovisual techniques in lesson presentations. A custodian might attempt to reorganize the floor waxing schedule to make better use of work time when students are not in school. This constitutes an objective for the custodian.

The next step in the evaluation development process is to decide on formal evaluation procedures. These procedures should be in written form and made available to the entire staff. A concern often voiced by employees is that they were not adequately informed about the evaluation process. Because evaluation procedures are applicable to all school district employees, a common practice is to incorporate them into the board of education policy manual that is distributed to all employees when they are hired. Other school districts have employee handbooks that outline working conditions and specify the procedures and forms used in the evaluation process.

Developing the actual procedures is a task that is best performed by involving employee representatives who both evaluate and will be evaluated. This committee approach produces a sense of involvement and accountability that will help to defend evaluation procedures in the face of possible criticism.

It is appropriate to divide the employees of the school district into two groups, professional and classified, when organizing the evaluation development committees. The work situations of these two groups are significantly different and consequently may necessitate different evaluation procedures. It is more defensible to have committee members elected by the employees they represent than to have them appointed. If a school district's employees belong to unions or professional associations, it would be appropriate to have these organizations appoint representatives to serve on the committees.

The number of committee members will vary depending on the size of the school district, the number of employees represented, and the number of unions and associations active in the district. However, the most important consideration is that the committee be composed of an odd number of members such as three, five, seven, or nine, which will avoid the possibility of deadlocked decisions.

Of course, the procedures will be tailored to the needs of the individual school district. However, the following questions should be addressed in every set of procedures:

1. Who, by position, has the primary responsibility for making evaluations? (*Examples:* assistant superintendent for elementary education, principals, director of transportation, director of food service.)

2. Who is evaluated by these designated positions? (*Examples:* assistant superintendent for secondary education evaluates secondary school principals; building principals evaluate teachers; director of maintenance evaluates carpenters.)

3. In what settings will formal evaluations take place? (*Examples:* a teacher will be evaluated in the classroom when he or she is teaching a lesson; a principal will be evaluated in how he or she conducts a staff meeting.)

4. On how many occasions will formal evaluations occur? (*Examples:* tenured teachers will be evaluated on one formal occasion each year; probationary teachers will be evaluated at a minimum on two formal occasions.)

5. In what setting will the results of formal evaluations be communicated to the person evaluated? (*Examples:* in a conference immediately after the evaluation in the teacher's classroom; in a conference held in the principal's office at the end of each semester.)

6. If an employee disagrees with his evaluation, what grievance procedure should be available? (*Examples:* written rebuttal may be attached to the evaluation form; appeal may be made to the superintendent.)

7. What effect will evaluation have on salary increase? (*Examples:* a teacher with an excellent rating may receive a double step on the salary schedule; an employee may receive a merit increase in addition to a step increase on the salary schedule.)

Appendix A, "Teacher Evaluation Policies and Procedures," presents a typical set of such procedures that speaks to most of the questions. In analyzing these procedures, it is important to realize that evaluation of all employees is a continual and ongoing process. However, it is just as important to have "formal" evaluations when an employee can demonstrate her or his performance capabilities. Formal evaluation is applicable to situations that involve interaction between an individual and a defined group. Teachers are subject to this process because of their interaction with students. Principals can be evaluated in this manner on how effectively they handle staff meetings. Bus drivers can be formally evaluated when transporting children to and from school.

Other employees perform jobs that are more appropriately evaluated on a continuing basis but not on a formal occasion. Cooks, custodians, and administrators can be evaluated on results obtained. This implies that the substance of the evaluation was obtained outside a formal setting but that the evaluation is communicated to the employee in a formal setting.

The final step in the evaluation process is analysis of the results that have been obtained through employee evaluations to determine if division objectives are being met. If objectives have not been reached, and if they are still relevant to implementing the objectives and goals of the school board, the divisional objectives should be retargeted. This suggests that the employee objectives apparently did not support the divisional objectives and should be realigned to support them. If both the divisional and employee objectives have been realized, new objectives can be identified that will further the goals of the organization and the development of individual employees. Figure 7.1 is a schematic representation of the evaluation process.

There are a number of popular evaluation techniques that have not been addressed in this section, such as self-evaluation, peer evaluation, and student evaluation. These techniques are aimed more at personal growth and do not directly affect the evaluation process from a central-office perspective. They are referred to more properly as supervisory techniques.

The Construction of Performance Evaluation Instruments

As with the development of evaluation procedures, evaluation instruments should be constructed by the committee process. Many management consulting firms have developed

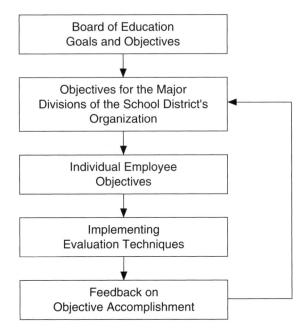

**FIGURE 7.1   Model for Developing an
Employee Evaluation Process**

evaluation forms that are easily adapted to the requirements of a given school district. However, the construction of evaluation forms is not a difficult task, particularly with the many prototypes available for the asking from neighboring school districts.

The basic format of an evaluation instrument has certain theoretical overtones. Most authors recognize two basic categories, trait forms and result forms. In the trait approach the employee is rated against a predetermined list of indicators in order to ascertain his or her level of performance. The results method compares the employee's performance against goals and objectives that were developed by the employee and agreed to by his or her supervisor. Using instructional assessment, the teachers and supervisor can document how the goals and objectives were reached.[4]

Many school districts are using standards that have been developed by several professional associations as guides in constructing performance-based evaluation instruments. The *Interstate New Teacher Assessment and Support Consortium* (INTASC) standards developed under the auspices of the Council of Chief State School Officers are currently considered to be best practice for licensure requirements in many states. INTASC standards are also compatible with the advanced certification standards of the new National Board for Professional Teaching Standards. These standards can be transformed into performance criteria.

[4]Charlotte Danielson and Thomas L. McGreal, *Teacher Evaluation: To Enhance Professional Practice* (Princeton, New Jersey: Educational Testing Service, 2000), 110–114.

Representatives from the teaching profession, colleges and universities, and representatives from a number of state educational agencies developed the INTASC standards. What follows are the ten core standards that INTASC considers essential for all teachers without regard to the subject or grade level that they teach.

1. The teacher understands the central concepts, tools of inquiry, and structures of the discipline(s) he or she teaches and can create learning experiences that make these aspects of subject matter meaningful for students.
2. The teacher understands how children learn and develop, and can provide learning opportunities that support their intellectual, social, and personal development.
3. The teacher understands how students differ in their approaches to learning and creates instructional opportunities that are adapted to diverse learners.
4. The teacher understands and uses a variety of instructional strategies to encourage students' development of critical thinking, problem solving, and performance skills.
5. The teacher uses an understanding of individual and group motivation and behavior to create a learning environment that encourages positive social interaction, active engagement in learning, and self-motivation.
6. The teacher uses knowledge of effective verbal, nonverbal, and media communication techniques to foster active inquiry, collaboration, and supportive interaction in the classroom.
7. The teacher plans instruction based on knowledge of subject matter, students, the community, and curriculum goals.
8. The teacher understands and uses formal and informal assessment strategies to evaluate and ensure the continuous intellectual, social, and physical development of the learner.
9. The teacher is a reflective practitioner who continually evaluates the effect of his or her choices and actions on others (students, parents, and other professionals in the learning community) and who actively seeks out opportunities to grow professionally.
10. The teacher fosters relationships with school colleagues, parents, and agencies in the larger community to support students' learning and well-being.[5]

There are also standards for art education, elementary education, English language arts, foreign languages, mathematics, science, social studies, and special education. The developers of the INTASC standards also developed knowledge, dispositions, and performance indicators.[6]

The appendices to this chapter exhibit a number of trait instruments that have roots in standards, knowledge, dispositions, and performance similar to those developed by INTASC. The focus may be different given the specific issues and concerns of individual school districts and individual state agencies. This is as it should be, because standards and indicators are only guides that must be individualized by school districts and state agencies.

The State Board of Education and the Department of Public Instruction of North Carolina have adopted the INTASC standards for licensure but have developed their own

[5]Council of Chief State School Officers, *New Teacher Assessment and Support Consortium (INTASC)* (May 2005), www.ccsso.org.

[6]Ibid.

indicators. However, the construction of the indicators has been guided not only by the standards but also by the knowledge, dispositions, and performance indicators. Here, for example, are the North Carolina *Key Indicators* for the first INTASC standard.

The candidate:

- Demonstrates an understanding of the central concepts of his or her discipline
- Uses explanations and representations that link curriculum to prior learning
- Evaluates resources and curriculum materials for appropriateness to the curriculum and instructional delivery
- Engages students in interpreting ideas from a variety of perspectives
- Uses interdisciplinary approaches to teaching and learning
- Uses methods of inquiry that are central to the discipline[7]

This author believes that the most appropriate method of evaluating performance is to use a trait instrument to ascertain overall performance and to target objectives to specify needed improvement in performance. The results method also helps to ascertain if employee objectives are supporting divisional and school board objectives. Employee objectives can be developed easily if overall performance has been measured. Although the simultaneous use of trait instruments and objectives is not a common practice, the exclusive use of one or the other has never proven in experience to be superior. Appendices B, D, and E represent various trait formats that have wide use in educational organizations.

Job descriptions play an important role in constructing appraisal instruments and in the developing of objectives. The job requirements of a position are the legal parameters within which evaluation must be confined. An employee performs job requirements to an acceptable, unacceptable, or superior level. To require an employee to assume responsibilities that are not within his or her job description and to evaluate how he or she carries out these responsibilities is poor management. The dismissal of an employee because he or she did not perform responsibilities omitted from the job description may not hold up in court.

Employee Discipline

The term *discipline* is often used with a negative connotation. However, the term itself refers to a condition in an organization created by employees conducting themselves according to the rules and regulations of the organization and in a socially accepted manner. Most individuals are self-disciplined and have little difficulty in following rules and regulations. Also, fellow employees can exert significant pressure on people who violate socially accepted norms. Using inappropriate language is a typical example of conduct offensive to most people.

There are two areas of misconduct that call for some action on the part of management: excessive absence from work and inappropriate on-the-job behavior. Absenteeism has become a major issue costing literally millions of dollars. Many theories have been proposed for this change in work ethic. However, the cause is usually rooted in the person, who must take responsibility for his or her actions.

[7]North Carolina State Board of Education and Department of Public Instruction, *The INTASC Standards* (May 2005), www.dpi.state.nc.us/pbl/pblintasc.htm.

"Inappropriate on-the-job behavior" is meant to cover a variety of offenses such as carelessness, failure to use safety devices, fighting, and alcohol and drug abuse. There are a number of variables that affect the seriousness of absenteeism and inappropriate on-the-job behavior. The administration must consider the nature of the problem, the duration of the problem, the frequency of the problem, the employee's work history, and other extenuating factors. However, it is clear to all practicing administrators that a response must be made that will correct the problem.

The response of the administration to such problems must be corrective rather than punitive; and the action taken must be progressive if it is to withstand the test of "due process." For example, if a custodian is tardy for work two times within a given week, the custodial supervisor should give that custodian a verbal warning. If the custodian is late the following week, the supervisor should then present the custodian with a written warning. If the tardiness continues for a third week, the custodian should be suspended from work for a week without pay. If the inappropriate behavior continues after the suspension period, the supervisor must continue with progressive discipline involving demotion, a pay cut, and finally, dismissal.

In terminating the employment of a person, it is critical for the supervisor and a designated staff member from the human resources department to carefully review the documentation of the reasons for the termination with the school district's attorney for assurance that defensible and appropriate procedures were followed. In preparing for the meeting at which the employee will be informed that his or her employment with the school district is being terminated, the individual's supervisor and a human resources staff member should have completed all the necessary reports and documents along with obtaining the individual's final paycheck. It is always important to have two people present at the meeting who will be representing the school district, usually the person's supervisor and a staff member from the human resources department. This provides a witness to the proceedings which may be important in the event of a lawsuit filed against the school district by the fired employee. It may be helpful to role-play what will take place at the meeting, including the anticipated reaction of the person to be fired.

Selection of the time and place of the meeting is important because the objective is to conduct the meeting in the most pleasant way possible for the person being fired and in the least disruptive way possible to other employees. For example, Monday afternoon may be the most appropriate time to have the meeting because the fired person will be able to use the rest of the week to search for another job, whereas Friday afternoon might result in intensifying the persons' anger during the weekend. Immediately after the meeting, district property should be returned and, after the individual collects his or her personal property, the fired person should be escorted out of the building by either the supervisor or the human resources staff member.

At the meeting, the following should take place: present the reasons why the person's employment is being terminated; make clear that the decision is final; allow the person to briefly respond; advise the employee of the school district's appeal process; and discuss severance and vacation pay along with information about fringe benefits such as COBRA.[8]

---

[8]Allen Fishman, "Firing Someone the Right Way Can Avoid Legal Hassles," *St. Louis Business Journal,* 20–26 July 1992, 13.

In a school district with a collective negotiated master agreement, such a progressive disciplinary process should be clearly outlined in the agreement.

This type of disciplinary process is very effective with classified personnel such as custodians, cooks, and bus drivers, but it is not very useful with teachers and administrators. Therefore, the following section deals with the due process that is more appropriately applied to certificated staff members. Both processes, however, may lead to the same outcome, termination of employment. It is important to keep in mind that a progressive discipline process does not supersede the evaluation process. Rather, it is a method of dealing with problems that cannot wait to be dealt with through the normal evaluation process.

Developing Termination Procedures

A universally accepted purpose for evaluating an individual's performance is to make a determination concerning the desirability of retaining that person as an employee of the school district. A decision to dismiss an employee, of course, is extremely difficult to make because of the importance of employment to a person's welfare and also because of the effects such a decision has on the employee's dependents.

Employment counselors have seen the devastating financial and psychological effects that getting fired has on a person's life. In fact, the trauma usually centers on the individual's self-concept. Feelings of inadequacy, failure, self-contempt, and anger are common to people who have their employment terminated. Although most individuals are able to cope with such a situation, others never fully recover from such an experience. Consequently, it is not only good human resources management but also a humane responsibility for school district administrators to develop termination procedures that are objective and fair, and that incorporate a due process that gives employees the opportunity to modify or defend their behavior. The *Missouri State Statutes Governing Revocation of License, Contract Management, and Termination Procedures* present a model that is being used here to explicate the nuances of due process and the grounds for terminating employment. Although the statutes pertain specifically to teachers, the concepts explained are applicable to other categories of employees.

Grounds for Terminating the Employment of Tenured Teachers

A tenured teacher may have his or her employment terminated for one or more of the following causes: physical or mental condition unfitting him or her to instruct or associate with children; immoral conduct; insubordination, inefficiency, or incompetency in the line of duty; willful or persistent violation of, or failure to obey, the state laws pertaining to schools; willful or persistent violation of the published policies and procedures of the school board; excessive or unreasonable absence from work; conviction of a felony or a crime involving moral turpitude.

The first cause listed must be understood within the context of the Rehabilitation Act of 1973. A disability does not constitute a physical condition that may in any way be construed as unfitting an individual from associating with children or students. In fact, the prevalent interpretation of the law is that an aide must be hired to assist an employee if the employee's disability interferes with the instruction or supervision of children. The only possible physical condition that would prevent an employee from associating with children is the contracting of a contagious disease. This would be a potential cause for dismissal only if the individual refused to get medical treatment and insisted on working while he or she was contagious. Emotional illness that produces dangerous or bizarre behavior is also a potential cause for dismissal if the employee refuses to receive medical treatment and insists on working while ill. In both cases, documentation from a physician is necessary to proceed with the termination process. Of course, the school district is responsible for all expenses incurred in securing the expert opinion of the physician.

Immoral conduct must be judged within the context of local standards but also must be reasonable and consistent with recent court decisions. A number of significant court cases have been reviewed and form the foundation for the following principles that should be used in judging employee conduct. First, the health of the pupil–teacher relationship is the criterion for judging employee behavior. A teacher or other employee who establishes a relationship with a student that goes beyond friendship and is exhibited in some form of "dating" is unacceptable. Second, illegal sexual acts are cause for immediate suspension. If an employee is convicted of performing such an act, his employment with the district must be terminated. Suspension is a justifiable practice while investigating allegations of sexual misconduct, if the employee receives his or her salary during this period. Third, private nonconventional sexual lifestyles are not a cause for employee dismissal. For example, homosexuality or cohabitation outside of matrimony may be unacceptable to many people in the community, but they do not inherently affect an individual's performance in the workplace. These and other practices are displayed publicly on television and in other media, which to an extent has nullified their impact on students. Fourth, if an employee advocates nonconventional sexual lifestyles at school, the employee has placed himself or herself in a position where termination is possible, because such lifestyles are in direct conflict with local standards.

Insubordination in the line of duty is always a cause for dismissal. Although the interpretation of what constitutes insubordination may appear to be self-evident, insubordination has restricted application. Employees can be insubordinate only if they refuse to comply with a directive of their supervisor that is clearly within their job expertise. If a principal asks a teacher to supervise the children on the playground during the teacher's preparation time and the teacher refuses, the teacher is insubordinate because teachers have the job-related responsibility of supervising children. On the other hand, if the principal were to direct a custodian to supervise the children on the playground and he refused, the custodian would not be guilty of insubordination because this is not within his occupational expertise. Nor would it be insubordination if a teacher refused to fill in for the principal's secretary, who was absent from work because of illness. The teacher was not hired to perform secretarial functions and may refuse this directive. The manner in which an employee responds to a directive does not usually constitute insubordination if the employee performs the task. Thus, if a teacher responds in a sharp tone to the principal when assigned to playground duty, but obeys the directive, the teacher is not guilty of insubordination.

Inefficiency is relatively easy to document. It usually refers to the inability of an individual to manage those tasks that are integral to a job responsibility. A teacher who never takes class attendance or who cannot account for the equipment, books, or materials assigned to his or her class is obviously inefficient. A principal who is always late in turning in building budgets or other reports also falls into this category.

Incompetency is perhaps the most difficult cause to document in terminating an employee. It also is directly related to the formal evaluation process. If a tenured teacher is performing in an incompetent manner, it means that he or she is hindering the instructional-learning process. The evaluations made by the principal must clearly indicate that major deficiencies have been identified and that objectives to remedy these deficiencies have not been met.

Claiming willful or persistent violation of state school laws or board of education policies and procedures as a cause for termination presupposes that school district employees have been informed of these. An effective method of notifying employees about these laws, policies, and procedures is through the publication and distribution of a handbook or manual that clearly outlines the employee's responsibilities.

Excessive or unreasonable absence from work is a relative circumstance that can be substantiated only through a policy defining what is meant by *excessive* or *unreasonable*. Local school boards probably will rely on patterns of absences in making their determination. Five consecutive days per month over a year's span, for example, could be considered excessive if the employee is not suffering from a chronic physical condition that interferes with attendance at work.

Conviction of a felony is obviously a reason to terminate the employment of an individual. The conviction for a crime involving moral turpitude, however, requires some explanation. Prostitution is usually classified as a misdemeanor, but because it involves morally offensive conduct according to most community standards, it is a reason to terminate a tenured teacher. The selling of pornography or a conviction for the use or sale of drugs also falls within the definition of moral turpitude.

In 1989 Congress passed the Drug-Free Workplace Act, which gives employers the choice of rehabilitating or dismissing staff members working in federal grant programs who are convicted of drug abuse offenses in the workplace. This law and federal administrative regulations require school districts to maintain a drug-free work environment by explicitly prohibiting employees from manufacturing, distributing, dispensing, possessing, or using unlawful drugs in the workplace. In addition schools must also provide a drug-free awareness program, which must include a description of the dangers of drug abuse, notification of the new requirements and penalties for violations, and information on available employee assistance programs. Employees must inform their supervisor within five days of a criminal conviction for a workplace drug crime. Job applicants must inform a potential employer of prior workplace drug conviction.

It is becoming common practice for school districts to give a second chance to persons convicted of a workplace drug offense by offering them the services of a drug rehabilitation program. This also points up the growing necessity of employee assistance programs as a voluntary fringe benefit for all employees.

This law also gives school district administrators the right to require persons to be tested for drugs when there is reason to suspect that these individuals are using or are under the influence of drugs on school premises or at school functions.[9]

[9]Staff, "The Administrative Angle on Policy Implementation," *National School Boards Association,* no. 2 (June 1989), 1.

Notification of Charges against a Tenured Teacher

After a behavior has been identified that could result in the termination of an employee, the next step in a due process is notification. This is a formal procedure of serving the employee with written charges specifying the alleged grounds that, if not corrected, will eventuate in dismissal. It must be kept in mind that notification with an opportunity to correct behavior is applicable only to charges arising out of incompetency, inefficiency, or insubordination in the line of duty. Physical or mental conditions as described above, immoral conduct, violation of school laws or board of education policies and procedures, excessive absences, and conviction of a felony or crime involving moral turpitude require a hearing before termination of employment, but they obviously do not require a period of time to correct the behavior. The behavior has already gone beyond what is rectifiable in an educational setting. A hearing is required, however, to determine if the facts substantiate the allegation.

Notification of charges, an extremely formal process, must not be confused with evaluation procedures that permit an employee the right to disagree with a written evaluation. As a normal course of action, employees may attach a written rebuttal to the evaluation instrument, setting forth points of disagreement and including any documentation to support their position.

Time periods are an essential component of the notification process. Three time periods are specified in these statutes: a thirty-day period during which time the employee has an opportunity to modify behavior; a twenty-day period before a hearing is held, which allows the employee time to gather evidence supporting his or her position; and a ten-day period after service on the teacher of a hearing during which time he or she must respond to the notification that he or she wishes to have the hearing. If the employee does not wish to have a hearing on the charges, the board of education may terminate his or her employment with the school district by a majority vote of the board members.

This statute also sets forth another common practice in termination proceedings. The teacher may be suspended with pay after notice of a hearing until the board of education makes a determination concerning the employment of the teacher.

Termination Hearing on Charges against a Tenured Teacher

This statute outlines a procedure that must be followed in conducting a hearing that might eventuate in the dismissal of a tenured teacher. Once again, these statutes present a model that is applicable to all termination proceedings.

1. The hearing shall be held in a public forum. There is a distinction between a public hearing and a hearing held in public. At a public hearing, those in attendance are usually allowed to address those conducting the hearing according to preestablished procedures; at a hearing held in a public forum, only those representing the party making the allegation and those representing the party against whom the allegation is made are allowed to speak and participate in the hearing.

2. Both parties may be represented by an attorney, who may cross-examine witnesses.

3. The testimony given at a hearing shall be under oath. Government agencies such as school districts are usually allowed the privilege of administering oaths in official proceedings. Normally, the president or secretary of the board of education is the official so empowered.

4. The board of education may subpoena witnesses and documentary evidence requested by the teacher. As with the power to administer oaths, school districts usually have subpoena rights and may limit the number of witnesses called on behalf of the teacher or school district administrators.

5. The proceedings at the hearing should be recorded by a stenographer employed by the school district. A tape recording of the hearing is usually acceptable in lieu of a stenographer. A transcript of the proceedings must be made available not only to the school board but also to the teacher. The transcript of a hearing held in public should be open to public inspection.

6. Except for the fee paid to the attorney representing the teacher, all expenses for conducting the hearing should be paid by the school district.

7. The decision by the board of education should be reached within a preestablished time period to ensure fair treatment to the employee.

The board of education is exercising judicial authority in conducting the hearing and reaching a decision on the possible dismissal of a tenured teacher. This is a unique circumstance because the school board acts in two capacities: prosecution, in the sense that the charges are brought against the employee in the name of the school board; and judiciary, because the school board renders the decision. In this respect the board of education is reviewing its own action. Consequently, it is extremely important to demonstrate, as much as possible, impartiality in the hearing structure. The evidence should be presented by an attorney representing the building principal and other line administrators because these administrators have the responsibility for evaluating and reviewing employee performance.

The room should be arranged to clearly delineate the functions that will be exercised at the hearing. The board of education will occupy a central place in the room seated at a table. A second table with a chair could be set up perhaps ten to fifteen feet in front of and facing the board members where witnesses will give testimony. To either side of the board table and facing each other should be two tables: seated at one, the teacher and his or her attorney; and at the other, the appropriate administrator with the school district's attorney. Those in attendance should be seated in a manner that clearly indicates that they are observers and not participants in the proceedings.

Another mechanism sometimes used in lieu of a formal hearing when discussing the possible termination of an employee is an executive session board meeting. Most states have statutes permitting government bodies to hold such private meetings at which public attendance is excluded. If a teacher or any employee is confronted with documentary evidence that could possibly result in his or her termination and if that employee had been given notice that his or her behavior must be modified, it may be possible to invite the employee to discuss his or her lack of improvement at an executive session of the school board. If the employee resigns in the face of the documentation, the expense and potential embarrassment of a public hearing are avoided.

Figure 7.2, Evaluation of a Permanent Teacher, schematically represents the relationship between the statutes elucidated in this section concerning the termination of a tenured teacher.

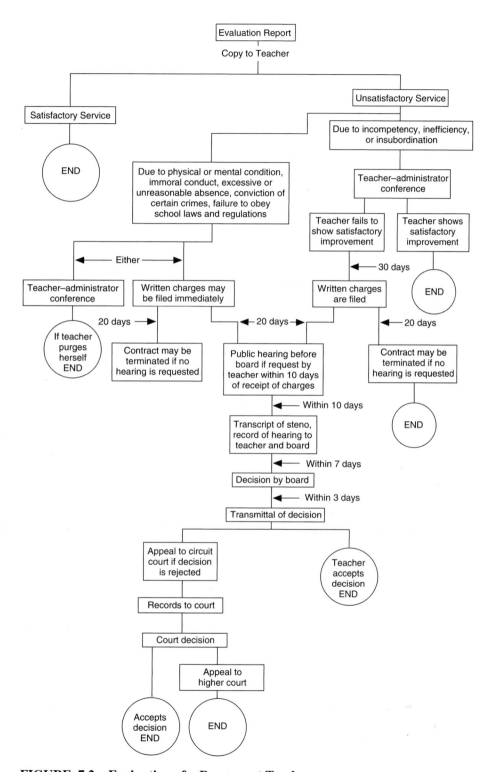

FIGURE 7.2 Evaluation of a Permanent Teacher

Source: Missouri State Department of Education, November 1970.

Appeal by a Tenured Teacher to a Termination Decision Issued by the Board of Education

Because school districts are state government agencies, appeal from the decision of a school board is made to the state circuit court, which is the court of original jurisdiction in state civil and criminal matters. In most states this appeal must be made usually within a set period of time. All evidence, documentation, records, and the transcript of the hearing probably will be requested by the court. Of course, the employee has the right to appeal the decision of the circuit court, as in all civil cases, through to a court of appeals and supreme court if there is a justifiable reason.

Termination Procedures for Probationary Teachers

A distinction must be made from the very beginning of this section between terminating the employment of a probationary teacher and not renewing a probationary teacher's contract. In the latter situation no formal due process is necessary; the employer–employee relationship simply ceases to exist with the expiration of the contract. This may occur if a probationary teacher is not performing at a level acceptable to the administration. A probationary teacher may have difficulty interacting with the students, staff, or parents in the school district or may be teaching at a minimal level. It is not only to the district's benefit but also to the teacher's benefit not to renew the contract, since the teacher might be more successful in another school district. Not renewing a contract presupposes that evaluations have been made by the teacher's principal, that deficiencies have been pointed out, and that advice and help have been offered on how to improve performance or correct the stated deficiencies. If such a process has occurred, nonrenewal of the teacher's contract is justified.

This statute refers to terminating the employment of a probationary teacher before his or her contract expires. As with all other school district employees, the teacher must be given a written statement setting forth the allegations along with a reasonable time period to correct deficiencies and improve performance. If such corrections or improvements are not made within the specified time, the employee may be dismissed by action of the board of education.

Grounds and Procedure for Revocation of a Teacher's License to Teach

A final formal procedure must be briefly alluded to when discussing termination procedures. A teacher's license to teach may be revoked if it can be proven that he or she has exhibited incompetency, cruelty, immorality, drunkenness, neglect of duty, or the annulling of a written contract with the board of education. As in the statute dealing with the termination of a tenured teacher, the reasons for revocation of a teacher's license have a very narrow interpretation.

Incompetency means that the teacher seriously hinders the instructional-learning process. A chronic mental illness or sociopathic behavior that has been diagnosed by a psychiatrist are examples of incompetency that could result in revocation of a teacher's license.

Cruelty refers not only to physical but also to mental or emotional abuse of children. The conditions that constitute cruelty may be summarized as follows: Any act that is meant to injure or bring serious ridicule and embarrassment to a child is abusive and cruel.

Of course, immorality is an extremely sensitive accusation. For practical considerations, this cause is commonly interpreted to mean that an individual has been convicted of a serious sexual offense or a crime involving moral turpitude. The examples provided earlier in this chapter are applicable to immorality as a cause for revocation of a teacher's license.

Drunkenness as a cause for revocation of an individual's license is usually interpreted to mean that the employee is either intoxicated or drinks alcoholic beverages while working. This cause is further strengthened by the fact that drinking alcoholic beverages in a government building such as a school is a misdemeanor in most states. A complicating factor is how drunkenness relates to the issue of alcoholism. Because alcoholism is considered to be a disease by the medical profession, the same considerations should be afforded the alcoholic as are granted to other employees with a medical problem. These considerations usually involve granting sick leave to an employee receiving medical treatment or reassigning the employee to a position with limited responsibilities during treatment. If an employee is not a diagnosed alcoholic and if he or she persists in drinking alcoholic beverages at work or continuously arrives at school intoxicated, license revocation is in the best interest of a school district's clientele, the children.

Neglect of duty presupposes that an employee has been informed about the responsibilities that are integral to his or her position with the school district. This is usually accomplished through written job descriptions or in policy manuals and handbooks specifying these responsibilities. Neglect of duty as a cause for revoking a teacher's license requires that the teacher be given an opportunity to rectify his or her behavior. Thus, evaluations that set forth the employee's deficiencies are necessary to such a situation. It also must be remembered that revocation of license is extremely serious and the neglect of duty, in like manner, must be extremely serious and chronic. A teacher who leaves young children unattended on a field trip—behavior that could result in an injury to a child—and who continues such irresponsible behavior after being informed of the danger by the principal has exhibited a lack of understanding that seriously affects his or her ability to supervise children. This is a reason not only to terminate the employment of the individual but also to safeguard against this teacher's potential employment with another school district by proceeding to have his or her license revoked.

Annulling of a written contract with the board of education is an improperly worded statement in this statute. Annulment means that both parties have agreed to the dissolution of the contract and the governing board has formally approved the dissolution. As cause for revocation of license, however, this aspect of the statute refers to the breaking of a contract by a teacher. Sometimes a teacher or other employee is offered a position with another school district or in private business and industry. If that teacher neglects to request a contract annulment from the school board and assumes another position, the board of education may proceed to have his or her license revoked. Most school boards are not resistant to annulling a contract except in those cases when the education of the students would be seriously affected. A teacher who tenders a resignation the day before the opening of school in September may not receive a contract annulment until a suitable replacement is obtained.

It should be clearly understood that the board of education does not have the authority to revoke a license; rather, the board may follow a statutory procedure that could eventuate in the revocation of a teacher's license. The state board of education, which issues teaching licenses, has the sole authority to revoke them.

Finally, revocation of a teacher's license is usually irreversible unless the statutory procedures were neglected or the evidence was faulty. It is, therefore, a very serious matter that should be initiated only if the education or health and safety of children will be significantly jeopardized not only now but also in future situations. Terminating the employment of an individual obviously removes him or her from injuring the children presently in his or her care. Revocation of license prevents the teacher from bringing such injury to children in another school district where he or she could be employed. A classic example involves the teacher who is convicted of child molestation and subsequently is fired from his position but who manages to get hired in another school district and commits a similar crime because his license was not revoked.

Humane Considerations in the Termination Process

The procedures described in this section may appear to overemphasize the legal and negative side of the evaluation process. It is, however, an aspect of evaluation that is seldom addressed and that is extremely important. Confusion over appropriate and fair termination procedures could result in a school district being saddled with an employee who hinders the instructional-learning process or who, in fact, may place children in an unsafe situation.

The educational welfare of children is the primary responsibility of a school district. The hiring, retaining, developing, and terminating of personnel should be guided by this mandate. However, employees also have rights that must be taken into consideration when developing procedures and dealing with employee evaluation. Due process is one right that has long been a fundamental principle in English common law and is basic to the legal procedures of American democracy.[10]

Chapter 6, *Staff Development,* makes the point that a legitimate objective of a staff development program is helping teachers and other employees to overcome deficiencies that affect their job performance. In like manner, Chapter 5, *Placement and Induction,* further provides guidelines for the transfer and placement of personnel to improve their performance. Humane human resources management presupposes that all alternatives have been exhausted in helping employees improve their performance or remove deficiencies before the process of termination is initiated.

Summary

There are three historical stages of development in U.S. education during this century concerning the evaluation of teachers. In the 1920s, efforts were primarily centered around analyzing if a given teaching style correlated with the philosophy and psychology of William James and John Dewey. The second stage was concerned with ascribing certain personality traits as being related to excellence in teaching. In the 1960s, the final stage emphasized generic teaching behaviors.

The last twenty years have ushered in a dramatic change in evaluation procedures. The traditional concept of teacher evaluation has been replaced by the broader concept of eval-

---

[10]See the American Association of School Administrators, *Teacher Tenure Ain't the Problem* (Arlington, VA: The Association, 1973), 24.

uation management. By this approach an employee is evaluated within the context of attaining certain preestablished objectives.

The reasons that justify the establishment and implementation of an evaluation process for all school district employees include the following: to foster self-development, to identify a variety of tasks which an employee is capable of performing, to identify staff development needs, to improve employee performance, to determine if an employee should be retained and what his salary increase should be, and to help in the proper placement or promotion of an employee.

A significant aspect of an appraisal process is measuring an employee's performance against his job responsibilities as outlined in his job description.

In developing an evaluation process, the board of education should establish a policy on employee evaluation that will give direction to the various divisions within a school district. These divisions are responsible for developing objectives aimed at implementing the goals of the school board. Each employee is then responsible for developing personal objectives that further the divisional objectives. Consequently, employee performance is measured against the degree to which each individual has attained his or her objectives. Feedback data is then available to analyze if divisional objectives have been reached. The actual evaluation procedures for implementing this process are best developed by involving representatives of the employees who will be evaluated.

Some school districts are using the standards developed by the Interstate New Teacher Assessment and Support Consortium (INTASC) as a guide in constructing performance-based evaluation instruments. In essence the standards then become performance criteria. The ten INTASC core standards are considered necessary for all teachers.

As with the development of evaluation procedures, evaluation instruments are more appropriately constructed by the committee process. There are two basic categories of evaluation instruments: trait forms and result forms. The trait approach rates an employee against a predetermined list of traits to ascertain overall performance. The results approach involves comparing an employee's performance against objectives that were developed by the employee and agreed to by his or her supervisor. Using both types of instruments helps to identify areas where improvement is needed.

Termination procedures, an aspect of the evaluation process that is seldom addressed, are extremely important. Because getting fired has such a devastating effect on the financial and emotional welfare of an individual, termination procedures must be fair and objective. Most states have statutory provisions outlining the due process that must be afforded teachers before termination. Such legislation, while applying to the professional staff, also provides a model for boards of education in establishing similar procedures for all employees. The educational welfare of students is the primary concern of a school district, but employees also have rights that must be taken into consideration when developing appraisal procedures and dealing with employee dismissal.

Discussion Questions and Statements

- What is the rationale for the performance evaluation of employees?
- How does performance evaluation benefit both the employee and the school district?
- Explain how performance evaluation can be an integral component of effective supervision.

- What type of evaluation report forms do you think are the most effective?
- Explain the relationship between the performance goals and objectives of the school district and of individual employees.

Suggested Activities

- You are the Assistant Superintendent for Human Resources in a school district with approximately 500 employees. Develop a due process procedure for the termination of an employee that you believe is both humane and also meets the responsibility of the board of education. Write a comparison of your procedure with the statutes that govern the termination process in the state where you live.
- In writing, compare and contrast these same state statutes and your procedure with the principles for teacher termination in this chapter.
- Obtain a copy of the evaluation report forms in a school district and write a comparison of them with the model forms in this chapter.
- Construct what you think is an ideal administrator evaluation form.
- Interview a human resources administrator in person or on the telephone about how the performance evaluation and termination processes are interrelated and further discuss the practical implications of both processes.

Selected Bibliography

Bridges, Edwin, *Managing the Incompetent Teacher.* Eugene, OR: ERIC Clearinghouse on Educational Management, 1990.

Brown, G., and B. Irby, *The Principal Portfolio.* Thousand Oaks, CA: Corwin Press, 1997.

Cederblom, Doug, and Dan E. Pemerl, "From Performance Appraisal to Performance Management: One Agency's Experience," *Public Personnel Management,* 31, no. 2 (Summer 2002), 131–140.

Coppola, Albert J., Diane B. Scricca, and Gerard E. Connors, *Supportive Supervision: Becoming a Teacher of Teachers.* A joint publication with the National Association of Secondary School Principals. Thousand Oaks, California: Corwin Press, 2004.

Danielson, Charlotte, and Thomas L. McGreal, *Teacher Evaluation: To Enhance Professional Practice.* Princeton, New Jersey: Educational Testing Service, 2000.

Darling-Hammond, Linda, and Jason Millman, eds., *The New Handbook of Teacher Evaluation: Assessing Elementary and Secondary School Teachers.* Newbury Park, CA: Sage, 1990.

Dwyer, Carol Anne, "Psychometrics of Praxis III: Classroom Performance Assessments," *Journal of Personnel Evaluation in Education,* 12, no. 2 (June 1998), 163–187.

Educational Research Service Staff, *Teacher Evaluation: Practices and Procedures Report.* Arlington, VA: Educational Research Service, 1988.

Emley, Ken, and Howard Ebmeier, "The Effect of Employment Interview Format on Principals' Evaluations of Teachers," *Journal of Personnel Evaluation in Education,* 11, no. 1 (April 1997), 39–56.

Gleave, Doug, "Bifocals for Teacher Development and Appraisal," *Journal of Curriculum & Supervision,* 12, no. 3 (Spring 1997), 269–281.

Glickman, Carl D., Stephen P. Gordon, and Jovita M. Ross-Gordon, *SuperVision and Instructional Leadership: A Developmental Approach,* 6th ed. Boston: Allyn & Bacon, 2004.

Guskey, Thomas R., ed., *High Stakes Performance Assessment: Perspectives on Kentucky's Educational Reform.* Thousand Oaks, CA: Corwin Press, 1994.

Hinkin, T. R., and C. A. Schriesheim, "Relationships between Subordinate Perceptions of Supervisor Influence Tactics and Attributed Bases of Supervisory Power," *Human Relations,* 43 (1990), 221–237.

Joint Committee on Standards for Educational Evaluation, *The Personnel Evaluation Standards: How to Assess Systems for Evaluating Educators.* Newbury Park, CA: Sage, 1989.

Kelley, Carolyn, Herbert Heneman III, and Anthony Milanowski, "Teacher Motivation and School-based Performance Awards," *Educational Administration Quarterly,* XXXVIII, no. 3 (August 2002), 372–401.

Manning, Renfro C., *The Teacher Evaluation Handbook.* Englewood Cliffs, NJ: Prentice-Hall, 1989.

Margulus, Lisabeth S., and Jacquelyn Ann Melin, *Peformance Appraisals Made Easy: Tools for Evaluating Teachers and Support Staff.* Thousand Oaks, California: Corwin Press, 2004.

Matlock, John, "Solving the Problem of Problem Employees," *The Executive Educator,* 14, no. 10 (October 1992), 39–41.

Mayo, Renate Weidner, "Trends in Teacher Evaluation," *Clearing House,* 70, no. 5 (May–June 1997), 269–270.

Meyer, C., "What's the Difference between Authentic and Performance Assessment?," *Educational Leadership,* 49, no. 8 (1992), 39–41.

National Association of Elementary School Principals, *Effective Teachers: Effective Evaluation in America's Elementary and Middle Schools.* Alexandria, VA: The Association, 1988.

Oakley, Karla, "The Performance Assessment System: A Portfolio Assessment Model for Evaluating Beginning Teachers," *Journal of Personnel Evaluation in Education,* 11, no. 4 (March 1998), 323–341.

O'Neil, Riley, I., and David R. Adamson, "When Teachers Falter," *The Executive Educator,* 15, no. 1 (February 1993), 25–32.

Pekoe Jr., Lawrence C., "Expert Evaluation," *The Executive Educator,* 13, no. 10 (October 1991), 39–40.

Peterson, Kenneth D., *Teacher Evaluation: A Comprehensive Guide to New Directions and Practices.* Thousand Oaks, CA: Corwin Press, 1995.

Rossow, Lawrence F., and Jerry Parkinson, *The Law of Teacher Evaluation.* Topeka, KA: National Organization on Legal Problems of Education, 1991.

Santeusanio, Richard, "Improving Performance with 360-Degree Feedback," *Educational Leadership,* 55, no. 5 (February 1998), 30–32.

Stein, Andrea R., "The Supervision Quandary," *The Executive Educator,* 14, no. 4 (April 1992), 33–35.

Sternberg, Robert J., and Joseph A. Horvath, "A Prototype View of Expert Teaching," *Educational Research,* 24, no. 6 (August/September 1995), 9–17.

Strange, James H., *Evaluating Professional Support Personnel in Education.* Thousand Oaks, CA: Corwin Press, 1991.

Sullivan, Kathleen A., and Perry A. Zirkel, "The Law of Teacher Evaluation: Case Law Update," *Journal of Personnel Evaluation in Education,* 11, no. 4 (March 1998), 367–380.

Sullivan, Susan, and Jeffrey Glanz, *Supervision that Improves Teaching: Strategies and Techniques,* 2nd ed. Thousand Oaks, California: Corwin Press, 2004.

Swanson, David B., Geoffrey R. Norman, and Robert L. Linn, "Performance-Based Assessment: Lessons from the Health Professions," *Educational Research,* 24, no. 5 (June/July 1995), 5–11.

Timperley, Helen S., "Performance Appraisal: Principal's Perspectives and Some Implications," *Journal of Educational Administration,* 36, no. 1 (1998), 44–58.

VanSciver, James H., "Using Rubrics to Support the Teacher Appraisal Process," *ERS Spectrum,* 16, no. 3 (Summer 1998), 36–40.

Wiles, Jon W., *Supervision: A Guide to Practice,* 6th ed. Upper Saddle River, New Jersey: Merrill/Prentice Hall, 2004.

Appendix A
Teacher Evaluation Policies and Procedures*

Professional Evaluation

I. Philosophy and Policy. The performance of all certified personnel in the Valley Park School District shall be periodically evaluated. Evaluation shall be thorough, fair, and objective. It shall be designed to improve instruction and to assist the professional staff in the growth and development of professional abilities, as well as to identify areas of strengths and weakness.

II. Goals of Evaluation
   1. Improvement of instruction
   2. Fairness in tenure decisions
   3. Foster community relations
   4. Improvement in staff supervision
   5. Aid in gauging the quality of instruction
   6. Encourage professional improvement and growth through constant self-evaluation

III. Rules of Procedure
   1. The building principal or supervisor has the primary responsibility for evaluation and shall be responsible for making recommendations concerning teachers to the superintendent.
   2. The teacher has a responsibility for continuous self-appraisal in relation to his or her areas of professional competence through discussion with the principal or supervisor.
   3. Evaluation is always functioning. It will occur through teacher–principal contacts, classroom visitations, teacher meetings, casual informal contacts, etc. This should not constitute any threat to effective principal–teacher relationships; no teacher need feel that he or she must be on his or her guard, watch his or her step or be wary of confiding in his or her principal, because each individual must be evaluated for and on the basis of what he or she really is, and is really doing, not on the basis of how well he or she can conceal reality. The professional knows what he or she is doing and why. The professional should not only welcome evaluation but also should seek it out to guarantee and substantiate his or her own self-evaluation and to resolve differences if there are any discovered.
      a. Probationary teacher's formal evaluation shall occur at least three times each year. The first evaluation of probationary teachers will be completed by November 1, the second by January 15, the third by March 1.
      b. Permanent teacher's formal evaluation shall occur at least one time each year, before March 1.
   4. Minimum formal evaluation shall occur as follows:
      a. The evaluator will visit the teacher's classroom informally a number of times throughout the year.
      b. Each classroom visitation should be recorded and included in the teacher's evaluation file as a record.
      c. All conferences and recommendations to the teacher shall be recorded with copies to the teacher. Both teacher and evaluator will sign these reports.
      d. The teacher should take the initiative to request spot visits by the principal over and above those indicated whenever the teacher feels that it will assist the principal in the evaluative process.

Source: Adapted from *Professional Evaluation,* Valley Park School District, St. Louis County, Missouri, 1981.

e. The principal will maintain a cumulative evaluation file of all pertinent data relating to each teacher. This file shall be available for the teacher's examination and use.

f. Prior to the date of the formal evaluation report, the principal or supervisor will schedule a formal evaluative interview with each teacher.

g. In the evaluative interview the evaluator and teacher will discuss classroom visits and compare the completed instruments. Any significant differences should be thoroughly analyzed and resolved if possible.

h. In the case of traveling or special teachers each principal to whom the individual is assigned shall be responsible for at least one classroom visitation. Reports on this visit shall be discussed with the teacher and recorded. The formal evaluative conference will be conducted in the manner described above by each building principal. The final evaluative report and recommendation may be prepared either jointly or individually by the principals concerned.

i. The formal evaluation in March shall contain recommendations concerning reemployment and tenure.

j. If a teacher is not satisfied with a given evaluation, he or she may submit in writing to the superintendent a rebuttal, which will be reviewed and will be placed in the teacher's personnel folder. A copy of the rebuttal should be submitted to the building principal. A conference may be scheduled with the superintendent by the teacher to discuss the evaluation.

k. The individual teacher's evaluation file shall be open to no one except the teacher, administrative personnel, and the Board of Education meeting in executive session.

5. *Training of evaluators.* An inservice program for training of personnel responsible for evaluation will be provided. Provision will be made to have annual training sessions. In addition constant efforts are to be made by the school district personnel to keep current on methods of improvement of instruction, learning theories, and methods.

6. *Record keeping.* It shall be the responsibility of the human resources office to keep necessary records required by the tenure law and the teacher evaluation procedure. The superintendent will provide the principal with necessary information concerning the tenure law at the beginning of the school year. Other information will be provided as needed. All records concerning teacher evaluation are confidential records and should be dealt with accordingly.

7. Evaluation in each of the evaluative categories will be determined during the interview conference between the evaluator and the teacher. The composite evaluation will be determined in accordance with the explanation attached.

Personal Traits

- Maintains adequate physical vitality
- Is punctual
- Is well-groomed
- Maintains appropriate emotional control
- Is conscientious
- Fulfills responsibilities without constant supervision
- Makes practical commonsense judgments
- Uses tact
- Can act in original situations without directions
- Is cooperative and a good team worker
- Is receptive to constructive criticism and suggestion
- Is self-confident

- Is reasonable in self-evaluation
- Is able to meet people on a courteous level of mutual self-respect

Executive Traits and Classroom Management
- Completes necessary paper work promptly and accurately
- Arranges to have materials at hand when needed
- Evaluates materials and keeps only applicable materials to meet curriculum objectives
- Recognizes each student as an individual within the framework of the school program
- Assumes the responsibility for discipline unless unusual factors are involved
- Makes authority understood and accepted in a gracious manner
- Transmits enthusiasm for the subject
- Assumes responsibility for appropriate evaluation of assignments
- Maintains a neat, clean classroom conducive to learning
- Is willing to use professional resource people within the school system
- Is in control of classroom at all times

Teaching Power
- Selects and organizes material with definite objectives compatible with the curriculum guides that are adapted to pupil needs, interests and capacities
- Has prepared unit lesson plans based on specific objectives
- Is aware of the importance of proper motivation
- Uses student experiences to enrich and give meaning to content
- Uses a variety of techniques and innovations to reach desirable goals
- Uses student responses to aid his teaching
- Accepts his responsibility to improve attitudes, work habits, and skills
- Uses grammatically correct, precise English
- Uses a well-modulated voice
- Evaluates instruction regularly and reteaches when necessary
- Shows imagination in adapting materials for classroom use
- Displays materials that stimulate students' desire to learn
- Can present ideas in a clear and concise manner

Professional Responsibility
- Develops a relationship with students that is warm and inspiring, yet professional
- Adheres to the NEA *Code of Ethics of the Education Profession*
- Is proud to be a teacher and lets this pride show
- Supports the profession, regarding this as a privilege to be able to participate in activities that improve the profession
- Takes personal responsibility for individual professional growth
- Contributes to the advancement of education by working effectively on committees, by assuming individual responsibility for improvement of schools
- Understands and follows school policies and procedures
- Respects group decisions
- Respects and is discreet in using professional information
- Can explain an educational point of view clearly and convincingly

- Maintains a spirit of mutual respect in teacher–student, teacher–teacher, principal–teacher, and parent–teacher relationships

Scholarship
- Works to develop a mastery of his or her chosen field of specialization
- Maintains a continuing spirit of learning and understanding
- Knows the psychology of learning, learning theories, and is aware of new trends in the field
- Surveys recent educational periodicals and reads information pertinent to her or his work

Community Relations
- Is informed about local school problems
- Is aware of the strengths and the problems of the Valley Park School community
- Realizes that the adequate support of free public schools in the community is based on a general understanding of and respect for the educational program
- Speaks and acts in community contacts to promote the general understanding of and respect for the educational program, distinguishing between personal opinion and district policy

Explanation of Composite Evaluation for Use in the Valley Park School District

Professional Staff Evaluation

Superior An individual receiving this evaluation is truly outstanding. He or she meets all the criteria under each evaluative category.

Strong An individual receiving this evaluation is a very definite asset to the children of the school district. He or she meets a large majority of the criteria under each evaluative category and receives a similar composite rating. This person is expected to recognize his or her determined weaknesses and to compensate by exercising strengths. Weaknesses are corrected or minimized.

Average An individual receiving this evaluation is fulfilling assigned tasks at a satisfactory level. He or she meets a majority of the criteria under each evaluative category and receives a similar composite rating. This person will be expected to show an affinity for correcting or minimizing the obvious weaknesses isolated during the evaluative process.

Unsatisfactory An individual receiving this evaluation is not adequately fulfilling assigned tasks. He or she does not meet the criteria under each evaluative category deemed necessary for continued employment in the Valley Park School District.

No Data Information is not available or does not apply to the position.

Appendix B
Teacher Evaluation Report Forms
and Performance Indicators

LINDBERGH SCHOOL DISTRICT

4900 So. Lindbergh Blvd.
St. Louis, MO 63126

TEACHER EVALUATION REPORT

Teacher _____ School _____ Year _____
Subject or grade _____ Years in system _____
Status of Teacher   ( ) Probationary   ( ) Tenured

Philosophy   Evaluation is a means of improving the quality of instruction.

Purposes

1. To improve the quality of teaching and service to students
2. To enable the teacher to recognize her/his role in the total school program
3. To assist the teacher in achieving the established goals of the curriculum
4. To help the teacher identify her/his strengths and weaknesses as a personal guide for her/his improvement
5. To provide assistance to the teacher to help correct weaknesses
6. To recognize the teacher's special talents and to encourage and facilitate their utilization
7. To serve as a guide for renewed employment, termination of employment, promotion, assignment, and unrequested leave for tenured teachers
8. To protect the teacher from dismissal without just cause
9. To protect the teaching profession from unethical and incompetent personnel

Implementation

The evaluation is to be made by the building principal, grade principal, assistant principal, or acting principal. If a teacher does not agree with an evaluation, she/he may request an additional evaluation to be made by another administrator of her/his choice.

Evaluation of a probationary (nontenured) teacher's services will be made semi-annually during the probationary period, with one of the evaluations completed during the first semester, and both completed before April 1. Each evaluation must be preceded by at least one classroom visit.

Evaluation of a permanent (tenured) teacher's services will be made every year with the evaluation completed before April 1. Each evaluation must be preceded by at least one classroom visit.

Source: Adapted from Lindbergh School District, St. Louis, Missouri, 1985.

Definition of terms

1. *Superior:* Consistently exceptional
2. *Strong:* Usually surpasses standards of Lindbergh School District
3. *Average:* Generally meets standards of Lindbergh School District
4. *Improvement needed:* Occasionally does not meet standards of Lindbergh School District
5. *Unsatisfactory:* Does not measure up to standards of Lindbergh School District

NOTE: The space at the end of this form marked "Principal's Comments" may be utilized to record the observations of the teacher's exceptional performances and/or to record the principal's recommendations for improvement.

The space at the end of this form marked "Teacher's Comments" may be utilized by the teacher to record any comment or comments which she/he wishes to make.

	Superior	Strong	Average	I-N	Unsatis-factory
I. TEACHING PERFORMANCE	1	2	3	4	5
A. Plans and organizes carefully					
1. Lesson is well planned					
2. Sets definite goals including student participation					
3. Makes clear, specific assignments					
4. Is familiar with appropriate guide and adapts to the recommendations therein					
5. Provides for individual and group instruction					
B. Is skillful in questioning and explaining					
1. Asks thought-provoking questions					
2. Gives clear explanation of subject matter					
3. Exposes students to varying points of view					
4. Is aware of both verbal and nonverbal acceptance or rejection of student's ideas, and uses this skill positively					
C. Stimulates learning through innovative activities and resources					
1. Encourages class discussion, pupil questions and pupil demonstrations					
2. Uses a variety of teaching aids and resources					
D. Displays knowledge of and enthusiasm for subject matter taught					
E. Provides a classroom atmosphere conducive to good learning					
1. Maintains a healthy and flexible environment					
2. Observes the care of instructional material and equipment					

Continued

	Superior	Strong	Average	I-N	Unsatis-factory
F. Keeps adequate and accurate records					
1. Records sufficient quantitative and qualitative data on which to base pupil progress reports					
G. Has wholesome relationship with pupils					
1. Knows and works with pupils as individuals					
2. Encourages relationships that are mutually respectful and friendly					
3. Uses positive language with students that is devoid of sarcasm					
H. Initiates and preserves classroom and general school management and discipline					
1. Rules of pupil conduct have been developed and teacher requires observance of these rules					
2. Rules of safety have been developed and teacher requires observance of these rules					

II. PROFESSIONAL QUALITIES

	Superior	Strong	Average	I-N	Unsatis-factory
A. Recognition and acceptance of out-of-class responsibilities					
1. Participates in the general and necessary school activities					
2. Sometimes volunteers for the "extra" duties					
3. Serves on school committees					
B. Intraschool relationship					
1. Cooperates effectively and pleasantly with colleagues, administration and nonprofessional personnel					
C. Public relations					
1. Cooperates effectively and pleasantly with parents					
2. Practices good relationships between school and community					
D. Professional growth and vision					
1. Accepts constructive criticism					
2. Participates in conferences, workshops, and study					
3. Tries new methods and materials					
E. Utilization of staff services					
1. Makes proper use of available special services					
F. Understands the growth patterns and behaviors of students at various stages of development and copes satisfactorily with situations as they occur					
G. Ethical behavior					
1. Protects professional use of confidential data					

DEFINITION OF TERMS FOR PERSONAL QUALITIES

S *Satisfactory:* Meets or surpasses standard for Lindbergh School District teachers.

I *Improvement needed:* Does not measure up to standards Lindbergh School District teachers meet.

III. PERSONAL QUALITIES

	S	I

A. Health and vigor
 1. Has a good and reasonable attendance record
 2. Is cheerful
 3. Displays a sense of humor

B. Speech
 1. Is articulate
 2. Can be heard and understood by all pupils in the room
 3. Speaks on the level of pupils' understanding

C. Grooming and appropriateness of dress
 1. Practices habits of good grooming

D. Promptness in meeting obligations
 1. Reports to classes on time
 2. Performs assigned tasks properly
 3. Completes reports on time

A copy of the written evaluation will be submitted to the teacher at the time of the conference following the observation(s). The final evaluation report form is to be signed and retained by the principal, and a copy is to be retained by the teacher. In the event the teacher feels the evaluation was incomplete, inaccurate, or unjust, she/he may put the objections in writing and have them attached to the evaluation report to be placed in her/his personal files. Teacher's signature acknowledges that the conference has taken place.

DATE OF OBSERVATION(S) _____

TIME OF OBSERVATION(S) _____

LENGTH OF OBSERVATION(S) _____

DATE OF EVALUATION _____

PRINCIPAL'S SIGNATURE _____

TEACHER'S SIGNATURE _____

PRINCIPAL'S COMMENTS

TEACHER COMMENTS

Performance Indicators

Indicators for the evaluation items in the Teacher Evaluation Report were developed by the administrators in the Lindbergh School District. The indicators are representative of the kinds of teacher-learning techniques the evaluator will be looking for when observing a teacher in a classroom situation. It is expected that each teacher will perform the skill as listed, but that the final evaluation will be based on the degree of performance.

I. TEACHING PERFORMANCE
   A. *Plans and organizes carefully*
      1. *Lesson is well planned*
         a. Written plans are available and followed by classroom teacher.
         b. Lesson includes preview, statement of objective, and review.
         c. Lesson fits within an alloted time frame.
         d. Lesson follows a logical sequence.
         e. Lesson meets the needs of the student group.
         f. Long- and short-range goals are clearly defined.
         g. Lesson indicates the teacher has used the concept of diagnosis and prescription.
         h. Lesson is flexible to permit spontaneous teaching.
         i. Plans and procedures are provided.
         j. Materials and equipment are readily available.
      2. *Sets definite goals including student participation*
         a. Long- and short-range goals are clearly defined.
         b. Students are involved in the goal-setting process when appropriate.
      3. *Makes clear, specific assignments*
         a. Reasonable and clear assignments are given in written form.
         b. Adequate time is given for clarification and discussion of assignment.
      4. *Is familiar with appropriate guide and adapts to the recommendation therein*
         a. Lesson reflects thorough knowledge of curriculum guide.
         b. Long-range planning for coverage of objectives in curriculum guide is indicated.
      5. *Provides for individual and group instruction*
         a. Lesson provides for individual instruction.
         b. Lesson provides for group instruction.
         c. Type of instruction is suited to lesson presented.
   B. *Is skillful in questioning and explaining*
      1. *Asks thought-provoking questions*
         a. Asks questions requiring more than a one-word answer.
         b. Questions stimulate critical and divergent thinking.
         c. Written questions are thought provoking.
         d. Questions asked stimulate a response from students.
      2. *Gives clear explanation of subject matter*
         a. Obtains response indicating understanding before continuing further explanation.
         b. Presents ideas in a logical sequence.
         c. Consistently uses correct grammar and vocabulary suited to student.
         d. Presents accurate and complete content information.
      3. *Exposes students to varying points of view*
         a. Establishes a background of general information on the topic before presenting varying points of view.

      b. Presents varying points of view consistent with curriculum.

      c. Elicits from students their points of view.

    4. *Is aware of both verbal and nonverbal acceptance or rejection of students' ideas, and uses this skill positively*

      a. Does not show rejection through verbal or physical expression.

      b. Does not allow peer-rejection.

      c. Praises, elicits, and responds to student questions and answers before proceeding.

C. *Stimulates learning through innovative activities and resources*

    1. *Encourages class discussion, pupil questions, and pupil demonstrations*

      a. Listens patiently to students' comments, questions, and answers.

      b. Questions are asked according to students' ability to answer correctly.

      c. Gives each student an opportunity to participate.

    2. *Uses a variety of teaching aids and resources*

      a. Looks for and uses models, manipulative materials, films, outside speeches, worksheets, records, etc.

      b. Materials and resources are appropriate for the lesson.

      c. Displays materials that are coordinated with the lesson.

D. *Displays knowledge of and enthusiasm for subject matter taught*

    1. *Displays knowledge of subject matter taught*

      a. Displays knowledge of content of textbook(s).

      b. Demonstrates competence and familiarity with subject matter.

      c. Has comprehensive knowledge of related disciplines and uses it when appropriate.

      d. Answers students' questions readily and thoroughly.

      e. Probes for knowledge of content presented (encourages questions and activities that are designed to stimulate critical thinking).

      f. Goes beyond the textbook to enhance the content (may be observed by use of films, resource persons, reference materials, charts, etc.).

    2. *Enthusiasm*

      a. Students respond positively to the teacher (Do the students appear interested? Are they listening to the teacher? Are they awake? Are they talking to other students? Do they appear bored?).

      b. Interest and enthusiasm are evidenced from the teacher's presentation.

      c. Responds positively to the students, both verbally and visually.

      d. Elicits enthusiastic response from the students to the questions and answers.

      e. Uses techniques that engender enthusiasm in students (a change of pace, voice inflections, body movement).

E. *Provides a classroom atmosphere conducive to good learning*

    1. *Maintains a healthy and flexible environment*

      a. Sets the tone for students to feel free to ask and to respond to questions (students are not intimidated).

      b. Classroom atmosphere is controlled but not dominated by the teacher (students interact with the environment).

      c. Differing views and values are allowed to be discussed.

      d. Positive interpersonal relationships are easily observed.

      e. Uses humor in proper perspective.

      f. Room reflects students' work.

    2. *Observes the care of instructional material and equipment*

      a. Equipment in use is carefully supervised.

      b. Equipment or material not in use is properly stored.

    c. Equipment is properly maintained and/or reported to the office for repair.

    d. Desks are devoid of writing and graffiti.

    e. Promotes respect for instructional materials and equipment.

F. *Keeps adequate and accurate records*

  1. *Records sufficient quantitative and qualitative data on which to base pupil progress reports*

    a. Records a number of written assignments, test scores, daily grades, and exam grades in the grade book (indicators of each student's performance).

    b. Quality of data recorded shows relationship between the objectives and grades.

    c. Daily attendance is correctly recorded.

G. *Has wholesome relationship with pupils*

  1. *Knows and works with pupils as individuals*

    a. Individual strengths and weaknesses of each student have been identified.

    b. Knows and calls each student by name.

    c. Listens carefully and politely to each student.

    d. Encourages student ideas and concentrates on their response.

    e. Students do not hesitate to ask for clarification.

    f. Students appear to be an active part of the class.

    g. Creative responses are encouraged.

  2. *Encourages relationships that are mutually respectful and friendly*

    a. Encourages positive behavior by maintaining complete control of self.

    b. Words and actions are positive.

    c. Exhibits qualities of warmth toward students.

    d. Elicits student responses.

    e. Sets an example of respect.

    f. Is sensitive to students' moods.

    g. Behavior is consistent with all students and situations.

    h. Handling of misconduct centers on the conduct or behavior, not the student.

    i. Requires student attention and gives attention in return.

  3. *Uses positive language with students that is devoid of sarcasm*

    a. Praises and elicits responses from students.

    b. Sarcasm is not used.

    c. Is positive in actions, voice tones, and movements.

    d. Tone of voice is moderate and even.

H. *Initiates and preserves classroom and general school management and discipline*

  1. *Rules of pupil conduct have been developed and teacher requires observance of these rules*

    a. Classroom incidents handled so as not to interrupt entire class.

    b. Pupils are aware of rules and regulations.

    c. Students understand and follow room routine readily without teacher's direction.

    d. Demonstrates behavior that is achievement oriented or businesslike.

    e. Is consistent and fair in expectations of behavior.

    f. Students enter room quietly and take seats.

    g. Students ask and receive permission to change patterns.

  2. *Rules of safety have been developed and teacher requires observance of these rules*

    a. Classroom behavior shows a concern for safety.

    b. Safety procedures are properly posted and followed.

    c. Horseplay is not tolerated.

    d. Plays an active and positive role in the supervision of halls, restrooms, lunchrooms, and pre/post class time as well as at assemblies.

    e. Classroom is free of hazards.

II. PROFESSIONAL QUALITIES
   A. *Recognition and acceptance of out-of-class responsibilities*
      1. *Participates in the general and necessary school activities*
         a. Performs assigned duties consistently.
         b. Follows the school time schedule.
         c. Attends and participates in school-related activities.
         d. Participates in assigned meetings.
      2. *Sometimes volunteers for the "extra" duties*
         a. Accepts responsibilities other than those considered general or necessary.
         b. Initiates volunteer services to the overall school program.
      3. *Serves on school committees*
         a. Serves on district and/or school committees.
         b. Attends school and/or district committee meetings.
         c. Participates in school and/or district level committees.
   B. *Intraschool relationship*
      1. *Cooperates effectively and pleasantly with colleagues, administration, and nonprofessional personnel*
         a. Relationships with other professionals indicate acceptance of differing views or values.
         b. Practices relationships that are mutually respectful and friendly.
         c. Shares ideas, materials, and methods.
         d. Informs appropriate personnel of school-related matters.
         e. Cooperates fairly and works well with all school personnel.
         f. Is effective in providing a climate that encourages communication between self and professional colleagues.
   C. *Public relations*
      1. *Cooperates effectively and pleasantly with parents*
         a. Maintains good communication with parents.
         b. Keeps best interest of student in mind.
         c. Provides a climate that opens up communication between the teacher and parent.
      2. *Practices good relationship between school and community*
         a. Enhances school involvement with communities.
         b. Encourages community involvement and attendance in school situations.
   D. *Professional growth and vision*
      1. *Accepts constructive criticism*
         a. Asks positive questions.
         b. Responds pleasantly to criticism.
      2. *Participates in conferences, workshops, and studies*
         a. Is engaged in activities that promote professional growth.
         b. Engages in professional activities that are not required.
      3. *Tries new methods and materials*
         a. Uses new methods and materials at appropriate times.
         b. Modifies materials when needed.
         c. Understands new techniques before using.
   E. *Utilization of staff services*
      1. *Makes proper use of available special services*
         a. Makes use of and cooperates with district service personnel (guidance, library, supervisory, specialists, as well as classified staff members).
         b. Makes student recommendations and referrals to appropriate staff members as needed.

F. *Understands the growth patterns and behaviors of students at various stages of development and copes satisfactorily with situations as they occur*
   a. Uses a variety of techniques to achieve desired work and skills, and adjusts the techniques to the age and maturity of the student.
   b. Does not expect identical behavior from all students, but allows for individual differences.
   c. Is understanding and sympathetic to students with special learning and behavior problems.

G. *Ethical behavior*
   1. *Protects professional use of confidential data*
      a. Confidential information concerning students and their parents and staff members is not discussed in the lounge, cafeteria, or in the classroom.
      b. Respects confidential information.
   2. *Supports the teaching profession*
      a. Has a positive attitude toward teaching.
      b. Uses positive statements regarding teaching, students, school, and profession.

III. PERSONAL QUALITIES
   A. *Health and vigor*
      1. *Has a good and reasonable attendance record*
         a. Absences are infrequent and justifiable.
         b. Places emphasis on assigned duties.
         c. Except in cases of extreme illness, is present at school and is prepared.
      2. *Is cheerful*
         a. Allows occasional humorous interruptions.
         b. Can relax and joke with students.
         c. Laughs with, not at, others.
      3. *Displays a sense of humor*
         a. Smiles easily.
         b. Has a friendly attitude.
   B. *Speech*
      1. *Is articulate*
         a. Consistently uses appropriate grammar.
         b. Communicates clearly.
      2. *Can be heard and understood by all pupils in the room*
         a. Consistently uses appropriate tone of voice.
         b. Is easy to hear and understand.
      3. *Speaks on the level of pupils' understanding*
         a. Uses appropriate vocabulary and examples according to student's level of understanding.
   C. *Grooming and appropriateness of dress*
      1. *Practices habits of good grooming*
         a. Is clean and neat.
         b. Clothes are appropriate for job task.
         c. Dress adds to rather than detracts from classroom performance.
   D. *Promptness in meeting obligations*
      1. *Reports to classes on time*
         a. Arrives at classroom before students.
         b. Classroom is open and in readiness prior to student arrival.

   c. Classroom preparations do not interfere with obligations.
   d. Arrives in the building at the required time.
2. *Performs assigned tasks properly*
   a. Tasks are completed on time.
   b. Tasks are completed to letter and in spirit of the assignment.
3. *Completes reports on time*
   a. Does not have to be reminded of reports that are due.
   b. Completes reports according to expectations of administrator.

LINDBERGH SCHOOL DISTRICT

4900 So. Lindbergh Blvd.
St. Louis, MO 63126

SHORT CLASSROOM VISIT FORM

The purpose of this form is to record data that will be pertinent in the overall evaluation of the teacher. The form will be used in conjunction with the Teacher Evaluation Report.

TEACHER _____ DATE OF VISIT _____
LENGTH OF VISIT _____ PERIOD _____

1. Did the lesson appear to be well planned? _____
   Topic being discussed _____
2. Was enthusiasm evidenced in the teacher's presentation? _____
   _____
3. Class reaction to the lesson _____
   Were the students involved? _____ Did they appear to be interested in the lesson?
   _____
4. Describe the type of interactions between the teacher and students, and students with students _____
5. Was there any unusual activity taking place? _____
6. Was there anything unusual about the physical appearance of the room? _____
   _____
7. Were personal qualities positive? _____
   _____

                              (speech, dress, grooming)

Principal's suggestions, comments _____
   _____
   _____

                              _____
                              Principal's Signature

Appendix C
Administrator Evaluation Report

Administrator Evaluation Report

ADMINISTRATOR _____ YEAR _____

POSITION _____ SCHOOL _____

YEARS IN LINDBERGH ADMINISTRATION _____

Purposes

Evaluation is to ensure that the administrator displays adequate management skills and leadership among the students, staff, and community. The evaluation process will ensure that the administrator has goals appropriate to his or her level of responsibility and in line with overall school system goals. This process will aid the administrator in the improvement of his or her performance and provide a basis for merit pay adjustment.

Implementation

1. The Superintendent will evaluate all building principals.
2. Evaluation of grade principals and assistant principals will be made by the building principal. The Superintendent will review these evaluations and confer with the principal prior to the formal evaluation.
3. The Evaluator will receive appropriate input from all Central Office Administrators prior to completing the evaluation.
4. Administrators will be evaluated on the standards and expectations of Lindbergh School District.
5. The evaluation will be made on a scale of one to nine ranging from improvement needed to consistently outstanding.
6. The overall rating will not be adversely affected by items marked not applicable.
7. The formal evaluation will take place following the close of the school year.

ADMINISTRATIVE SKILLS	Consistently Outstanding							Needs Improvement	NA
1. Has implemented procedures for budget preparation and accounting methods for monitoring the budget									
2. Has implemented a plan for the effective cleaning and maintenance of the facility									
3. Has implemented a process for inventorying, acquiring, and replacing of equipment									
4. Has implemented safety and energy conservation procedures									
5. Has established procedures for the use of student, teacher, and parent feedback									

Source: Adapted from Lindbergh School District, St. Louis, Missouri, 1985.

ADMINISTRATIVE SKILLS	Consistently Outstanding							Needs Improvement	NA
6. Has developed and follows procedures for administrative scheduling and reporting									
7. Has completed written communications accurately and on schedule									

Total points _____ ÷ _____ number of items marked = _____ average marking.

INSTRUCTIONAL LEADERSHIP	Consistently Outstanding							Needs Improvement	NA
1. Has demonstrated knowledge of curricular issues in various subject areas									
2. Has assisted classroom teacher in the implementation of the curriculum									
3. Has evaluated the instructional program and used the results to plan program improvements									
4. Has knowledge of good teaching methods and assists teachers to improve diagnostic skills and teaching strategies									
5. Has carried out procedures to evaluate and maintain a building climate conducive to learning									

Total points _____ ÷ _____ number of items marked = _____ average marking.

SUPERVISION	Consistently Outstanding							Needs Improvement	NA
1. Has coordinated the work of special and support personnel with the programs of the school									
2. Has conducted a program of faculty and staff supervision that includes periodic visits, conferences and evaluation of all personnel									
3. Has carried out a procedure for the orientation and supervision of all new personnel									

Continued

SUPERVISION	Consistently Outstanding						Needs Improvement	NA
4. Has developed and implemented procedures to maintain effective school discipline								
5. Has maintained a system of supervision of all after school activities								

Total points _____ ÷ _____ number of items marked = _____ average marking.

SCHOOL AND COMMUNITY	Consistently Outstanding						Needs Improvement	NA
1. Has promoted good relationships between the school and community through positive interpretation and implementation of district policy								
2. Has conducted a comprehensive and effective system of communication with the students of the school								
3. Has conducted a comprehensive and effective system of communication with the parents of the school								
4. Has coordinated and maintained a volunteer program in the school								
5. Has participated in various civic, service, and community groups and community functions to help assure public knowledge and understanding of the school program								
6. Has provided support and guidance to P.T.O., Mothers' Club, and other parent groups								

Total points _____ ÷ _____ number of items marked = _____ average marking.

PERSONAL QUALITIES	Consistently Outstanding						Needs Improvement	NA
1. Has exhibited professional growth through staff development activities, conferences and conventions, membership in and participation in professional organizations, and continuing formal education.								
2. Has displayed appropriate decision-making skills by recognizing problems, evaluating facts, and implementing decisions								

PERSONAL QUALITIES

	Consistently Outstanding							Needs Improvement	NA
3. Has displayed good personal relationships with administration, faculty, staff, parents, and students									
4. Has evidenced personal and professional ethics in all relationships									
5. Has shown sustained effort and enthusiasm in the quality and quantity of work accomplished									

Total points _____ ÷ _____ number of items marked = _____ average marking.

Building Priorities

Each building priority is rated separately on a combination of the following criteria:

1. Building priorities are identified with input from teachers, students, and/or parents.
2. The design to meet each priority is clearly written with definitive steps and a timetable.
3. Periodic review of progress toward accomplishing each priority is carried out, and necessary adjustments are made during the year.

	Consistently Outstanding						Needs Improvement	NA
Priority I								
Priority II								
Priority III								
Priority IV								
Priority V								
Priority VI								
Priority VII								

Total points _____ ÷ _____ number of items marked = _____ average marking.

4. Accomplishment of building priorities involves participation and input from the school faculty and other affected groups when appropriate.
5. Each priority is completed according to the timetable and definitive steps in the original written design. Deviations from that design are stated and explained.

Rating System

1. The *average marking* in each category is multiplied by the percentage weight given that area.
2. The weighted scores for each area are added. The sum will fall in a range from one to nine. The total score will be carried out to the third decimal place.
3. The sum of the weighted scores is applied directly to the merit portion of the administrators' salary schedule.

Continued

	Average Marking		Percentage Weight	Weighted Score
Administrative Skills	_____	×	.10	_____
Instructional Leadership	_____	×	.20	_____
Supervision	_____	×	.20	_____
School and Community	_____	×	.10	_____
Personal Qualities	_____	×	.10	_____
Building Priorities	_____	×	.30	_____
			Total	_____

EVALUATOR'S COMMENTS:

ADMINISTRATOR'S COMMENTS:

Evaluator's Signature _____ Date _____
Administrator's Signature _____ Date _____

Appendix D
Rating Scale to Evaluate Administrator Performance

RATING SHEET
Administrator Evaluation Form

Instructions: Place an X on numbered line for each item. Leave item blank if you have no opinion.

	Negative						Positive
	1	2	3	4	5	6	7
1. Maintains an open, positive working relationship with							
A. Parents							
B. Staff							
C. Pupils							
D. Nonteaching staff							
E. Other administrators							
2. Is supportive of the classroom concerns of teachers							

Source: Adapted from Thomas S. Butera, "Principal, Know Thyself," *NASSP Bulletin,* 60 (September 1976), 85.

	Negative					Positive	
	1	2	3	4	5	6	7
3. Is understanding of the personal concerns of teachers							
4. Takes definite steps to aid teachers' professional growth							
5. Evaluates teachers in objective manner							
6. Takes time to praise teachers							
7. Is open to suggestions and ideas							
8. Allows teachers to try new ideas							
9. Encourages new ideas							
10. Is able to mediate differences among staff							
11. Plans and executes inservice programs for staff							
12. Displays knowledge of curriculum							
13. Displays knowledge of new methods and materials							
14. Displays knowledge of budget and business procedures							
15. Delegates work to right people							
16. Helps establish a positive guiding climate							
17. Helps create and maintain high morale							
18. Is flexible							
19. Has knowledge of characteristics of this age group student							
20. Has general knowledge of the students in this building							
21. Treats students with respect							
22. Helps develop student control and responsible discipline							
23. Is aware of "what's going on" in building							
24. Makes commitments to educational beliefs							
25. Is respected by staff							
26. Is respected by students							
27. Availability							
28. Personality							
29. Appearance							
30. Visibility							

Using the items listed above as a guide, please use the remaining portion of this form to make any suggestions you feel would aid in improving this administrator's performance. You might indicate what you feel are some strong assets and then some areas that need improvement.

Appendix E
Performance Appraisal—Custodial, Landscape, Maintenance*

Employee's Name _____

Position _____

Location _____ School Year _____

Instructions

The Supervisor is to complete this form by placing the number of the rating on each item in the space provided. If an item is rated 1 or 2 then a statement is to be written in the comment area clarifying what needs to be done to improve. A form is to be completed at the end of three months on new employees and a second evaluation is to be completed by June 1 of each year. One copy of the form is to be given to the employee and a second copy is to be sent to the Personnel Department to be placed in the employee's file.

I. *Quality of Work*   Rating _____
    Indicators: Neatness, accuracy, consistency of quality.
    5. Exceptionally neat and accurate. Practically no mistakes.
    4. Usually accurate. Very neat. Seldom necessary to check work.
    3. Acceptable. Usually neat. Occasional errors—some supervision required.
    2. Acceptable work if closely supervised.
    1. Unacceptable work. Too many errors.

    Comment: _____
    _____

II. *Job Knowledge*   Rating _____
    Indicators: Experience, special training, education.
    5. Well informed on all phases of the job.
    4. Knowledge is thorough enough to perform without assistance.
    3. Knows job fairly well.
    2. Requires assistance frequently.
    1. Inadequate knowledge.

    Comment: _____
    _____

III. *Quantity of Work*   Rating _____
    Indicators: Amount of work required under normal conditions.
    5. Exceptional quantity. Rapid worker. Usually good production.
    4. Good volume—will do more than is expected.
    3. Average volume—does what is expected.
    2. Does not always complete expected amount of work.
    1. Slow worker. Frequently does not complete duties.

    Comment: _____
    _____

Source: Adapted from Lindbergh School District, St. Louis, Missouri, 1985.

IV. *Dependability*   Rating _____
     Indicators: Tasks are completed on time.
     5. Work is always completed on time.
     4. Work is almost always completed on time.
     3. Work is usually completed on time.
     2. Work is completed on time only under close supervision.
     1. Work is rarely completed on time.

     Comment: _____
     _____

V. *Initiative*   Rating _____
     Indicators: Develops new ideas, develops efficient ways of doing jobs, takes charge
     when something needs to be done, is self-reliant.
     5. Highly motivated and contributes new ideas frequently. Does other jobs without
        being told.
     4. Very resourceful. Can work on own. Occasionally contributes new ideas and
        methods. Does small jobs without being told.
     3. Does job very well. Will do other jobs when told to.
     2. Rarely volunteers to help in other areas. Usually waits for instructions.
     1. Needs constant supervision. Not motivated. Displays little interest in improving.
        Does only what is told to do.

     Comment: _____
     _____

VI. *Cooperation and Relationship with Others*   Rating _____
     Indicators: How employee works with coworkers, supervisors, subordinates,
     parents, teachers, students, visitors.
     5. Goes out of the way to cooperate with others. Always has a positive attitude.
        Takes and gives instructions easily.
     4. Gets along well with others. Does not complain about others. Good attitude.
     3. Satisfactory relationship with others and only occasionally complains.
     2. Shows reluctance to cooperate and complains often.
     1. Very poor cooperation. Does not follow instructions. Complains often.

     Comment: _____
     _____

VII. *Ability to Learn*   Rating _____
     Indicators: Speed of understanding new routines, ability to understand explanations,
     how well instructions are carried out, ability to retain knowledge.
     5. Exceptional ability to learn assigned work and adjust to new conditions.
     4. Learns rapidly. Follows instructions well. Retains instructions.
     3. Usually understands instructions and masters new ideas reasonably well.
     2. Requires extra instruction. Necessary to repeat instructions.
     1. Very slow to understand instructions. Cannot remember instructions. Very slow
        to master new ideas.

     Comment: _____
     _____

Continued

VIII. *Attendance*   Rating _____
       Indicators: Number of days of absenteeism, number of tardies (consider the reasons
       for absenteeisms).
       5. Less than three days absent and less than three days tardy.
       4. Three or four days absent and less than three days tardy.
       3. Five or six days absent and less than five days tardy.
       2. Seven or eight days absent and less than seven days tardy.
       1. Nine or more days absent and more than six days tardy.

       Comment: _____
       _____

 IX. *Appearance*   Rating _____
       Indicators: Cleanliness, appropriate dress (uniforms where applicable).
       5. Always neat and clean and appropriately dressed.
       4. Almost always neat and clean and appropriately dressed.
       3. Usually neat and clean and appropriately dressed.
       2. Usually neat and clean but not appropriately dressed.
       1. Often not neat and clean and often carelessly dressed.

       Comment: _____
       _____

Directions for Overall Evaluation

   1. Add the ratings for all nine categories   _____
   2. Divide by nine   _____
   3. Circle the category that corresponds to the average.

                         4.6–5.0   Doing an excellent job.
                         3.6–4.5   Doing a very good job.
                         2.6–3.5   Doing a satisfactory job.
                         1.6–2.5   Work needs to be improved.
                         1.0–1.5   Work is unacceptable.

Employee Comments: _____
_____
_____
_____
_____

_____   _____
Signature of Supervisor   Signature of Employee

_____   _____
Date   Date

Employee's signature indicates the employee has had this form reviewed with him/her. The
signature does not indicate agreement. An employee may appeal the decision of the supervisor to the next line supervisor. The decision of the superintendent is final.

Compensation

Before engaging in any activity, every human being consciously or subconsciously asks the same question, "What will I get out of this?" Psychologists have recognized for a long time that satisfaction of needs is the motivation behind all actions. This satisfaction or reward might be money, a promotion, recognition, acceptance, receipt of information, or the feeling that comes from doing a good job.[1]

This self-interest motive often carries a negative connotation, yet it is a reality of life. People act in ways that they perceive to be in their own best interests. Whether a given act is truly in an individual's best interest is irrelevant; what counts is that he or she believes it to be so. Even if an action appears to be irrational, such as handing in a resignation because of a minor misunderstanding at work, to the individual resigning, the act may be totally in keeping with what he or she believes to be in his or her best interest.

From an administrative standpoint, managers can develop a unique compensation system if they understand what their employees believe to be in their best interest. Not all individuals value the same type of compensation. Consequently, a compensation program must be flexible enough to meet the expectations of individual employees. It is also necessary to structure a compensation program in such a way that people realize they are acting in their own best interest when they are acting in the best interest of the school district. This exemplifies the importance of compensation in an "expectancy model." As a result of this model, several things become clear.[2]

1. Compensation must be linked to behaviors that the school system classifies as desirable.

2. The employee should recognize that good job performance is compatible with self-interest.

3. Employees should recognize that the compensation system also will satisfy their own needs.

4. Administrators must analyze and interpret the needs of the employees.

---

[1] Pamela Babcock, "Find What Workers Want," *HR Magazine,* 50, no. 4 (April 2005), 50–57.

[2] Stephen P. Robbins, *Personnel: The Management of Human Resources,* 2nd ed. (Englewood Cliffs, NJ: Prentice-Hall, 1982), 349. (Some major concepts elucidated in this chapter have also been patterned after Robbins' work, 349–387.)

The fourth statement requires further explanation. In recommending that administrators analyze and interpret employees' needs, the major question that arises is how this can best be accomplished.

The most obvious way of learning about an individual's needs is to ask the person. However, some people do not always understand their own needs and self-interests; others find it difficult to put such needs into words. The most immediate way for an administrator to learn about employees' needs is to observe and develop an awareness of employee behaviors. Behavior is usually a stronger indicator than the verbal utterances of employees. Unfortunately, developing skill in interpreting behavior takes time and practice. The only reliable method of determining needs is through social scientific research aimed at determining patterns of needs, quantified and analyzed through statistical applications. A number of consulting firms are capable of providing this service, and some packaged programs are available that can be administered by staff employees.

Variables Affecting Compensation

The main purpose for establishing a compensation policy is to attract and retain qualified employees who will provide the type of service expected by the public. It is essential that employees understand the compensation structure and have confidence in the objectivity by which the system is implemented. Five major variables must be taken into consideration by the administration in constructing and recommending a compensation policy to the board of education for approval: performance, effort, seniority, skills, and job requirements. It is not important how appropriations are allocated for the compensation system; whether through board approval of the budget or collectively negotiated with employee unions, these variables are necessary to the policy.

Performance

The evaluation of performance is concerned with a basic question, Did you get the job done? Compensating individuals requires criteria that define performance. The task of constructing valid and reliable criteria for evaluating performance was treated in Chapter 7. The importance of using performance as a basis for compensating employees is critical to all effective compensation systems.

Effort

School districts have required teachers to consider the effort put forth by students as a determinant in evaluating student performance. Even if effort does not directly influence a grade, some method is usually employed to indicate whether a given student is putting forth his or her best effort. It is ironic, therefore, that school districts have long neglected using the degree of effort put forth by employees as a component in their compensation systems. Yet, without such an orientation, a school district will fall prey to compensating quantity rather than quality and the end rather than the means. Also, there are some situations in which an outcome is difficult to evaluate and effort becomes a primary determinant of compensation. One such instance is cited by Stephen Robbins. A major eastern university was attempting to increase its research efforts and had designated the objective of obtaining grants or funded research as a critical benchmark towards that end. All faculty members were informed that compensation for the coming year would be based on performance in obtaining grants. Approximately 20 percent of the faculty made grant applications; however, after the first year of the program, none were approved. When the time came for performance evaluation and the distribution of salary increases, the dean chose to give the majority of the funds available for pay raises to those faculty members who had applied for grants. Performance, defined in terms of obtaining funded research grants, was zero, so the dean chose to allocate salary increases based on effort.[3]

This discussion is obviously concerned with a topic much debated in education: performance incentives. There is no one best method for rewarding performance with money; however, the following comments will help to clarify this issue.

A performance incentives system will be ineffective unless it has the following components:

1. Effective teacher evaluation procedures
2. Training programs for management and supervisory personnel who will implement the plan
3. School board and management commitment to the plan in time and resources
4. Staff involvement in developing the program
5. Teacher acceptance and satisfaction
6. Adequate financing
7. Merit pay for all who meet the criteria
8. Plausible, fair, and equitable performance criteria
9. Valid and verifiable measures of results
10. Objectivity and consistency in applying assessment measures
11. Increased student learning promoted[4]

Seniority

Length of time in a particular position plays a significant role in compensation systems in the public sector. The civil service system of the United States is the best example of how seniority operates in a compensation program. The master salary schedule approach used by many school districts, incorporating channels for credentials and an incremental dollar amount for years of service, testifies to the influence of seniority in compensation systems. In business and industry, seniority has some impact on the compensation systems collectively bargained by unions. However, for management positions, seniority has little or no effect on rewards.

---

[3]See Robbins, *Personnel,* 365.

[4]Glen H. Tecker, *Merit, Measurement, and Money: Establishing Teacher Performance Evaluation and Incentive Programs* (Alexandria VA: National School Boards Association, 1985), 14.

The reason that seniority has been used by educational organizations to determine financial compensation is because it can be applied so easily. A principal may evaluate a given teacher's performance either higher or lower than another teacher's performance; but if both teachers perform within the limits of what is considered satisfactory, both will get the same salary increase if they both have served the same number of years in the school system. This relieves the principal from recommending to the superintendent different dollar amount compensation for each teacher based on his or her evaluation of their performance.

Nevertheless, seniority is a variable to be incorporated into a compensation system because the basic purpose of establishing a compensation policy is to attract and retain qualified employees. A compensation system is ineffective when its sole criterion for rewarding employees is seniority.

The necessity of retaining some form of seniority in a compensation plan that also rewards performance has led to the establishment of what is commonly referred to as "career ladders." Two of the more frequently discussed programs are the Charlotte-Mecklenburg Schools Career Development Plan and the Tennessee Better Schools Program. The objective of these two and most other programs is to encourage teachers to direct their careers along a path that will lead to refined skills and higher levels of responsibilities. For example, a person entering the education profession as an apprentice teacher must have met the following requirements:

a. Completed a teacher education program offered through an approved college or university
b. Attained a Bachelor's degree
c. Successfully completed student teaching
d. Successfully passed the National Teacher's Examination

This apprentice teacher could progress to subsequent higher levels of designation such as "professional teacher," "senior teacher," and finally "master teacher." The path to these levels requires additional education and the assuming of more and more responsibilities. For example, a master teacher could be expected to serve as a curriculum specialist, seminar presenter in a staff development program, or a resource person to apprentice teachers. Each level of attainment could be rewarded with perhaps a more lucrative salary schedule. A bonus upon attaining each successive level would be another method of rewarding those reaching such levels. Exhibit 8.1 shows the career paths for teachers in Tennessee.

Skills

A common practice in organizations, particularly in the private sector, is allocating compensation based on the skills of employees. Those who possess the most advanced skills receive the highest compensation. When an individual is hired by an organization, his or her skill level is usually a major consideration in determining the amount of compensation to be received.

EXHIBIT 8.1   Career Paths for Teachers

Apprentice Teacher

Entry Routes

- Completion of a teacher training program and recommendation by an approved institution of higher education
- Trade shop personnel who meet appropriate standards

Qualifications/Requirements

- Student teaching
- Successful completion of the National Teacher's Examination
- Bachelor's degree
             or
- Employment standards required for trade shop personnel

Certificate

- Three-year
- Nonrenewable

Contract/State Salary

- Regular school term of 200 days
- State salary schedule based on training and experience

Professional Teacher

Entry Routes

- Three (3) years as an apprentice teacher
- A currently certified teacher with three (3) or more years of experience who wishes to enter the new career paths

Qualifications/Requirements

- Knowledge of subject matter
- Acceptable student achievement
- Participation in professional growth activities
- Observation by evaluating team/teacher interview

Certificate

- Five-year
- Renewable

Contract/State Salary

- Regular school term of 200 days
- State salary schedule based on training and experience *plus* state incentive pay supplement of $1,000

Continued

EXHIBIT 8.1 *Continued*

Senior Teacher

Entry Routes

- Three (3) to five (5) years as a professional teacher
- A currently certified teacher who has eight (8) or more years of appropriate experience

Qualifications/Requirements

- Acceptable student achievement
- Participation in professional growth activities
- Observation by evaluation team/teacher interview
- Exceptional classroom practice
- Evaluations by local supervisors and administrators

Certificate

- Five-year
- Renewable

Contract/State Salary

- Contract for 10 months (200 days)—*current teachers only*—state salary schedule based on training and experience *plus* state incentive pay supplement of $2,000
- Contract for 11 months (220 days)—state salary schedule based on training and experience *plus* state incentive pay supplement of $4,000

Master Teacher

Entry Routes

- Five (5) years as a senior teacher
- A currently certified teacher who has twelve (12) or more years of appropriate experience

Qualifications/Requirements

- Acceptable student achievement
- Participation in professional growth activities
- Observation by evaluation team/teacher interview
- Classroom effectiveness
- Capability and willingness to assume additional duties
- Evaluations by local supervisors and administrators
- Skill in supervising, evaluating, and improving the performance of other teachers

Certificate

- Five-year
- Renewable

Contract/State Salary

- Contract for 10 months (200 days)—*current teachers only*—state salary schedule based on training and experience *plus* state incentive pay supplement of $3,000

Source: Tennessee Better Schools Program (Tennessee: Master Teacher–Master Administrator Act, 1983), 3.

Competition, therefore, to hire individuals with certain skills becomes an element in the compensation package. The standard as to what constitutes a desirable skill is imposed from either the human resource requirements of the organization or from the occupational category itself. If the board of education has mandated having a community education program, individuals possessing the experience and educational qualifications necessary for implementing such a program have skills that will demand a quality compensation package.

Job Requirements

The complexity and responsibility of a job are often criteria by which compensation is distributed. A job that is difficult to perform because of stress, unpleasant working conditions, or level of responsibility must also offer higher compensation to attract capable individuals. A major determinant of job difficulty is the degree of discretion a job requires. The greater the discretion, the greater need for good judgment and, consequently, the greater need for commensurate compensation.

Any good compensation system must recognize effort, seniority, skills, and job requirements; performance, however, must also be given a primary emphasis. Quality individuals are attracted to school districts that reward performance, which in turn affects the quality of education offered by a school district.

Types of Compensation

If compensation is to motivate performance, employees must recognize the relationship between performance and compensation. Most school districts have traditionally used non-performance criteria, such as seniority-based salary schedules, for allocating compensation. However, this chapter views compensation primarily as a payoff for performance. This concept is in keeping with the outcry for accountability and, if properly applied, might be the only realistic approach to improving the quality of education. For too long, teachers and other employees of school districts have been placed apart from the rest of mankind by taxpayers who believe that they should be more dedicated to service than concerned about making a living. Teachers and other public employees have fought this long-held belief by engaging in unionism and collective negotiations for wages and fringe benefits. A reasonable compensation system that recognizes quality performance and that is objectively administered could help remedy some of the dissatisfaction voiced by school district employees.[5]

The most obvious kinds of compensation are wages and fringe benefits. However, a truly effective compensation system must be multifaceted, incorporating both intrinsic and extrinsic aspects. Although modern school districts employ people in many different occupational categories, many of the possible rewards are applicable only to particular job positions. For example, teachers, administrators, bus drivers, and custodians would receive a salary; administrators, in addition, would have greater job discretion; and custodians could receive overtime pay.

[5]William C. Cunningham and Paula A. Cordeiro, *Educational Administration: A Problem-Based Approach* (Boston: Allyn & Bacon, 2000), 307.

In addition, rewarding performance and encouraging higher levels of performance must be fashioned into a comprehensive system that is ongoing and integral to the operation of the school district. Thus, Figure 8.1 has many functions; first and foremost it demonstrates that compensation can be weaved into a complete system for both rewarding performance and creating organizational commitment that encourages improvement of performance.

Intrinsic compensation is a reward that the employee receives from doing the job itself. The employee's satisfaction on the job is usually increased by the following: participation in the policy-making process, greater job discretion, increased responsibility, and opportunities for professional development.

Extrinsic rewards are divided into direct and indirect compensation. The most common forms of direct compensation are salary, overtime pay, holiday pay, and merit pay for performance. Direct compensation is also the part of a compensation system that generates the most controversy and disgruntlement among employees. Industrial psychologists have long contended that rate of pay is not the most important determinant of job satisfaction. However, it is an indispensable part of every compensation package and, because of its importance, is treated at length under a separate title in this chapter.

Indirect compensation usually includes insurance programs, pay for time away from work, and services. There is a widespread attitude among human resources administrators who view indirect compensation as that which helps to retain individuals in an organization rather than motivating them to greater performance. Direct compensation is considered the stimulus to better performance. Because of the complexity and importance of

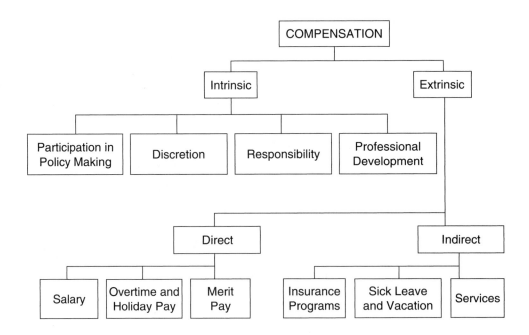

FIGURE 8.1 Structure of Compensation

indirect compensation, more frequently referred to as *fringe benefits,* this also is treated under a separate heading in this chapter.

Nonfinancial rewards have begun to appear in some school districts. These rewards may either motivate an employee to greater performance or help to retain his or her services. The limits to the kind and extent of nonfinancial compensation is established only by the creativity of those responsible for establishing a compensation program. Nonfinancial compensation, however, is effective only if it meets the needs of specific employees. What one person considers desirable might seem superfluous to another. For example, a very status-conscious employee might be motivated by a job title, a reserved parking place, the services of a private secretary, or a paneled and carpeted office. Another individual might value working without close supervision that could both motivate performance and retain his or her services. The significant point is that organizations can use a variety of nonfinancial means as part of a total program and that these means may be more appreciated by certain individuals than direct or indirect forms of compensation.

Direct Compensation: Salary and Wage Administration

The basic philosophy underlying pay systems in school districts is compensation for services rendered. However, the subjective nature of administrative judgments, of collectively bargained agreements, of state and federal pay guidelines, and of salary rates in the public and private sectors have a definite influence on actual wage programs. To ensure external and internal wage comparability, a school district must continually gather data on the wage and salary policies of other school districts and also of public and private employers in the community and region. Most organizations are cooperative in sharing information concerning salary programs because they too understand that their systems are influenced by others. Surveys by telephone and letter, governmental publications, and literature published by employee organizations and unions are also valuable resources in gathering information.

Because the principle of compensation for services rendered is somewhat elusive, the following guidelines should help a school district in developing a salary and wage policy aimed at fair treatment for all employees.[6]

- *Equitable salary system.* All salary systems must recognize the skills required in various positions. Therefore, every position must be evaluated to determine its importance in relation to other positions. All positions are then arranged in order of their relative value, with the position of greatest value and responsibility at the top. This establishes a gradation classification system that serves as a basis for the uniform administration of salaries and wages.
- *Comparability.* The salary system must be competitive with other school districts and, as much as possible, with other public agencies and private industry.
- *Position evaluation.* The relative value for every position should be established cooperatively through a salary committee composed of employees and administrators.

[6]Charles W. Foster, ed., *Wage and Salary Administration: A Handbook for School Business Officials* (Chicago: Research Corporation of the Association of School Business Officials, 1969), 7–8.

- *Performance incentives.* The primary focus of a compensation program is improvement of performance. Because salary is a major component of a compensation program, the salary system should be constructed so as to encourage employees to improve performance and assume greater responsibility. This, of course, requires that the district establish a uniform and fair method of appraising an individual's performance and a suitable personnel records system to maintain performance evaluations. Once again, Figure 8.1 presents an array of performance incentives that can be utilized to encourage all employees to strive for higher levels of performance. The key, of course, is demonstration by human resources administrators that there is a direct link between incentive rewards and the quality of performance.
- *Salary review.* Salary schedules must be reviewed annually to ascertain if they are competitive with other school districts and are keeping pace with the increases received by employees in other public agencies and in the private sector.

The Effects of Salary on Motivation

An interesting question central to all pay systems is, "Does money stimulate an employee to put forth more effort?" The answer to this question is closely related to individual needs, because money in itself is rarely an end but rather a means to "purchasing an end." A $4,000 raise for an employee making $40,000 a year would help that individual maintain the standard of living in the face of ordinary inflation. That same raise would considerably improve the standard of living for an individual earning $20,000 a year, but it would have much less effect on the life style of someone earning $80,000 per year. From this perspective, money does have a potential to motivate if individuals are seeking to maintain or improve their standard of living. We rarely find a person who is not concerned when his or her life style deteriorates because salary increases have not been keeping pace with inflation.

A study based on the responses of 157 professionals in an electronics company further supports the position that each dollar of merit increase had a value to the employee.[7] This research suggests that money is important to employees, regardless of the job level in the organization or the amount of salary that the individual earns. In addition, money has a great deal of symbolic value in our society, even though it has varying degrees of importance to individuals having different backgrounds and experiences.

If money is to motivate an individual within an organization to greater performance, it must be very clear that such performance is indeed rewarded with more money. The behavior that is thus rewarded will be repeated, and the behaviors that are not rewarded with money will not be repeated. This, of course, is not the modus operandi of most school systems in the United States. The common position has been one of emphasizing intrinsic motivation. Teachers and other school district employees are expected to perform to the best of their abilities because of the importance of educating children and because of the status afforded to these individuals. The accountability movement, with taxpayers demanding a return on their dollar from school district employees by way of increased student performance, and the number of teacher strikes for higher wages should dispel the myth that the performance of any group of employees in any organization, public or private, is unaffected by money.

---

[7]See Brian A. Giles and Gerald V. Barrett, "Utility of Merit Increases," *Journal of Applied Psychology,* 55, no. 2 (April 1971), 103–109.

In addition to this experientially proven conclusion, statistical data support the position that money increases intrinsic motivation under the following two conditions: (1) monetary rewards must closely follow performance so as to be reinforcing, and (2) the employee must perceive the monetary rewards as being related to work behavior.[8]

A reasonable conclusion concerning the relationship of money to motivation is that money definitely affects performance under certain circumstances. Unfortunately, most school districts use a seniority-based salary schedule, which does not reward performance but rather rewards an individual's survival for another year.

However, developing monetary incentives is only limited by the creativity of the human resources department. For example, giving a double step increase on the salary schedule to an outstanding teacher is a way of using a traditional salary schedule in an innovative way. Salary bonuses for exceptional performance, longevity pay for a certain number of years that outstanding teachers have committed to a school district, and signing bonuses to encourage excellent teachers to continue teaching in a school district are other examples of performance incentives.

Public Disclosure of Salaries

Because school districts are public agencies, salary schedules and budget information are disclosed not only to school district employees but also to the general public and at times to the news media. However, many school districts consider the salaries of individual employees to be confidential. This situation brings up a number of concerns. First, in public agencies supported by tax money, the public would seem to have a right to know how tax money is being spent and for what. Second, secrecy regarding salaries sometimes leads to misperceptions, which in turn may lead to the dissatisfaction of employees with their pay.

An open salary policy may also affect management effectiveness. If pay information became common knowledge among employees, individuals could compare their salaries, and inequities in the pay system would soon become apparent. Of course, there also would be petty complaints and misperceived inequities. However, an open pay system would demonstrate that the administration has confidence in the management of the pay system and this may increase the trust individual employees have in the school district's administration.

Although very few statistical data are available on the preferences of employees concerning an open salary policy, experience suggests that most Americans are sensitive about their wages and would probably prefer to have their salaries undisclosed.

The Equal Employment Opportunity Commission continues to receive cases alleging that women are being paid less than men for doing comparable work. This, of course, is contrary to the provisions of the Equal Pay Act of 1963 and Title VII of the Civil Rights Act of 1964.[9] In like manner, school districts receiving federal funds must disclose wage and salary information to demonstrate commitment to the principles of affirmative action. Further, a company cannot prohibit employees from discussing salary

---

[8]See Fred Luthans, Mark Martinko, and Tom Kess, "An Analysis of the Impact of Contingency Monetary Rewards on Intrinsic Motivation," *Proceedings of the 19th Annual Midwest Academy of Management* (St. Louis, 1976), 209–221.

[9]Stites, Janet, "Equal Pay for the Sexes," *HR Magazine,* 50, no. 5 (May 2005), 65–69.

issues during working hours because this is an abridgement of the constitutional rights of employees.

Compensation Packaging (Cafeteria Plans)

Because individual employees have individual needs, no compensation program will satisfy everyone. A number of corporations, recognizing this fact, have developed compensation programs commonly referred to as cafeteria plans, which allow each employee to choose a combination of programs most attractive to that person. Thus, employees are informed that their compensation is X dollars, and they then choose a mix of salary and other benefits suited to their particular situation and offered by the corporation. Such benefits might include:

- Major medical and hospitalization insurance
- Pharmaceutical insurance
- Dental insurance
- Optical insurance
- Flexible spending plan
- Life insurance
- Extended care insurance
- Dependent care plan
- Accidental death and dismemberment insurance
- Long-term disability insurance
- Travel accident insurance
- Adoption assistance
- Annuities
- Others limited only by the creativity of human resources administrators

The concept underlying this approach is that an employee will be motivated towards higher performance if such performance carries a dollar value that can then be "spent" by the individual for compensation tailored to meet his or her needs.

Although it is difficult to generalize, younger employees appear to be more concerned with salary and educational reimbursement programs than with life insurance and retirement plans. Married employees are usually more concerned about life insurance and medical programs than single individuals; older employees are justifiably interested in retirement benefits.

With this type of compensation packaging, a considerable amount of information must be made available to employees for them to have adequate data on which to base decisions. This will obviously increase the administrative costs of the compensation programs. However, the potential benefit in terms of increased performance and the retention of employees could significantly offset the additional costs.

Equity of Pay and Performance

In any organization, employees tend to compare what they get from their job with what they must put into it. At the same time, they are comparing what they make in wages with what coworkers make and how productive their coworkers are. The inevitable outcome of this comparison process is that an individual will see his or her compensation as either equal or unequal to that of fellow employees. Those who feel inequality exists will view themselves as under-rewarded or over-rewarded.

Three variables can color an employee's perception.[10] The first variable, usually termed the "other" category, includes colleagues, friends, and neighbors. With information received from these individuals and from newspapers and other communication media, the employee compares his or her pay to that of others. The "system" category is the second variable and includes organizational pay policies, pay procedures, and administration of the pay system. The final category is the "self," which refers to the input–output ratio unique to the individual. This category is also influenced by past jobs and current family role commitments.

An employee who perceives an inequality may choose one or more of the following alternatives: distort his or her own inputs or outputs or those of others; attempt to induce others to match his or her inputs or outputs; change his or her own inputs or outputs; choose a different frame of reference for comparing pay; or quit the job.[11] Administrators must realize that employees are not only concerned about the absolute amount of money they are paid but also with the relationship of that dollar amount to what others are paid. When an inequality is perceived, tension is created. The implication for human resources administrators is very clear. Employees are motivated not only by their absolute compensation but also by the relativity of compensation. Where employees perceive inequality, quality of performance may diminish, absenteeism may increase, and resignations may even rise.

Employee Relations in Salary Management

Employees who believe they are unfairly compensated will certainly create a morale problem for the administration. However, low wages alone will not necessarily create a morale problem if employees believe the administration and board of education are doing everything possible to improve wages. Therefore, how salary decisions are presented to the employees is of great importance. The method, of course, will vary with each individual school district because of local traditions and the number of employees.[12] However, most presentation plans must be formulated with a sensitivity to the process used in making salary decisions. The two most commonly used processes are briefly explained here.

In the first process, the administration analyzes the fiscal condition of the school district; formulates a recommendation that appears reasonable; receives approval from the board of education; and, finally, informs the school district employees of the decision. This method is the most efficient in terms of time spent by the administration, but it is also the most vulnerable in terms of good staff morale because it is basically a "take it or leave it"

---

[10]See Paul S. Goodman, "An Examination of Referents Used in the Evaluation of Pay," *Organizational Behavior and Human Performance,* 12, no. 2 (October 1974), 170–195.

[11]See Robbins, *Personnel,* 358.

[12]See John W. Boyle, "Techniques for Consultation and Presentation," in *Wage and Salary Administration: A Handbook for School Business Officials,* Charles W. Foster, ed. (Chicago: Research Corporation of the Association of School Business Officials, 1960), 39–40.

approach. Although this method is traditional in education, it is also highly suspect even in those school districts where it is used successfully because it has all the markings of a benevolent dictatorship.

In the second process, which is the more defensible, administration and employee representatives work together to develop a mutually acceptable salary and wage package. In over half the states this process is mandated in varying degrees by state collective negotiations legislation. However, the process is certainly valid even in those states that prohibit collective negotiations by public school employees. Where such a prohibition exists, salary decisions remain with the board of education, but the task of formulating a recommendation becomes a mutual concern of both administrators and employees.

This collaborative process is not without its drawbacks. It can be very time consuming, and the administration may disagree with the proposals presented by the employee representatives. Chapter 9 discusses in detail the process of collective negotiations as practiced in public school districts.

Whatever process is used, the administration must ultimately present the salary plan and the decision of the board of education to the school district employees. A significant advantage of the bilateral model is that the employees through their representatives have some knowledge of the administration's position. The sensitive nature of salary and wage decisions cannot be overemphasized. Wages affect an individual's ability to support his or her family and maintain an adequate standard of living; a paycheck represents security in a highly materialistic society. Therefore, effective communication is essential in explaining policies and decisions.

There are four basic principles that, if followed, will maximize the effectiveness of presenting salary and wage decisions to the employees: (1) the board of education must place top priority on paying adequate wages when it draws up and approves the school district's budget; (2) the administration must make complete disclosure of the fiscal condition of the school district; (3) the administration must avoid presenting too many technical details of the financial conditions, which could give the semblance of a "snow job"; and (4) the administration should prepare a position statement to distribute to all employees and to the news media. This document may take various forms, but at a minimum it should contain the decision on salary and wages, the process used in reaching the decision, facts about the financial condition of the school district, and data about wages in comparable school districts and the business community.

It is also effective in minimizing confusion and misrepresentation to invite employees to call a designated office, which will be responsible for answering questions about the salary and wage document. The most obvious central-office component to take this responsibility, of course, is the business and finance office. However, those districts that maintain a public relations office would more properly place this responsibility with the director of community relations.

A final, yet very important, point should be made concerning employee relations in salary management. The building principal is often the last person to be informed about central-office and board of education decisions, but he or she is usually the first person contacted by teachers and other building level employees when they have questions. Therefore, it is both good administrative procedure and good public relations to inform the principals first about salary decisions. This will also help principals identify themselves as members of the school district's administrative team.

Collecting Community Wage Data

A defensible technique in developing cooperation is to establish salary parameters compatible with wages paid by other government agencies and by business and industry in the community served by the school system. In metropolitan areas, this would include more than the immediate vicinity; salaries in the surrounding area would probably give a better indication of the adequacy of salary levels within the district. Thus, a school district located in suburban Chicago should be concerned with the wages paid by private business and industry, municipal governments, and other school districts in the entire metropolitan Chicago area.

If salaries are to be competitive and comparable enough to sustain a reasonable standard of living for school district employees, they must be relative to the salaries received by other individuals living in the same community. Another reason for seeking salary data from other employers in the area is because these corporations and their employees support the school district through taxation; and school district salaries must not be out of proportion with the wages paid and received by these constituents.

A source of information on salaries and wages paid in the community to individuals with occupations similar to noninstructional employees of a school district is the employment agency. Although the quality of such agencies varies, both private and public employment agencies usually have valuable data on wages. The civil service commissions of state and municipal governments also have readily available information on salary systems used in their respective jurisdictions.

The most effective way to gather data on salaries and wages is through a survey. Such a technique has the advantage of clarity and precision. If the survey instrument is accompanied by a cover letter explaining its purpose, most agencies and corporations will cooperate with the school district by supplying the data because they usually view this type of cooperation as a public service.

The following guidelines are applicable to wage and salary surveys for noninstructional positions and should be valuable to those school districts using this technique for the first time.[13]

Surveys dealing with instructional and administrative positions generally follow these guidelines, substituting appropriate position titles, salary, and job descriptions.

1. The material for the survey must be obtained on a confidential basis. All summaries must be prepared in a manner that preserves the anonymity of each firm or school asked to participate. Also, let it be known that the data in the summary will be restricted to confidential management use, and that no publicity will be given to the data or the survey.
2. Every effort must be made to make this an objective, unbiased survey. Statistical techniques should be used to select a sample of firms that would produce an unbiased representation, since it is too expensive to survey all the firms in a given locality.
3. Request wage rates that are the averages for each occupation. Use straight-time day work rates for regularly employed full-time employees and show as an equivalent forty-hour week rate.
4. The occupations should be grouped into two general categories—craft and clerical. The occupations selected for the survey will cover such a wide range of experiences

[13]Foster, *Wage and Salary Administration,* 10–12, with modifications.

and skills that they cannot be considered typical of any one firm or group of firms. Rather, the intent is to represent occupations found widely throughout industry in general, as well as certain special occupations of particular interest. If a single occupation is reported by fewer than three firms, the occupation should be eliminated from the summary to preserve the confidential nature of the information.

5. The job descriptions to be used in the survey should provide for the "slotting" of jobs (see Exhibit 8.2)

6. Samples of other craft occupations
   Mechanic
   Sheet metal worker
   Electrician
   Plumber
   Carpenter

7. Samples of clerical occupations
   Bookkeeping—machine operator
   Accounting clerk
   Payroll clerk
   Administrative assistant
   Transcriptionist
   Switchboard operator/receptionist

The practice of keeping school district wage and salary rates comparable to the wages paid in the community is becoming imperative not only because of the teacher shortage in some fields but also because more and more school district employees are attracted to jobs in business and industry. This, of course, is particularly true of craft and clerical positions because of the ease of transferring from public to private sector employment. Administrative assistants, electricians, cooks, and bus drivers are sometimes "in training" with public school districts until an appropriate job becomes available in business or industry. Thus, the principle of like pay for public employees for like work in corporations and other organizations is becoming a necessary human resources policy. Such a policy not only helps a school district to be competitive with the private sector for quality employees but also helps a school district retain its employees and reduces the expense involved with high turnover.

EXHIBIT 8.2   Sample Job Description

Janitor, Porter, or Cleaner

Cleans and keeps in an orderly condition, factory working area and washrooms, or premises of an office, apartment house, school building, or commercial establishment. Duties involve a combination of the following:

Sweeping, mopping, or scrubbing, and polishing floors; removing trash and other refuse; dusting equipment, furniture, or fixtures; polishing metal fixtures or trimmings; providing supplies and minor maintenance services; cleaning lavatories, showers, and restrooms. Workers who specialize in window washing are excluded.

The salary rates being offered in the private sector are also attracting instructional and administrative personnel. Mathematics, industrial arts, and science teachers are finding many more opportunities in business and industry than ever before. This trend is also reaching into the liberal arts disciplines as corporations recognize that they can train an individual for almost any job if that person is motivated and has a basic college education. Salaries have motivated many teachers to seek employment in the private sector and in jobs where the rewards systems recognize performance.

Thus, collecting data about salaries and wages is extremely important. Although school districts individually gather information through the survey method, many cooperative ventures also have emerged with most or all of the school districts in a metropolitan area jointly sponsoring salary and wage surveys.

The following techniques for establishing the survey purpose, preparing the schedule, and tabulating the data should prove valuable to school districts planning to use this method.[14]

1. Collect basic factual data to provide a basis for establishing the rates of pay for employees in the school district.
2. Determine the degree and amount of wage movement that occurs in the community within a given period of time.
3. Determine wage relationships among categories within the school district.
4. Collect data on basic working conditions such as the length of the work week, general pay practices, overtime practices, prerequisites, and so on.

Prepare the schedule or questionnaire so that the following are taken into consideration:

5. Include only those technical terms commonly used in the pertinent industries and schools.
6. Indicate the amount of training and experience required by job description or by implication.
7. Define the processes, equipment, or terms specific to the benchmark job.
8. Prepare detailed guide notes which clearly define in both negative and positive terms what the survey field person should be looking for and what he or she should avoid in job comparisons.
9. Consider the desirability of obtaining organization charts which indicate the relationship between the benchmark job and other related jobs.
10. For accuracy in the results of the survey, computerized data processing must be used.
11. Consultation with data processing personnel at the time the survey is being constructed will facilitate the proper tabulation of the data.
12. Preparation of the report can easily be made from the data processing tabulation runs.

Salary and Wage Review

Since approximately 80 percent of most school districts' budgets is spent on wages, salary planning and review is an essential part of the entire compensation process. Two methods

---

[14]Foster, *Wage and Salary Administration,* 13–14.

are commonly used by school systems to review compensation programs: continual salary review and annual review.

A continual salary review system is usually tied into a cost of living index. Government agencies use a number of indicators to determine inflation rates, with the Consumer Price Index being the most commonly used. A major problem with such a measure is the fact that this is an average; the actual cost of living in a community may be higher or lower than the average reported.

Under a continual salary review system, adjustments are automatically made on salary schedules as the selected cost of living indicator changes, necessitating a change in the hourly rates for classified employees and the contracts for administrative and instructional personnel. Such a system does not of itself reward performance; it merely adjusts the basic salary of all employees. Merit increases, therefore, are not addressed by the continual review process.

The annual salary review process functions from a much different perspective. Salary schedules are adjusted annually in relation to the prevailing wages in other school districts and businesses in the community. The adjustment may or may not be in keeping with a recognized cost of living indicator; rather, its major focus is on the local community as the appropriate measure. The concern of the annual salary review process is that wages in other school districts and businesses in the community, which continually change, may steal away the more talented employees. As with the continual salary review process, the annual review method does not of itself reward performance. Therefore, merit increases must be viewed as a separate component of the compensation program.

The decision of a school district as to what method best meets the needs of the employees must be tempered with the constraints of the budget. There are two significant differences between public sector and private sector financing: First, school districts are financed primarily by tax revenue, which is usually not received on a consistent monthly basis but rather as taxes are collected; second, in most states, taxes can be raised to meet higher costs only by voter approval, whereas in the private sector, the price of an item can be raised at any time to offset costs. These financial considerations would make the continual salary review process difficult to implement in a school district.

Salary Schedule Construction

In the public sector and particularly in the civil service systems of the state and federal governments, salary schedules are divided into a number of grades, each of which has several step rates. The use of salary schedules can have three distinct advantages.[15] First, recruitment of personnel can be more effective because a potential employee may be offered a step above the minimum in the grade—often a necessary inducement to hire the most qualified applicant. Second, an employee will be able to see potential salary increases, assuming satisfactory performance. Finally, with multiple steps within a grade system, an employee may receive step increases for meritorious performance.

A major question in establishing such an approach is deciding on the appropriate number of steps to be included within a grade. If the steps are numerous and small, employees will be unhappy because salary increases will be small. If the steps are large and few, an

---

[15]Cyrus Knutson, "Development of a Master Salary Schedule," in Foster, *Wage and Salary Administration,* 15.

employee will reach the maximum within a grade in a relatively short time and consequently will have no place to progress to over the long term.

A realistic approach, therefore, could be a compromise setting up six or seven steps within each grade, with each representing a certain percentage increment. Each grade may be further improved by adding longevity steps to the top and expressing these in even dollar amounts rather than percentages. For example, a salary schedule could grant an employee a longevity increase for every two years of service after reaching the last step within a grade.

Each position in the school district is assigned to one of the salary ranges, and each employee is assigned to one of the steps. As new people are hired, they are placed within the range assigned to that position and on a step negotiated with the administration. Advancement from one step to another is based on performance. Consequently, an employee who is performing unsatisfactorily could remain on the same step until termination or resignation. An employee performing satisfactorily could receive a step advancement that would represent a certain percentage salary increase. A meritorious employee could be granted a two- or three-step advancement.

Some school districts have initiated a policy of placing a new employee on the first step for a probationary period, then advancing the employee as he or she demonstrates satisfactory performance. For example, an employee might be moved to the second step after six months. This method is usually effective only with classified employees who, unlike teachers, are not working under an individual contract.

Advancement from one salary range to another is usually based on either a promotion or an increase in educational qualifications. A teacher who becomes an assistant principal will usually advance to the salary range established for the assistant principalship. In like manner, a teacher who receives a master's degree would be advanced to the salary range established for teachers with master's degrees. This same process is applicable to classified employees. A custodian who is promoted to a head custodial position with supervisory responsibilities over the other custodians in a building would be placed on the appropriate salary level. It is important to note that advancement to a higher salary grade will not necessarily result in a higher wage for an employee. For example, Step 5 of the bachelor's degree teacher salary range may be higher than Step 1 of the master's degree salary range. Consequently, when moving employees to a higher grade, it is important to place them on a step that will ensure an increase in wages for having upgraded their academic qualifications or for taking on greater responsibilities.

Although the types of salary ranges will vary from one school district to another, a few examples of common designations are:

ADMINISTRATIVE	INSTRUCTIONAL	CLASSIFIED
Central Office Director (Example: Director of Federal Programs)	Bachelor's degree	Custodian
	Bachelor's degree plus 30 graduate hours	Head Custodian
Secondary School Principal		Maintenance Employee
Secondary School Assistant Principal	Master's degree	
Elementary School Principal	Master's degree plus 30 graduate hours	Maintenance Supervisor
Elementary School Assistant Principal	Doctoral degree	

Each of these designations would have a salary range with multiple steps.

Exhibit 8.3 is an example of the type of teacher salary schedule to be found in most school districts. There are five categories that correspond to the academic requirement necessary for placement in each category. The categories progress from the "Bachelor's Degree" level on through to the "Doctoral Degree" level. The steps in each category are listed down the left side of the schedule. Those teachers in Category 1 could receive a step increase with satisfactory performance up through ten steps. At that point, they would not receive a step increase until they acquired fifteen graduate hours of additional education in their subject area and thus would move to Step 11 in Category 2. Therefore, this method encourages teachers to upgrade their knowledge and skills. Such is the case with all categories. There are two categories that have experience requirements in addition to the academic ones. The "Master's Degree" level also requires two years of successful teaching experience; the "Doctoral Degree" level requires three years. Thus, a person who is pursuing a master's degree or doctoral degree on a full-time basis without experience in teaching would be placed in the preceding category until completing the successful teaching requirement.

Exhibit 8.4 indicates the percent of increase between categories and steps. Such a salary schedule is commonly referred to as an "index" system. The designation "incremental" system refers to those salary schedules that have an equal dollar amount between steps, such as $500 between Step 1 and Step 2; also, $500 between Step 2 and 3, etc.

EXHIBIT 8.3   Salary Schedule

Step	Category 1 Bachelor's Degree	Category 2 Bachelor's Degree plus 15 graduate hours	Category 3 Master's Degree plus 2 years experience	Category 4 Master's Degree plus 15 graduate hours	Category 5 Doctoral Degree plus 3 years experience
1	35,000	36,575		38,150	
2	36,575	38,150		40,425	
3	38,150	39,725	40,512.50	42,700	
4	39,725	40,300	42,087.50	44,975	46,550
5	41,300	42,875	43,662.50	47,250	48,825
6	42,875	44,450	45,237.50	49,525	51,100
7	44,450	46,025	46,812.50	51,800	53,375
8	46,025	47,600	48,387.50	54,075	55,650
9	47,600	49,175	49,962.50	56,350	57,925
10	49,175	50,750	51,537.50	58,625	60,200
11		52,325	53,112.50	60,900	62,475
12			54,687.50	63,175	64,750
13				65,450	67,025
14					70,000
15					72,275
16					74,550
17					76,825
18					79,100
19					81,375
20					83,650

EXHIBIT 8.4   Indices

STEP	INDEX	INDEX	INDEX	INDEX	INDEX
1	1.0000	1.0450		1.0900	
2	1.0450	1.0900		1.1550	
3	1.0900	1.1350	1.1575	1.2200	
4	1.1350	1.1800	1.2025	1.2850	1.3300
5	1.1800	1.2250	1.2475	1.3500	1.3950
6	1.2250	1.2700	1.2925	1.4150	1.4600
7	1.2700	1.3150	1.3375	1.4800	1.5250
8	1.3150	1.3600	1.3825	1.5450	1.5900
9	1.3600	1.4050	1.4275	1.6100	1.6550
10	1.4050	1.4500	1.4725	1.6750	1.7200
11		1.4950	1.5175	1.7400	1.7850
12			1.5625	1.8050	1.8500
13				1.8700	1.9150
14					2.0000
15					2.0650
16					2.1300
17					2.1950
18					2.2600
19					2.3250
20					2.3900

Multiple Salary Ranges

There will probably be multiple salary ranges in most school districts for administrative and instructional positions. These ranges are necessary to recognize the various levels of academic preparation and responsibility. A secondary school principal with a master's degree, usually a minimum academic qualification, should not receive as much compensation as a secondary school principal with a doctorate. Thus, when a salary plan has multiple ranges, it is usually designated as a "salary schedule." The teachers' salary schedule would usually have a range for each of the following: bachelor's degree, bachelor's degree plus thirty graduate hours, master's degree, master's degree plus thirty graduate hours, and doctorate. Consequently, it is common to find multiple salary schedules with multiple ranges in most school systems. For these professional positions, it is relatively easy to identify appropriate ranges, which is not the case with classified positions.

The use of *negotiated contracts* is a new phenomenon taking shape in some school districts across the nation, and particularly in school districts that are experiencing difficulty finding qualified administrators and teachers. This refers to the practice of providing salary and benefit packages that are tailored to meet the employment demands of desirable candidates. Such candidates might be applying for superintendent, assistant superintendent, principal, or special education positions. For example, there is great demand for secondary school principals with successful experience in large urban school districts, for teachers and administrators experienced in providing quality services to children with autism, and for assistant superintendents with extensive and successful experience in curricular and instructional planning and assessment.

Compensation packaging could include a salary enticement that extends beyond the usually salary schedules or benefits, which might include annuities, professional development financial allowances, extended periods of vacation, use of a school-owned vehicle, or an automobile allowance. However, negotiated contracts could have some limitations because of Internal Revenue Service codes. In addition, it is always a good practice to make known the terms of negotiated contracts because they are being financed by taxpayer money. Also, public disclosure militates against exaggerated claims that may accompany agreements that are out of the ordinary.

For classified employees, it is necessary to designate job families based on similarity in duties and responsibilities and similarity in qualifications. From time to time, it might be necessary to reevaluate a position to determine if these criteria are still applicable. An example of a family of jobs with similar responsibilities, duties, and qualifications is the designation, "secretarial-clerical." Not all school district secretaries and clerical personnel have exactly the same working conditions. Therefore, a salary schedule for this designation could be constructed with ranges established to discriminate between the various working conditions. The highest range could be reserved for executive secretaries working for the superintendent and assistant superintendents. Another range would be assigned to building secretarial positions and the lowest range to clerk-typist positions. Similarly, a job family for classified transportation supervisory personnel could include ranges for transportation supervisor, mechanic foreman, and dispatcher, with salary ranges appropriate to these designations.

Establishing Base Salaries

There are two processes that can be used to establish the basic wage for each salary schedule range. The preceding discussion of types of salary ranges illustrates the various methods used to calculate step increases but provides no indication of base salaries.

The first process centers on gathering salary data from other school districts and from the business–industrial community. There is little difficulty in analyzing the data in relation to administrative and teaching positions. Classified positions, on the other hand, present a more challenging situation because of the multitude of job categories with responsibilities unique to the individual organization.

A successful method of setting classified salaries is by designating certain jobs as benchmark positions. The following four-step process exemplifies how the benchmark positions are used to set the salaries of other positions in a job family.

- *Step 1.* Through the procedures of job description and analysis, classes of noninstructional positions can be determined. These classes are grouped into broad job families as follows:

   Clerical. Clerk-typist, senior clerk, accounting clerk, school secretary, administrative secretary, superintendent's secretary
   Maintenance and operations. Custodian, gardener, head custodian, maintenance person, maintenance supervisor

- *Step 2.* Benchmark positions are selected which can be compared reliably with prevailing rates for comparable jobs in local industry and other public agencies. In this hypothetical example, the benchmarks chosen could be clerk-typist and custodian.
- *Step 3.* Salary survey data are applied to the benchmark positions. The best-fitting ranges on the master salary schedule, using the survey statistics of central tendency (mean and median) and dispersion (interquartile range), are selected for the benchmark positions.
- *Step 4.* The alignment of other positions is determined according to their skill relationships, using for each position the predetermined benchmark position as a reference point.[16]

The second process involves gathering data from individual employees within the organization concerning the extent of their responsibilities, the tasks they perform, and their qualifications. The data can be analyzed and used to establish salaries as part of the annual review process. The data also provide a vehicle for reevaluating jobs to ascertain if they are properly assigned to the appropriate salary schedule and in the correct range. The Appendix illustrates an employee questionnaire that can be used for this position analysis; it also contains samples of job evaluation forms. The use of this questionnaire and the evaluation forms is predicated on a procedure that utilizes a salary review committee.

In most situations where this procedure is used, the salary review committee is composed of administrators, supervisors, teachers, and noninstructional personnel who are not directly employed in the job categories being evaluated but who have a knowledge of the working conditions involved. This gives credibility and objectivity to the process. A committee of three or five people is optimal for the evaluation task. Thus, if a secondary school principal's position is being evaluated, the committee could be composed of one or two elementary school principals, one or two secondary school teachers, and the assistant superintendent for secondary education. In like manner, if a building-level secretarial position is being evaluated, the committee could be composed of one or two central-office executive secretaries, one or two clerk-typists, and the director of staff development.

Each committee member studies the questionnaire completed by the employee and his or her supervisor. Using a scale of one to five with five indicating the highest requirement, each person evaluates the position in terms of the factors indicated on the evaluation form. Finally, a tally sheet summarizing the evaluations is completed. From these data, the assistant superintendent for human resources or another central office administrator can establish the salary range appropriate to the position.

Payroll Deductions

Making deductions from an employee's salary is such a common practice that most individuals take it for granted. Yet it has significant consequences because of legal and

---

[16]Richard Maxfield, "Application of Classes Within the Classified Service to the Master Salary Schedule," in Foster, *Wage and Salary Administration,* 26.

personal considerations. Therefore, the board of education should have a comprehensive payroll deduction policy covering such areas as the minimum and maximum amounts that may be deducted, the number and types of deductions authorized, deduction procedures, and the opening and closing dates for entering deductions on the payroll records.

No payroll deduction should be initiated without written authorization from the employee unless authorized by law or the courts. John Ramsey has put together a list of payroll deductions, which describes not only the commonly accepted categories but also information about procedures (see Exhibit 8.5).

Pay Periods

The complexity and size of modern school districts has raised a question for education that has been answered in the private sector for many years: Should salaries be paid on a monthly, semimonthly, biweekly, or weekly schedule? School districts no longer employ just a few people in simple jobs, and their payrolls can no longer be managed by a hand-worked method. The complexity of multiple deductions for extensive employee classifications has mandated computerization of payroll management, and this in turn has increased the importance of deadlines. The basic principles for determining pay periods are the type of work done by the employee, the amount earned, and the cost to the school district.

Different classifications of employees have different expectations about how often they should be paid. Custodians, bus drivers, and cafeteria workers are more accustomed to being paid on a weekly basis in the business community, and such employees expect a weekly check when working for a school district. Skilled employees such as plumbers, electricians, and carpenters generally receive higher wages than unskilled workers and are more accustomed to being paid on a monthly or biweekly basis. Finally, professional employees such as administrators and teachers are usually paid on a monthly basis; they normally have individual contracts for a set dollar amount, which is divided into equal payments. Some school districts allow teachers to be paid in either nine or twelve payments, at the discretion of the individual teachers. Some building principals, in like manner, work ten months and are given the option of receiving their salary in ten or twelve monthly payments.

The size of the school district will determine the complexity of the payroll process. In larger school systems, of course, more people are employed, which usually increases the number of job classifications having different payroll periods. This will demand more computerization as well as deadlines and specific procedures for handling the payroll. More payroll specialists and equipment will be needed, which will increase the school district's cost in managing the payroll process.

In conclusion, the importance of the payroll process to the school system is unquestioned. "It is essential that each person, as soon as he is employed, knows just how much he will earn, what deductions will be made, what retirement benefits he will receive, how often he will be paid, and when. Good payroll administration can do more to establish good morale in the school system than any other single factor."[17]

---

[17]Thomas E. Smith, "Pay Periods and Discussion of Monthly, Semi-Monthly, Bi-Weekly and Weekly Pay Periods," in Foster, *Wage and Salary Administration,* 45.

EXHIBIT 8.5   Categories of Payroll Deductions

1. **Income Tax Deductions.** Government income tax legislation requires each employee to execute a certificate of exemptions to be used as a basis for calculating income tax deductions. In most instances the certificate will provide the following information:

   a. *Full name*. It is recommended that it be typed or printed for legibility. In the case of married women, use first name, maiden name, and last name.

   b. *Employee account number*. This is needed for identification on payroll tax returns as well as for employee record cards. All employees should be required to show their account card and also to copy the name as it appears on the card. The existing U.S. Income Tax Regulations require a Social Security (FICA) Account Number for all employees subject to withholding taxes. If an employee has not filed an account number, he or she should be advised to fill out an application form and send it to the nearest district office of the U.S. Social Security Administration. Forms to obtain lost account cards are also available at the same office.

   c. *Home address*. Print or type this information, including city, state or province, and other identifying postal information.

   d. *Claim for withholding exemptions*. The school district must allow exemptions to each employee on the basis of the withholding certificate. If an employee fails to furnish a certificate, the school district is required to withhold tax as if the employee had claimed no withholding exemptions. A certificate filed by a new employee is to be made effective upon the first payment of salary. Once filed with the school district, a withholding exemption certificate will remain in effect until an amended certificate is furnished.

   The following classifications of exemption are usually considered:

   a. *Single*. This refers to persons not married and who desire to claim an exemption. A mark, number, or other designation is made on the form for this claim of exemption.

   b. *Married*. This classification allows one exemption each for husband and wife if not claimed on another certificate. If claim is made for both exemptions, then an indication is inserted on the certificate; if one of the exemptions is claimed, or no exemptions are claimed, this is also indicated on the form.

   c. *Other exemptions*. This classification covers such exemptions as:
      i. Age (over 65)
      ii. Blindness
      iii. Other relatives who qualify as dependents

   Employees may file an amended exemption certificate, increasing the number of exemptions, at any time. Normally the deductions are reflected in the next payment of wages.

   School districts will usually find it convenient to determine the amount of income tax required to be withheld from wage bracket tables. Government agencies provide these tables free of charge—commercial tax tables may also be purchased from office supply houses, professional accountants' organizations, and suppliers of tax services. Tax tables are available for various pay periods; that is, weekly, biweekly, semimonthly, monthly, daily, or miscellaneous periods.

   In addition to making payroll withholding as specified by Internal Revenue Service tax tables, a percentage method may be used. Additional amounts may be withheld under

Continued

EXHIBIT 8.5 *Continued*

a written agreement between the school district and the employee. This agreement will be effective for such periods as may be mutually agreed upon.

The school district usually is assigned a reporting number for purposes of transmitting and accounting for payroll taxes deducted. Returns are usually rendered monthly or quarterly; and an annual reconciliation is required.

Some cities or local government units require collection of an occupational license or payroll tax. The law serves as the basis for the deduction and no authorizing action is required of the employee. In most instances, this tax is based on a percentage of gross salary, with no provision for exemptions.

The same employer reporting is required as mentioned above.

2. **Retirement Deductions.** These deductions usually come under one of three classifications—a government retirement plan for all employees, a program specifically limited to certificated or noncertificated personnel, or a commercial underwriting program. Some school districts may permit certificated employees to participate in all three plans or only one plan. This is usually determined by the school board or a governing board or by law. Deductions are usually based on a fixed percentage of gross salary.

3. **Court-Ordered Deductions.** The problems of deductions relative to garnishments, bankruptcies, levies, and other deductions of this nature are sometimes vexing to school districts. Employees should be encouraged to keep their personal financial affairs in sufficient order to prevent this type of action. Of course, the employee should be given every opportunity to rectify the situation if it is and oversight or an honest error on the debtor's part.

In determining this deduction, care must be taken to note the following important information:

a. Name of plaintiff or debtor
b. Date of garnishment served and received by school district
c. Amount of garnishment
d. Court costs—advisable to verify with Court
e. Amount of pay due as of date of garnishment
f. Number of days permitted to answer the garnishment

An information copy of the garnishment or order should be sent to the employee. It is possible that a form entitled "Release" may be obtained by the employee which will alter the sum of money to be deducted from salary. In no instance should the school district accept the word of the plaintiff's or defendant's attorney, or the debtor, relative to reduction in the principal amount of the debt unless a written form is furnished by the Court responsible for the original garnishment order.

At this time, it is appropriate to stress these four points:

a. Recover the amount required by the Court up to the date of the garnishment. If the salary earned is not sufficient to take care of indebtedness, there is a possibility that a subsequent garnishment will be initiated.
b. File with Court the necessary answer, within the specified time permitted. Deduction check should be made payable to the Court.
c. Always advise employee of the garnishment and give him or her every opportunity to clear the matter up prior to actual deduction.
d. Establish a policy relative to number of garnishments permitted and acquaint all employees of the policy requirements.

EXHIBIT 8.5

4. Miscellaneous Deductions. The preceding paragraphs have dealt with deductions that are mandatory in nature and which are based on government regulations or court orders. Reference has been made to the control of deductions through an approved policy of the school district. In this connection, surveys of other school district deduction policies may be made to assist in development of the individual district policy.

The deductions discussed in the ensuing paragraphs are on a voluntary basis, and are usually identified as fringe benefits. The types of deductions are varied in scope. However, only a few will be presented here, to be used for guidance and direction.

a. *Health, accident, and hospital plans.* These deductions are based on a predetermined premium made by the underwriting company. Rates are based on the type of coverage desired by the employee—the more coverage desired, the higher the premium. Apart of the premium may or may not be paid by the school district depending upon the policy of the board along with applicable state laws. Some school districts may pay all of the premiums. In most instances, an application form is required of the employee in which personal information as well as family health history is indicated. A deduction authorization should also be signed by the employee and mayor may not be included as a part of the application form. Group insurance certificates or individual policies are usually issued to the employee and confirm the coverage authorized on the deduction form.

b. *Life insurance plans.* These deductions generally follow the same outline as the plan for health, accident, and hospitalization. Many retirement plans now include life insurance as apart of their comprehensive program.

c. *Employment association dues.* Deductions for association dues are becoming increasingly popular among school districts. These include such deductions as local unit, state or province association dues which may be paid in one or more installments out of the salary of the employee. Many associations also provide for other deductions as a part of their overall program. This could include a life insurance program, disability income protection, and personal liability insurance.

d. *Credit union.* This is becoming a more popular deduction for school district employees. The Credit Union has as its major purpose the encouragement of savings as well as the providing of a source of financial assistance. It is suggested that the deduction authorization form be worded in such a way that the deduction amount will not he identified as to whether it is a savings or a loan payment. The Treasurer of the Credit Union should determine the monthly amount to be paid or the savings desired and secure the signed authorization for payroll records. Many Credit Unions pay for deduction service on the basis of the number of accounts serviced.

e. *Community fund contributions.* Considerable pressure is exerted on the school districts to participate in various solicitations for the welfare of the under privileged in the community. Many localities have combined all the campaigns into one, on an annual basis. It is emphasized that every attempt be made to combine these appeals into one amount for deduction purposes. A signed deduction form should be obtained which would indicate the amount to be deducted, and the period covered.

Source: John L. Ramsey, "Payroll Deductions," in Foster, *Wage and Salary Administration,* 47–51. Modified for this presentation.

Principles for Presenting Recommendations to the School Board

It is assumed that all salary recommendations presented to the board of education will be based on sound wage and salary practices. The previous sections in this chapter outline defensible procedures that, if followed, will place the administration in such a position. The next objective, then, is to present the recommendations in a manner that will evoke favorable approval by the school board.

Dr. W. E. Campbell identified three factors that will affect the presentation of salary recommendations: fiscal condition of the school district, the administrative organization of the school district, and the unions and associations to which the various categories of employees belong.[18]

The Fiscal Condition of the School District

In the present economy, salary recommendations almost always call for an increase, and in some cases a substantial increase, in wages. Salary appropriations account for 80 percent of school district budgets. Clearly, an increase in salaries will create one of the following situations: less money will be available for other categories of school operations, the school district will have enough revenue and/or balances to accommodate the salary increases, or the board of education will have to find additional sources of revenue to meet the increases. In most states, additional revenue can be obtained only through a tax levy increase which, of course, requires voter approval. Inflation has generally created scarcity for most school districts. Therefore, a board of education may be unable to approve a recommendation if the cost is unrealistically high.

The Administrative Organization of the School District

Usually, only two administrative structures affect salary recommendations. If a school district does not engage in collective bargaining, the superintendent of schools, with the advice of the school business administrator, is directly responsible for making the salary recommendations. However, if the school district engages in collective bargaining, the board will be asked to ratify a master contract, which will normally have major sections devoted to salary and wages. The chief negotiator for the school district, with input from the superintendent of schools, will have negotiated within preestablished fiscal considerations. In this latter situation, the salary recommendations along with working conditions and fringe benefits, which also have a dollar value, must be evaluated by the board.

Employee Unions and Associations

The American Federation of Teachers, the National Education Association, and many unions representing noninstructional personnel have official positions on salary and wage policies. Most of these unions and associations seek comparability with the private sector and negotiate for their membership along this line. Within recent years, these organizations have come to realize that, because of the large numbers of people they represent, they have

---

[18]W. E. Campbell, "Presentation of Salary Recommendations to the Board and the Community," in Foster, *Wage and Salary Administration,* 59–62.

a great deal of political influence. This influence has had an effect on the election not only of school board members but also of state legislators and even national candidates. An endorsement by a national labor or teacher organization such as the National Education Association is much sought after by all presidential candidates.

Salary Recommendation Procedures

The procedure for presentation of salary schedules to the board, of course, will vary with the particular needs of the locality. Campbell has put together a set of procedures that can act as a guide to the superintendent of schools in formulating salary recommendations to the board of education. Following are his suggestions for adaptation to local needs.

1. Be sure that the recommendations are sound, that they have the backing of the staff, and that the employees themselves are reasonably satisfied. On these bases the administrator should have full confidence in his recommendations.

2. Prepare as much supporting data as needed to verify the soundness of the recommendations. Present schedules from comparable school systems and from private enterprise. Provide information relative to previous increases and show whether the recommendations will keep the noninstructional personnel at a desirable rate of increase in comparison with the increase granted the professional personnel.

3. Try to make recommendations as part of a package deal for all employees. Salary increases for teachers are generally favored in the community, even though funds may not always be available to pay as well as the public sentiment indicates. A factor especially in favor of the package deal is that the funds necessary to meet the salaries of the noninstructional personnel will represent a relatively small proportion of the total salary needs of the school system.

4. Secure when needed the services of a consulting firm to compile data regarding prevailing rates in the community. A consulting firm can also be of assistance in establishing classifications of employees and in writing job descriptions.

5. Emphasize the importance of the noninstructional personnel to the educational program. Show how instruction can be improved by having capable, well-paid employees to drive the busses, to provide the food services, to maintain the buildings and grounds, to care for and clean the physical facilities, to furnish the needed classroom materials at the appropriate time, and so on.

6. Appeal to the business side of the board members by showing the need for capable people to care for the board's property—to protect its investment. School buildings now require services beyond the level of the ordinary custodian. Efficiency reduces waste and breakdown and produces savings in time and funds.

7. Bring about realization on the part of the board of the value of the noninstructional employees to community life and their influence on how the community may view the schools. The noninstructional personnel are more likely to live in the immediate community than are the professional personnel. Employees satisfied with their salary schedules are more likely to be proud of their work and should be more likely to perform at a level of work efficiency which will benefit the school system and have beneficial effects in the community.

8. Emphasize the business and financial aspects of the school system to the community. The school system may be operating the largest bus system in the community. It may be selling more meals than the largest restaurant or possibly more than all the restaurants combined. Its program of maintenance and operation of buildings and grounds may be the largest in the community. Its total expenditures in the community for goods and contractual services may be among the highest in dollar volume in the community.[19]

Small Business Job Protection Act of 1996

This legislation[20] is commonly referred to as the "Minimum Wage Law," because the intent of the legislation was to increase the take-home wages of employees. The passage and signing into law of this act attracted much attention in the news media. When President Clinton signed the bill in August, 1996, the ceremony featured minimum-wage workers and their children, labor union officials, Congressional leaders, and Vice President Al Gore. To sign the bill, President Clinton used the desk of President Franklin Roosevelt's Labor Secretary, Francis Perkins.

The minimum wage was increased in two stages, $.50 per hour on October 1, 1996, which raised the total to $4.75; and on September 1, 1997, the minimum wage was increased by $.40 per hour to $5.15. Each increase impacted approximately 10 million workers who received an increase in their pay checks. However, individual states can raise the minimum wage to even higher levels. Further, cities may increase the minimum wage beyond federal and state levels.

Because the law was opposed by many small businesses, Congress included approximately $9 billion in tax breaks for businesses, which took effect over a seven-year period. For example, in the year of purchase the total cost of new equipment that a small business can claim for tax exemption was raised from $17,500 to $25,000.

A major implication for school districts, of course, is that budgets must be adjusted to account for the required increase in wages. Custodians, cafeteria workers, and bus drivers are probably the employees most affected by the new law.

Conclusions

A few final comments are appropriate at the end of this section on salary and wage administration. First, executive salaries are usually negotiated on a personal basis and do not fall within the limits of a salary schedule. The executive positions in school districts are relatively few and commonly pertain to the superintendency and associate or assistant superintendencies.

Second, it is extremely important to consider each salary schedule as a separate entity. In some school systems increases to teacher salary schedules are reflected in an additional percentage increase being applied to administrator schedules. This, of course, defeats the integrity of the salary schedule objective, which is to reward performance within salary limits that are competitive with other school districts and businesses in the community. This can only be done by analyzing each individual salary schedule.

---

[19]Campbell, *Presentation of Salary Recommendations,* 62–63. Modified for this presentation.

[20]Small Business Job Protection Act of 1996, H.R. 3448, 104th Cong., 2nd Session (1996).

When collective bargaining is involved, such a tied-in procedure also violates the distinction between management and employees. If an administrative salary schedule is affected by an increase to the teacher salary schedule resulting from collective negotiations, the administrators are in actuality being represented by the teachers' bargaining agent.

Third, extra pay for extra duty, which is the common language applied to overtime pay for instructional personnel and overtime pay for classified employees, should be determined by the same procedure used to establish regular salary and wages. The rewards of performance and competitiveness are also primary considerations in overtime compensation.

Fourth, this chapter was written from the viewpoint that salary and wage increases are rewards for performance and are not simply rewards for seniority with the school district. Many districts have developed salary schedules with channels reflecting academic preparation (bachelor's degree, master's degree, and so on) and steps reflecting seniority in the school district. The salary schedules recommended in this chapter provide for ranges reflecting job classification with step increases based on performance.

The practices in most public school districts are not in keeping with the principles set forth in this chapter, which essentially recommend establishing competitive compensation programs that will attract quality personnel. Allan Ornstein's predictions are even more ominous:

> These data and projections pose a grave threat to the teaching profession, affecting entry standards, job performance, and teacher morale. The bleak prospect will put tremendous pressure on teacher organizations to resort to strikes for improved salaries. Strikes, in turn, will pit teachers against the public. Departments and colleges of education will not escape unscathed. Fewer students—especially the academically talented—will seek careers in teaching. Unless we can convince the public that education is a wise investment, the future looks grim indeed.[21]

Indirect Compensation: Fringe Benefits Administration

Fringe benefits may be defined as benefits available to all employees resulting from a direct fiscal expenditure. Because fringe benefits are available to all employees and are not contingent upon performance, such services are not motivators but are more properly considered maintenance factors. Nevertheless, fringe benefits are commonly considered to be an important part of an effective compensation program. Retirement programs, medical and hospitalization insurance, and life insurance are only a few of the many fringe benefits offered to employees in school systems. Because these services are essential in our society, the quality of these and other fringe benefit programs can have a significant effect on the ability of a school district to attract and retain good employees. Conversely, absenteeism and employee turnover, which are signs of employee dissatisfaction, can possibly be kept to a tolerable level with good fringe benefit and salary programs.

---

[21]Allan C. Ornstein, "Teacher Salaries: Past, Present, Future," *Phi Delta Kappan* (June 1980), 679.

High employee turnover across the nation costs school districts millions of dollars each year. Recruiting, and hiring new employees, which creates direct expenditures of money, should be minimized to a reasonable turnover rate. This factor, however, does not begin to address the problem of meeting the primary objective of the school district to educate students when there is a continual flow of new employees.

Absenteeism costs corporations in the United States an average of $20 billion each year. Although figures on the cost of absenteeism to public education are not readily available, millions of dollars would be a conservative estimate. A substitute teacher must be hired whenever a teacher is absent. The students are still present, and the task of teaching them cannot be passed on to another of the district's regular teachers, nor can it wait until the absent teacher returns.

The key factor in addressing high employee turnover and absenteeism is to establish a positive approach. Attracting individuals with excellent credentials and a desire for excellence in performance, from the outset, will ultimately correct high turnover and absenteeism. Quality fringe benefits attract quality candidates for positions and will maintain employee commitment to the school district.

Types of Fringe Benefits

The prediction made by John Sullivan in 1972 has come to pass.[22] The cost of fringe benefits in the United States has risen to approximately 35 percent of total salary and wages paid to employees.

School districts across the country are experiencing severe financial problems. With financial problems continuing to spread, school districts have found that fringe benefit enrichment is an alternative when large wage and salary increases are not feasible. As more school districts develop elaborate fringe benefit programs, greater pressure has been placed on competing school districts to develop similar programs to attract and keep employees.

There is also a growing recognition that fringe benefits are nontaxable, which has been another major stimulus towards their expansion. If a teacher wants a certain amount of life insurance, there are two advantages in having it purchased by the school district. First, the premium will be lower because the school district will be purchasing a large degree of protection. Second, the teacher would pay the premium for the insurance out of his or her net pay, which is the dollar amount left over after paying taxes. If the school district pays the premium, the teacher has more wages left to pay for other needs and, therefore, this becomes an attractive fringe benefit.

Benefits Required by Law

Certain benefits must be provided by the school district: social security premiums, state retirement insurance, unemployment compensation, and workers' compensation. These benefits provide the employee with financial security and protection at retirement or termination, or when an injury occurs in the workplace; they also provide survivors' benefits to dependents in the event of the employee's death.

---

[22]John F. Sullivan, "Indirect Compensation: The Years Ahead," *California Management Review,* (Winter 1972), 73.

The social security program usually covers classified employees. Instructional and administrative personnel are normally included in state retirement programs. Social security is the major source of income for U.S. retirees. This program is financed by the contributions of employees, which are matched by the employer and computed as a percentage of the employee's earnings. Survivors' benefits for the dependents of a deceased employee and disability benefits for an employee who is unable to be gainfully employed are provided through the social security administration.

The Social Security Act is an important aspect of the United States government's attempt to care for and protect the aged by ensuring a minimal standard of living for them. Although social security is often referred to as an insurance program, this is a misnomer. Rather, it is a transfer program of a trust fund from one generation to another. We, the currently employed, pay a social security tax that is used to support yesterday's retired workers, dependents, and the disabled. It is important for human resources administrators to be cognizant of the fact that social security benefits and the program itself are subject to legislation. Thus, changes are certain to occur and must be continually monitored to ensure that adequate budgetary appropriations are available to meet the demands of these potential changes.

Unemployment compensation laws in most states provide benefits to individuals who are without a job. To qualify for these benefits, a person usually submits an application to the State Employment Agency for unemployment benefits and registers with that agency with a willingness to accept suitable employment offered through the agency. In addition, the person must have worked a minimum number of weeks before becoming unemployed.

Unemployment benefits are derived from a tax levied against employers calculated on a percentage of the employer's total salary payroll. Benefits received by unemployed workers are calculated from the individual's previous wage rate plus the length of previous employment. Unemployment benefits are provided on a limited basis, typically for a twenty-six week period.

Unemployment compensation also serves the total economy of our nation because it provides a stability in spending power during periods of high unemployment, as when a recession occurs.

Workers' compensation programs provide benefits to individuals injured or disabled while engaged in a job-related activity. Benefits paid to employees for injuries are based on schedules for minimum and maximum payments, depending on the type of injury sustained. For example, the loss of a hand is compensated with a higher dollar amount than the loss of a finger. In like manner, disability payments are calculated based on the individual's current salary, future earnings, and financial responsibilities.

The funds for workers' compensation programs are borne entirely by the employer. Although the programs are mandated by state laws, the method of obtaining workers' compensation insurance is usually left to the discretion of the employer, who may buy such protection from public or private agencies or provide the protection through a self-insuring program. Like social security and unemployment insurance, workers' compensation is subject to the legislative process. Thus, requirements and benefits will certainly change with the passage of time.

Where mandated by state laws, retirement programs for administrators and teachers generally follow the prescriptions of these other protection programs. Contributions are calculated on the basis of an employee's wages and are usually matched by the school district. Benefits based on contributions are paid upon retirement, with survivors benefits being available for the dependents of deceased employees.

In 1986 the United States Congress passed the Consolidated Omnibus Budget Reconciliation Act (COBRA). This federal law requires employers that provide group health plans for their employees and their dependents to offer an extension of the coverage on a temporary basis under certain conditions when coverage would usually end. An employee covered by the group health plan is eligible for continuation of coverage if his or her employment is terminated except in cases of gross misconduct, if he or she is laid off for economic reasons, or if he or she is reduced to part-time employment and thereby would usually lose coverage.

Family members of an employee are entitled to continued coverage under the following qualifying events: death of the employee; divorce or legal separation from the employee; medicare becoming the employee's primary health care coverage; termination, layoff, or part-time status of the employee; ceasing to be considered a dependent child under the plan.

There are notification requirements under this law and the employee or family members must pay the premiums for the extended group health plan coverage. Extended coverage may last for eighteen, twenty-nine, or thirty-six months dependent on certain qualifying conditions.

Voluntary Fringe Benefits

This category of benefits may be further divided into insurance programs, time away from the job, and services. Group insurance programs are available for almost every human need. Among the most common are major medical and hospitalization insurance, dental insurance, term life insurance, errors and omissions insurance, and optical insurance. The number of such programs made available to employees depends on the fiscal condition of the school district and the wishes of the employees. A school district is usually restricted by state statute to paying insurance premiums only for employees. Therefore, an employee who wishes to include dependents under such insurance programs, must pay the additional premium for this coverage.

Under federal law and Internal Revenue Service regulations, school districts can design "cafeteria" fringe benefit plans, which will allow individual employees to choose the benefits that most meet their needs. In addition, if the employee is to bear the cost of some of these programs, the premiums he or she pays can be deducted from his or her gross salary or wages before federal income taxes are levied.

This tax advantage for employees and the opportunity to choose their benefits from a predetermined list are two reasons why such programs are quite desirable. The administrative expense of such a program and the availability of insurance coverage that does not demand a high percentage of participation are problems. For example, a company may offer a dental insurance program to a school district only if there is 60 percent participation by employees.

Federal tax-qualified plans must not be offered to only highly compensated employees. Beginning in 1997, the definition of a *highly compensated employee* was changed to include an employee who was compensated for the preceding year in excess of $80,000 and which placed him or her in the category of the 20-percent highest paid employees. Federal tax-qualified plans are those that are exempt from taxation, such as 401(k) salary deferral plans.[23]

A fringe benefit that is often taken for granted by employees but creates an additional expense for a school district is time spent away from work. Therefore, sick leave, vacation time, paid holidays, and sabbatical leave are, in fact, benefits provided at the discretion of the school system. In very large school districts, this amounts to a considerable expenditure.

Corporations have long recognized the value of *services* in a fringe benefit program. Social and recreational events, employee assistance programs, wellness programs, cultural activities, credit unions, company cafeterias, company-provided transportation to and from work, tuition reimbursements, and child care centers are only a few of the services found in many large corporations.

School systems usually provide much more limited services. Services, such as time away from work, are seldom recognized by employees as fringe benefits. Those most commonly found in public education are expenses paid for attendance at workshops, professional meetings, and conventions; tuition reimbursement; and free lunches and coffee. In some districts experiencing a decrease in pupil enrollment and, thus, a reduction in staff, career counseling is provided to teachers in order to help them prepare for jobs outside education. In large school districts, central-office administrators are usually provided with district-owned automobiles to use when engaged in school business, or they receive mileage reimbursement.

Fringe benefits are certainly an important component of all compensation programs, and they are becoming even more important as alternatives to large salary and wage increases.

Managed Health Care

Health care costs continue to increase at an alarming rate. An alternative approach to traditional insurance programs that is meant to maintain a high quality of care but at a lower cost and in a more efficient manner is *managed health care.*

Managed health care coordinates services around the patient and thereby produces a more efficient delivery system. In order to accomplish this, school districts must employ *case management specialists* who have the job responsibility of evaluating cases that require extensive and/or expensive medical treatment. As an alternative to hiring case management specialists, a school district can contract with a company specializing in *third party health care administration.* These case managers or third party administrators work with patients and physicians in order to identify alternatives that are medically sound yet cost effective. A common example is developing a plan that incorporates outpatient care after sufficient inpatient hospital care rather than a prolonged hospital stay. Such specialists should also develop employee programs that encourage healthy lifestyles and the prevention of illness. It would probably be cost effective for a school district to offer mammograms or diabetes testing at a nominal cost to employees.

[23]Newkirk Products, Inc., "Nondiscrimination Provisions," *1996 Tax Law Summary,* 1996, 13.

There are various levels of managed health care. *Utilization management* attempts to control the cost of a school district's health benefit plan. This is best accomplished through *catastrophic case management* and *utilization review*. When an employee suffers a catastrophic illness, the case manager begins the process of assisting the patient and his or her physicians to access the best treatment at the lowest cost. This could include care in a rehabilitation center, nursing home, extended care facility, or outpatient services in the patient's home. The case manager will help negotiate rates with these various facilities.

Utilization review usually includes the reviewing of all inpatient admissions, outpatient surgical procedures, inpatient substance cases, and inpatient psychiatric care. The purpose is to ascertain if such services are medically sound. In addition, before a claim is paid, the case manager will review the charges for accuracy.

An alternative to hiring case management specialists or contracting with a third party health care administrator, is for a school district to join a *managed care network*. Physicians who are members of the network have agreed to certain fee guidelines and medical facilities that belong to the network have agreed to a certain quality of service and fee guidelines. The network provides the school district with the efficient processing of paperwork and also with cost information that will help the school district in its financial planning.

There are various types of networks. One type is called a *preferred provider organization* or PPO. Both hospitals and physicians belong to such a network. Physicians treat patients in their own offices. If a school district employee chooses a physician or hospital outside the network, most PPOs will pay a much smaller percentage of the bill. Hospitals and physicians outside the network cannot be monitored to insure quality care and cost containment.

A second type is a *health maintenance organization* or HMO. In this arrangement, each patient is provided with a network primary care physician who controls access within the network to care for the employee and his or her dependents. A prepaid fixed monthly fee for all services is another important feature of the HMO. Typically, HMO's are organized around four models: group, staff, individual practice, and point-of-service. In the group model, a group or groups of physicians provide care to patients at one or more locations. In the staff model, physicians are actually employed by an HMO and provide services at one or more locations. In the individual practice association model, an HMO contracts with physicians who practice out of their own offices. In the point-of-service model, an HMO allows school district employees to chose physicians outside the network but the employee will pay a higher percentage of the cost.

Many PPOs and HMOs have prescription drug plans whereby certain pharmacies within a network offer medication at a reduced cost. This kind of network can also be found outside of PPOs and HMOs.

Health Insurance Portability and Accountability Act of 1996 (HIPAA)

There was little media coverage of this bill[24] until August 21, 1996 when it was signed into law by President Bill Clinton. The law addresses the needs of approximately 25 million Americans who are denied health insurance coverage because of an illness or who cannot

[24]Health Insurance Portability and Accountability Act of 1996, H.R. 3103, 104th Cong., 2nd Session (1996).

change jobs because they, their spouse, or their dependents would be denied insurance coverage because of a preexisting medical condition such as diabetes. The law became effective at the beginning of a new plan year after July 1, 1997. The following are major provisions of HIPAA:

- Immediate coverage for the employee, spouse, and dependents by the new employer if the employee, spouse, and dependents were covered by the previous employer's health care plan for twelve months or eighteen months if they enter the new employer's plan late.
- Immediate coverage for pregnant women, newborns, and children placed in the employee's home pending adoption.
- The new employer can deny coverage for up to one year for a preexisting condition, if the employee, spouse, and dependents were not covered by the previous employer for twelve or eighteen months respectively. If there was a break in the previous coverage for more than sixty-three days, the waiting period could start over again.
- Employers can limit a new employee, spouse, and dependents to the same coverage they had with the previous employer even if other employees have additional coverage.
- The health care plan with the new employer could exclude coverage for certain illnesses and could place a cap on benefit coverage
- Local and state government health care plans may exempt themselves from this law.
- Employers can make premium adjustments to their plans or increase copayments and deductibles in order to offset high claims experience as long as these modifications are applicable to all employees.
- If the new employer does not provide a health care plan, the state in which the school district is located is responsible for providing unrestricted access to a choice of individual health insurance policies to those individuals, their spouses and dependents who were covered by a group health care plan for at least eighteen months with a previous employer.

The law does not address the needs of people who are uninsured because they cannot afford to pay insurance premiums. Additionally, individuals who have insurance for long-term care can receive a tax deduction for the cost of the premium and the cost of the care. Finally, the law authorized a pilot program, *medical savings accounts,* as an alternative to conventional health insurance policies for self-employed people and for employees of small companies. The law also required medical plans to cover illnesses arising from genetic defects. Further, accidents which are caused through participation in recreation activities or hobbies such as skiing must now be covered by health care plans.

School districts must now require their insurance companies to delete provisions from insurance policies that discriminate against employees, employee spouses, and their dependents because of preexisting medical conditions. Small school districts could also be eligible for medical savings accounts.

Medical Savings Accounts
The Health Insurance Portability and Accountability Act of 1996 established a pilot Medical Savings Accounts (MSAs) program in an attempt to control the rising cost of health

care.[25] The program began in 1997 and continued through the year 2000. After the year 2000, employees of school districts that had already established MSAs were allowed to continue with this program. In order to qualify, a school district had to provide a health care plan with a large deductible and had to meet the "small employer" designation. Under this approach, employees can choose the physicians, hospitals, and treatment options they want. Major illnesses are paid for by school districts' insurance companies while money withdrawn from the Medical Savings Accounts is used to pay for minor health care costs. Health insurance coverage with a high deductible creates a much lower costing premium than coverage with a low deductible. A high-deductible plan is one with an annual deductible of at least $1,500 but not more than $2,250 for single coverage or for family coverage with at least a $3,000 but no more than a $4,500 deductible.

Thus, the employer could purchase high-deductible health care insurance and would establish MSAs for each employee. The amount of money saved by the district could then be placed in each employee's medical savings account. Also, the employee can authorize the employer to deduct a certain amount of money from his or her payroll check before taxes are assessed to be placed in the medical savings account to pay for dependent spouse and/or children health care costs that are minor. If the deductible is reached, the health insurance company will pay for the incurred cost.

A small school district is one with no more than fifty employees during the preceding or second preceding year. An employer may continue to establish an MSA for new employees or employees who previously did not have an MSA until the year following the first year when a school district has two hundred employees. After reaching this plateau, no new MSAs may be established.

The medical savings account is under the control of the employee, and each year additional contributions could be made to MSAs from the employee through the employer for his or her dependent coverage. The account should be interest bearing and unspent funds can grow from the contributions and interest. The employee could make withdrawals for nonmedical purposes but such withdrawals would be taxed and penalized.

It is estimated that only 5 to 10 percent of employees would reach the deductible each year. Former employees on Medicare have an option of receiving health insurance and a large contribution to a medical savings account from Medicare funds.

The advantages of MSAs are considerable. Among the most obvious are:

- National reduction of health care costs
- Increased savings for employers
- Increased saving for employees
- Retirement savings for health and nonhealth expenses
- Patients' control of health care choice
- Health care coverage for people and their dependents between jobs (portability)

Procuring Health Care and Related Insurance

In large school districts, the process for procuring fringe benefit insurance is usually the responsibility of the purchasing and procurement departments along with significant involvement of the director of employee benefits who reports to the assistant superintendent for

[25]Newkirk Products, Inc., "Health Care-Related Provisions," *1996 Tax Law Summary,* 1996, 1–3.

human resources.[26] In medium-size districts, an assistant superintendent may be assigned this responsibility; while in small school districts, the superintendent of schools will probably implement the procurement process. Of course, many school districts hire an insurance consultant or broker, who will not be permitted to place a bid, to help in developing the bid specifications and may also oversee the bidding process including the analysis of the bids.

The health care industry has been experiencing a period of significant change and modification; Exhibit 8.6 sets forth categories of coverage in a typical health care program which must be considered when developing such a program.

EXHIBIT 8.6   Categories of Coverage in a Typical Health Care Program

Physician and Hospital Selection
Annual Deductible
Copayment
Preventive Care
   Routine Physical
   Gynecological Exams
   Eye Exams
   Immunizations
   Well-Baby and Pediatric Care
   Pediatric Dental Exams
Health Education
Home Care
Physician Care
Diagnostic Services (including X-ray and laboratory tests)
Surgery
   Outpatient
   Consultations and Second Opinions
Physical Medicine and Occupational Therapy
Hospital Services
Maternity Care
   Prenatal Care
   Postnatal Care
   Delivery
Mental Health Benefits
   Outpatient
   Inpatient
Chemical Dependency Benefits
   Outpatient
   Inpatient
Emergency Care
Prescription Drugs and Medications
Away from Home Care
Maximum Out-of-Pocket Costs to the Employee
Maximum Cost Paid in Claims for the Employee

---

[26]William T. Rebore, Ronald W. Rebore, *Financial and Business Administration in Public Education* (Needham Heights, MA: Allyn & Bacon, 1993), 271–278.

The Insurance Agent and Broker

An insurance policy is a legal contract between an insurance company and the school district. The provisions of insurance policies are usually developed by a third party, an insurance agent, or broker. The majority of insurance companies do business under the American Agency System whereby insurance companies contract with individuals within a given territory. This individual is referred to as an agent because he or she is authorized to issue policies, collect premiums, and solicit renewals. Independent agents represent several insurance companies, whereas exclusive agents only represent a single company.

Insurance brokers are not under contract to any specific insurance company, and they act on a freelance basis. Thus, brokers buy insurance coverage for clients. The broker can purchase insurance directly from an insurance company or may place business through an insurance agent. The major difference, therefore, between an agent and a broker lies in the fact that the agent may act on behalf of the company. If an agent states that the school district is covered by an insurance policy even before the policy is issued, then it is covered. A broker must receive written verification from an insurance company.

Selecting Insurance Companies

There are literally thousands of insurance companies selling some form of health care and related insurance in the United States. Companies differ significantly due to their financial capacity to assure timely and accurate processing and payment of claims. In addition, third party management companies that process claims for school districts that are self-insured also vary depending on their fiscal solvency and performance.

Thus, when bids are received from health care and related services insurance companies or third-party management companies, it is essential to check their performance and financial solvency with well-established rating firms. Among the nationally recognized rating firms are A.M. Best of Oldwick (New Jersey), Duff & Phelps of Chicago, Moody's of New York, and Standard & Poor's of New York. These firms use a letter grade that they award to insurance provider companies based on each company's performance and viability. A.M. Best awards a range of grades from a top grade of A++ to a low grade of F; Duff & Phelps uses AAA to CCC; Moody awards range from a top of AAA to a low grade of C; and Standard & Poor's uses AAA to R. School districts can directly contact at least one of these rating firms with the list of insurance companies that have submitted a bid. The rating firms may charge the school district a fee for their services. Insurance companies desiring a rating must pay an annual fee to the rating firms; thus, many insurance companies may not request a rating from all the rating companies. Consequently, school districts should request in the bidding process that the insurance companies identify the firm or firms by whom they are rated.

The specifications in the request for proposals bid package should be written in such a way that the school district can select a single company to provide all the lines of health care and related insurance or a group of companies with each providing a different benefit. In selecting one or more health care and related insurance companies or third party companies, the following criteria should constitute the minimum required: successful experience in providing coverage or management in at least two other school districts with an equal number of employees and similar benefits; written references from other school districts stating that claims were accurately and promptly processed; useful communication literature for employees concerning the coverage and claims process; evidence that the school district will be required to provide only reasonable administrative assistance; affordable premiums for the district and the employees; and evidence that the insurance companies or management companies will use accurate and appropriate data in establishing future premiums.

Of course, there is a direct relationship between the premium a school district pays for health care and related insurance and the claims experience of the group of employees covered by the insurance. When the sum of money paid in claims is high, premiums are correspondingly higher. Most insurance companies are "for profit," and therefore the premium includes a profit for the company. Premiums also include not only enough money to pay claims but also to build up a reserve for cash flow purposes. In addition, the premium includes a reserve to pay outstanding claims if the school district takes bids and awards a contract to a different insurance company.

There is a significant financial advantage to the school district if the health care and related insurance lines have a deductible that must be paid by the employee before the district's insurance program incurs a claim. There is a direct relationship between the amount of the premium paid by the district and the size of the deductible. For example, if an employee must pay the first $250 in medical costs, the cost of premium paid by the district will be less then if the employee has to pay only the first $100. The reason for this is obvious—a claim is incurred after the $100 rather than after the $250.

There are several reasons why a school district should require a deductible for all premium related fringe benefits. The most important reasons are:

- Deductibles encourage employees to retain some responsibility for controlling costs.
- Deductibles avoid nuisance claims.
- Deductibles help to preserve a competitive market for the district's insurance program.
- Deductibles help to reduce administrative costs.

A *copayment* is an alternative to deductibles that is also a financial benefit to a school district if it is incorporated into the district's health care and related insurance program. For example, a district's program could require a $10 copayment for an office visit to a physician; the insurance program would pay the remainder of the cost for the visit. The copayment approach is more commonly used for prescription drugs and medications. Like deductibles, the copayments would encourage employees to be more responsible in controlling health costs.

Even if a school district has self-funded health care and related insurance programs, deductibles and copayments can bring about the same advantages cited above. The single most important reason why a school district would create a self-funded health care and related benefits program is to save money. There are two ways that a school district can save money if it uses a self-funded approach: first, the premium set aside by the district will not include a profit; second, the money budgeted from the district's revenue for health care and related benefits can be invested, and the interest will help to reduce the cost of the benefits programs during periods of time without large claims.

Self-funding, however, will require a school district to purchase "stop loss" insurance. The purpose of stop loss insurance is to pay a portion of the cost of claims arising from catastrophic illnesses that would significantly deplete the pool of money set aside to pay claims. Insurance should be purchased for individual claims after a certain amount has been paid through the district's self-funded programs and for claims in the aggregate after a certain amount has been paid. For example, the birth of a premature baby will result in a costly hospital bill. Stop loss insurance could pay for that portion of the hospital bill over

$100,000, or any other limit set by the school district. In like manner, stop loss insurance could pay for claims from all employees taken together that exceed $3,000,000. The cost of the premium for stop loss insurance depends on the amount of money that the school district pays in claims. Obviously, the more money the school district pays in claims, the less the district will pay in premiums for stop loss insurance.

In those school districts where employee benefits are bargained collectively, these issues are affected by the master agreement. If a school district and its employees do not bargain collectively or do not include these benefits in the negotiations, it is very important for the superintendent to establish an employee advisory committee. This committee should be charged with reviewing the district's health care and related programs, making suggestions for improvements in benefits, making suggestions for containing costs, reviewing specifications for bidding benefit insurance, reviewing the analysis of bids, and for annually making recommendations to the assistant superintendent for human resources through the director of employee benefits.

Health Risks in the Workplace

A major issue facing many school districts across the nation is the rising cost of workers' compensation. In the early years of this century, workers who were injured on the job had to pay for their own medical treatment and probably received no wages during the recovery period. If a worker was seriously injured with an extensive recovery period, he or she most likely would not have a job even when able to return to work. Around 1910 individual states began to adopt various systems of workers' compensation. This approach required employers to compensate workers injured on the job regardless of who was at fault. In return the workers were not allowed to sue their employers. The system has been beneficial not only for workers but also for employers.[27]

However, medical costs associated with workers' compensation has risen over the last ten years. There are probably three major reasons for this dramatic rise in cost. First, in trying to contain general health care costs, employers have initiated cost-cutting measures such as higher deductibles, copayments, case management, utilization reviews, and the establishment of health maintenance and preferred provider organizations. Although these measures contained costs in general health care, employees are now utilizing workers' compensation to receive the same level of benefits prior to initiating the cost-cutting measures. Workers' compensation usually pays the total cost of medical treatment. Second, the original "no fault" approach has deteriorated into a massive legal bureaucracy where lawyers and judges have become the central figures in workers' compensation cases. Finally, the nature of the workplace has dramatically changed with the effect of producing more complicated injuries. In addition there has emerged a new category of injuries termed "cumulative trauma," which is associated with repetitive work such as exposure to a video display terminal for long periods of time. Psychological stress is also a form of cumulative trauma.[28]

---

[27]Greg Steinmetz, "States Take On the Job of Holding Down Medical Costs of Workers' Compensation," *Wall Street Journal,* 3 March 1993, sec. B, B1.

[28]Michael S. Pritula, "Workers' Comp: Tranquilizing a Benefit Gone Mad," *Wall Street Journal,* 13 January 1992, sec. A, A16.

For school district employees, there are three major categories of health risks. School facility environmental risks are the first. These include: radon gas, lead in the drinking water, asbestos in floor tile and other building materials, tobacco smoke, fungi, mold and spores, pesticides, cleaning materials, and so on.[29] The second category is violence. Today, teachers and staff members are working with students who have a history of committing violent acts. The emergence of gangs is a contributing factor to the increasing number of violent acts committed against teachers and staff members. Finally, there is the risk of contracting infectious disease that comes with working with children. For special education teachers who work with children who are multiply impaired or physically impaired, there is the risk of back injuries because many of these children must be lifted from one position to another.

Employees need and want health information that will help them manage the work environment in such a way that they can be as health conscious as possible. It is the responsibility of human resources administrators to devise methods for providing this information to employees. Such information could prevent an employee from being injured or from contracting diseases.[30]

As set forth in Chapter 1, fringe benefit management is a component of the human resources function and because workers' compensation is such a complicated and expensive fringe benefit, more and more school districts have established the position of risk manager. This position usually reports to the assistant superintendent for human resources. The responsibilities of this position include identifying and evaluating the school district's exposure to risks. It is possible to seek assistance from the school district's insurance agent or broker or underwriter to help the risk manager conduct an audit in order to ascertain the exposure of the district to injuries on the job. When these risks are identified, the next step is to minimize or eliminate the potential risk.[31] For example, if a school has a problem with gangs, the most appropriate method of dealing with this issue is to develop a comprehensive security program. This plan might include hiring security guards; developing gang prevention or self-esteem curricula; targeting at-risk students for special prevention programs; increasing job opportunities and drug education; strengthening extracurricular and recreational programs, and so on.[32] The development of the strategy which will eventuate into such a security program becomes the responsibility of the director of risk management.

A second example of a method for minimizing or eliminating risk is a comprehensive staff development program. For example, maintenance and custodial staff members are consistently utilizing potentially dangerous equipment and hazardous chemicals. The manufacturer's sales representative or distributor of cleaning chemicals is usually available to train employees in the proper use of equipment and supplies.

Finally, if it is impossible to eliminate or significantly minimize a risk, it will be necessary to develop procedures that will ensure that the workers' compensation program is effective in meeting the needs of the employees.

[29]Cathryn Ehrhardt, "Environmental Policy—a Priority for Schools in the 90's," *Updating School Board Policies,* 20, no. 8 (September 1989), 2–3.

[30]Lin Grensing-Pophas, "Health Education Turns Proactive," *HRMagazine,* 50, no. 4 (April 2005), 101–104.

[31]William T. Rebore and Ronald W. Rebore, *Financial and Business Administration in Public Education* (Needham Heights, MA: Allyn & Bacon, 1993), 272–273.

[32]Cathryn Ehrhardt, "Gangs, Cults, and Hate Groups: Where Does Rebellion End and Trouble Begin?" *Updating School Board Policies,* 21, no. 4 (April/May 1990), 3.

Crisis Event Managment

Crises have been a concern in schools and school districts throughout the history of public education. However, the tragic violence that took place at Columbine High School in Littleton, Colorado, in 1999 brought not only the issue of student violence but also the issue of crisis event management to the attention of the U.S. public. In terms of risk management, violence is one of an entire range of crises that need to be addressed in all schools and school districts. Crises occur because of a variety of situations, such as the following:

- *Accidents.* Arising out of human error, equipment malfunction, or inadequately maintained facilities
- *Misconduct.* Including bullying of students and staff members, theft, threats, sexual harassment, and immoral public behavior
- *Natural disasters.* Including earthquakes, droughts, floods, landslides, tornadoes and hurricanes, and storms
- *Technology malevolence.* Sabotage of computer equipment and software, unauthorized entry into computer programs, and breaching the confidentiality of computer records
- *Violence.* Ranging from self-inflicted deadly physical injury, as in suicide, to the injuring and killing of others

Of course, these are not the only crises facing school administrators nor the full range of possible crises. However, they do represent some of the more common occurrences that require the attention of the director of risk management.

When a crisis occurs, it is usually without warning, and the response that is required to manage the event is time-sensitive. Immediate action is required that could catch off-guard administrators in the unprepared school district. If a school district has a director of risk management, he or she should have the responsibility of managing the entire crisis event. He or she will need the assistance of other administrators including the assistant superintendents and other central office administrators and staff members who should have specific responsibilities in a crisis. For example, the director of maintenance and custodial services could be responsible for notifying public services such as the police and fire departments. The director of community relations could be responsible for contacting the news media and for issuing statements and other communications about the crisis. The director of employee benefits could be responsible for making certain that injured staff members and students are receiving proper medical attention. If the event occurs in a school, the building principal along with the counselor and other professional staff members will be responsible for communicating with parents and students. The director of transportation could be responsible for evacuating other students and staff members from the crisis scene. Securing the facility and equipment could be the responsibility of the maintenance or custodial supervisors.

Summary

Psychologists have long recognized that satisfaction of needs is the primary motivation behind all human actions. In satisfying their needs, individuals will act in ways that they perceive to be in their own best interest. A manager who understands human motivation and what employees believe to be in their best interests is able to develop a unique compensation system.

School district administrators should attempt to utilize an "expectancy model" as the vehicle for developing a compensation system. With this model, compensation is linked to employee behaviors that both meet the objectives of the school district and satisfy the needs of the employees.

Five variables must be taken into consideration in a compensation program: employee performance, effort, seniority, skills, and job requirements. The rewarding of performance, however, must be the primary objective of a compensation program.

An effective program must include both intrinsic and extrinsic compensation. Intrinsic compensation consists of those that pertain to the quality of the job situation; they may include participation in the policy-making process, increased responsibility, and greater job discretion. Extrinsic rewards are divided into direct and indirect compensation. Direct compensation is commonly referred to as salary or wages; indirect compensation is frequently referred to as fringe benefits. Nonfinancial compensation has begun to appear in some school districts and is limited only by the imagination of the administration. It is tailored to meet the needs of individual employees. For example, a very status-conscious employee might consider a reserved parking place as a reward for exceptional performance.

Direct compensation, salary and wages, can be effectively administered only if the following principles are incorporated into the pay policy: Skills required in various positions must be recognized; salaries must be competitive; the primary focus of salary increases must be improved performance; and salary schedules must be reviewed annually.

An important question central to all pay policies is, "Does money motivate?" A reasonable conclusion, supported by experience and research, is that money does affect performance if it is clear that performance is rewarded by a salary increase.

There are a number of other issues in salary and wages management that must command the attention of human resources administrators. These issues will have an effect on pay policy development and include public disclosure of salaries, compensation packaging, equity of pay and performance, techniques for collecting community wage data, methods of making salary recommendations to the school board, payroll deductions, employee reactions to salary decisions, appropriate pay periods, annual wage review, and salary schedule construction.

Indirect compensation, or fringe benefits, may be defined as benefits that are available to all employees and that help a school district to attract and retain good employees. Certain fringe benefits are required by law. These include social security, state retirement programs, unemployment insurance, and workers' compensation.

Federal law requires school districts that provide group health plans for their employees and their dependents to offer an extension of the coverage on a temporary basis under certain conditions when coverage would usually end.

Voluntary fringe benefits may be divided into insurance programs, time away from the job, and services. Group insurance programs are available for almost every human need and include medical and hospitalization insurance, dental insurance, term life insurance, errors and omissions insurance, and optical insurance.

A fringe benefit often taken for granted by employees is time away from the job—including sick leave, vacation time, paid holidays, and sabbatical leave. In like manner, certain services offered by school districts are in reality fringe benefits. These include expenses paid for attendance at workshops, professional meetings, and conventions; tuition reimbursement; and free lunches. Central-office administrators are usually given use of a school district automobile or receive mileage compensation. In districts experiencing decreasing enrollments, teachers are being offered career counseling services in order to help them look for a job outside education.

Health care costs continue to increase at an alarming rate. Managed health care is an alternative approach to the traditional insurance programs and is meant to maintain a high quality of care but at a lower cost and in a more efficient manner. Many school districts hire case management specialists who have the job responsibility of helping to contain costs while still providing quality health care to employees of the school district. Two alternatives to this approach are for a district to contract with a third party health care administration company or to join a managed health care network.

A major issue facing many school districts across the nation, is the rising cost of workers' compensation. For school district employees, there are three major categories of health risks: environmental risks; the risk of violence; and the risks, such as contracting infectious disease, that come from working with children. Many school districts have created the position of risk manager. The responsibilities of this position include identifying risks and then developing a plan to minimize risks.

Crises occur because of a variety of situations which include: accidents, misconduct, natural disasters, technology malevolence, and violence. Crises are time sensitive and require immediate action. The director of risk management should be responsible for managing the entire crisis event, but will need the assistance of other administrators.

The director of employee benefits supervises the staff in the fringe benefits department. Of course, the director reports to the assistant superintendent for human resources.

Fringe benefits, as an alternative to large salary and wage increases will continue to play a significant role in compensating employees.

Discussion Questions and Statements

- From an expectancy model perspective, what elements would you include in compensation programs?
- Describe the variables that affect compensation programs.
- Define direct compensation and explain what should be taken into consideration in developing such a program.
- Identify and describe the most common types of mandatory and voluntary fringe benefits.
- What is the relationship between compensation and higher levels of employee performance?

Suggested Activities

- You are the Director of Employee Benefits in a large metropolitan school district with more than 5,000 employees. The state where your school district is located does not have a strong collective negotiations law for public employees. Develop, in writing, a process that you would use to create a voluntary fringe benefits program.

- Visit the payroll office of a school district and discuss how position control is maintained so that someone inside the organization cannot create a fictitious employee who receives a salary.
- Ask a human resources administrator in a school district about what percentage of the personnel budget goes for workers' compensation claims and discuss if this is a reasonable amount.
- Find websites that deal with health risks in the workplace. Also, interview a human resources administrator about the most effective way to conduct a safety and security audit.
- Interview a human resources administrator in person or on the telephone and discuss the advantages of managed health care.

Selected Bibliography

Abel, Gene B., "School District Health Care Expenses: Moderating the Escalating Rate of Growth," *School Business Affairs,* 57, no. 12 (December 1991), 26–28.

Andrews, Hans, *Merit in Education.* Stillwater, OK: New Forums Press, 1988.

Brandt, Richard M., *Incentive Pay and Career Ladders for Teachers.* Albany, NY: University of New York Press, 1990.

Christmann, Robert W., "Getting Behind Pay-for-Performance," *School Business Affairs,* 63, no. 8 (August 1997), 7–11.

Conley, S., and A. R. Ogden. "Linking Teacher Compensation to Teacher Career Development: A Strategic Examination," *Educational Evaluation and Policy Analysis,* 17, no. 2 (1995), 219–238.

Deeb, William S., "Curbing Workers' Comp," *School Business Affairs,* 64, no. 8 (August 1998), 44–46.

DiCello, Jim, "Safety Procedures for Emergencies," *School Business Affairs,* 64, no. 7 (July 1998), 16–17.

Dickson, Lou Ann S., Mary Walton, and Virginia Guy, "Teacher Attitudes Toward a Career Ladder," *Spectrum: Journal of School Research and Information,* 10, no. 2 (Spring 1992), 27–34.

Educational Research Service Staff, "Changes in Salaries and Wages for Public School Employees," *Spectrum: Journal of School Research and Information,* 11, no. 2 (Spring 1993), 44–47.

Firestone, William A., "Merit Pay and Job Enlargement as Reforms: Incentives, Implementation, and Teacher Response," *Evaluation and Policy Analysis,* 13, no. 3 (1991), 269–288.

Firestone, William A., "Redesigning Teacher Salary Systems for Educational Reform," *American Educational Research Journal,* 31, no. 3 (Fall 1994), 549–574.

Grensing-Pophas, Lin, "Health Education Turns Proactive," *HRMagazine,* 50, no. 4 (April 2005), 101–104.

Garvey, Charlotte, "Philosophizing Compensation," *HRMagazine,* 50, no. 1 (January 2005), 73–78.

Hatry, Harry P., John M. Greiner, and Brenda G. Ashford, *Issues and Case Studies in Teacher Incentive Plans,* 2nd ed. Lanham, MD: University Press of America, 1994.

Heneman, Robert L., and Gerald E. Ledford, "Competency Pay for Professionals and Managers in Business: A Review and Implications for Teachers," *Journal of Personnel Evaluation in Education,* 12, no. 2 (June 1998), 103–121.

Jenkins, G. D., G. E. Ledford, N. Gupta, and D. H. Doty, *Skill-Based Pay: Practices, Payoffs, Pitfalls, and Prescriptions.* Scottsdale, AZ: American Compensation Association, 1992.

Joiner, Lottie L., "Life-Saving Lessons: What Have Schools Learned Since Columbine About Keeping Students Safe?" *American School Board Journal,* 189, no. 3 (March 2002), 14–18.

Kelley, Carolyn, and Allan Odden, *Reinventing Teacher Compensation Systems.* Madison, WI: Consortium for Policy Research in Education, 1995.

Kennedy, M., "Crisis Management: Every School Needs a Plan," *American School and University,* 71 (1999), 25–28.

King, Richard A., and Judith K. Mathers, "Improving Schools through Performance-Based Accountability and Financial Rewards," *Journal of Educational Finance,* 23, no. 2 (Fall 1997), 147–176.

Lankford, Hamilton, and James Wyckoff, "The Changing Structure of Teacher Compensation," *Economics of Education Review,* 16, no. 4 (October 1997), 371–384.

Martini, Jr., Gilbert R., "Wellness Programs: Preventive Medicine to Reduce Health Care Costs," *School Business Affairs,* 57, no. 6 (June 1991), 8–12.

Milanowski, Anthony, Allan Odden, and Peter Youngs, "Teacher Knowledge and Skill Assessments and Teacher Compensation: An Overview of Measurement and Linkage Issues," *Journal of Personnel Evaluation in Education,* 12, no. 2 (June 1998), 83–101.

Mohrman, Allan M., Jr., Susan Albers Mohrman, and Allan R. Odden, "Aligning Teacher Compensation with Systemic School Reform: Skill-Based Pay and Group-Based Performance Rewards," *Educational Evaluation and Policy Analysis,* 18, no. 1 (Spring 1996), 51–71.

Natale, Jo Anna, "Shopping for Health Benefits," *The American School Board Journal,* 179, no. 1 (January 1992), 38–40.

Odden, Allan, and Carolyn Kelley, *Paying Teachers for What They Know and Do: New and Smarter Compensation Strategies to Improve Schools.* Thousand Oaks, CA: Corwin Press, 1996.

Petersen, George J., Dale Pietrzak, and Kathryne Speaker, "The Enemy Within: A National Study on School Violence and Prevention," *Urban Education,* 33, no. 3 (September 1998), 331–359.

Progressive Policy Institute. *Better Pay for Better Teaching—Making Teacher Compensation Pay Off in the Age of Accountability.* Washington, DC: The Institute, 2002.

Rowe, Roger E., "Risk Management: A Leader's Responsibility," *Facilities Manager,* 13, no. 6 (November–December 1997), 35–36.

Southern Regional Education Board, *Paying for Performance—Important Questions and Answers.* Atlanta, GA: The Board, 1990.

Stemphens, Ronald D., "Ten Steps to Safer Schools," *American School Board Journal,* 185, no. 3 (March 1998), 30, 32–33.

Stites, Janet, "Equal Pay for the Sexes," *HRMagazine,* 50, no. 5 (May 2005), 64–69.

U.S. Department of Education, *Teacher Incentive Programs in the Public Schools.* Washington, DC: Office of Educational Research and Improvement, 1989.

U.S. Department of Education, *Teacher Salaries—Are They Competitive?* Washington, DC: OERI/ Education Information Branch, 1993.

Appendix
Position Description Questionnaire

Instructions to Employee

1. Please read through the entire questionnaire carefully to familiarize yourself with all questions asked.
2. Once you have read the questionnaire, answer each question as carefully and completely as possible. If additional space is needed to answer any question, please indicate "over" and use back side of the sheet.

Source: Adapted from *Wage and Salary Administration: A Handbook for School Business Officials,* Charles W. Foster, ed. (Chicago: Research Corporation of the Association of School Business Officials, 1960), 65–77.

   If the question asked does not apply to your position, please write "does not apply" or "not applicable" in the space provided. Only in this way can we be certain you have considered each question and can you be certain you have not missed an important question.

3. When you have completed the questionnaire, return it to your department head or supervisor.

   You are urged to use care and deliberation in the completion of the questionnaire. The information you provide in your replies will be one of a number of means used to develop an official description of your position.

   When this questionnaire has been completed and reviewed by your supervisor or department head, it should be forwarded to the director of human resources. After a description has been written, the job evaluation committee of the school system will evaluate the position and recommend assignment to the appropriate salary classification.

Position Description Questionnaire

I. GENERAL INFORMATION

1. Your full name: _____ Date: _____
   (First)　　(Middle or Maiden)　　(Last)

2. Title of your position: _____
   When appointed to this position: _____
   　　　　　　　　　　　　　　　　　(Date)

3. To your knowledge, is this position ever referred to by another title? If so, what title or titles are used? _____
   _____

4. To which major division is your position assigned? (e.g., Division of Business Administration, Division of School Administration, Division of Instruction) _____
   _____

5. To which specific unit (office, department, school) is your position assigned? _____
   _____

6. Regular daily hours of work:　　From _____ to _____

7. What is the position title and name of your immediate supervisor? (i.e., the person or persons who assign work to you regularly and to whom you report)
   　　　　　TITLE　　　　　　　　　　　　　　　NAME
   _____　　　　_____

8. If your immediate supervisor is someone other than your department head, what is the title and name of your department head? (If same person, write "same.")
   　　　　　TITLE　　　　　　　　　　　　　　　NAME
   _____　　　　_____

9. What are the position titles and names of the persons whom you supervise directly? (i.e., the persons to whom you give work assignments and from whom you receive reports on work progress. If no one, write "none.")

Continued

TITLES	DEPT. OR DIVISION	NAMES
_____	_____	_____
_____	_____	_____

10. What employees do you regularly train or instruct on the job?

	FREQUENCY			ONLY NEW EMPLOYEES
POSITION TITLE	WEEKLY	MONTHLY	SEVERAL TIMES A YEAR	JOIN DEPARTMENT
_____	_____	_____	_____	_____
_____	_____	_____	_____	_____

11. To what position, or positions, within the school system would a person normally consider a logical promotion from your position?

_____

12. What jobs or positions within the school system do you feel have responsibilities about equal to yours?

_____   _____
_____   _____

13. What position in the department, bureau, section or office to which you are now assigned is the next more responsible position?

_____

II. ASSIGNED FUNCTIONS AND RESPONSIBILITIES

1. What is the basic function or purpose of your position? (e.g., to provide typing assistance to the _____ department; to receive all persons entering building and direct them to desired office; to direct and coordinate the instructional program)

_____
_____

2. What regular duties or assigned responsibilities do you perform in your position? (Please list all of the duties you can think of, and be as specific as possible, e.g., clean windows, prepare purchase requisitions, conduct staff conferences.) Indicate frequency of performance by code letters as follows:

Daily or several times weekly   Code "D"
Weekly   Code "W"
Monthly   Code "M"
Occasionally during the year   Code "Y"

DUTIES	CODE
_____	_____

3. What machines requiring special skills do you use in your work?

	FREQUENCY (CHECK ONE)	
CONTINUOUSLY	FREQUENTLY	OCCASIONALLY
_____	_____	_____
_____	_____	_____

4. What special nonmachine skills do you use in your work? (e.g., bookkeeping, creative writing, higher mathematics, etc.)

FREQUENCY (CHECK ONE)

CONTINUOUSLY	FREQUENTLY	OCCASIONALLY
_____	_____	_____
_____	_____	_____

5. What grade level of education did you complete? (check one)

8th grade (or below)	_____	1 yr. college	_____
9th grade	_____	2 yrs. college	_____
10th grade	_____	3 yrs. college	_____
11th grade	_____	4 yrs. college	_____
12th grade	_____	5 yrs. college	_____
or equivalent to above grade		6 yrs. college	_____
checked in special courses	_____	7 yrs. or more college	_____

Up to

1 year special courses after high school	_____
2 years special courses after high school	_____
3 years special courses after high school	_____
4 years special courses after high school	_____

6. If you have completed a college or university program, what degree(s) did you earn and in what major subject area?

_____

_____

7. Have you taken other courses, not covered above, to enable you to qualify for your present position or another position in the school system? (Please explain type of course, length, etc.)

_____

_____

8. Is accuracy or working within close precision limits a requirement of your job? _____
YES OR NO

If yes, which of the following would best describe the effect of errors you might make?

_____ Errors would be corrected early and would not be significant.

_____ Errors might involve small losses of money. Corrections can be made with minor inconvenience to other employees or supervisor.

_____ Errors might involve significant losses of money or would cause considerable delay, confusion or bad public relations. Can be corrected but with loss of time and expense.

_____ Errors would seriously hamper financial operations of school systems or involve loss of prestige of school board. Difficult and costly to correct.

III. DETAILS CONCERNING RESPONSIBILITIES

1. For what specific activities, programs, and/or services do you have responsibilities for formulating objectives and goals? (Please list.)

_____

_____

Continued

2. What is the extent of your responsibilities for objectives? (e.g., formulate and recommend to department head; recommend to School Board; establish)

_____

_____

3. Which of the following statements best describes your responsibilities relative to objectives and goals for your program or service? (check one)

____ None

____ My opinions are sometimes requested.

____ My opinions are regularly requested.

____ Formulate and recommend objectives to supervisor or department head

____ Formulate objectives for department, program or service and recommend to division head

____ Formulate objectives for division and recommend to Superintendent

____ Formulate objectives for school system

____ Other (Specify) _____

4. For which specific programs and/or services do you have responsibilities for analyzing requirements and whose requirements are analyzed for each? (e.g., purchasing and warehousing for all schools and services)

5. For which departments, programs, and/or services are you responsible for planning the organization, staffing, facilities or finance? (List and describe your planning responsibilities.)

6. For which specific programs and/or services do you have responsibilities for evaluating effectiveness and results?

7. Which of the following statements best describes your responsibilities for evaluating the results of programs and/or services? (check one)

____ None

____ Opinions may be requested.

____ Opinions are regularly requested.

____ Participate in evaluation regularly with supervisor or department head

____ Responsible for evaluation

____ Other (Specify)_____

8. For which specific activities, programs, and services do you have responsibility for developing and evaluating plans of organization? _____

_____

9. Approximately how many staff members are included in plans of organization which you develop and evaluate? _____

_____

10. If you have supervisory responsibilities, what is the nature of the tasks performed by the majority of the persons you directly or indirectly supervise?

____ Repetitive tasks

____ Semiroutine tasks of moderate complexity but not of a highly professional or technical nature

_____ Activities of a highly technical or professional nature
_____ Other (Specify)_____

11. For what specific activities, programs, and/or services do you have staff recruitment and/or selection responsibilities?

_____

_____

12. What type of responsibility do you have for facilities planning? (e.g., recommending amounts and layouts of space) _____

_____

13. What responsibility do you have for supervising the use of facilities and equipment? (e.g., supervising one office and office machines; supervising carpenter shop, saws, joiners)

_____

_____

14. What responsibilities do you have for supervising the care and maintenance of buildings or equipment? _____

_____

15. What kind of financial planning responsibilities do you have and for what programs or services? (e.g., estimating current costs, formulating budget, financial projection)

_____

_____

_____

16. What is total amount of annual budgets for which you have planning responsibility?
_____ None
_____ Less than $100,000.
_____ $100,000 to $499,000.
_____ $500,000 to $999,000.
_____ $1,000,000 or over.
_____ Please explain: _____

_____

17. What responsibilities do you have for evaluating the management of finances; for which programs and/or services? (e.g., evaluating expenditures for maintenance or repairs; analyzing program costs)

_____

_____

_____

18. What is the total amount of annual expenditures for which you are responsible to evaluate financial management?
_____ None
_____ Less than $100,000
_____ $100,000 to $499,000
_____ $500,000 to $999,000
_____ $1,000,000 or over
_____ Please explain: _____

_____

Continued

19. In performing your job, in what ways do you come into contact with the public, employees in other departments, other department heads, etc.? (Briefly describe.)

20. How would you characterize your contacts with the public, employees and others, as you have described them? (check one)

   _____ Little or no contact
   _____ Requires only good manners/no pertinent communication
   _____ Regular and frequent contact; manner and attitude are important, but giving and receiving information is not a principal requirement
   _____ Includes giving and receiving information; requires ability to handle varied face-to-face situations
   _____ A predominant feature of the job, necessitating a high degree of tact, courtesy, and ability to work effectively with individuals and groups

21. What responsibilities do you have for planning the external relations (including public relations) of your service, department or program? (Please specify to the extent that you contribute to planning, are responsible for planning, or otherwise.)

   _____

   _____

22. With regard to all of your planning responsibilities, for what period of time are you usually concerned in making plans?

   _____ Current academic or fiscal year
   _____ Current and next academic or fiscal years
   _____ Current and next 4 academic or fiscal years
   _____ Current and next 5 to 9 academic or fiscal years
   _____ Current and next 10 or more academic or fiscal years

IV. OTHER INFORMATION

1. Are there any other aspects of your responsibilities that are unusual and should be taken into account in evaluating your position?

   _____

   _____

2. Are there any unique requirements not identified above that should be taken into account in establishing the qualifications of a person to fill the position you now occupy?

   _____

   _____

3. How would you characterize general working conditions necessitated by the nature of your job?

   _____ Work in normal temperatures, clean, comfortable surroundings—normal office conditions.
   _____ A few disagreeable conditions exist such as noise, congestion, drafts.
   _____ Several disagreeable conditions accompany the job such as abnormal temperatures, humidity, excess noise, and dirt, offensive odors and fumes.

4. Are there any personal hazards related to your job? (e.g., work on high ladders, use sharp knives, electricity)

   _____

   _____

V. DEPARTMENT HEAD OR SUPERVISOR'S SECTION

(To be completed by immediate supervisor or department head.)

1. I have read the staff members' responses to the attached questionnaire and believe they accurately reflect the duties, responsibilities, and characteristics of the position with the following exceptions: _____

   _____

   _____

2. I believe the minimum educational requirement for this position should be: (List grade completion such as 8th grade, 2–3 years high school, high school graduation, A.B. degree, doctor's degree, etc. Be realistic.) _____

   _____

   _____

3. Which one of the following statements do you feel accurately describes the general work schedule of this position?

   _____ Normal work schedule; some gaps in the work cycle
   _____ Little or no pressure
   _____ Steadily paced with occasional pressure
   _____ Frequent pressure of work with almost constant accumulation of tasks
   _____ Very high and unusual pressure created by important decisions or frequent emergency situations

   _____
   (Signature, Supervisor or Department Head)

SCORE SHEET

JOB EVALUATION COMMITTEE NO. 1
OFFICE, CLERICAL AND MANUAL POSITIONS

Job Title _____ Department _____

Factors:

Technical Demands	_____
Experience	_____
Complexity	_____
Accuracy	_____
Supervision and Training	_____
Independent Action	_____
Contacts	_____
Mental Effort	_____
Physical Effort	_____
Working Conditions	_____
Total	_____

Date: _____   _____
(Signature of Committee Member)

JOB EVALUATION COMMITTEE NO. 1

OFFICE, CLERICAL AND MANUAL POSITIONS

TALLY SHEET

Job Title _____

Department _____ Date _____

Committee \ Factors	Technical Demands	Experience	Complexity	Accuracy	Supervision and Training	Independent Action	Contacts	Mental Effort	Physical Effort	Working Conditions	TOTAL

SCORE SHEET

JOB EVALUATION COMMITTEE NO. 2
ADMINISTRATIVE AND PROFESSIONAL POSITIONS

Job Title _____ Department _____

Factors:

Planning Responsibilities	_____
Professional and Technical Demands	_____
Supervision	_____
Staffing	_____
Facilities	_____
Finance	_____
External Relations	_____
Evaluating Responsibilities	_____
Total	_____

Date: _____   _____

(Signature of Committee Member)

JOB EVALUATION COMMITTEE NO. 2

ADMINISTRATIVE AND PROFESSIONAL POSITIONS

TALLY SHEET

Job Title _____

Department _____ Date _____

Committee / Factors	Planning Responsibilities	Professional and Technical Demands	Supervision	Staffing	Facilities	Finance	External Relations	Evaluating Responsibilities	TOTAL

CHAPTER 9

Collective Negotiations

Collective negotiations has become an accepted part of American education. The first significant collective bargaining contract was negotiated in 1962 with the teachers in New York City. Since that time many state legislatures have enacted collective bargaining laws. Personnel considerations such as salaries, fringe benefits, and working conditions constitute the major negotiable items. Membership in teacher organizations has stabilized and consequently, because of dues, so have the fiscal resources of these organizations. Because human resources expenditures constitute approximately 80 percent of school budgets, virtually every aspect of education has been influenced either directly or indirectly by the phenomenon of collective negotiations.

Experience indicates that the underlying consideration in collective negotiations is participation in the decision-making process. It is a natural evolution in our democratic society that individuals continually look for more significant ways to participate in governance, whether in the political sphere or in our employing institutions. It is important for teachers, administrators, and school board members to understand that collective negotiations is about fostering workplace democracy and providing a way for people to be heard. Thus, it is a political process.[1]

Furthermore, as a process, collective negotiations is working successfully in both the private and public sectors. This chapter deals with the major components of the collective negotiations process as it operates in education.

The attitudes of teachers, administrators, and members of the board of education are critical to the success of collective negotiations because their attitudes affect the relationship between the negotiating parties.[2] If the teachers and representatives of the school district approach the negotiating process with a sense of respect for each other, resentment will be diminished, and the prospect of reaching an acceptable agreement will be enhanced.[3]

---

[1]Kathryn Tyles, "Good Faith Bargaining," *HR Magazine,* 50, no. 1 (2005), 51.

[2]P. D.V. Marsh, *Contract Negotiation Handbook,* 3rd ed. (Burlington, VA: Gower, 2001), 224.

[3]Ibid.

The terms *collective bargaining* and *collective negotiations* have been used with various shades of meaning when referring to this process in public education. To avoid confusion and because the process is invariable, these terms are interchangeable.

When representatives of an organized group bargain collectively over salaries, fringe benefits, and working conditions for their membership with management, the group is in essence a labor union. Therefore, the terms *labor union* and *professional association* are also interchangeable when referring to the involvement that teacher organizations have in the negotiations process. The above definition holds true for administrator associations when they engage in collective negotiations, which appears to be a trend in public education.

Historical Perspectives

Collective Bargaining in the Private Sector

Collective actions by employees have a history going back to the medieval guilds. These actions have always been influenced by the economic, political, and social conditions of the times. Such influences are even stronger today because the technology of the news media allows daily updating on economic, political, and social trends.

Four major congressional acts provide legal guidelines for collective bargaining in the private sector: the Norris–LaGuardia Act of 1932, the National Labor Relations Act of 1935 (Wagner Act), the Labor–Management Relations Act of 1947 (Taft–Hartley Act), and the Labor–Management Reporting and Disclosure Act of 1959 (Landrum–Griffin Act).

The Norris–LaGuardia Act was the first general public policy position on labor unionization. The act supported the concept that workers have a right to organize, if they so desire, into unions. Particularly, the act restricted the U.S. courts from issuing injunctions that would restrict labor activities. It also outlawed the yellow-dog contract, an agreement that employers required employees to sign as a condition of employment stating that they were not members of a union and would not join a union as long as they worked for that company.

The Wagner Act is perhaps the most important piece of labor legislation. This act guaranteed workers the right to organize and join labor unions for the purpose of collective bargaining with employers. The Wagner Act also prohibited employers from engaging in the following unfair labor practices:

1. Interfering with or coercing employees in exercising their rights to join labor unions and bargain collectively
2. Interfering with the formation or administration of any labor union
3. Discriminating against an employee because of union activity
4. Discharging or discriminating against an employee who filed charges or gave testimony under this act
5. Refusing to bargain with the representatives chosen by the employees.

The National Labor Relations Board (NLRB) was established and given the responsibility for conducting elections to determine union representation and for applying this law against the stated unfair labor practices.

The Taft–Hartley Act was passed to amend the Wagner Act and to prevent unfair labor practices by unions. It sought to protect a worker's right not to join a union and to protect employers from mistreatment by unions. The Taft–Hartley Act specifically outlawed the closed shop; allowed the federal government to seek an injunction preventing work stoppages for eighty days in a strike defined as injurious to the national welfare; prohibited the use of union funds in connection with national elections; required union officers to swear that they were not members of the Communist party; required unions to file financial statements with their membership and the U.S. Department of Labor; allowed the states to pass right-to-work laws; and made it illegal for any collective agreement to contain a clause requiring compulsory union membership.

The Taft–Hartley Act also prohibited unions from engaging in the following unfair labor practices:

1. Refusing to bargain collectively with an employer

2. Causing an employer to discriminate against an employee who was refused membership in a union or expelled from a union

3. Engaging in secondary boycotts, which is exerting pressure on an employer not directly involved in a dispute

4. Causing an employer to pay for services that were not rendered

5. Engaging in a conflict between two or more unions over the right to perform certain types of work

6. Charging excessive or discriminating initiation fees

The Landrum–Griffin Act was passed as a result of internal corruption in some unions. This act contained a bill of rights for union members, including freedom of speech at union meetings, secret ballot on proposed dues increases, and protection against improper disciplinary action. It also established the conditions to be observed in electing union officers.

The Landrum–Griffin Act, in addition, contained the following amendments to the Taft–Hartley Act:

1. Repealed the requirement that union officials take a non-Communist oath

2. Gave states authority over cases outside the jurisdiction of the NLRB

3. Prohibited picketing by a union when a rival union had been recognized to represent employees or an NLRB election had taken place within twelve months

4. Guaranteed the right of a striker to vote in union representative elections for twelve months

5. Prohibited agreements by which an employee could seek to bring economic pressure on another employer by refusing to handle, sell, use, or transport his or her products

6. Authorized union shops in the construction industry and required membership after seven days of employment rather than the traditional thirty days

Collective Negotiations in the Federal Government

In 1962 President John Kennedy issued Executive Order 10988, which affirmed the right of federal employees to join labor unions and bargain collectively. It required federal agency heads to bargain in good faith, defined unfair labor practices, and established a code of conduct for labor organizations. However, it prohibited the union shop and banned strikes by federal employees.

In 1968 a presidential committee reviewed employee–management relations in the federal service and recommended improvements to the provisions of E.O. 10988. As a consequence, President Richard Nixon issued E.O. 11491 in 1969 to supersede the previous directive.

The objectives of E.O. 11491 were to standardize procedures among federal agencies and to bring federal labor relations more in line with the private sector. It gave the assistant secretary of labor the authority to determine appropriate bargaining units, to oversee recognition procedures, to rule on unfair labor practices, and to enforce the standards of conduct on labor organizations. E.O. 11491 also established the Federal Labor Relations Council, which has the responsibility to supervise the implementation of this executive order, to handle appeals from the decisions of the assistant secretary of labor, and to rule on questionable issues.

Collective Negotiations in Local and State Governments

Although some professional organizations support passage of a federal teacher collective bargaining law, most educators see this as a state issue. In fact, public school employees are working for a state agency operating at the local level, the school district.

Over three-fourths of the states have permissive or mandatory statutes governing the rights of public school employees to organize, negotiate, exercise sanctions, and strike. There are, of course, substantial differences between these state laws. In a number of states, legislation covers all public employees; in others, a specific law covers only school employees.

Model Board of Education Policy on Collective Negotiations

The following is a sample policy on collective negotiations.

> The board of education believes that collaborative decision making is the most effective way to govern a school system. If school district employees have the right to share in the decision-making process affecting salaries, fringe benefits, and working conditions, they become more responsive and better disposed to exchanging ideas and information concerning operations with administrators. Accordingly, management becomes more efficient.
>
> The board of education further declares that harmonious and cooperative relations between itself and school district employees protect the patrons and children of the school district by assuring the orderly operation of the schools.
>
> This position of the board is to be effectuated by:
>
> 1. Recognizing the right of all school district employees to organize for the purpose of collective negotiations.
> 2. Authorizing the director of employee relations to negotiate with the duly elected employee representatives on matters relating to salaries, fringe benefits, and working conditions.

3. Requiring the director of employee relations to establish administrative procedures for the effective implementation of the negotiations process. This is to be
accomplished under the supervision of the assistant superintendent for human
resources who, in turn, is directly responsible to the superintendent of schools.

Upon successful completion of the negotiations process, the board of education will enter into written agreements with the employee organizations.

Emanating from this board of education policy is the following definition for negotiation: Collective negotiations is the process by which representatives of the school board
meet with representatives of the school district employees in order to make proposals and
counterproposals for the purpose of mutually agreeing on salaries, fringe benefits, and
working conditions covering a specific period of time.

Recognition and Bargaining Unit Determination

This section is concerned with answering the basic question, "Who represents whom?" In
labor history, most of the violence that occurred in the private sector centered around this
query. Unions fought each other for the right to represent workers against management. The
prize was power. In education, the prize is still the same, but the contest is usually nonviolent.

Recognition is defined as the acceptance by an employer of some group or organization as the authorized representative of two or more employees for the purpose of collective negotiations. Without recognition each teacher is left to make his or her own
arrangements with the school board, which is the antithesis of collective negotiations.

There are two basic types of representation in education—multiple and exclusive.
Multiple representation does not occur in many school districts because of the inherent
problems when two or more organizations or unions represent a specific bargaining unit.
In New York City prior to the collective negotiations elections in 1961, ninety-three organizations were accorded equal representational rights by the board of education.[4] Although
this situation was extreme, there are communities in which more than one organization
claims the right to represent a segment of the professional staff.

In multiple representation, recognition is usually granted by the board of education on
the basis of organizational membership. This recognition is operationalized by one of the
following methods: The board meets with representatives of each union separately; the
board meets in joint sessions with equal numbers of representatives from each union; or
the board meets in joint sessions with representatives of the unions proportionally determined. For example, if union A has 500 members and union B has 250 members, A is entitled to twice as many representatives on the negotiating team as B.

Exclusive recognition occurs when a single union represents all members of a bargaining unit. The technical designation for the union in this role is *bargaining agent.* The
bargaining unit consists of all the employees whose salaries, fringe benefits, and working

---

[4]Myron Lieberman and Michael H. Moskow, *Collective Negotiations for Teachers* (Chicago: Rand McNally,
1966), 92.

conditions are negotiated by the bargaining agent. The paramount importance of exclusive recognition is that the employer cannot negotiate with anyone in the unit except through the designated bargaining agent.

Exclusive recognition is the most accepted form in education for three reasons: First, it is supported by both the National Education Association and the American Federation of Teachers; second, exclusive recognition is mandated by law for the public sector in many states and widely accepted in most communities even in the absence of state legislation; and finally, private business and industry witnesses to the fact that this is the most effective form of recognition.

Recognition procedures take various forms in education. The three most commonly used are membership lists, authorization cards, and elections. If a union can demonstrate that it has 51 percent membership of the employees in a bargaining unit or if 51 percent of the employees in a unit present their signatures on a card authorizing a certain union to represent them, the board may recognize this union as the exclusive bargaining agent.

A more common practice is the "representation election," which also is necessary in the absence of membership lists or authorization cards that signify majority support. Most school boards prefer an election as a requisite to recognizing a union as exclusive bargaining agent for a number of reasons. Some teachers who join a union may not want that union to represent them in negotiations. Teachers join certain unions for social, professional, or other reasons that have nothing to do with negotiations. In some cases, a teacher may be a member of more than one teacher union.

The representation election poses several questions that must be addressed by both the school board and the unions seeking recognition:

- Who conducts the election?
- Who will pay the costs for the election?
- What are the ground rules for electioneering?
- Who is eligible to vote?
- Who will certify the results?
- What will be the duration of the certification?

There are no correct answers to these questions. Rather, they must be answered within a framework that takes into consideration the variables affecting local situations. A cardinal principle is that the board and unions must maintain credibility and, therefore, a third party is often requested to intervene in finding a workable answer to these questions. The Federal Mediation and Conciliation Service or the League of Women Voters are examples of two independent agencies with the public image necessary to act as the appropriate third party. In many states with collective bargaining laws, recognition procedures and bargaining unit determination are mandated by state legislation. This discussion pertains to those states without legislation and to those states where the law allows latitude on these issues. Some states have public employee relations boards that conduct the elections and make a determination on who belongs to the bargaining unit.

It is necessary to more closely define the term *bargaining unit*. School districts not only employ teachers of many different subjects and levels but they also employ a wide variety of specialists, such as psychologists, nurses, social workers, and attendance officers.

In addition, there are noncertificated employees: cooks, custodians, bus drivers, maintenance workers, administrative assistants, and clerks. To have collective negotiations, there
must be a determination on what specific category of employees is represented by the bargaining agent who wins the representation election. In practice, this determination must occur
as part of the recognition process, because only those employees in a given bargaining unit
will be allowed to vote on which union will represent them. The definition most commonly
accepted states that the bargaining unit is composed of all those employees who are covered
by the negotiated agreement or master contract.

The fundamental criterion for determining who belongs to the bargaining unit is formulated on the "community of interest" principle.[5] Although it may sound elusive, the principle is not difficult to implement. Employees have a community of interest if they share
skills, functions, educational levels, and working conditions. Elementary-school teachers of
all levels, secondary-school teachers of all subjects, and guidance counselors clearly have a
community of interest and should belong to the same bargaining unit. Clerks and administrative assistants, on the other hand, could not be effectively represented by such a unit and
should constitute a separate unit by themselves. It is conceivable that a medium to large
school districts might have the following units bargaining separately with the representatives of the school board:

1. Certificated educators exclusive of supervisors and administrators
2. Building level administrators
3. Subject matter coordinators
4. Administrative assistants and clerks
5. Cooks and cafeteria workers
6. Bus drivers
7. Custodians
8. Maintenance workers

Each of these bargaining units would have a separate agreement or master contract, specifying salaries, fringe benefits, and working conditions, that could be quite different from
the others.

Besides community of interest, there are two additional considerations determining a
bargaining unit. Size of the group is important; an extremely small unit of five or ten employees will have little impact acting alone. In this case employees would have a more
strategic base from which to bargain if they combined with other categories of employees.
In a small school district, for example, there might be two bargaining units: a certificated
employees' unit including teachers, nurses, psychologists, and so on; and a noncertificated
employees' unit including cooks, custodians, maintenance personnel, and others.

A final consideration in determining bargaining units is effective school administration. An unreasonably large number of units would be unworkable. For example, if guidance counselors, classroom teachers, speech therapists, music teachers, physical education
teachers, and safety education teachers were each covered by different agreements speci-

---

[5]Lieberman and Moskow, *Collective Negotiations,* 129.

fying different working conditions, a building principal would have a difficult job of supervising the staff.

Two other issues have an influence on future negotiations—the agency shop and administrator bargaining units. *Agency shop* is a term borrowed from industry and is used when referring to a question of equity: An employee who is a member of a given bargaining unit may not be a dues-paying member of the union that is the bargaining agent. If the negotiated agreement with the school board includes an agency shop clause, such an employee would be required to pay a fee, usually the equivalent of dues, to the union. Although the employee would not be allowed to participate in internal union affairs, he or she would be allowed to participate in such unit activities as attending meetings called by the negotiating team and voting on ratification of an agreement.

A growing number of educational administrators, particularly building principals, are organizing into unions and negotiating with school boards. The reasons administrators are turning to collective negotiations include decreasing autonomy and power, and economic concerns. It appears that this trend will continue during the next two decades, and school board representatives will be negotiating with increasing numbers of administrator bargaining units.

The Scope of Negotiations

Scope of negotiations refers to those matters that are negotiable. In some school districts, negotiations are limited to salaries; in other districts, literally hundreds of items are discussed.

Negotiations must not be limited to unimportant matters, or the process will be considered a failure by teachers. What constitutes an important item, of course, is dictated by local circumstances. A school board might be willing to negotiate only on salaries and refuse to consider such items as a grievance procedure or reduction-in-force policy. Experience indicates that some of these nonmonetary items are just as important to teachers as salaries. Therefore, it is extremely important to place only mandatory limitations on the scope of negotiations. These limitations refer to items that are illegal by reason of state and federal constitutions, state and federal laws, or those items that are contrary to the policies of a given State Board of Education.

Most state laws on collective negotiations stipulate that negotiations must be confined to "working conditions." However, this phrase usually refers to salaries, fringe benefits, and working conditions. The meaning of *salary* is self-evident, but there is some confusion over what is meant by the terms *fringe benefits* and *working conditions.*

A fringe benefit may be defined as a service made available to employees as a direct result of a fiscal expenditure by the school district. Such services might include major medical insurance, hospitalization insurance, pension benefits, sick pay, dental insurance, and professional liability insurance.

Working conditions pertain to the quality of the employment situation. Teaching for a particular school district might be more desirable than teaching in other districts located in the same geographic area because that district has desirable policies concerning class size, duty-free lunch periods, preparation periods, sabbatical leave, and so on.

A major concern in defining the scope of negotiations for a particular situation centers around the concept of educational policy. School boards are required by state law to set educational policy. Although many teachers are deeply interested in educational policy and believe that they should be consulted in formulating such policy, it is commonly understood that such policy is not subject to negotiations.

The following are examples of policy issues:

1. Should the school district provide a foreign language program in the elementary grades?
2. Should statistics be offered in the high school mathematics program?
3. Should extracurricular activities be sponsored or supported by district funds?

The obvious problem is that virtually all educational policy decisions have implications affecting working conditions. For example, funds expended to introduce a foreign language program in the elementary grades could leave less money available to lower class size. Therefore, it is often impossible to decide issues pertaining to policy apart from those pertaining to working conditions.

Lieberman and Moskow make an observation about the scope of negotiations that summarizes and clarifies this aspect of the process:

> Finally, it must be remembered that the scope of negotiations is itself negotiated or at least affected by the process of negotiations.
>
> When the parties meet to negotiate, there is no formula which prescribes what is negotiable. Good administration does not eliminate the need for negotiations, but the scope of negotiations is likely to include those matters which have been administered in an inequitable manner. The relative strength of the parties may affect the scope of negotiations much more than academic versions of what progressive school administrators or organization leaders should negotiate. Legal, personal, political, economic, and organizational factors may have some impact on the scope of negotiations as well as on the resolution of items actually negotiated. In other words, the process of negotiations inevitably affects its scope and vice versa.[6]

The Bargaining Process

The Negotiating Team

The purpose of this section is to analyze those factors that influence the "at-the-table" process of negotiations. The first issue that must be addressed is the composition of the school board's negotiating team. There is no universally accepted practice in forming a negotiating team; however, the size of a school district appears to have a significant influence on the makeup of the team. In small school districts, a committee of school board members

[6]Lieberman and Moskow, *Collective Negotiations,* 247.

usually negotiates directly with a team of teachers. In medium to large districts, the assistant superintendent for human resources along with other central-office or building-level administrators might be designated by the superintendent to negotiate with the teachers union. In some large districts, a chief negotiator is employed on a full-time or ad hoc basis.

In keeping with the model presented in Chapter 1, medium to large school districts should employ a director of employee relations who has responsibility for managing the entire process of collective negotiations and who acts as the chief negotiator on the board's team. The size of the team is relative, but it should have an odd number of members to avoid a deadlock in making strategy decisions. Therefore, a team of three, five, or seven members would be appropriate. Experience also dictates that a team composed of more than seven members impedes decision making.

Membership on the team may be by job description, appointment, or election. This author prefers a team of five members. The chairperson and chief negotiator, of course, is the director of employee relations, by virtue of job position. Additional membership on the team should include building-level principals, because they are the first-line supervisors who will be managing the master agreement. Also, many principals have been critical of school boards for "negotiating away" their authority. On a five-member team, one principal from each level (elementary school, junior or middle school, high school) elected by the other principals would give the team high credibility among building administrators. The final member of the team should have some specific expertise and knowledge of the district's financial condition. Thus, the assistant superintendent for administrative services or the business manager would be an appropriate appointee.

This team must function as an entity over the entire academic year. As will be pointed out later in this section, the development of strategies and the construction of proposal packages cannot be accomplished only during a few months of the year. Although a major portion of work will fall to the director of employee relations, the team will be required to expend a great deal of time. In fact, it is desirable for the teachers' and board's teams to meet routinely throughout the year to discuss mutual concerns and goals.[7] Such meetings will hopefully create a sense of trust that will facilitate the negotiations sessions.[8] Consequently, it is advisable to provide those principals who serve on the team with some compensation such as a stipend or with additional administrative assistance in their buildings.

The negotiating team for the teachers, of course, is composed of teachers. Sometimes the officers of the local association or union act as the team; in other situations a negotiating team is appointed by the union officers or elected by the teachers. If the local is affiliated with a national union, experts in the bargaining process are made available to advise union officers.

A final issue concerning the board's negotiating team must be addressed. What if the building administrators organize, form a bargaining unit, and elect a bargaining agent to represent them concerning salaries, fringe benefits, and working conditions? This, of course, is the current trend, especially in large urban school districts. In this case the same structure for the board's negotiating team may be maintained with the substitution of assistant superintendents for principals. Because each bargaining unit negotiates a separate master

[7]Ildiko Knott, "Collective Bargaining Can Enhance the Quality of Worklife," *Community and Junior College Journal* (December/January 1983–84), 20.

[8]"Unions, Employers Try New Paths to Labor Peace," *U.S. News & World Report,* 10 March 1984, 74.

agreement, which reflects salaries, fringe benefits, and working conditions for employees in a given job category, it is not inconsistent with good administration for principals on the one hand to negotiate for the board and on the other hand against the board.

Developing Strategies

The negotiating team is responsible for the entire bargaining process, which must begin with strategy development. The quality of this planning will determine the effectiveness of the negotiations sessions.[9] This entails two activities, assessing the needs of the school district and establishing goals for negotiations.

Needs assessment may take various forms, but certain tasks must be completed:

1. Review the current master agreement to determine if its provisions meet the goals of the district and if they allow for effective administration.

2. Study the previous negotiating sessions to determine if the ground rules provide for effective negotiations.

3. Analyze the formal grievances filed by both the union and administration.

4. Study the arbitration decisions rendered on these grievances.

5. Meet with school district administrators to gather input concerning the provisions of the current master agreement.

6. Meet informally with the union to ascertain their concerns over the current agreement.

7. Confer with the board of education and superintendent to learn their concerns and to establish fiscal parameters.

From this information the team sets the goals and objectives for negotiations, which are formulated into operational language in the proposal package.

Setting the Ground Rules

With the advice and consent of the negotiating team, the chairperson should meet with the union negotiators to determine rules for the "at-the-table" process. Key points that must be determined include

- The time and place for the sessions
- The number of participants who will sit at the table
- The role of each participant
- The manner in which each side will present its proposals
- The target date for completing negotiations
- The kinds of school district data that will be needed by each side
- The conditions governing caucuses
- The provisions for recording the sessions
- The method to be used in recording counterproposals and agreements
- The policy on press releases
- The types of impasse procedures that will be employed and when

[9]Lewis T. Kohler, ed., *Negotiations and the Manager in Public Education* (Park Ridge, IL: ASBO, 1980), 1.

- The format for the written agreement
- The procedure for agreement approval by the school board and union membership
- The procedure that will be used in publishing the ratified agreement

At-the-Table Sessions

There are two objectives for being "at the table." First, through making proposals and counterproposals, the negotiating teams should be able to ascertain what issues are critically important to each side. Second, each team should be able to assess the other side's bargaining power. This is the ability to get the other team to agree on an item or the entire proposal package based on your terms. This can be represented schematically as

$$\text{Bargaining power of the school board} = \frac{\text{Teachers' cost of disagreeing with the terms of the school board}}{\text{Teachers' cost of agreeing with the terms of the school board}}$$

$$\text{Bargaining power of the teachers} = \frac{\text{School board's cost of disagreeing with the terms of the teachers}}{\text{School board's cost of agreeing with the terms of the teachers}[10]}$$

Political pressures, negotiating skill, and psychological elements are important sources of bargaining power. Although it is impossible to measure bargaining power exactly, it is apparent that, at some time, the overall advantages of agreement outweigh the overall disadvantages of agreement. During the bargaining sessions, it is very important to keep the board and entire administrative staff informed as to the progress being made. If this is not effectively accomplished, rumors may adversely affect the bargaining power of the board's team.

When an agreement is reached by the negotiating teams, ratification by the respective governing bodies is the final step in the process. The board's team meets with the superintendent and board of education to explain and recommend the agreement. In like manner, the union's team meets with the bargaining unit membership to explain and recommend the agreement. Formal ratification occurs when a majority of school board members vote to accept the agreement and when a majority of the bargaining unit membership similarly votes approval.

Because negotiating is an art rather than a science, it is extremely difficult to develop a formula for success. Nevertheless, a number of practical hints may be in order. The following are recommendations made to local boards of education by the Ohio School Board Association.

- *Keep calm—don't lose control of yourself.* Negotiation sessions can be exasperating. The temptation may come to get angry and fight back when intemperate accusations are made or when "the straw that broke the camel's back" is hurled on the table.

---

[10]Adapted from Neil W. Chamberlain, *The Labor Sector* (New York: McGraw-Hill, 1965), 248.

- *Avoid "off the record" comments.* Nothing is "off the record." Innocently made remarks have a way of coming back to haunt those who said them. Be careful to say only what you are willing to have quoted.
- *Don't be overcandid.* Inexperienced negotiators may, with the best of intentions, desire to "lay the cards on the table face up." This may be done in the mistaken notion that everybody fully understands the other and utter frankness is desired. Complete candor doesn't always serve the best interests of productive negotiations. This is not a plea for duplicity; rather, it is a recommendation for prudent and discriminating utterances.
- *Be long on listening.* Usually a good listener makes a good negotiator. It is wise to let your "adversaries" do the talking—at least in the beginning.
- *Don't be afraid of a "little heat."* Discussions sometimes generate quite a bit of heat. Don't be afraid of it. It never hurts to let the "opposition" sound off even when you may be tempted to "sound" back.
- *Watch the voice level.* A wise practice is to keep the pitch of the voice down even though the temptation may be strong to let it rise under the excitement of emotional stress.
- *Keep flexible.* One of the skills of good negotiators is the ability to shift position a bit if a positive gain can thus be accomplished. An obstinate adherence to one position or point of view, regardless of the ultimate consequences of that rigidity, may be more of a deterrent than an advantage.
- *Refrain from a flat "no."* Especially in the earlier stages of a negotiation it is best to avoid giving a flat "no" to a proposition. It doesn't help to work yourself into a box by being totally negative too early.
- *Give to get.* Negotiation is the art of giving and getting. Concede a point to gain a concession. This is the name of the game.
- *Work on the easier items first.* Settle first those things that generate the least controversy. Leave the tougher items until later in order to avoid an early deadlock.
- *Respect your adversary.* Respect those who are seated on the opposite side of the table. Assume that their motives are as sincere as your own, at least until proven otherwise.
- *Be patient.* If necessary, be willing to sit out tiresome tirades. Time has a way of being on the side of the patient negotiator.
- *Avoid waving red flags.* There are some statements that irritate teachers and merely heighten their antipathies. Find out what these are and avoid their use. Needless waving of red flags only infuriates.
- *Let the other side win some victories.* Each team has to win some victories. A "shut out" may be a hollow gain in negotiation.
- *Negotiation is a way of life.* Obvious resentment of the fact that negotiation is here to stay weakens the effectiveness of the negotiator. The better part of wisdom is to adjust to it and become better prepared to use it as a tool of interstaff relations.

Third Party Negotiations

In recent years, some parents and other school district patrons have been clamoring for an active involvement in collective negotiations. Proponents of this position have eagerly sought an extension of the sunshine laws to require negotiations sessions to be open to the public. Other forms include trilateral negotiations, by which a citizen group becomes an equal participant with the board's team and union's team in the negotiating process; public response to proposals before an agreement is reached; and public referendum, by which proposals are voted on by the citizens of the school district. There are other variations on this theme. However, the ultimate objective is the same: citizen participation in the bargaining process.

Collective negotiations demands refined skills of those sitting at the table. Citizens generally do not possess these skills. Furthermore, a third party will bring confusion and can interfere with the employment relationship between the board and employees. In addition, school board members have been elected to represent the interests of parents, students, and district patrons. Third party involvement seeks to usurp this responsibility.[11]

Impasse Procedures

It is extremely difficult to define the term *impasse*. Negotiators often have trouble knowing when an impasse has been reached. However, for this discussion, an impasse will be considered as a persistent disagreement that continues after normal negotiation procedures have been exhausted.

Impasse must be expected to occur from time to time, even when both parties are negotiating in good faith. There are, unfortunately, no procedures that are guaranteed to resolve an impasse. Some procedures have been more successful than others, and the objective of this section is to outline these procedures. Also, it must be kept in mind that improperly used impasse procedures can aggravate rather than resolve a disagreement. Therefore, a working knowledge of procedures is essential to all participants in the negotiating process.

Twenty-two of the states that have passed collective negotiations laws also have established public employee relations boards. Each board is charged with implementing the law and, in most cases, with administering impasse procedures, including mediation, fact finding, and arbitration.

Mediation

Mediation is usually the first procedure used when an impasse has been reached. The negotiators for both labor and management must agree on the need for third party assistance. The role of the mediator is advisory, and consequently, the mediator has no authority to dictate a settlement. Some mediators use the tactic of first meeting with both parties separately and thereby attempt to ascertain what concessions each party might be willing to make in order to reach an agreement. This procedure has been most effective when one or both parties consider making concessions to be a sign of weakness. Meeting jointly with both parties is helpful, particularly in assessing the actual status of negotiations and in obtaining agreement from the parties on the importance assigned to each unresolved issue. Most mediators will use a combination of separate and joint meetings to facilitate an agreement.

Mediators usually refrain from recommending a settlement until they are sure that their recommendations will be acceptable to both parties. Up until the time of recommendation,

[11]Ronald W. Rebore, *Educational Administration: A Management Approach* (Englewood Cliffs, NJ: Prentice-Hall, 1985), 213.

the mediator acts only as a clarifier of issues and through the process attempts to defuse the antagonism between the parties, which is frequently the cause of the impasse.

A mediator may be called into a dispute at any time. In some cases the mediator may even practice preventive mediation by making suggestions useful to the parties early in the negotiations.

Because mediation is a voluntary process, in the stages preparatory to the actual negotiations, the parties must decide who will mediate and what the mediator's role will be. In approximately one-third of the states, this issue is settled by statute and a formal declaration of "impasse" is all that is required to put the process in motion. Often a master agreement will contain provisions outlining impasse procedures to be followed in negotiating the agreement. When mediator services are not provided by a governmental agency, the fee for a private mediator is borne equally by both parties to the dispute.

Fact Finding

Fact finding is the procedure by which an individual or a panel holds hearings to review evidence and make recommendations for settling the dispute. Like mediation, the fact-finding process is either governed by a state statute, provided for in a master agreement, or established by both parties before negotiations begin.

The formal hearing is usually open to the public. Parties having a vested interest in the dispute are given the opportunity to offer evidence and arguments in their own behalf. Fact finders are sometimes requested by both parties to mediate the dispute and avoid the formal hearings.

The fact-finding report and recommendations are usually made public. The process is voluntary, and the parties may reject all or part of the report. To a certain extent, the action of the parties will depend on the public's reactions, which in turn depend partly on the prestige of the fact finders.

Arbitration

Arbitration is the process by which the parties submit their dispute to an impartial third person or panel of persons that issues an award the parties are required to accept. Arbitration can be either compulsory or voluntary. Compulsory arbitration must be established by statute; nineteen states have such legislation. The voluntary use of arbitration has gained some acceptance in the public sector for handling grievances arising from the interpretation of master agreements.

The Federal Mediation and Conciliation Service

The Federal Mediation and Conciliation Service (FMCS) works annually to resolve disagreements arising out of collective negotiations in the public sector, which amounted to approximately 8 percent of the agency's caseload. The Federal Mediation and Conciliation Service is an independent agency of the federal government created by Congress in 1974 with a director appointed by the President of the United States. The primary purpose of the FMCS is to promote labor–management peace. To more effectively carry out this mission, the agency has established regional offices and field offices staffed by professional mediators.

Federal labor laws do not cover employees of state and local governments. However, if state legislatures fail to establish mediation services for public employees, the FMCS may voluntarily enter a dispute. The FMCS also has an Office of Arbitration Services in Washington. This office maintains a roster of arbitrators located in all parts of the country. On request, FMCS will furnish a randomly selected list of arbitrators from which the parties to a dispute may choose a mutually acceptable arbitrator to hear the dispute and make a decision.

In summary, it is too difficult to promote one impasse procedure as the most effective approach to handling all persistent disputes that arise at the bargaining table or in grievances over master agreement interpretation. It is more appropriate to think in terms of sequence. Mediation should be utilized first, followed by fact-finding, and then, where it is permitted by law, arbitration. This sequence places the responsibility for resolving the dispute first on the parties themselves. Experience teaches that better and more effective agreements are reached when the parties can resolve their own disputes. Yet, when disputes cannot be resolved and when it is mandated by law, arbitration curtails strikes, which always have a devastating effect on school districts.

Work Stoppage Strategies

The Scope of Strikes

Nothing is more disruptive to a school district than a strike. As board members, administrators, teachers, and support personnel engage in heated and public argument, schisms occur that often last for years. Community groups also become divided over who is right and who is wrong. When a strike occurs, the administrative team has the responsibility to keep the schools open; to protect students who report to school; to protect school property; and to maintain communications with parents, teachers, and the public.

Strikes by public school employees are illegal or, at least, limited by most state laws. However, this has not prevented strikes from occurring each year in many states. The news media daily remind us of the magnitude of this issue. There is also no indication that strikes will go away as school employees, administrators, and teachers become more proficient in the negotiations process.

In past decades most teachers felt that striking was not in keeping with their professional status. This thinking has vanished, and the personal traumas once associated with this type of action also are gone. Today teachers strike over many issues, including recognition of their unions, salary increases, curriculum control, reduction in force, and lack of community support. Teachers also have honored strikes by nonteaching personnel and have attempted to get their unions to support them in their work stoppages.

School Employee Strike Tactics

A strike by school employees is usually the result of failure at the bargaining table. The objective of all strikes is to gain as favorable a settlement as possible from the board of education within the shortest period of time.

A few key issues have been used by teacher unions to rally support for a strike. These include the pupil–teacher ratio; planning time, particularly for elementary-school teachers;

and, extra pay for extra duty, particularly for secondary-school teachers. With the onslaught of the accountability reform movement, the rallying call centers around job security and compensation issues.

Teacher unions have almost unlimited resources from their state and national affiliates at their disposal in a strike. In very sensitive strikes, as many as a hundred field staff members may be available to help the local union.

A careful examination of several strikes will verify the following tactics as some of the most commonly used by teacher unions.

1. Inundating the community with the reasons for the strike. Handbills, advertisements in the local press, and news coverage are the main vehicles usually employed.

2. Placing the blame on a specific person such as the superintendent of schools or board president, thus channeling the pressure exerted by parents and the community.

3. Encouraging local and state politicians to become involved in the dispute. School employee groups represent a sizable number of votes.

4. Working diligently to gain support from other unions in the community.

5. Staging a strike in the late spring because this will interfere not only with graduation but also with state aid, which is usually calculated on a certain number of days in attendance before the end of the school year.

Although some strikes do occur spontaneously because of unexpected developments, most teacher strikes are well orchestrated. Teacher unions generally are aware weeks or even months in advance that certain negotiation demands are strike-producing issues.

Administrative Strategies

If a school system finds itself in the middle of a strike without an adequate plan of action, the administration and the board of education have not been paying attention to the tenor of the times or the situation in their own school district. In fact, the superintendent and his or her cabinet should have a carefully developed strike plan even in the most tranquil of school settings. This strike plan should operate at both the district and building levels. The American Association of School Administrators (AASA) has developed a series of steps in a plan that can serve as a guide for administrators in establishing their own individual district plans (see Exhibit 9.1).

When the Decision-Making Center mentioned in Exhibit 9.1 is established at the central office, duties are assigned by the superintendent of schools with the advice of his or her cabinet. Central-office administrators are assigned specific tasks to be performed during the strike, which correspond to the provisions of the above stated AASA plan. The director of labor relations could be given the task of notifying staff members of the state law and board policy concerning strikes and the legal ramifications of striking. The director of community relations would have the responsibility of notifying the news media of the times and the place for daily briefings concerning the strike. In like manner, the building principal and, if it is a large school, his or her administrative team are responsible for implementing the building-level provisions.

EXHIBIT 9.1   Sample Strike Plan

Before a Strike

District Level

1. Develop the overall district plan as well as a board policy statement well in advance of an anticipated strike (preferably, when there is absolutely no indication of a strike).
2. Provide as early as possible for the notification of news media, parents, and staff, of the likelihood or possibility of a strike.
3. Notify staff members of the applicable state law and school board policy concerning a work stoppage and the legal ramifications of such action.
4. Establish provisions for a Decision-Making Center to have the overall direction of a strike and assign specific responsibilities to those key people in the Center.
5. Make contacts with police, fire, health, telephone, and other community or state agencies likely to be needed or contacted during a strike.
6. Prepare a list of names and telephone numbers for the specific individuals in each agency who can be contacted day or night in emergency situations.
7. Provide for "hot line" telephones for citizens and staff members so they may receive strike information.
8. Install a bank of unlisted telephones in the Decision-Making Center to facilitate on-going and continual communications.
9. Obtain, or make provisions to obtain, two-way radio systems for strategic places in the district (or mobile car radios, beeper systems).
10. Develop building strike plans and reporting systems for daily status reports from each building.
11. Notify the news media of the media area and provide the time(s) and place of daily (or more often) briefings concerning the strike.
12. Have the board of education pass the necessary legal resolutions required to deal with the strike (restraining orders, injunctions, picket line restrictions, formal notification to personnel on strike, etc.).
13. Continue to seek a solution to the strike and keep such initiative on the side of the administration and board.

Building Level

1. Develop with each building principal a building Strike Plan in conformance with the overall district plan.
2. Secure back-up personnel for each building principal to act in his or her stead during the work stoppage.
3. Make provision within the building Strike Plan for a daily, early-morning report to the Decision-Making Center.
4. Make provision for a daily written report listing the names of staff who reported for duty and the number of pupils in attendance at the building.
5. Make provision for continuity of communications in the event that telephone lines are unusable.
6. Make provision for each building principal to have specific guidelines and authority to close the building when the safety and health of the pupils are threatened, or when it is impossible to carry on an educational program.
7. Make provision for adequate building security (leaving lights on at night, security guards, etc.).

Continued

EXHIBIT 9.1   *Continued*

After a Strike

District Level

1. Notify all groups.
2. Hold briefing session for all administrators and board members.
3. Prepare building principals for the return of teachers.
4. Issue public statement detailing strike settlement to news media.
5. Begin making plans to defuse "anti-climactic" emotions.

Building Level

1. Do not allow striking teachers to return to the classrooms until all substitute teachers are out of the building.
2. Make plans to focus major attention on the educational program and learning environment for students.

Administration of the Master Agreement

The process of collective negotiations is usually ineffective unless the agreements reached are put into writing. Written master agreements are essential because they formalize the basic rights governing the parties to each agreement and reduce controversy over the meaning of what was agreed upon.

Provisions of the Agreement

Most master agreements are extremely detailed and replace board of education policies covering those working conditions negotiated. Certain provisions are included in most agreements and are deemed essential. These are

1. Recognition of the union as the exclusive bargaining agent
2. A statement of purpose
3. The duration of the agreement and a method for renegotiating the agreement before the expiration date
4. Incorporation of a grievance procedure
5. Incorporation of impasse procedures
6. Description of who is a member of the bargaining unit
7. A statement concerning dues check-off
8. A fair practices statement
9. Salary schedules and guidelines for the duration of the agreements[12]

---

[12]Lloyd W. Ashby, James E. McGinnis, and Thomas E. Pering, *Common Sense in Negotiations in Public Education* (Danville, IL: The Interstate Printers and Publishers, 1972), 59–60.

As an example of the types of articles and appendices that operationalize these provisions, the Table of Contents for the Dade County, Florida, master agreement is reproduced in Appendix A of this chapter.

The style and format of the master agreement will sometimes be dictated by state statutes; but in the absence of legislation, school boards and unions must look elsewhere for help. In many cases, teacher associations affiliated with national unions have access to model master agreements that can be adapted to local situations. In fact, some models are complete in every detail except for filling in the blanks with the proper data.

Implementing the Master Agreement

It is the responsibility of the administration to implement and interpret the provisions of the agreement. Furthermore, the administration is limited only by the specifics of the master agreement, which is commonly referred to as "management prerogative."

In the day-to-day interpretations of the agreement, it is certainly possible for violations to occur. Most written agreements, therefore, provide for a grievance procedure by which individuals or the union can allege that the master agreement is being violated or misinterpreted. Most grievance procedures contain the following elements:

1. A careful definition of the term *grievance*
2. The purpose of the grievance procedure
3. A clause stating that a person alleging a grievance or testifying in a grievance will not face prejudicial treatment by the other party
4. A clear outline of the appropriate steps to be taken in a grievance and the time allotments between each step
5. In the case of arbitration, who will bear the costs of arbitration and the qualifications required for an arbitrator

The grievance procedures used in the Dade County School District is reproduced in Appendix B of this chapter because it is an excellent example of how the above provisions can be put into operation.

Labor–Management Relations Committee

In an attempt to diffuse the adversarial relationship that sometimes exists between the board of education/administration and unions, labor–management committees have been organized in some school districts. The charge to these committees is to work through concerns, problems, and issues before they appear at the table in the next round of negotiations. In a large school district, the director of employee relations will have the responsibility of chairing the board/administration team, which should include first line supervisors. In smaller districts an assistant superintendent or even the superintendent may wish to assume this responsibility. Shop stewards or other representatives of a given union will constitute labor's membership on the committee.

The approach to labor–management committee meetings should be informal with the emphasis on mutual interests and collaboration. Compromise is the key to a successful relationship as is true in at-the-table negotiations. A win–win strategy should also prevail, with each party attempting to come away with something that it wants. Whatever is agreed to at these sessions should be put into writing, which, in turn, will help avoid confusion at a later time.

Of course, a labor–management committee should not deal with monetary and fringe benefits issues but, rather, with working conditions. If this committee is to be successful, it must meet throughout the term of the master agreement.

Collaborative Bargaining

In the mid 1980s, a movement began with the hope of defusing the hostility that sometimes accompanies collective negotiations. This has resulted in a derivation of the collective negotiations model presented in this chapter.

In collaborative bargaining there are not two teams but just one composed of teachers, board members, and administrators. This team's mission is to problem-solve rather than to engage in bargaining.

The collaborative model was operationalized in the Ashland, Oregon School District in 1986. As part of the process, their team went through a seven-part training program that included communication skills; problem-solving skills; creative-thinking skills; orientation to collaborative bargaining; the development of group agreements; the development of superordinate goals; and group recorder, convener, and process observer roles.

Superordinate goals, such as "enhancing teaching and learning," are highly valued, attainable, and commonly sought after by the group members. These goals provide the framework within which the various issues are addressed and solved. Consensus is the essence of the decision-making process. Thus, if the district's teacher transfer policy is a concern for the teachers, questions are posed which lead to clarification of the issue. For example, What is the purpose of the teacher transfer policy? When the issue is clarified, the team begins the process of problem-solving which might require a review of the district's budget or other documents that have a bearing on the transfer policy.[13]

Collaborative bargaining usually requires more time than the more traditional model. It can be a very effective approach especially if the traditional model has resulted in overt hostility. However, it is important to approach collaborative bargaining with caution; it is not a panacea.

Summary

Collective negotiation has become an accepted part of American education, as evidenced by the fact that over three-fourths of the states have enacted collective negotiations laws affecting teachers. The underlying consideration in collective negotiations is participation in the decision-making process, which is a natural extension of our democratic life style.

---

[13]John M. Daggett, "Collaborative Bargaining: Ashland, Oregon's Experience," *Updating: School Board Policies,* 22, no. 1 (January/February 1991), 1–4.

Teachers and administrators want to have input into the priorities established by school boards when these affect their salaries, fringe benefits, and working conditions.

Collective negotiations may be defined as the process by which representatives of the school board meet with representatives of the school district employees in order to make proposals and counterproposals for the purpose of agreeing on salaries, fringe benefits, and working conditions for a specific period of time. To operationalize this process, it is necessary for the board of education to adopt a policy that will give the administration authority to implement negotiations.

Collective actions by employees have a long history in the private sector, reaching back to the time of the medieval guilds. These actions are directly affected by the economic, political, and social conditions of life. Four major congressional acts provide legal guidelines for collective bargaining in the private sector: the Norris–LaGuardia Act of 1932, the National Labor Relations Act of 1935, the Labor–Management Relations Act of 1947, and the Labor–Management Reporting and Disclosure Act of 1959. Executive Orders 10988 and 11491 affirm the right of federal employees to organize and bargain collectively, but strikes are forbidden.

Public school teachers are state employees working in a local unit, the school district. As such they are not covered by federal legislation but rather by the acts of state legislatures. There are substantial differences in those state statutes granting collective negotiations rights to teachers.

There are six aspects to the collective negotiations process: recognition and bargaining unit determination, the scope of negotiations, the bargaining process, impasse procedures, work stoppages, and the administration of the master agreement.

Recognition and bargaining unit determination answer the question, "Who represents whom?" Recognition is the acceptance by an employer of a bargaining agent as the authorized representative of a bargaining unit. There are two types of recognition, multiple and exclusive. Experience indicates that exclusive recognition is the most effective. The three most commonly used recognition procedures are membership lists, authorization cards, and elections. In an election, a third party, such as the Federal Mediation and Conciliation Service, should be engaged to handle the mechanics of the election process.

The bargaining unit is composed of all employees to be covered by the negotiated master agreement. The criteria for deciding who belongs to the unit include a community of interest among the members, effective bargaining power, and effective school administration.

The scope of what is negotiable usually includes salaries, fringe benefits, and working conditions. A major problem in defining the scope is the fine line between educational policy, which is the prerogative of the school board, and working conditions, which are negotiable.

The at-the-table bargaining process must begin with the formation of a negotiations team. An odd-numbered team composed of the director of employee relations, building principals, and a central-office fiscal administrator has the greatest potential for being effective. This team is responsible for developing strategies, formulating goals, setting the ground rules, preparing proposals, and participating in negotiating sessions. Once an agreement is reached, the team makes a recommendation to the superintendent and school board members, who formally ratify the agreement.

If there is persistent disagreement at the table after normal negotiations procedures are exhausted, an impasse has been reached. The three procedures usually employed in an impasse are mediation, fact finding, and, where permitted by law, arbitration. Mediation is the voluntary process of bringing in a third party who intervenes for the purpose of ending the disagreement. Fact finding is a procedure by which an individual or panel holds hearings for the purpose of reviewing evidence and making a recommendation for settling the dispute. Arbitration occurs when both sides submit the dispute to an impartial third person or panel that issues an award which the parties are required to accept.

Nothing is more disruptive to a school district than a strike, a tactic that is sometimes used by unions when negotiations reach an impasse. Although strikes by teachers are illegal in most states, a number of strikes occur each year throughout the country. It is extremely important, therefore, for the administration to develop a strike plan, even in the most tranquil of school settings.

The process of collective negotiations is usually ineffective unless the agreements reached are put in writing, thus formalizing the basic rights governing the parties and reducing potential controversy. It is the responsibility of the administration to implement and interpret the master agreement. Furthermore, the administration is limited only by the specifics of the agreement, which is commonly referred to as "management prerogative."

In the day-to-day interpretation of the master agreement, it is certainly possible for violations to occur. Most written agreements, therefore, provide for a grievance procedure by which individuals or the union may allege that the agreement is being violated.

In some school districts, labor–management relations committees have been formed for the purpose of working through concerns, problems, and issues before they appear at-the-table when the existing master contract is renegotiated.

An innovative approach to collective negotiations was developed in the mid-1980s. Called "collaborative bargaining," its purpose is the defusing of the hostility that sometimes accompanies the traditional negotiations process. In this process there is one team composed of teachers or other categories of employees reflecting the bargaining unit, administrators, and board members. The goal is to problem-solve issues, and the essence of the process is consensus.

Discussion Questions and Statements

- What are the significant differences between collective negotiations in the public and private sectors?
- What provisions do you think should be included in a state statute on collective negotiations for teachers?
- Explain the differences between the impasse procedures of mediation, fact-finding, and arbitration and further explain which procedures would be the most effective in collective negotiations with teacher organizations.
- Should public school employees have the right to strike?
- Explain the differences between a master contract and an individual person's employment contract.
- Explain how the labor movement in the United States has impacted professional teacher organizations and teacher unions.

Suggested Activities

- You are the Director of Employee Relations in a small suburban school district with approximately 75 teachers. The state where the school district is located has a strong collective negotiations law for public employees. Create, in writing, a process for conducting collective negotiations from a central office perspective that meets the principles in this chapter.
- Write a board of education collective negotiations policy that you think will meet the needs of employees for a school district in a state with a weak collective negotiations law for public employees.
- Review the statutes in the state where you live on collective negotiations for public employees and write a comparison of them with the principles in this chapter.
- Interview a human resources administrator in person or on the telephone and discuss the implementation of the policies in his or her district concerning collective negotiations.

Selected Bibliography

Abel, Gene P., "Equity, Accountability and Teacher Negotiations in the '90s," *School Business Affairs,* 57, no. 5 (May 1991), 30–31.

Ayers, Steven V., "Collective Bargaining as an Instrument of Change," *School Business Affairs,* 64, no. 2 (February 1998), 19–22.

Bland, Michael, and Peter Jackson, *Effective Employee Relations.* London: Kogan Page, 1990.

Conley, Sharon, and Jewell Gould, "Knowledge and Skill-Based Pay through a Collective Bargaining Lens," *Educational Policy,* 11, no. 4 (December 1997), 403–425.

Decker, Robert H., "Helping the Board of Education & Negotiating Team Understand their Roles in Collective Bargaining," *School Business Affairs,* 57, no. 2 (February 1991), 6–10.

Eiler, Edward E., "When Collective Bargaining Isn't Working," *School Business Affairs,* 57, no. 2 (February 1991), 18–21.

ERIC Clearinghouse on Educational Management, *Collective Bargaining and Alternatives.* Eugene, OR: University of Oregon, 1987.

Frombach, John W., "Negotiations—Are You Prepared?" *School Business Affairs,* 57, no. 2 (February 1991), 14–18.

Gerardi, Robert, "Strikes: Some Lessons from a Yankee Past," *Thrust for Educational Leadership,* 14 (September 1984), 27–28.

Glaser, John P., and James W. Tamm, "Better Bargaining," *The Executive Educator,* 13, no. 12 (December 1991), 22–25.

Godshall, Clark J., "Managing Success: Collective Bargaining," *School Business Affairs,* 68, no. 4 (April 2002), 2–3.

Grossman, Robert F., "Unions Follow Suit," *HR Magazine,* 50, no. 5 (2005), 46–51.

Herman, Jerry J., "The Two Faces of Collective Bargaining," *School Business Affairs,* 57, no. 2 (February 1991), 10–14.

Kerchner, Charles Taylor, *Labor Policy in School Districts: Its Diffusion and Impact on Work Structures.* Eugene, OR: University of Oregon Center for Educational Policy and Management, 1986.

Marsh, P. D. V., *Contract Negotiation Handbook,* 3rd ed. Burlington, Virginia: Gower, 2001.

Murphy, John F., "The Thanksgiving Dinner: An Allegory of the School Negotiation Process," *School Business Affairs,* 68, no. 4 (April 2002), 9–11.

Ramming, Thomas M., "Alternative Approaches to Negotiating," *School Business Affairs,* 63, no. 8 (August 1997), 3–6.

Rauth, Marilyn, "Exploring Heresy in Collective Bargaining and School Restructuring," *Phi Delta Kappan,* 71 (1990), 781–790.

Sharp, William L., *Collective Bargaining in the Public Schools.* Dubuque, IA: William C. Brown Communications, Inc., 1993.

Smith, Stuart C., Diana Ball, and Demetri Liontos, *Working Together: The Collaborative Style of Bargaining.* Eugene, OR: ERIC Clearinghouse on Educational Management, 1991.

Streshly, William A., and Todd A. DeMitchell, *Teacher Unions and TQE: Building Quality Labor Relations.* Thousand Oaks, CA: Corwin Press, Inc., 1994.

Tyler, Kathryn, "Good Faith Bargaining," *HR Magazine,* 50, no. 1 (2005), 48–53.

Vidak, Jim, "Take the Sting Out of Negotiations," *The Executive Educator,* 13, no. 3 (March 1991), 24–25.

Appendix A
Contract Table of Contents

Contract Between the Dade County Public Schools and the United Teachers of Dade FEA/United, AFT, Local 1974, AFL-CIO

Appendix B
Grievance Procedures

A. Purpose

It is recognized that complaints and grievances may arise between the bargaining agent and the employer or between the employer and any one or more employees concerning the application or interpretation of the wages, hours, terms and conditions of employment as defined in this agreement. The employer and the bargaining agent desire that these grievances and complaints be settled in an orderly, prompt, and equitable manner so that the efficiency of the Dade County Public Schools may be maintained and the morale of employees not be impaired. Every effort will be made by the employer, employees, and the bargaining agent to settle the grievances at the lowest level of supervision. The initiation or presentation of a grievance by an employee will not adversely affect his standing with the employer. No reprisals of any kind will be made by the Board or its representative or any member of the administration against any party in interest, any Union representative or any other participant in the grievance procedure by reason of such participation. All documents, grievance forms, communications, and records dealing with the processing of a grievance shall be filed separately from the personnel files of any party in interest, including final disposition, except for and exclusively for awards resulting from arbitration.

Source: Adapted from *Grievance Procedure from the Contract Between the Dade County Public Schools and the United Teachers of Dade* (Miami, FL: Dade County Public Schools, 1977), 53–66.

B. Definitions

1. *Grievance.* Formal allegation by an employee and/or the bargaining agent that there has been a violation, misinterpretation, or misapplication of any of the terms and conditions of employment set forth in this contract, *or its appendices.*

2. *Bargaining agent.* The bargaining agent shall mean the employee organization certified as the exclusive bargaining agent pursuant to 447.009 Florida Statutes Chapter 74.100.

3. *Aggrieved employee.* The aggrieved employee shall mean any full-time or part-time teacher and such other persons who are members of the bargaining unit as certified pursuant to Section 447.009 Florida Statutes Chapter 74.100.

4. *Party in interest.* A party in interest is any person who might be required to take action or against whom action might be taken in order to resolve the grievance.

5. *Supervising administrator.* The individual having immediate administrative authority over the aggrieved employee(s).

6. *Immediate superintendent.* The area, assistant, or associate superintendent having immediate administrative authority over the supervising administrator.

7. *Days.* As referred to in the time limits herein, days shall mean working days.

8. *Letter of inquiry.* Request in writing on proper CDPS form, by the bargaining agent to the Division of Legislative and Employee Relations seeking clarification of Dade County Public Schools rules, state law, or this agreement.

C. Special Provisions

The time limit set forth herein may be extended and/or modified by mutual agreement, using the stipulated Grievance Form.

In the event a grievance is filed at such time as it cannot be processed through all steps in the grievance procedure by the end of the aggrieved employee's contract year, and, if left unresolved until the beginning of the following year could result in irreparable harm to a party in interest, the time limits set forth herein will be reduced so that the grievance procedure may be exhausted as soon as practicable.

If the employer violates any time limits, the bargaining agent may advance to the next step without waiting for the employer response.

The parties acknowledge that as a principle of interpretation, employees are obligated to work as directed while grievances are pending.

The employer and the bargaining agent shall have the right of free choice in designating representatives for the purpose of resolving grievances. Aggrieved employees, or employees who are called as witnesses, will be allowed released time without loss of pay to process or assist in the processing of a grievance.

The bargaining agent in accordance with its own nondiscriminatory internal rules shall have the sole and exclusive right to determine whether any grievance warrants processing through this procedure. In the event the bargaining agent determines at any step of the grievance procedure that a grievance does not warrant processing, a written notification of that determination, using the stipulated Grievance Form, shall be sent to the Special Counsel for Legislative and Employee Relations and to the employee(s) involved who shall then be free to process it themselves or through legal counsel.

If the bargaining agent has declined to process or further process any grievance presented to it, and if any employee or group of employees desire to process it or further process their own grievance through this procedure, the bargaining agent shall be sent copies of all written communications sent by the employer or the employee(s) involved. Further, nothing herein contained shall be construed to prevent any public employees from representing, at any time, their own grievance in person or by legal counsel to the employer and having such grievance(s) adjusted without the intervention of the bargaining agent, provided however, that the adjustment is not inconsistent with the terms of the collective bargaining agreement then in effect, and provided further that the bargaining agent has been given notice and a reasonable opportunity to be present at any meeting called for the resolution of such grievances.

The bargaining agent shall not be responsible for any costs attendant to the resolution of any grievance it has not processed.

The parties acknowledge that multiple grievances may be combined with mutual agreement of the employer and the union.

One set of School Board rules at each work location shall be made available to Union building representatives for the purpose of reference and information as well as for the purpose of expediting the provisions of this grievance procedure.

The use of tape recorders or other mechanical devices is expressly forbidden.

D. Letter of Inquiry

Either the immediate superintendent or bargaining agent may send a Letter of Inquiry on the stipulated Letter of Inquiry form, to the Special Counsel for the Division of Legislative and Employee Relations for the purpose of seeking a clarification of a Dade County Public Schools rule, state law, and/or terms and conditions of employment as set forth in this agreement.

The Division of Legislative and Employee Relations shall respond within ten (10) working days of receipt of the Letter of Inquiry. If the interpretation of the Letter of Inquiry is not satisfactory, a formal grievance may be filed.

E. Implementation

Step I

1. The grievance shall be filed within thirty (30) days of the alleged violation, misinterpretation or misapplication of the terms and conditions of employment set forth in this agreement.

2. The grievance shall be filed in writing stating the specific article, section and language alleged to have been violated, misinterpreted or misapplied to the supervising administrator of the aggrieved employee(s). It is further understood and agreed that the aggrieved employee(s) shall be granted released time to attend formal proceedings, as described herein, which are held during working hours. No Dade County Public Schools employees, other than the aggrieved employee(s), shall be granted released time to either represent the aggrieved employee(s) or to observe the proceedings as representatives of the bargaining agent.

3. The supervising administrator shall note the date of receipt of the grievance and shall seek to meet with the aggrieved employee at a mutually agreeable time within five (5) working days of receipt of the grievance.

4. The bargaining agent for the unit shall be advised in writing as to the date of the proposed meeting, and shall have the right to send one (1) observer to the proceeding if the bargaining agent is not involved in the actual representation of the aggrieved employee(s).

5. Within five (5) working days of the meeting, the supervising administrator shall render a decision and shall immediately communicate that decision in writing to the aggrieved and the appropriate immediate superintendent or his designee. Additional copies of the decision shall be sent to the Division of Legislative and Employee Relations, and to the exclusive bargaining agent.

6. The aggrieved employee(s) and/or the bargaining agent may appeal the decision of the supervising administrator within five (5) working days of its rendering.

7. The notice of intent to appeal shall be communicated in writing to the immediate superintendent. Failure to appeal the decision of the supervising administrator within five (5) working days shall constitute acceptance by the aggrieved employee(s) and the bargaining agent of the decision as being a satisfactory resolution of the issue raised.

Step II

1. If the aggrieved employee(s) appeals the decision, the immediate superintendent shall schedule a meeting to take place at a mutually agreeable time not more than ten (10) days after receipt of notice of appeal. The immediate superintendent shall immediately communicate notice of appeal to the Division of Legislative and Employee Relations.

The exclusive bargaining agent shall be advised in writing as to the date of the proposed meeting and shall have the right to send one (1) observer to the proceedings if the agent is not involved in the actual representation of the aggrieved employee(s).

2. Within ten (10) working days of the meeting, the immediate superintendent shall render a decision and shall immediately communicate that decision in writing to the aggrieved employee(s). Copies of the decision shall be sent to the Division of Legislative and Employee Relations, and to the exclusive bargaining agent. A copy is to be retained by the immediate superintendent.

3. The aggrieved employee(s) may appeal the decision of the immediate superintendent within five (5) working days of its rendering. The notice of intent to appeal shall be communicated in writing to the Special Counsel for Legislative and Employee Relations. Failure to appeal the decision of the immediate superintendent within five (5) working days shall constitute acceptance by the aggrieved employee(s) and the bargaining agent of the decision as being a satisfactory resolution of the issue raised.

Step III

1. If the aggrieved employee(s) appeals the decision, the Superintendent or his designee shall schedule a meeting to take place at a mutually agreeable time not more than twelve (12) days after receipt of notice of appeal.

2. Within twelve (12) working days of the meeting, the Superintendent or his designee shall render a decision and shall immediately communicate that decision in writing to the aggrieved employee(s). Copies of the decision shall be sent to the supervising administrator, the immediate superintendent, and to the exclusive bargaining agent.

3. Failure to appeal the decision rendered in Step III within five (5) working days by notice of intent to submit to arbitration, shall deem the decision at Step III to be final and no further appeal will be pursued.

F. Arbitration

If the employer and the aggrieved employee(s) and/or the bargaining agent fail to resolve the grievance, the grievance may be submitted to final and binding disposition by an impartial neutral mutually selected by the parties. Nothing contained in this Appendix or elsewhere in this agreement shall be construed to permit the Union to file an issue for arbitration unless by mutual consent, that has not been processed through applicable steps of the grievance procedure.

1. Notice of intent to submit the grievance to arbitration shall be communicated in writing to the Special Counsel for Legislative and Employee Relations within five (5) working days of the decision at Step III.

2. Prior to the submission of the appeal to arbitration, the arbitrator may hold a prehearing conference to consider and determine

    a. The simplification of the issues

    b. The possibility of obtaining stipulation of facts and documents that will avoid unnecessary proof

    c. Such other matters as may aid in the disposition of the grievance

    d. Matters of jurisdiction or applicability

3. In the event that an employee desires, on his own behalf, to process his grievance to arbitration, the bargaining agent reserves the right to intervene in the arbitration proceeding up to and including the full right to participation as a party. Should the bargaining agent intervene, it shall bear half the employee's cost.

4. Within ten (10) days after written notice of submission to arbitration, the parties will attempt to agree upon a mutually acceptable arbitrator and obtain a commitment from said arbitrator to serve. If the parties are unable to agree upon an arbitrator or to obtain such a commitment within the specified time, a request for a list of arbitrators may be made to the Federal Mediation and Conciliation Service by either party. The parties will be bound by the rules and procedures of the Federal Mediation and Conciliation Service in the selection of an arbitrator and the holding and conduct of an arbitration hearing.

5. The arbitrator, selected by the parties, or pursuant to the rules of the Federal Mediation and Conciliation Service, will issue a decision not later than twenty (20) days from the date of the close of the hearings, or if oral hearings have been waived, then from the date final statements and proofs are submitted. The arbitrator's decision will be in writing and will set forth findings of fact, reasoning and conclusions on the issue submitted and where permitted by law may include a monetary award. The arbitrator will be without power or authority to make any decision which requires the commission of an act prohibited by law, or which adds to, subtracts from, modifies, or alters the terms of this collective bargaining agreement. The decision and award of the arbitrator shall be final and binding.

6. All arbitration costs, including the cost of stenographic reporting of the arbitration hearing if agreed to by the parties, shall be divided equally between the employer and the bargaining agent, or if the bargaining agent has determined not to process the grievance through arbitration, between the employer and the employee(s). Each party will pay the cost of presenting its own case; however, the aggrieved employee(s) or the employee(s) who is called as witness for an arbitration hearing will be allowed released time to process or to assist in the processing of their own grievance, or to testify.

7. It is understood and agreed by the employer, members of the unit, and the bargaining agent, that the resolution of complaints which are grievable or litigable shall be pursued through the grievance procedure until such remedy is exhausted. At that time the employer, the aggrieved employee(s) and/or the bargaining agent may seek other legal remedies as are available.

Refusal to discuss a grievance in good faith shall constitute an Unfair Labor Practice and shall be subject to the penalties provided for in Section 447.017 Florida Statutes 74–100.

8. Both parties agree to negotiate and mutually agree to the rules and procedures which govern arbitration. In the event mutual agreement cannot be reached, the American Arbitration Association will be utilized to process arbitration cases.

CHAPTER 10

Legal, Ethical, and Policy Issues in the Administration of Human Resources

This final chapter is concerned with legal, ethical, and policy issues in the administration of human resources. An understanding by current and future human resources managers of contract management and the nuances of litigation has become more important within the last decade because of the ever-increasing societal emphasis on legal rights and responsibilities. Human resources managers are as vulnerable to litigation as teachers and principals. In fact, with the multitude of federal and state laws, regulations, and procedures that impinge on human resources functions, defensibility and accountability must be continuing concerns in the human resources department.

Relevant, concise, and clear personnel policies become the foundation upon which the eight human resources functions rest. Administrative processes and procedures operationalize these policies and provide the internal structure necessary to accomplish the school district's primary mandate—to educate children. Consequently, this chapter has been written with these issues in mind and should provide direction to all persons concerned with human resources administration including boards of education, superintendents, assistant superintendents, and human resources managers.

Contract Management

Teachers and administrators usually work under the provisions of an individual contract; classified personnel such as clerks, bus drivers, and custodians are employed at an hourly rate or for an annual salary. In school districts where a master contract has been negotiated by a union, teachers and/or administrators belonging to the bargaining unit do not have individual contracts but rather work under the provisions of the master agreement. There are exceptions to these general statements; however, for all practical purposes these are the alternative methods by which employees are hired to work in a school system.

The question may legitimately be asked, "What is the purpose of issuing individual contracts to teachers and administrators?" The most accurate response is tradition. As professionals, teachers and administrators are employed to perform a service for which they receive a certain amount of financial compensation. The performance of the service may require a teacher to take student projects home to be graded or may require a teacher to remain after the school day to talk with the parents of a student having problems. The time it takes to perform the service and the amount of work involved are not considerations under the contract method of employment.

Classified employees also are paid to perform a service, but the time and work involved does make a difference in the amount of money received. When such employees are required to work after the regular eight-hour day, they receive overtime pay. If they are required to perform a task not specified by the categories outlined in their job descriptions, they receive additional compensation.

Those professional employees who are covered by the terms of a master agreement have a closer identity to classified employees than to teachers and administrators with individual contracts. Their working conditions are spelled out in the master agreement.

Board of education policies sometimes address working conditions, but these policies are usually not as specific as the terms of a master agreement. Teacher and administrator handbooks also may contain references to working conditions, but these are usually more concerned with internal procedures.

Although using individual contracts for teachers and administrators is a matter of tradition, this is mandated by statute in some states. Individual contracts also distinguish an individual's working conditions from those termed "classified." A teacher's or administrator's contract must meet the requirements of general contract law. Because school districts are legal entities with a corporate character, they may sue and be sued; purchase, receive, or sell real and personal property; make contracts and be contracted with. The contracts entered into by a school district must conform not only to contract law but also to state statutes governing contracts and to the precedents established through case law.

A *contract* is an agreement that must possess five basic components in order for it to be valid. The components are: offer and acceptance, competent persons, consideration, legal subject matter, and proper form.[1]

Offer and Acceptance

A valid contract must contain an offer and an acceptance. In the selection process, therefore, it is poor procedure to notify unsuccessful candidates for a position that the job has been filled until after the prospective employee has accepted the offer of employment. If the board of education approves a contract for a specific person to teach high school English, there is no agreement until the contract is executed, which constitutes acceptance.

A few other facts about the legal nature of an agreement must be kept in mind. First, an offer can be accepted only by the person to whom it was made. For example, the husband of a candidate for a teaching position cannot accept the offer for his wife. Second, an offer must be accepted within a reasonable time after it is made. If an individual does not sign and return a contract within a few weeks in the hope that another job offer will be made by a different school district, the board of education may offer the contract to another can-

---

[1]An extended treatment of the essential matter in this section may be found in the following reference: Steven Knowles, *Contracts* (Larchmont, NY: Emanuel Law Outlines, Inc., 1993–94 edition).

didate. Finally, a newspaper advertisement is not an offer of a position but rather an invitation to become a candidate for a job.

Competent Persons

A contract is not valid unless it is entered into by two or more competent parties. This means that the persons have the legal capacity to enter into a contract. As a corporate entity, a school district has the power, through the legal action of the school board, to enter into a contract. Certain classes of individuals, however, have a limited capacity to contract. The most commonly identified classes include minors, mentally ill persons, and individuals who are intoxicated. If a person was mentally ill or intoxicated to the extent that he or she did not understand the significance of the action at the time of entering into a contract, he or she may have the contract set aside because there was no agreement, which is essential to the validity of every contract.

Consideration

For a contract to be valid, it must be supported by a consideration, which is usually defined as something of value. The type of consideration found in an employment contract is referred to as "a promise for an act." For example, in a teacher's contract the board of education promises to pay an individual $40,000 to teach third grade for one year. The teacher fulfills the act by teaching during the designated time period.

Legal Subject Matter

In all fifty states an individual may teach only if he or she possesses a license to teach issued by the respective state department of education. Consequently, if a board of education enters into a contract with a person who does not possess a license to teach the third grade, such a contract would involve illegal subject matter and would be invalid.

Proper Form

For a contract to be enforceable, it must be in the form required by law. The courts recognize both oral and written contracts. However, most states have statutory provisions that require teachers' and administrators' contracts to be in writing and even specify the proper wording for the contracts.

Litigation in Human Resources Management

School districts have experienced an increase in litigation partially due to the fact that sovereign immunity has been abrogated by many state legislatures. Sovereign immunity is the common law principle that protects government officials from lawsuits resulting from the performance of their duties. School districts are governmental subdivisions of the state operating on the local level, and thus, school board members have been protected from such lawsuits. However, many states have taken away this cloak of immunity.

The ripple effect from this situation has caused human resources administrators to become more vulnerable to judicial review of their decisions and actions. Even if human resources administrators act in good faith and with reasonable deliberation, they may find themselves defending their actions in court.

Therefore, it is imperative that all administrators have a rudimentary understanding of the U.S. judicial system and are capable of carrying out their daily responsibilities in such a manner that they can legally defend themselves if they are sued. The following discussion is meant to provide future human resources administrators with a better understanding of their potential liabilities.

The U.S. Judicial System

There are two systems of law. The first, known as "civil law," is descended from Roman law; the rule of law in this system is established through statutes enacted by a legislative body. The second system, known as "common law," is the basis of law in England. Under this system, the decisions rendered by a court become a guide or precedent to be followed by the court in dealing with future cases. The system of law found in the United States is a mixed system, using both civil and common law principles.

Sources of Law

There are three major sources of law that form the foundation of the U.S. judicial system: constitutions, statutes, and case law. There are two additional sources of law that affect education even though they are not primary sources: administrative law and attorney general opinions.

Constitutions
Constitutions are bodies of precepts that provide the framework within which government carries out its duties. The federal and state constitutions contain provisions that secure the personal, property, and political rights of citizens.

School districts have been continually confronted with constitutional issues, many of which have resulted in lawsuits. Some of these issues have dealt with racial discrimination in hiring practices, due process rights for individuals faced with employment termination, and the privacy right of employees in relation to their personnel records.

Statutes
Statutes, more commonly called "laws," are the enactments of legislative bodies. Thus, the U.S. Congress or a given state legislature may enact a new law or change an old law by the passage of legislation. A statute is subject to review by the respective state or federal court to determine if it is in violation of the precepts set forth in a state or federal constitution.

The presumption is that laws enacted by legislative bodies are constitutional, and the burden of proving otherwise is determined only through litigation. Thus, if a state legislature passes a law that allows school administrators the right to terminate tenured teachers without a hearing before the school board, a teacher or group of teachers could initiate a lawsuit asking the state's supreme court to consider the constitutionality of the new law. The basis for the lawsuit might be a provision in the state constitution dealing with the permanent employment status of tenured teachers.

Because public schools are state agencies, the legislature of every state has created statutes governing school districts. School operation, therefore, must be in compliance with such state statutes, and it is the responsibility of the board of education and the superintendent of schools to ensure compliance. Further, the board of education cannot establish policies that are in conflict with state statutes or the acts of the U.S. Congress; in addition, the policies must not be in conflict with either the federal or state constitutions. If a school board, for example, creates a policy prohibiting the employment of individuals with disabilities as teachers, this policy would be in violation of federal law—in particular, the Rehabilitation Act of 1973—and probably violates the due process guaranteed by the Fourteenth Amendment to the U.S. Constitution; it might also violate a given state constitutional provision stipulating that all citizens have a right to employment opportunities.

Case Law

The third source, common law, is more properly called "case law" because it is derived from court decisions rather than from legislative acts. Past court decisions are considered to be binding on subsequent cases if the material facts are similar. This is the doctrine of precedent. Lower courts usually adhere to the precedent (rule of law) established by higher courts in the same jurisdiction. The U.S. Supreme Court and state supreme courts can reverse their own previous decisions and thereby change the rule of law. Thus, a state circuit court may apply a rule of law established by a state supreme court as to what constitutes due process in the termination of a tenured teacher. In a later case, the supreme court may redefine what constitutes due process and thus change the rule of law.

Administrative Law and Attorney General Opinions

Administrative law has developed through the creation of state and federal boards and commissions charged with administering certain federal and state laws. In carrying out their responsibilities, these boards and commissions establish rules and regulations. For example, school employees are likely to be affected by the regulations of the Social Security Administration, the Employment Security Administration, or the Workers' Compensation Commission. Of course, the actions of these boards and commissions are subject to review by the courts.

A second and frequently initiated legal procedure is the requesting of an opinion from a state attorney general on the interpretation of a certain statute. In the absence of case law, this opinion can be used by educators in addressing legal issues.

Human resources administrators must continually research professional journals that speak to significant court decisions and legislation. Most state departments of education also notify school administrators concerning recent state court decisions and laws that affect school district human resources practices and policies. The agencies of the federal government are very diligent in notifying school districts across the country about regulations with which they are required to be in compliance.

Major Divisions of Law

There are two broad classifications of law: criminal and civil. Criminal law is concerned with protecting the rights of society; and as such, the state, representing the people, is responsible for prosecuting wrongs committed against society by individuals or corporate entities. Civil law is concerned with protecting the rights that exist between individuals, between an individual and a corporate entity, or between two corporate entities. Most of the litigation that arises out of human resources management, of course, will deal with civil law. Civil law embraces many areas including contracts, wills and estates, corporate law, divorce, and torts. Human resources administrators are most vulnerable in lawsuits dealing with contracts and torts.

The Court Structure

The municipal court structure is of little or no concern to human resources administrators. These courts are usually concerned with enforcing the ordinances of municipal governments, which include housing and building codes and traffic ordinances.

The federal court structure, of course, is divided into three levels: the federal district courts, the courts of appeal, and the U.S. Supreme Court. The district courts are courts of original jurisdiction where all suits involving federal law will be filed. Civil suits that involve agencies of the U.S. government also are heard in the federal district courts. Thus, both the Bakke and Weber cases originated in the respective federal district courts. Both cases were eventually appealed to the U.S. Supreme Court and have become landmark decisions. Human resources administrators should be familiar with the nuances of the federal court system due to the multitude of federal employment laws, which are potential areas of litigation.

The state court structure is analogous to the federal system. The court of original jurisdiction in most states is termed the circuit court and is where all civil lawsuits are filed. Cases involving tenure and contract management will be heard in the circuit court. The decisions of the circuit court may be appealed, usually to an appellate court and, finally, to the state supreme court. Once again, it must be stated that human resources administrators should become very familiar with the workings of the state court system because of the high incidence of litigation involving state laws as they relate to human resources management.

There is a distinction in the manner by which certain courts can hear cases that is important for human resources administrators to understand. Certain issues are traditionally tried in "equity" by the state circuit courts and federal district courts. The most familiar to human resources administrators are injunctions. For example, a school district may go to a state circuit court to ask for an injunction directing a group of teachers to leave the picket lines and to return to their classrooms, if there is a state statute prohibiting strikes by teachers. Obviously, if the parties named in an injunction fail to obey the court order, they are in contempt of court and may be punished by a fine or by jailing.

The Role of the Attorney in Human Resources Management

A common misconception about the role that a school district's attorney fulfills in a lawsuit against a school district is that he or she will entirely handle the litigation. An attorney's expertise centers around his or her ability to take the material facts in a case and research the statutes and the precedents of other court cases for the purpose of organizing a reasonable defense. An attorney must begin with what you, the human resources administrator, can offer by way of documentation. The defense will only be as strong as the level of accountability that has been demonstrated through human resources procedures and policies. Consequently, a good test of the workability of procedures and policies is whether they will be a help or a hindrance in a lawsuit.

The Anatomy of a Lawsuit

Although lawsuits do not follow a set pattern, there is enough commonality in litigation to make a few general observations (see Fig. 10.1). The plaintiff files a petition with the appropriate court of jurisdiction, setting forth the cause of action, which is the allegation. A summons is then delivered by the court to the defendant, who is required to appear in court on a given date for the purpose of pleading to the petition.

The next step involves clarifying the allegation and the material facts supporting it. This may be accomplished by the taking of depositions, a formal procedure in which the parties to the lawsuit answer questions posed by the respective attorneys. Also, written queries may be required by the attorneys in lieu of or in addition to the depositions.

Then a motion may be filed to dismiss the petition if the material facts do not appear to support the allegation. If the judge does not dismiss the petition, a trial date will be set. In civil cases involving tenure, a contract, or a tort, the defendant usually has the option of a jury trial or may rely on the judge to make a decision.

Who the defendant is in a civil lawsuit is determined by the nature of the petition and the material facts. In a tenure or contract dispute, the board of education as a corporate body is usually the defendant because the board approves all personnel contracts. If it is a tort, an individual or a group of individuals may be named as the defendant because the petition may allege that a civil wrong has been committed against the plaintiff by one person or a group of persons. In a judgment favoring the plaintiff, damages are assessed in dollar amounts to be paid by the defendant.

Tort Liability in Human Resources Administration

There is a tendency to take a shotgun approach in some types of civil lawsuits, particularly torts, when identifying defendants in a litigation. If a student is injured as a consequence of using gymnastics equipment, the teacher might be sued for being negligent in supervising the student or for not properly instructing the student on how to use the equipment. The building principal might be sued for neglecting to properly evaluate and remove the teacher who allegedly did a poor job of supervising the student. The superintendent might be brought into the lawsuit because he neglected to remove the principal who inadequately supervised the teacher. The board of education might be sued because the members neglected to supervise and monitor the superintendent in evaluating the performance of the principal. This path then follows the chain-of-command in a school district and ensures that the responsible party or parties will be identified by the court.

This same type of situation is applicable to human resources management. A case could be made alleging that a given teacher's references were not properly investigated by the assistant superintendent for human resources, which eventuated in the hiring of an unqualified applicant. It goes without saying that employment situations may carry more vulnerability

Plaintiff Files a Petition

Court Serves a Summons on
the Defendant

Defendant Pleads the Petition

Depositions and/or Written Queries
Are Taken by Both Parties

Defendant May File a Motion
for Dismissal or Plaintiff May
Drop the Lawsuit

Trial Is Held If the Lawsuit
Is Not Dismissed or Dropped

Decision of the Judge or Jury
Is Rendered

If the Decision Is in Favor of
the Defendant—the Case
Is Dismissed

If the Decision Is in Favor of
the Plaintiff—a Remedy
Is Addressed

Appeal by the Defendant

FIGURE 10.1   Anatomy of a Lawsuit

Source: Ronald W. Rebore, *Educational Administration:
A Management Approach* (Englewood Cliffs, NJ:
Prentice-Hall, 1985), 69.

than those involved with instruction. Therefore, it is important for human resources managers to be well-informed about tort liability. With this knowledge, they will be able to establish human resources processes and procedures that will accomplish the objectives of the human resources department and also will be easy to defend in court. A tort is a civil wrong, other than a breach of contract, committed against a person or a person's property.

Tort law emanates from common law, which is composed of those principles established through court cases that are usually referred to as *precedent.* The acts of legislatures have either broadened or narrowed these common law principles. For example, at common law, an individual wrongfully causing the death of another person incurs no civil liability; the Missouri legislature has enacted a statute that imposes civil liabilities in favor of certain persons, including the surviving spouse and children.

There are two major types of torts: intentional torts and negligence. Intentional torts are further classified as to whether the action interfered with a person or with the person's property. Assault, battery, and defamation are the most common types associated with personal interference; malicious trespassing is the most common interference with respect to property rights.

In human resources management, defamation of character is a potential area of litigation with regard to the giving of references and communicating the contents of an individual's personnel file. Defamation occurs when false information is communicated either by word of mouth (slander) or in writing (libel), brings hatred or ridicule on a person, and produces some type of harm to the person. With regard to the human resources function, the harm produced by defamation might be the loss of an employment opportunity or a job promotion.

To protect against such litigation, established procedures should outline who is responsible for writing references and under what circumstances the contents of an individual's personnel file can be released. Although each situation will vary, the following guidelines should be observed:

1. The employee has a right to review the contents of his or her personnel file in the presence of a human resources administrator.
2. The supervisor of an employee has a right to review the contents of an employee's file in the presence of a human resources administrator.
3. Only official and approved documents may be added to an employee's file (for example, attendance records, payroll records, performance evaluation forms).
4. No document may be removed from an individual's personnel file without notification to the employee, who has the right to question the removal.
5. The contents or partial contents of an employee's personnel file may not be released to other parties without the written permission of the employee (for example, attendance records being requested by a potential employer).
6. Under no circumstances should a human resources administrator discuss over the telephone information in an employee's file.

Negligence is that type of tort which involves some form of injury to another person as a result of conduct that falls below an established standard. It is the duty of an assistant superintendent for human resources and other human resources administrators to establish processes and procedures that do not violate federal and state laws and that accomplish the objectives of the human resources function. Therefore, in the recruitment and selection of new employees, affirmative action procedures must be followed so that the rights of protected groups are not violated. A human resources administrator who neglected to properly initiate or follow such procedures could be guilty of a tort if a minority applicant was denied an opportunity to be interviewed for a position and, as a result, lost a job opportunity. Even though a charge of discrimination would probably be filed in this case with the

Equal Employment Opportunity Commission, there is also the possibility of a civil lawsuit being brought against an individual administrator.

In a tort liability lawsuit that involves a question of negligence, the court will apply the principle of the *reasonable person*, which has some limitations in a pluralistic society.[2] This concept has a very specific application and definition. The reasonable person is someone who

1. Possesses average intelligence, normal perception, and memory
2. Possesses such superior skill and knowledge as the defendant has or purports to have
3. Possesses the same level of experience that the defendant has
4. Possesses the same physical attributes that the defendant has

Thus, the conduct of a human resources administrator involved in a lawsuit is compared against the conduct of a mythical reasonable person. If a reasonable person could have prevented the consequence, the administrator will be found negligent by the jury. The moral of the example is that all administrators should examine their professional responsibilities to determine if their conduct in fulfilling these responsibilities can withstand the test of the reasonable person.

In a civil lawsuit resulting in a judgment favoring the plaintiff, the defendant usually will be required to pay actual damages, which is the amount of money that the injury cost. The loss of a job opportunity has a potential for costing the defendant a considerable amount of money, which could conceivably reach into the hundreds of thousands of dollars. If it can be demonstrated in court that the defendant deliberately caused the injury, punitive damages may also be levied. This dollar amount is a punishment for intentionally bringing about a civil wrong. In some cases, punitive damages may equal or supersede the actual damages assessed by the court. A human resources administrator who publicly disagrees with the concept of affirmative action and who tells ethnic jokes to fellow employees might be laying the foundation for the allegation that he or she deliberately neglects to follow affirmative action procedures.

Errors and Omissions Liability Insurance

It should be clear from this presentation that every human resources administrator should be protected by errors and omissions liability insurance. Sources for obtaining such coverage include professional organizations and the school district's insurance carrier.

Many professional educator associations offer this type of insurance as a part of the regular membership benefits. Many of the large insurance companies will be happy to provide such protection under a group policy for all central-office administrators or for any other group of employees. The members of the board of education also may be included in this coverage and should be covered, particularly in those states where sovereign immunity has been abrogated. Finally, it should be remembered that most errors and omissions liability insurance policies do not cover punitive damages, because this would amount to condoning an act that was deliberately perpetrated.

---

[2]Moran Mayo, *Rethinking the Reasonable Person: An Egalitarian Reconstruction of the Objective Standard* (New York: Oxford University Press, 2003), 315–316.

Ethical Considerations in Human Resources Management

People in the United States have become increasingly aware of the vulnerability of those who occupy leadership positions in private business, government, churches, and in public education. The news media constantly reveal crimes committed even by those who hold not only leadership positions but also positions of significant trust. Lawyers, too, have exhibited less than exemplary conduct.[3] However, nothing is more disheartening than to read about a member of the clergy or teacher who sexually abuses a child. These occurrences are easily judged as being immoral or unethical.

The central issue in this treatment is the fact that all people must make decisions on a daily basis where the lines of appropriate behavior are somewhat blurred—the grey area. Human resources administrators are particularly vulnerable because their decisions affect people in that most important area of life—employment. Students are also affected because the quality of their education depends on the quality of the people employed by a school district.

The basis for making ethically sound decisions is usually grounded in religious beliefs or philosophical assumptions. The Judeo-Christian-Islamic tradition sets forth norms of appropriate conduct that are accepted by most U.S. citizens. Many of these religious beliefs and philosophical assumptions are contained in the documents upon which the United States was founded. The philosophical assumptions are commonly understood to proceed from human reason fortified by natural law.[4]

The American Association of School Personnel Administrators has adopted the *Statement of Ethics for School Administrators,* which was developed by the American Association of School Administrators. Although this statement is appropriate, it is intended for all categories of administrators and does not go far enough to provide guidance in the many diverse and complicated situations that face contemporary school human resources administrators. There are three principles that have been gleaned from the above sources and that constitute the foundation upon which the responsibilities in Exhibit 10.1 have been developed.

First, the exercise of these responsibilities in making judgments for decisions, over time, will help an individual to determine the sort of person and human resources professional he or she wants to become. Any given decision usually does not determine an individual's central ethical orientation unless it is a decision of monumental significance such as deliberately committing a felony. Rather, a person is constantly in the state of becoming either a better person and professional or a person who gradually loses his or her integrity. Even inappropriate decisions about issues that might appear to be rather insignificant can chip away at the edges surrounding a person's central core of integrity.

Second, the decisions of school human resources administrators have a definite effect upon school districts as institutions. This effect will be either positive or negative depending on the motivation for the decision and its magnitude. For example, an assistant superintendent for human resources who attempts to influence the hiring of a candidate solely

---

[3]Richard B. Schmitt, "Ethics Courses for Lawyers Draw Comers," *Wall Street Journal,* 8 July 1993, sec. B, 82.

[4]Milton A. Gonsalves, *Fagother's Right & Reason: Ethics in Theory and Practice,* 9th ed. (Columbus, OH: Merrill Publishing Company, 1989), 124–125.

EXHIBIT 10.1 Responsibilities for the Ethical Management of the School Human Resources Function

School districts have a moral and legal obligation to provide children and young adults with the best education possible given the human and financial resources available to them. The quality of education depends on the quality of personnel who directly or indirectly provide the educational service. Consequently, boards of education and superintendents of schools must be diligent in the selection of human resources administrators who will manage the human resources function. Once employed, human resources administrators will be held accountable for the following responsibilities:

Responsibilities to the School District and Its Staff

The responsibilities to the school district and its staff are to

- Support and implement the policies of the board of education in a positive and effective manner
- Support and implement administrative processes and procedures in a positive and effective manner
- Through appropriate means, pursue changing board polices, administrative processes and procedures that are not consistent with sound practice
- Project a positive image of the school district to the community-at-large and the education community
- Promote the equitable treatment of individuals, groups, and companies
- Help colleagues and subordinates fulfill their obligations and aspirations
- Help subordinates achieve their maximum potential
- Treat colleagues and subordinates with dignity and fairness
- Maintain confidentiality in carrying out the obligations of a school human resources administrator

- Promote adherence to all local, state, and national ordinances and laws

Responsibilities to the School Human Resources Profession

The responsibilities to the school human resources profession are to

- Promote membership in and the activities of school human resources professional associations at the local, state, and national levels
- Accept leadership roles in school human resources professional associations
- Promote research in school human resources administration that will enhance the effectiveness of the profession
- Promote professional development activities that will enhance the performance of school human resources administrators

Personal Responsibilities

Personal responsibilities are to

- Fulfill the obligations of a school human resources administrator in an open manner
- Seek consultation from colleagues or other professionals when faced with an ethical or professional problem for which there appears to be no appropriate solution
- Continue to grow as a person and as a school human resources professional through attendance at conventions, seminars, conferences, or through university coursework
- Develop the virtues of prudence, honesty, and justice so your behavior will enhance not only your integrity as a person but also the integrity of the school district in which you work and the school human resources profession that you represent

because that person is his or her friend has made a decision that will have a negative effect on the school district for which he or she is employed. If this type of action is repeated over time, the school district could take on a negative image that would affect morale among other employees and among other educators in the surrounding school districts. In a similar manner, the decisions of human resources administrators will have a positive or negative effect upon the school human resources professional associations in which the administrator is a member or has a position of leadership. Human experience indicates that it is virtually impossible to keep inappropriate actions from becoming common knowledge.

The third principle is taken from the Declaration of Independence. "[A]ll men are created equal, . . . they are endowed by their creator with certain unalienable rights, that among these are life, liberty, and the pursuit of happiness." Any action by a school human resources administrator to show preferential treatment to certain people, groups, or companies is contrary to this principle. The human resources administrator has a duty to ensure that such rights are manifested not only in the daily actions of employees but also in the policy and procedural processes of the school district.

Ethical Responsibilities of School Human Resources Administrators

The responsibilities set forth in Exhibit 10.1 are grouped under three separate headings: those pertaining to the school district and its staff, those pertaining to the school human resources profession, and those pertaining to the human resources administrator as a person. This approach has been selected over the more traditional approach wherein a list of prohibitions is presented as a code of ethics. The emphasis here is on carrying out responsibilities that will have a positive effect on the school district, the human resources profession, and the human resources administrator. Also, because each human being is constantly in the state of becoming either a better person or a person of decreasing integrity, just avoiding certain types of actions is not enough to steer the process in a positive direction. Each person must be proactive. This is the reason why, in this presentation, the ethical administrator is portrayed as a person who seeks to fulfill responsibilities.

Responsibilities to the School District and Its Staff

This first group of ten responsibilities clearly addresses the *communal* aspect of public school administration and, in particular, the *communal* aspect of school human resources management. School human resources administrators have obligations to the institution for which they work, the school district. Further, they have obligations to their colleagues and subordinates. Thus, loyalty to the board of education, superintendent of schools, colleagues, and subordinates becomes the vehicle for fulfilling these responsibilities. Sometimes it happens that a certain human resources administrator cannot ethically accept the policies or practices of the school district for which he or she works. If the administrator is unable to effect changes in the policies or practices of the district by using the chain-of-command process, he or she should seek other employment.[5]

---

[5]National School Boards Association, "Ethics in Education," *The Administrative Angle on Policy Implementation* (Arlington, VA: The Association, December 1992), 2.

Responsibilities to the School Human Resources Profession

The next group of responsibilities defines the professional obligations of the human resources administrator. Emphasis is placed on participation in professional associations and working within these associations to enhance the profession. This is particularly important in the areas of research and professional development.

Personal Responsibilities

The final group of responsibilities are concerned with the personal growth of the human resources administrator. This growth is nurtured through professional development activities and the practice of certain virtues. The virtue of honesty should help administrators avoid conflict of interest situations and the virtue of prudence should help them to avoid even the appearance of such a conflict. Thus, accepting gifts, services, or anything of value because of an act performed or withheld certainly violates the virtue of honesty. Accepting gifts, services, or something of value even though "no strings" were attached violates the virtue of prudence. Honesty is also violated when administrators use their position in a professional association for personal gain. When an employee receives preferential treatment simply because of friendship with a certain administrator, the virtue of justice is violated.

All people need help at times. Seeking consultation from other professionals when the need arises is viewed here as an obligation. Therefore, to continue an inappropriate practice or to persist in behavior that could bring derision on the school district, the human resources profession, or the administrator is a violation of this obligation.

Human Resources Policy Development

Chapter 1 enumerated the advantages of having board of education policies. Now that the eight human resources functions have been elucidated in detail, it should be very clear that well-defined human resources policies are absolutely necessary. In fact, creating such policies is a major task of the human resources department. The difference between board of education policies and administrative procedures also should be kept in mind. Policies are usually broad statements of direction; procedures are a sequence of steps to be followed in implementing a policy. In practice, however, there is a fine distinction in some situations between the wording of a policy and the wording of a procedure that makes it operational.

Appendix A presents a set of sample policies adapted from those collected by the Educational Policies Service of the National School Boards Association. These policies demonstrate a variety of construction models; they also demonstrate the overlapping characteristics of policies and procedures. Of course, EPS/NSBA is an exceptional service that would be of benefit to all school districts.

The index to the human resources policy section of the Educational Policies Service has also been included to show the scope that professional staff human resources manuals should entertain. Included for the same reason is Appendix B, which gives the table of contents for a classified employee human resources manual.

Summary

This chapter is concerned with legal, ethical, and policy issues in human resources administration. These issues have become important within the last decade because of the increased emphasis on legal rights and responsibilities.

Teachers and administrators usually work under the provisions of an individual contract; classified personnel are employed at an hourly rate or for an annual salary. Using individual contracts for teachers and administrators is a matter of tradition that also is mandated by law in some states and that distinguishes a professional employee's working conditions from those of classified employees.

Teachers' and administrators' contracts must meet the requirements of general contract law, state statutes, and the precedents established through case law. A contract is an agreement between two or more competent persons for a legal consideration on a legal subject matter in the form required by law. The five basic components, therefore, to every valid contract are offer and acceptance, competent persons, a consideration, legal subject matter, and proper form.

School districts have experienced an increase in litigation. In addition, human resources administrators are far more vulnerable today to judicial review of their actions than previously. It is imperative, therefore, that administrators have a rudimentary understanding of the American judicial system and are capable of making decisions that are legally defensible.

There are basically two systems of law. The first, called a civil law system, attempts to establish all laws in the form of statutes enacted by a legislative body. The second is referred to as a common law system. It is the basic approach used in England and was adopted in theory by most of the states in our country. Under this system the decisions rendered by a court become a precedent to be followed by the court in dealing with future cases. The system of law in the United States is a mixture of both civil and common law.

There are three major sources of law that form the foundation of the American judicial system: constitutions, statutes, and court cases. Constitutions are bodies of precepts that provide the framework within which government carries out its duties. Statutes are the enactments of legislative bodies; they are more commonly called "laws." As stated above, common law emanates from the decisions of courts rather than from legislative bodies. There are two additional sources of law that affect education even though they are not traditionally considered primary sources: administrative law and attorney general opinions. Administrative law consists of those regulations set forth by agencies established by Congress and state legislatures. In the absence of case law, the state attorney general may be requested to render an opinion on the interpretation of a certain statute.

The two broad classifications of law are criminal and civil. Civil law is concerned with protecting the rights of individuals and corporate entities; criminal law is concerned with protecting the rights of society.

The judicial system is composed of municipal, state, and federal courts. Most states have three categories of courts: circuit courts, courts of appeal, and supreme courts. In like manner, there are three categories of federal courts: district courts, the U.S. Courts of Appeals, and the U.S. Supreme Court.

The U.S. judicial system also preserves the concept of equity. The state circuit and U.S. district courts may handle both law and equity issues. Certain issues are traditionally tried in equity, the most common being injunctions.

Human resources administrators should become familiar with the nuances of the state and federal court systems because of the great number of laws affecting employment and because of the potentiality for tort liability lawsuits.

In human resources management it is also extremely important to understand the role of the attorney. The attorney takes the material facts in a case and researches the statutes or laws and precedents of court cases for the purpose of organizing a reasonable defense. The defense will be only as strong as the level of accountability that has been demonstrated through human resources procedures and policies.

A lawsuit begins with the filing of a petition, setting forth the allegation in the appropriate court of jurisdiction. The next step is clarifying the allegation and the material facts. The final step is the trial.

A tort is a civil wrong, other than a breach of contract, committed against a person or a person's property. The two major types of torts are classified as intentional torts and negligence. Assault, battery, defamation, and trespassing are the most common types of intentional torts. In human resources management, defamation is a potential area of litigation with regard to the giving of references and the communicating of the contents of an individual's personnel file.

Negligence is a tort that involves conduct falling below an established standard that results in some type of injury to another person. Negligence, therefore, implies neglect of a duty. The duty of human resources administrators is to establish processes and procedures that do not violate federal and state laws and that meet the objectives of the human resources department. A human resources administrator who neglected to initiate or follow such procedures could be guilty of a tort if a minority applicant was denied an opportunity to be interviewed for a position and, as a result, lost a job opportunity.

In a civil lawsuit resulting in a judgment favoring the plaintiff, the defendant may be assessed actual damages and even punitive damages if the injury was deliberately perpetrated. Each and every human resources administrator, therefore, should be protected by an errors and omissions liability insurance program.

People in the United States have become increasingly aware of the vulnerability of those who occupy leadership positions. The central issue is that all people must make decisions on a daily basis when the lines of appropriate behavior are somewhat blurred. Human resources administrators are particularly vulnerable because their decisions affect people in that most important area of life—employment.

The basis for making ethically sound decisions is usually grounded in religious beliefs or philosophical assumptions. There are three principles that have been gleaned from these beliefs and assumptions. First, the exercise of responsibilities in making judgments for decisions, over time, will help an individual to determine the sort of person and human resources professional he or she wants to become. Second, the decisions of school human resources administrators have a definite effect upon school districts as institutions. The third principle comes from the Declaration of Independence, which sets forth that all people are created equal and have certain unalienable rights among which are life, liberty, and the pursuit of happiness.

The ethical responsibilities of school human resources administrators are grouped around the following: responsibilities to the school district and its staff; responsibilities to the school human resources profession; and personal responsibilities.

Effective policies are the key to effective human resources management. Boards of education should take a deliberate approach to policy development that will ensure defensible human resources operations.

Discussion Questions and Statements

- Explain the elements that must be considered in creating an individual employment contract for teachers.
- In what ways are human resources administrators vulnerable to lawsuits, and what are the guidelines that will help protect them?
- Identify the common stages in the development of a lawsuit.
- What are the ethical responsibilities of human resources administrators?
- How does the reasonable person concept influence the practice of human resources administration?

Suggested Activities

- You are the Director of Risk Management in a large metropolitan school district serving approximately 30,000 students. You and your staff have conducted the yearly safety and security audit and have found a number of safety hazards and security needs in several of the district's schools. The Assistant Superintendent for Human Resources has informed you that the facilities budget has been reduced by ten percent due to a shortfall in state aid, which will keep many of your safety and security recommendations from being implemented. Given this situation, set forth in writing your ethical and legal responsibilities and what you would do.
- Write a policy dealing with an issue in human resources administration that can serve as a model for policy construction.
- Attend a state court proceeding concerning a school personnel issue and write a reflection paper about your observations.
- Interview an attorney, in person or on the telephone, who specializes in school law and discuss with him or her the role and function of a school district's legal counsel.
- Interview a human resources administrator, in person or on the telephone, about the process he or she uses when the school district is sued over a personnel issue.

Selected Bibliography

Beck, L., "Why Ethics? Thoughts on the Moral Challenge Facing Educational Leaders," *The School Administrator,* 54, no. 9 (October 1996), 8–11.

Beck, Lynn G., and Joseph Murphy, *Ethics in Educational Leadership Programs: An Expanding Role.* Thousand Oaks, CA: Corwin Press, 1994.

Boothe, James W., Leo H. Bradley, T. Michael Flick, Katherine E. Keough, and Susanne P. Kirk, "Questions of Ethics," *The Executive Educator,* 14, no. 2 (February 1992), 17–24.

Data Research, Inc., *U.S. Supreme Court Education Cases,* 4th ed. Rosemount, MN: Data Research, 1996, 135–191.

Essex, Nathan L., *School Law and the Public Schools: A Practical Guide for Educational Leaders,* 3rd ed. Boston: Allyn & Bacon, 2005.

Fullan, Michael, *The Moral Imperative of School Leadership.* Thousand Oaks, CA: Corwin Press, 2003.

Kalish, Judith, and David Perry, "Setting Ethical Standards," *The Executive Educator,* 14, no. 2 (February 1992), 24–27.

Lamorte, Michael, *School Law: Cases and Concepts.* Englewood Cliffs, NJ: Prentice-Hall, 1981.

Looney, Susan D., *Education and the Legal System: A Guide to Understanding the Law.* Upper Saddle River, NJ: Merrill/Prentice Hall, 2004.

Mayo, Moran, *Rethinking the Reasonable Person: An Egalitarian Reconstruction of the Objective Standard.* New York: Oxford University Press, 2003.

Menacker, Julius, *School Law: Theoretical and Case Perspectives.* Englewood Cliffs, NJ: Prentice-Hall, 1987.

Rebore, Ronald W., *The Ethics of Educational Leadership.* Upper Saddle River, NJ: Prentice Hall, 2001.

Rebore, Ronald W., *A Human Relations Approach to the Practice of Educational Leadership.* Boston: Allyn & Bacon, 2003.

Russo, Charles J., "Letters of Recommendation: A Legal Update," *School Business Affairs,* 68, no. 7 (July/August 2002), 30–33.

Starratt, Robert J., *Ethical Leadership.* San Francisco: Jossey-Bass, 2004.

Uerling, Donald F., "Constitutional Due Process and Educational Administration," *Spectrum: Journal of School Research and Information,* 3, no. 3 (Summer 1985), 41–46.

Zirkel, Perry A., and Sharon Nalbone Richardson, *A Digest of Supreme Court Decisions Affecting Education,* 2nd ed. Bloomington, IN: Phi Delta Kappa Educational Foundation, 1988, 53–85.

Appendix A
An Index of Appropriate Policies
with Sample Human Resources Policies

The policies contained herein are meant to exemplify various policy formats employed by a number of school districts. They have been modeled after actual policies currently in effect in different parts of the United States. The source from which the original policies have been drawn is the Educational Policies Service of the National School Boards Association (EPS/NSBA).

The main purpose of this service is to assist school boards with their responsibility to establish and maintain updated written policies. Further, EPS/NSBA assists school boards in developing those kinds of policies that improve the education process and establish productive relationships between the school board, staff, students, and the public.

Along with an index of policies that outlines the scope of common and professional policies necessary for most school districts, two statements are included concerning human resources policy goals and objectives. Specific policies covering the following dimensions of the human resources function also are included:

- Staff Recruiting and Hiring
- Professional Staff Probation and Tenure

- Professional Staff Hiring
- Evaluation of Professional Staff
- Professional Staff Development Opportunities
- Professional Staff Probation and Tenure (administrators)
- Professional Staff Termination of Employment (administrators)
- Staff Complaints and Grievances
- Professional/Support Staff Employee Assistance Fringe Benefits Program
- Professional Staff Contracts and Compensation Plans
- Personnel Records

The variety in content and style of these policies should provide some insight into the nuance of policy development.

Index of Policies

- Human Resources Policies Goals
    - Human Resources Policies Priority Objectives
- Equal Opportunity Employment
- Staff Involvement in Decision Making
- Staff Ethics
    - Staff Conflicts of Interest
    - Staff Conduct
- Board–Staff Communications
- Staff Health and Safety
- Staff Participation in Community Activities
- Staff Participation in Political Activities
- Staff–Student Relations
- Staff Gifts and Solicitations
- Smoking on School Premises by Staff Members
- Personnel Records
- Staff Complaints and Grievances

Professional Staff
- Professional Staff Positions
- Professional Staff Contracts and Compensation Plans
    - Professional Staff Salary Schedules
        - Professional Staff Merit System
    - Professional Staff Supplementary Pay Plans
    - Professional Staff Fringe Benefits
    - Professional Staff Leaves and Absences
    - Professional Staff Vacations and Holidays
- Professional Staff Recruiting
    - Posting of Professional Staff Vacancies
- Professional Staff Hiring
- Part-Time and Substitute Professional Staff Employment
    - Arrangements for Professional Staff Substitutes
- Professional Staff Orientation

- Professional Staff Probation and Tenure
- Professional Staff Seniority
- Professional Staff Assignments and Transfers
- Professional Staff Time Schedules
- Professional Staff Work Load
    Professional Staff Extra Duty
    Professional Staff Meetings
- Professional Staff Development Opportunities
- Professional Staff Visitations and Conferences
- Supervision of Professional Staff
- Evaluation of Professional Staff
- Professional Staff Promotions
- Professional Staff Termination of Employment
    Reduction in Professional Staff Work Force
    Resignation of Professional Staff Members
    Retirement of Professional Staff Members
    Suspension and Dismissal of Professional Staff Members
- Miscellaneous Professional Staff Policies
    Nonschool Employment by Professional Staff Members
        Professional Staff Consulting Activities
        Tutoring for Pay
    Professional Research and Publishing
    Exchange Teaching
    Professional Organizations

Human Resources Policy Goals

The personnel employed by the district constitute the most important resource for effectively conducting a quality learning program. Important contributions to a successful education program are made by all staff members. The district's program will function best when it employs highly qualified personnel, conducts appropriate staff development activities, and establishes policies and working conditions that are conducive to high morale and that enable each staff member to make the fullest contribution to district programs and services.

The goals of the district's human resources program shall include the following:

1. To develop and implement those strategies and procedures for personnel recruitment, screening, and selection that will result in employing the best available candidates; that is, those with highest capabilities, strongest commitment to quality education, and greatest probability of effectively implementing the district's learning program

2. To develop general deployment strategy for greatest contribution to the learning program, and to utilize it as the primary basis for determining staff assignments

3. To develop a climate in which optimum staff performance, morale, and satisfaction are produced

4. To provide positive programs of staff development designed to contribute both to improvement of the learning program and to each staff member's career development aspirations

5. To provide for a genuine team approach to education, including staff involvement in planning, decision making, and evaluation

6. To provide attractive compensation and benefits as well as other provisions for staff welfare

7. To develop and utilize for personnel evaluation positive processes that contribute to the improvement of both staff capabilities and the learning program

Human Resources Policies Priority Objectives

In support of its stated human resources policies goals, the board endorses the following set of priority objectives:

1. By *(month/year)*, all staff assignments will be reviewed to ensure the most effective utilization possible of staff time and capabilities. To the maximum degree possible, each staff member is to be assigned duties that employ his or her talents to the utmost.

2. By *(month/year)*, job descriptions for all staff positions will be reviewed and updated by all employees and their supervisors. All job descriptions are to integrate program requirements with related positions; itemize specific and realistic job performance responsibilities; and provide for measures of assessing job performance. This objective will be considered successfully achieved when there is a consensus by the employee and his or her immediate supervisor.

3. By *(month/year)*, the superintendent will develop a comprehensive Staff Talent Bank, which will provide access to many special skills, talents, and capabilities that district personnel have at their command and which the district may draw on from time to time to meet specialized needs. This objective will be considered accomplished when the central office can provide immediate answers to questions such as the following: Which staff members can speak the Navajo language, Spanish, Cantonese? Which are published authors? Which have degrees in law? Which know how to climb a mountain, build a house, ride a horse, quilt a rug, or drive a tractor trailer?

4. By *(month/year)*, procedures and methods for recruiting, screening, selecting, and assigning personnel shall be revised to (1) integrate with program needs, and (2) provide humanistic procedures that meet needs and concerns of applicants and employees as adequately as feasible. Measures of success shall be prepared under the district superintendent's supervision and shall include increased success in program operation, subjective judgments of program managers and others, and perceptions of applicants and employees.

Staff Recruiting/Hiring

Through its human resources policies, the board of education shall maintain an effective recruitment program designed to attract, secure, and hold the highest qualified personnel for all professional, nonprofessional, and paraprofessional positions. The recruitment program shall be based on an alertness to candidates who will devote themselves to the education and welfare of the children of this school system.

It is the responsibility of the superintendent and of persons delegated by him or her to determine the human resources needs of the school district and to locate suitable candidates to recommend for employment to the board. Through effective administration procedures, the superintendent shall recommend to the board the retention of personnel who are motivated to do their best work and to be creative.

No inquiry in regard to religion, creed, race, color, or national origin shall be made of a person proposed for or seeking employment.

It shall be the duty of the superintendent to see that persons nominated for employment shall meet all qualifications established by state statute, the rules and regulations of the state board of education, the commissioner of education, the county superintendent, and policies of the board of education for the type of position for which nomination is made.

Priority shall be given to the best qualified *local* applicant when two or more applicants seem equally qualified for a position.

An employee shall be appointed by the board only on the recommendation of the superintendent. Should a person nominated by the superintendent be rejected by the board, it shall be the duty of the superintendent to make another nomination.

An estimate of the cost of the recruitment and selection program will be made annually by the superintendent and presented to the board for inclusion in the annual budget.

Professional Staff Probation and Tenure

In accordance with state law, all certificated personnel will be granted tenure on reemployment after three consecutive years of successful service under contract with the district. The board will expect thorough and competent evaluations of all personnel before they become candidates for tenure. This requires critical evaluation at four stages:

1. At the time of selection
2. During the first year, when emphasis on self-evaluation will help the teacher decide whether he or she commands the necessary skills to contribute to the profession
3. During the second year, when emphasis is on whether the first year's success can be sustained and developed
4. During the third year, when it must be determined whether the teacher will be a permanent asset to the staff

If evaluations are regular and thorough, and discussed carefully with teachers, candidates for tenure will be aware of their status. The board wishes no teacher to be taken by surprise if he or she is not reappointed, and will direct that due notice of nonrenewal of contracts be served in accordance with state law.

The contract of employment of a probationary or continuing teacher for a school year will be deemed automatically renewed for the ensuing school year unless, on or before April 15, the board, a member thereof acting on behalf of the board, or the superintendent of the school district gives notice to the teacher of the termination of his or her contract.

The probationary or continuing teacher will indicate acceptance of the contract for the ensuing year by signing and returning the contract or by an acceptance in writing that is delivered to the school board within 30 days after receipt of the contract.

Notice of termination of a contract will be delivered personally to the teacher or sent by registered or certified mail bearing a postmark of on or before April 15, directed to the teacher at his or her place of residence as recorded in the school district records. The notice will include a statement of the reasons for not reemploying the teacher.

All continuing teachers will be issued a contract annually.

The superintendent will present to the board of education, on or before April 1 of each year, lists of appointments, reappointments, and non-reappointments for the following school year. These lists will indicate the following information for each employee:

1. Location of employment
2. Name and position
3. Sex
4. Race

Professional Staff Hiring

The board of education has the legal responsibility of approving the employment of all employees. Although this responsibility cannot be waived, the board assigns to the superintendent the process of recruiting staff members. In carrying out this responsibility, the superintendent will involve various administrative and teaching staff members as needed. All personnel selected for employment must be recommended by the superintendent and approved by the board. To aid in obtaining the best available staff members for our schools, the board adopts the following general criteria to be utilized in the selection process for initial employment.

1. There will be no discrimination in the hiring process due to age, sex, creed, race, color, or national origin.
2. Candidates for high school and middle school positions should have a major or its equivalent—30 semester hours—in the teaching field. Elementary candidates should have a major or its equivalent—30 hours—in elementary education or in the special area to which they will be assigned.
3. Candidates for all teaching positions should have an overall grade-point average of 2.5 (A–4, B–3, C–2, D–1). High school and middle school candidates should have a grade-point average of 2.75 in their teaching field.
4. The highest quality of instruction is enhanced by a staff with a wide variation in educational preparation, background, and previous experience. Concerted efforts will be exerted to maintain this variation in the staff.
5. Candidates for teaching positions should provide evidence of meeting the state requirements for regular certification status. In cases of absolute necessity, holders of provisional or temporary certificates may be employed in regular full-time capacity not to exceed one year.

In addition to the previous general criteria, the superintendent will submit to the board for approval specific criteria dealing with each vacancy. These specific criteria will describe those competencies needed for success in the position.

In the event that the specific or general criteria are not being met by a particular candidate being recommended, it shall be the responsibility of the superintendent to point out the deficiencies to the board so that it may act accordingly. Should the board not approve the employment of a candidate being recommended by the superintendent, it shall be the duty of the superintendent to make another recommendation.

The employment of each staff member is not official until the contract is approved by the board and signed by the candidate. The employment sequence shall be as follows:

1. The verbal offer of employment to the candidate
2. Verbal acceptance by the candidate
3. Approval of candidate by board
4. Contract sent to the candidate
5. Candidate's acceptance as signified by a signed contract returned to superintendent within 15 days

Evaluation of Professional Staff

The primary purpose of teacher appraisal will be the development of staff and the improvement of teaching. This appraisal will be an ongoing program, important for beginning teachers, but equally as important for teachers with experience. As teachers appraise their present performance and set goals for future performance, they gain in stature and add stature to their profession.

Appraisal procedures will be designed to help teachers define their areas of greatest strength as well as the areas in which improvement is needed. Plans will be made to capitalize on those strengths. Procedures will be set up to help them improve in areas where help is needed. At later conferences, progress will be noted and plans for further improvement made. The appraisals will not be used for merit rating or merit pay. Staff improvement is the goal.

The regulations, procedures, and instruments for the evaluation of teachers will be developed cooperatively by administrators and the teaching staff.

Professional Staff Development Opportunities

Today's dynamic and rapidly changing society, with its tremendous accumulation of new knowledge and the attending obsolescence in some areas of practice, makes it imperative that all staff members be engaged in a continuous program of professional and technical growth in order that they may be qualified to provide a quality educational program for all students being served by this school system.

It is the policy of the school board that a program of staff development be established to provide an opportunity for the continuous professional and technical growth of teachers of this school district.

As a result of the operation of this policy, staff members will become knowledgeable regarding new developments and changes in their specialized fields and will utilize new and improved methods in practice.

The administrative staff will provide leadership in establishing a staff development program, which will assist each staff member to make a maximum contribution to the school district's effort to provide a quality educational program.

Professional Staff Probation and Tenure Administrators

School-level administrators shall be on two years' probation on entry into this school district. On promotion to a new position, an administrator's probation shall not exceed one year.

A year's probation shall be determined on the basis of a full twelve-month period commencing from the effective date of appointment. The probationary year may be interrupted by any leave approved by the board of education. Approved leaves with full pay will not alter the probationary period. Long-term leaves of absence shall result in the probationary period being altered by the exact number of calendar days absent.

On satisfactory completion of his or her probationary period, an administrator shall have tenure in all positions in the same class and salary range or lower classes and salary ranges. Administrators with tenure shall not be suspended, demoted, discharged, or terminated without due process. However, the foregoing is not intended to interfere with the right of the board to relieve employees from duty for legitimate reasons.

Administrator Termination Procedures

This policy sets forth procedures to be used by the board to nonrenew or immediately terminate the contract of a certified administrator. These procedures are designed to protect the rights of both the employee and the board and to ensure that a spirit of fairness prevails.

Procedures for Nonrenewal of Contract Are as Follows:

A. When it becomes evident to a unit superintendent that an administrative employee is not doing an acceptable job, the unit superintendent will arrange a conference to discuss the problem and try to find a solution to it.

B. Within three days of the conference the unit superintendent will make a report in duplicate outlining the problems as seen by the unit superintendent and by the administrator, and the recommendations for resolving the problem. A copy of this report will be sent to the superintendent of schools.

C. Approximately two weeks after the first conference, a second conference will be held and a report made as outlined in (B) above.

D. At least two weeks and not more than four weeks after the second conference, a third conference will be arranged and a report made as outlined in (B) above.

E. If a solution to the problem is found after one or more meetings, the unit superintendent will notify the administrator in writing that his or her work is now satisfactory and further conferences are not necessary.

F. After the third conference, if the problem has been resolved, the unit superintendent will notify the administrator in writing that his or her work is now satisfactory and further conferences are not necessary. If the problem still exists, the unit superintendent may schedule another conference or may recommend to the superintendent of schools that the administrator's contract not be renewed. (This procedure is to ensure that there will be at least three formal conferences before a recommendation is made not to renew a contract. There may be any number of conferences before a problem is solved or a recommendation is made.)

G. In the event the superintendent of schools decides to recommend to the board that an administrator's contract not be renewed, he or she will give written notice to the administrator of his or her pending action.

H. After an administrator receives written notification of the superintendent's intention to recommend that his or her contract not be renewed, he or she will have ten (10) days to file a written request with the president of the board, with a copy to the superintendent of schools, for a hearing before the board. The hearing before the board will be conducted in accordance with provisions outlined in state statutes.

I. Within ten (10) days of the hearing, the school board will render a final decision and the administrator will be notified in accordance with state statutes.

Procedures for Immediate Termination of Contract Are as Follows:

A. Any person serving under annual contract may be placed on probation or suspended for cause with pay by the superintendent of schools, who will report such action to the board at its next meeting for final action. Cause includes, but is not limited to, the following: immorality, conduct unbecoming a professional teacher, insubordination, failure to follow reasonable written regulations and policies, physical or mental disability impairing the performance of duties or any conditions that may require immediate action to protect the safety or welfare of the children.

B. While the board may terminate the employee's contract at any time for cause, such action will not take place prior to the employee's receipt of a notice of the specific charges and an opportunity for a hearing before the board of education in accordance with state law.

Staff Complaints and Grievances

All employees of the board of education shall have the right to appeal the application of policies and administrative decisions affecting them. Each employee shall be assured freedom from restraint, interference, coercion, discrimination or reprisal in presenting his or her appeal with respect to a personal grievance.

All grievances shall be handled expeditiously.

Those grievances that involve a complaint of an employee who has sustained a personal loss, injury, or inconvenience because of a violation, misinterpretation, or misapplication of a contract with a collective bargaining unit of which the employee is a member shall be presented and heard according to the procedures established in the particular contract.

All other grievances shall be handled according to the following procedures, which also outline the general pattern for grievance processing established by the negotiated contracts.

Steps in Grievance Procedure

1. *First level.* Any complainant who has a grievance shall discuss it first with his or her principal/other supervisor.

2. *Second level.* If as a result of the informal discussion, the matter is not resolved, the grievant shall initiate a grievance in writing to his or her principal/other immediate supervisor within five (5) school days, giving the full details of his or her grievance. The principal/other immediate supervisor shall communicate his or her decision to the grievant in writing within three (3) school days of the receipt of the written grievance.

3. *Third level.* If the grievance remains unresolved, the grievant no later than five (5) school days after receipt of the above decision may appeal it to the appropriate department head (superintendent, school business administrator, board secretary). The appeal must be made in writing and must give details as to why the decision was unsatisfactory. The department head shall give his or her decision in writing to the grievant within ten (10) school days.

4. *Fourth level.* If the grievance is not resolved, the grievant may, no later than five (5) school days after receipt of the department head's decision, request a review by the board of education. The request shall be made in writing through the department head, who shall attach all papers relating to the grievance. The board, or a committee thereof, shall review the grievance and shall, at the option of the board, hold a hearing with the grievant and render a decision in writing within forty-five (45) days of receipt of the appeal. If the board decides not to hold a hearing, the grievant shall be notified of this decision no later than thirty (30) days after receipt of the appeal.

Representation

An employee shall have the right to present his or her own grievance or may designate a representative of his or her recognition unit to appear with him or her at any level of the above procedure.

The employee who chooses to have representation shall provide advance notice of such in writing to the superior at the respective procedural level at least two (2) days prior to the hearing on the grievance.

Professional/Supportive Staff Employee Assistance Program Fringe Benefit

The school board, the State Teacher Education Associations, and the State Association of Supporting Services Employees recognize that a wide range of problems not directly related to a job may have an effect on an employee's job performance. The problems may be behavioral or medical in nature and involve physical, mental, or emotional illness, alcohol abuse or alcoholism, and drug abuse or chemical dependency; or may involve marital, family, financial, or legal concerns. Alcoholism and other chemical dependencies are recognized as being progressive illnesses and potentially fatal.

In most instances, employees will overcome such personal problems independently, and the effect on job performance will be negligible. However, employees who have a problem they feel may affect their work performance are encouraged to seek voluntarily information and referral by contacting the director or advisors of the employee assistance program.

All requests for help will be considered confidential.

The purpose of this policy is to assure employees that if personal problems are or may be the cause of current and/or future unsatisfactory job performance, they will receive an offer of assistance to help resolve such problems in an effective and confidential manner. Specifically,

1. It is agreed that almost any problem can be successfully treated provided it is recognized in its early stages and the assistance of an appropriate medical, psychiatric, counseling, and/or self-help service is sought.

2. This aid will be made available to employees through the employee assistance program.

3. Employees are assured that their job, tenure, future, and reputation will not be jeopardized by using this employee service.

4. It is the responsibility of an employee who is chemically dependent or who abuses drugs or alcohol to seek early intervention, assistance, and treatment.

5. Treatment for alcoholism and other chemical dependencies is covered by the present sick leave policy. Extended leave for treatment can be arranged under accumulated sick leave, annual leave, sick leave banks, or leave without pay on the same basis as for other physical or mental health problems.

6. Efforts will be made to ensure that the disease of alcoholism and/or chemical dependency will receive the same employee benefits and insurance coverages provided for other illnesses under established employee benefit plans.

7. All records pertaining to clients in this program will be maintained with the strictest of confidentiality in accordance with the highest medical and ethical standards and state and federal laws. All records will be segregated from an individual's personnel records.

8. Since employee work performance can be affected by the problems of an employee's spouse and other dependents, the program is available to the families of employees as well.

9. School district retirees may also use the services of the employee assistance program.

Professional Staff Contracts and Compensation Plans

It shall be the general policy of this district to pay salaries commensurate with the duties and responsibilities involved and with regard to prevailing practices in other comparable jurisdictions.

It shall be the policy of the board to establish all salaries and benefits for employees insofar as possible by June 1 and no later than June 30 of each year.

It is the intent of the board of trustees to take into consideration the Area Consumer Price Index in its deliberation of employee salaries.

A. Placement on Schedule

Placement within classification shall be made as accurately as possible. At the time of employment each certificated employee shall submit to the personnel department a complete transcript of college units and verification of all previous experience. Contracts shall not be effective until complete transcripts have been received and approved. It is the responsibility of the employee to provide the personnel department with transcripts. Credit for previous experience will be granted as follows:

1. *Regular teaching.* Previous verified experience as a full-time regularly credentialed teacher in the public schools shall be recognized for the purpose of placement on the salary schedule on a year-to-year basis. A year for the purposes of this section is defined as 75 percent of the school calendar year.

2. *Military service.* One year of credit on the salary schedule for each two (2) years of honorable military service shall be granted for a maximum of two (2) years on the salary schedule.

3. *Other experience.* Participation in Peace Corps, Vista, National Teacher Corps and noncombatant service under the direction of the Selective Service System shall be awarded experience credit in the same manner as military experience.

Experience credit may be rewarded for directly related experience (e.g., business for business education; recreation for P.E.; public library for librarians; teaching, counseling, or nursing in private accredited schools, colleges or universities) as determined by the superintendent or his or her designated representative.

The employee at all times is responsible for providing verifications and certification as required in this section. This section shall apply only to personnel entering the district following date of adoption.

B. Intern Teachers

In recognition of the district's commitment to the progress of education and the professional development of educators, the board of trustees authorizes the administration to employ intern teachers when such employment shall benefit the educator in training and the school district.

The purpose of the intern teaching program is to provide a program for specially selected young people to become fully credentialed teachers. Close supervision of the interns is provided throughout the year by the vice principal for curriculum, department chairperson, and the supervising instructor from the college or university.

All teacher interns shall be placed on step 1 of column 1 and will be eligible for all benefits in direct proportion to their contracts.

Intern teachers whose contracts are for less than a full-time assignment shall receive a prorated salary equal to the contractual percentage of their assignments.

C. Salary Adjustments for Part-Time Teachers

Salary for less than a full year of service shall be paid to certificated personnel in accordance with state statute, which limits payment of the salary to the ratio of days worked to the total number of working days required of that position for the school year by the board of trustees.

Teachers employed part time shall receive remuneration equal to the contractual percentage of their assignments.

A certificated employee absent for reasons other than illness, accident, personal necessity, or bereavement shall be paid his regular salary less the amount actually paid the substitute, except as otherwise stipulated herein.

Full salary shall be deducted for all periods of unauthorized absences. Salary adjustments for authorized absences shall follow the leave of absence policy.

D. Increments

In general the board of trustees has followed a policy of providing increments for employees on a yearly basis, based on the current published salary schedule. However, the board reserves the right to approve a salary schedule prior to July 1 of each school year. This approval may include the granting of increments and the stipulation of any and all salary benefits accruing to employees by virtue of the previous salary schedule. The board further reserves the right to delay the operation of a salary schedule in the event of any emergency.

In general, each certificated employee shall receive the annual salary increase provided that

1. He or she holds a regular teaching credential.
2. He or she has not yet reached the highest step in his or her classification.
3. He or she has fulfilled the staff development education requirements as stipulated in the professional development policy.

E. Minimum Salaries

The minimum salary provision of the salary schedule shall not be less than the minimum salary requirements of the state for certificated employees of the public schools as established by the current law.

F. Horizontal Movement on Salary Schedule

A staff member shall provide written notice to the personnel department of the district of the intention to qualify for horizontal movement on the salary schedule prior to March

1 of the school year preceding the year for which advancement is desired. Staff members shall advance no more than one column a year. The official transcripts from the colleges or universities showing credits earned must reach the personnel department by October 1 of the school year for which horizontal advancement has been requested. An employee who qualifies for horizontal advancement on the salary schedule shall be advanced one column and shall then be advanced one increment step if he or she has not already reached the maximum step in the new column. (An employee shall advance only one step per school year.)

With these exceptions, only credits earned for upper division or graduate study in accredited universities and colleges shall be counted for advancement on the salary schedule. Such credits shall be earned in the major or minor areas on the teachers' or counselors' credential or as part of a graduate degree program.

1. Undergraduate credits shall be counted toward advancement on the salary schedule only when prior written approval has been obtained from the personnel department.

2. Credit earned under the professional development policy shall be counted toward advancement on the salary schedule at the rate of one unit for every fifteen hours of class attendance in staff development educational programs conducted by the district. Study in accredited colleges and universities undertaken for the purpose of fulfilling the requirements of the professional development policy shall be granted credit according to that awarded by the educational institution. The maximum number of credits earned under district sponsored staff development programs that may be applied to the salary schedule advancement shall be fifteen units.

3. The credit awarded by the professional growth committee also may be used to qualify for horizontal movement on the salary schedule.

G. Professional Development Required
for Vertical Movement on Salary Scale

The professional growth of certificated personnel in the district shall include the acquisition or improvement of skills in the areas of high priority as identified by the board of trustees in its goal-setting process. In order to ensure continual professional growth, all certificated staff members are required to complete a minimum of four (4) semester units or the equivalent (one semester unit equals 15 hours) in professional development every three years for this service (professional growth period) to qualify for vertical movement on the salary schedule. Fulfillment of the requirement may be met by any of the options listed below. Professional development activities described in options 3, 4, and 5 require approval of the district's professional growth committee.

1. Successful completion of any course, workshop, or similar activity offered by an accredited college or university.

2. Participation in staff development education programs offered by this or other districts.

3. Participation in seminars or workshops sponsored by educationally oriented agencies.

4. Successful completion of an individual professional development program approved in advance.

5. Active participation in professional organizations, conferences, and other educational groups related to the individual's teaching area.

The initial professional growth period shall begin on September 1 of the first year of employment for new employees and on September 1, 1990, for current employees of the district.

Personnel Records

The school administration shall maintain a personnel file in the office of the superintendent for each teacher it employs. The personnel file shall include the following sections:

1. *Evaluation section.* The evaluation section shall include all complaints against and commendations of the teacher, written suggestions for corrections and improvements, and evaluation reports made by the administration.

2. *Supplementary section.* The supplementary section shall include teacher certificates, health certificates, academic records, preemployment references, and application forms.

Additions to the Evaluation Section

No complaint, commendation, suggestion, or evaluation may be placed in the evaluation files unless it meets the following requirements:

1. The comment is signed by the person making the complaint, commendation, suggestion or evaluation.

2. The superintendent or teacher's principal has notified the teacher by letter or in person that the comment is available in the superintendent's office for inspection prior to its placement in the teacher's evaluation section.

The teacher may offer a denial or explanation of the complaint, commendation, suggestion, or evaluation, and any such denial or explanation shall become a part of the teacher's evaluation section.

General Access to the Teacher's Personnel File

Access to a teacher's personnel file may be given to the following persons without the consent of the teacher:

1. The superintendent, the teacher's principal, the teacher's supervisor, and a school board member if it relates to his or her duties or responsibilities as a board member.

2. Members of the review panel if the teacher requests a review by the Professional Review Committee.

No other person may have access to a teacher's personnel file except under the following circumstances:

1. When the teacher gives written consent to the release of his or her records. The written consent must specify the records to be released and to whom they are to be released. Each consent to release must be handled separately; blanket permission for release of information shall not be accepted.

2. When subpoenaed under court order.

Teacher's Access to His or Her Personnel File

A teacher may have access to his or her own personnel file at all reasonable times; that is, during regular office hours. The right to access includes the right to make written objections to any information contained in the file. Each written objection must be signed by the teacher and it shall become part of the personnel file.

Records Management

The superintendent shall be the records manager for teacher personnel files and shall have the overall responsibility for maintaining and preserving the confidentiality of teacher personnel files. The superintendent, however, may designate another official to perform the duties of the records manager. The records manager is responsible for granting or denying access to records on the basis of these regulations.

Human Resources Administration Policy on Evidence-Based Decision Making

The administrators and staff of the Human Resources Department recognize that the effective administration of human resources functions depends on the full and proper utilization of both quantitative and qualitative data in formulating human resources procedures and in making decisions about human resources.

In order to facilitate this responsibility, the board of education mandates the ongoing collection and analysis of both qualitative and quantitative data by human resources administrators in the following areas: human resources planning, recruitment of personnel, selection of personnel, placement and induction of personnel, staff development, evaluation of personnel, compensation of personnel, and collective negotiations.

The assistant superintendent for human resources, under the direction of the superintendent of schools, is directly responsible for the collection and analysis of data. Of course, he or she must involve all members of the human resources department including the director of employee relations, director of staff development, director of affirmative action, director of employee benefits, and director of risk management in fulfilling this responsibility.

The assistant superintendent for human resources is expected to develop a schedule for the collection and analysis of data by July 1 of each year. The annual human resources report will be presented to the superintendent of schools and the board of education by April 1 of each year in order for the superintendent and board to be able to utilize the report in developing the annual budget.

The report will not only set forth data along with an analysis but also will clearly identify the methodology that was used to collect data. Further, the report will set forth what statistical and qualitative treatments were used in the analysis process.

Appendix B
Table of Contents for a Classified Employee Personnel Manual

GOODVILLE SCHOOL DISTRICT

Classified Employee Personnel Manual

This manual constitutes the human resources policies and regulations for classified employees of the Goodville School District. Accountability for the implementation and maintenance of this manual is dedicated to the Assistant Superintendent for Human Resources. The policies contained in this manual may be deleted or amended, and additional policies may be included by action of the Board of Education.

Regulations contained herein may, in like manner, be deleted or amended, and new regulations may be included by administrative memorandum.

Each employee will receive a copy of this manual and every employee is expected to become familiar with its contents.

TABLE OF CONTENTS

Continued

Epilogue

This book has covered a lot of material in relatively few pages, describing the various dimensions of the human resources function. The reader who has just finished this book must keep in mind that politics and the human condition in general will affect the processes, procedures, and techniques used in human resources administration. For example, a human resources administrator may recommend the employment of a teacher who is turned down by the board while another with fewer qualifications is hired. The human resources administrator may never know the reason why this occurred. There are always hidden agendas!

There is no issue more important in our contemporary times than *ethical behavior.* This is true not only for teachers and educational administrators but also for governmental officials, business people, and the clergy. The media continually focus on illegal and unethical conduct. Although professional educational administrators have always recognized the necessity of being above-board, the climate in contemporary society is such that administrators must be able to demonstrate that their actions are based on a system of ethics. It is for this reason that I developed the section in Chapter 10 dealing with ethics in school human resources management along with a corresponding set of *responsibilities.* It is vital that every administrator learn to carry out his or her professional responsibilities in such a manner that his or her integrity cannot be questioned. Short-term solutions and arbitrary decisions, therefore, must be judiciously avoided.

Technological advances present educational administrators with unique opportunities and significant challenges. Administrators must become competent in the use of technology, or the administration of our schools will slip even further behind the private sector. Administrators must learn how to utilize computers not only to perform administrative tasks such as pupil scheduling, attendance reporting, grade reporting, inventory reporting, and fiscal accounting, but also in the management of the various dimensions of the human resources function. Some larger school districts have already installed very sophisticated information-management systems, which make for more efficient and accurate human resources management. Computer technology advances so rapidly that it is impossible to recommend hardware and software in this book.

In order to balance involvement in the new technologies, human resources administrators must also become more humanistic. Technology tends to isolate individuals from one another and emphasizes solitary activities. What happens, in essence, is that information collection, storage, and use increase while human interaction decreases. In the final analysis, we will know more but understand less, with an accompanying decrease in human relations skills.

The human resources administrator, therefore, must see the necessity of developing innovative ways to interact with teachers and staff members. Utilizing a collaborative approach to human resources management as set forth in this book will provide such an opportunity.

Thus, human resources administrators of the future must be scrupulously ethical. At the same time, they must understand and make use of technological advances, as well as appreciate the necessity of creating ways to improve human interaction.

Glossary

This glossary is divided by chapters in order to provide easy reference to selected terms, phrases, and acronyms that will help readers understand the terms used in each chapter as well as other terms and acronyms that are not used in the chapters but which contribute to a grasp of its concepts and ideas.

Chapter 1: Organizational Dimensions

Assistant superintendent for human resources The chief human resources administrator in a school district who is charged with developing the strategies and implementing the policies, processes, and procedures necessary to the effective management of the human resources function. Alternative titles are director of personnel or director of human resources.

Asynchronous Refers to the experience of using technology independent of *real-time* constraints. Thus, a person can log on to a school district's website and process a medical claim after normal working hours.

Automatic patch management software Computer security software patches for programs and systems. The most promising patches detect unidentified viruses by recognizing virus-like patterns.

Board of education Elected or appointed policy-making body of a school district.

Client/server When personal computers are networked with a larger school district computer, the PCs are referred to as the clients and the mainframe as the server.

Datamart Technological term that refers to a specialized depository of data created from a school district-wide data warehouse and used only by specific departments such as the human resources and the business departments.

Data mining Refers to an array of analytical applications used to identify patterns in a database.

Data warehouse School district–wide database designed to support the activities of an entire district. It is usually batch-updated and provides rapid online information and summaries.

Decision support system   An interactive computer-based system that allows a user to solve problems through databased modeling.

Employee relations   Strategies, policies, processes, and procedures used in collective negotiations that implement the preparatory phase for negotiations, at-the-table bargaining, managing the master agreement, and grievance management.

Encryption   Data-security method that allows only the user to view or receive the information.

Ethernet   Technology that is used to connect computers, printers, and other devices in the same location.

Human resources administration   Management of the processes, procedures, and techniques necessary to implementing the following dimensions of the human resources function in a school district: planning, recruitment, selection, placement and induction, staff development, performance evaluation, compensation, and collective negotiations.

Human resources information systems   Refers to the technology utilized in carrying out the functions, systems processes, and procedures of a human resources department.

Information technology   Describes the technology that produces, manipulates, warehouses, and disseminates information.

Interactive voice response   A telephone system using text-to-speech technology whereby a user can receive current status information and transact business through prompts indicating a series of options.

Internet   The worldwide network of connected computers.

Intranet   The application of Internet technology to a school district's internal computer networks.

Kiosk   A standalone data center that allows users to transact business through data entry commands.

Management approach   Approach to human resources administration that centers on developing strategies and carrying out processes, procedures, and techniques.

Metadata   A summary and directory of the kinds of data that are stored in a warehouse.

National Council of Chief State School Officials   The professional organization that supports the role and function of state commissions and superintendents of education.

No Child Left Behind Act (NCLB)   Federal legislation signed into law by President George Bush in 2002. The law requires all children to be proficient in reading and mathematics by 2014. Other provisions mandate improved communications with parents and improved safety at school for children.

Online analytical processing   An interactive computer-based system that allows a user to reframe multidimensional data gathered from various sources and stored in a warehouse; allows data to be organized into many different representations.

Personnel administration   Alternative designation for human resources administration.

Relational database   A database that permits the sharing of information from multiple files, which can be linked or related.

Risk management   The strategies, policies, processes, and procedures necessary for implementing a health and safety program for a school district that includes safety and security audits, training and education, monitoring, and crisis event management.

Superintendent of schools   The chief executive officer of the board of education and administrative leader of a school district.

Synchronous   Refers to the experience of interacting with another person through technology in *real time*. Thus, a retiree may be communicating through email with a staff member in a school district's benefits office during normal working hours.

Transcendental leadership A leadership theory that is predicated on the premise that a person acts from the totality of who he or she is as a human being. The theory requires administrators to reflect on the fact that their decisions are prompted by more than just the immediate circumstances and have an effect that goes beyond the present situation.

TQM An approach to administration based on the philosophy of W. Edwards Deming that views all employees as stakeholders and empowers them to make strategic decisions about how to meet the goals and objectives of an organization.

Workflow The technological capability to initiate multiple transaction through a single data entry.

Chapter 2: Human Resources Planning

Acquired Immune Deficiency Syndrome (AIDS) A viral infectious disease; those who contract it are protected under Section 504 of the Rehabilitation Act of 1973. Fear of contagion by itself does not permit federal agencies and federally assisted employers to discriminate against employees infected with the AIDS virus.

Affirmative action This refers to detailed and results-oriented programs whose objective is compliance with the equal employment clauses found in most civil rights legislation.

Age Discrimination in Employment Act of 1967 A federal law, as amended, that promotes the employment of workers between the ages of forty and seventy based on ability rather than age. It makes it illegal to discriminate against older workers in all areas of employment.

Americans with Disabilities Act of 1990 (ADA) The most comprehensive legislation ever passed protecting the rights of individuals with disabilities. This legislation extends the Rehabilitation Act of 1973 in that it pertains to the private sector and to local and state governmental agencies that receive no federal monies. Both the United States Department of Justice and the Equal Employment Opportunity Commission have been given jurisdiction for the enforcement of ADA.

Civil Rights Act of 1964 Title VII of this federal law, as amended, provides that a person cannot be denied a job or fair treatment on a job because of race, color, religion, sex, or national origin.

Civil Rights Act of 1991 A federal law that extends compensatory and punitive damages and jury trials to employees who have been discriminated against because of race, national origin, sex, disability, or religion.

Enrollment prediction A estimate of the number of students who will attend specific schools at specific grade levels over a five- to ten-year period of time. The cohort-survival method is commonly used in many school districts.

Equal Employment Opportunity Commission (EEOC) Established by Title VII of the Civil Rights Act of 1964 and strengthened by the passage of the Equal Employment Opportunity Act of 1972, this agency investigates charges of discrimination, attempts conciliation, and can litigate cases.

Equal Pay Act of 1963 A federal law that requires employers to pay males and females the same salary or wage for equal work.

Executive orders In the federal government, the presidential orders that have the force of law. They have been issued by several presidents to address issues of employment discrimination.

Family and Medical Leave Act of 1993   A federal law, the fundamental purpose of which is to provide eligible employees with the right to take twelve weeks of unpaid leave per year because of personal or family health reasons and for first-year parenting purposes.

Hostile environment sexual harassment   Occurs when unwelcome sexual conduct interferes with an employee's job performance.

Human resources forecasting   Estimating future human resources needs, usually established through expert estimates, historical comparison, task analysis, correlation, and modeling.

Human resources inventories   A human resources profile of the employees of a school district that includes age, job title, education and/or training, placement, sex, special skills, and certification.

Human resources planning   The process whereby a school district ensures that it has the right number of people, with the right skills, in the right place, and at the right time in order to effectively carry out the goals and objectives of the district.

Pregnancy Disability Amendment   An amendment to Title VII of the Civil Rights Act of 1964 that makes it illegal to discriminate against pregnant women in all employment-related situations including hiring, promoting, assigning, the granting of medical benefits, and receiving seniority credit.

Quid pro quo **sexual harassment**   Occurs when personnel decisions are made because of an employee's submission to an employer's or supervisor's sexual advances.

Reduction in Force (RIF)   A process required when decreasing student enrollments produce a surplus of teachers in a given school district. The reduction can be humanely carried out through attrition, early retirement incentive programs, enhancing curricular programs, and helping employees acquire new skills or find other positions.

Rehabilitation Act of 1973   Title V of the Rehabilitation Act contains five sections, four of which relate to affirmative action for people with disabilities and one which deals with voluntary actions, remedial actions, and evaluation criteria for compliance with the law.

Sexual harassment   In 1980 EEOC declared sexual harassment to be a violation of Title VII of the Civil Rights Act of 1964. There are two types of sexual harassment: *Quid pro quo* and hostile environment harassment.

Social justice   The concept that people have certain rights and responsibilities simply because they are members of a given society.

The Omnibus Transportation Employee Testing Act of 1991   The provisions of this federal law allow certain employers to conduct preemployment, postaccident, random, reasonable suspicion, and return-to-duty alcohol and controlled substances testing on persons in safety-sensitive jobs.

Title IX   Title IX of the Education Amendments of 1972 prohibits discrimination against women in educational programs and activities, including employment, when an educational agency receives federal financial assistance.

TRICARE   The Department of Defense's health insurance plan for military personnel and their families (formerly CHAMPUS, the Civilian Health and Medical Program of the Uniformed Services). When employees are called up for active military service, they are immediately covered by this military health care system. Their dependents may be covered by TRICARE under certain conditions, including length of mobilization.

Vietnam Era Veterans Readjustment Assistance Act of 1974   The purpose of this federal law is affirmative action for veterans with disabilities, especially those who served in the Vietnam War.

Chapter 3: Recruitment

Advertisement The techniques used to communicate position vacancies; also important verification of a school district's efforts to promote affirmative action and equal employment opportunity.

Alternative certification programs College and university programs designed for people with bachelor's degrees that give them the opportunity to become licensed as teachers in a relatively short period of time. These programs have been designed in many states where there is a shortage of teachers.

Employment agency Private companies that help clients search for employment opportunities and charge either the client or the hiring school district a fee for this service.

Online recruitment Use of the Internet by school districts to post job vacancies, provide information about the districts, provide information about a given job, and indicate how to apply for positions.

Recruitment Process used to ensure that a school district has qualified candidates for positions which become vacant because of retirements, resignations, terminations, and enrollment growth.

Recruitment brochure Specialized type of advertisement commonly used to recruit principals and superintendents that provides extensive information about the school district, the position, the community, and the application process.

Theories of occupational choice Set of theories concerning the interaction between a person's psychological makeup, his or her vocational and occupational choices, the availability of appropriate jobs, and the culture of various communities.

U.S. Training and Employment Service Federal government agency that supervises state employment agencies which provide services to people who are without employment, including the management of unemployment benefits and job searches.

Chapter 4: Selection

Assessment center Places where candidates for jobs can be observed as they work through a series of simulations—usually taking the form of case studies and decision-making exercises—dealing with administrative problems.

Criminal-background investigation Process used by school districts to check both the references and credentials, and the records of law-enforcement agencies to identify candidates who might have been convicted of a criminal act.

Employment test Intelligence, aptitude, ability, and interest tests constitute the usual battery of tests that are used in the selection process for certain types of jobs.

Immigration Reform and Control Act of 1996 Federal law that makes it unlawful to knowingly hire an unauthorized alien, to continue the employment of one who becomes an unauthorized alien, or to hire any individual without first verifying his or her employability and identity.

Job analysis Process of gathering information about a given job that centers on that job's parameters; how tasks are carried out; skills, education, and training requirements; physical and environmental conditions that affect it; and its relationship to other jobs.

Job description   Formal job designation that includes the job title, duties, authority and responsibility, and specific qualifications.

Job vacancy announcement   Based on the job description; provides potential candidates with sufficient information to decide whether to apply for a position.

National Association of State Directors of Teacher Education and Certification (NASDTEC)   A professional organization that promotes the role and function of state certification officials and maintains the Teacher Identification Clearinghouse.

Online application   The use of the Internet by school districts to receive applications and resumés via email and to post job vacancies on a school district's web page. Through the intranet, an administrator can check the status of an applicant in relation to the selection process or can search the human resources database to find a candidate whose profile fits a certain job description.

Open-ended interview   Type of interview that encourages the candidate to talk freely and at length about the topics introduced by the interviewer(s).

Organizational change   An organizational learning theory that is implemented in school districts under two rubrics. First, all stakeholders are identified with the organization; second, an organization must be focused on a vision that gives it direction.

Selection criteria   Those ideal characteristics that if possessed by a person to a minimal degree would ensure successful performance of a given job.

Selection interview   Structured conversation with direction and format between one or more interviewers and a candidate for a job in order to generate information about the person being interviewed; to learn about the candidate's opinions, beliefs, and attitudes; and to experience the candidate as a person.

Selection process   Process designed to hire people who will be successful on the job; includes developing a job description, establishing selection criteria, advertising the job vacancy, interviewing candidates, checking reference and credentials, making the job offer, and notifying unsuccessful candidates.

Teacher Identification Clearinghouse   National database of all teachers who have been denied certification and whose certification has been revoked or suspended for moral reasons.

Chapter 5: Placement and Induction

Induction   Process designed to acquaint both newly employed and newly assigned employees with their job positions, the community, and their colleagues. With newly employed individuals an orientation to the school district is most beneficial.

Mentoring   Practice of pairing newly employed teachers, staff members, and administrators with experienced colleagues to provide support and encouragement.

Personal adjustment   The aspect of an induction program which focuses on helping a new employee establish professional relationships with colleagues and others with whom he or she is required to interact. It also refers to helping the employee acquire a sense of job satisfaction.

Placement   Job assignment of an employee based on the best judgment of the superintendent of schools or a designee in relation to the school district's programming, staff balancing, and the welfare of the students.

Chapter 6: Staff Development

Apprenticeship training   Oldest form of training whereby a person understudies a master worker for a given period of time or until the trainee acquires the necessary skills.

Conditions of learning   In order to facilitate learning, which is a change in human capability, the instructor must utilize stimulus, response, reinforcement, and motivation techniques.

Education   Process of helping an individual understand and interpret knowledge through the development of reasoning processes that allow him or her to analyze the relationship between variables.

Off-the-job training   Refers to various kinds of training techniques such as lectures, seminars, workshops, case studies, programmed instruction, and simulations.

On-the-job training   Refers to training in which employees are placed in the actual work situation in order for them to learn by doing but are monitored by a supervisor.

Professional learning community   A school or school district that has four focuses: on learning rather than teaching, on collaboration, on viewing all members of the community as learners, and on self accountability.

Program design   Process of matching needs with available resources through an effective delivery method.

Staff development   Because of knowledge expansion and advances in technology, every employee is in need of acquiring new information, understanding, and skills in order to meet the goals and objectives of a school district. The staff development dimension consists of conducting needs assessments, establishing staff development goals and objectives, designing programs, implementing delivery plans, and evaluating the programs.

Teacher centers   Places where teachers determine their own staff development needs and, on their own initiative, implement staff development programs.

Training   Process of learning a sequence of programmed behaviors that can be broken down and analyzed in order to determine the best way to perform certain tasks. Training is most effective in learning routine tasks.

Chapter 7: Performance Evaluation

Drug-Free Workplace Act of 1989   Federal law that gives employers the choice of rehabilitating or dismissing employees working in federal grant programs who are convicted of drug abuse offenses in the workplace.

Due process   Procedures enacted to safeguard the rights of an employee, including the right to a fair and impartial hearing on allegations of noncompliance with the policies, goals, objectives, rules, and regulations of a school district.

Employment termination   Cessation of a person's employment for cause based upon documentation that can stand up against legal scrutiny.

Evaluation instrument   Formal document used by supervisors in evaluating the performance of personnel in relation to behavior traits and/or goals and objectives.

Evaluation process   In human resources administration from a central-office perspective, refers to the development of policies, procedures, methods, and instruments used in evaluating the performance of personnel with emphasis on legal and due process considerations.

Interstate New Teacher Assessment and Support Consortium (INTASC)   A national consortium that developed standards considered to be best practice for the licensure of teachers in many states.

Progress discipline   Corrective action taken by a supervisor when an employee does not meet socially acceptable standards or comply with the rules and regulations of a school district. The severity of such corrective measures depends on the type of behavior exhibited by the employee and the number of incidences.

Results evaluation   Method of evaluating the performance of an employee based upon objectives that were developed by the employee and agreed to by his or her supervisor.

Trials evaluation   Method of evaluating the performance of an employee against a predetermined set of performance indicators.

Chapter 8: Compensation

Administrative Service Organization (ASO)   Refers to a third party administrator under contract to a school district and responsible for monitoring and processing claims when a school district is self-insured.

Career ladder   Advancement to a higher level of recognition and financial rewards because of attaining a higher level of professional proficiency.

Catastrophic case management   When an employee, his or her spouse, or his or her dependent suffers a catastrophic illness and a case manager assists the patient and his or her physician to access the best treatment at the lowest cost.

Consolidated Omnibus Budget Reconciliation Act of 1986 (COBRA)   Federal law that permits an employee, employee's spouse, and dependents to continue health care coverage through the school district's group insurance programs under certain conditions when the employee is no longer employed by the district.

Compensation packaging   The distribution of an individual employee's compensation into a certain amount of salary and into certain fringe benefits based on his or her expressed desire and needs.

Copayment   Amount of money an employee pays for medical services in addition to that paid by the school district's medical plan; usually, a significantly smaller amount than the district's portion.

Deductibles   Amount of money, usually within a calendar year, that an employee must pay for medical and hospital services before a school district's insurance programs begin to pay the remaining cost of the services.

Direct compensation   That part of a compensation program that comprises salary, overtime pay, holiday pay, and merit pay.

Expectancy model   Model for compensating employees by which they can readily understand that when they act in the best interest of the school district, they are acting in their own best interests.

Extrinsic compensation   Usually divided into direct and indirect compensation.

Fringe benefits   Benefits available to all employees resulting from a direct fiscal expenditure; usually classified as insurance programs, paid time away from work, and services.

Garnishment   Legal summons to deduct a certain amount of money from an employee's salary for remission to a court in order to satisfy a creditor.

Health Insurance Portability and Accountability Act of 1996   A federal law guaranteeing certain health insurance coverage to employees, their spouses, and their dependents, even if they have preexisting medical conditions.

Health Maintenance Organization (HMO)   In this approach to health care management, health insurance and the delivery of health care are combined. Physicians receive a salary for providing services or, through a contract, the physicians receive a fixed per-patient payment regardless of the number of visits.

Indemnity health care plan   Traditional health care insurance plan that allows the employee, employee's spouse, and dependents to choose any physician and hospital in order to receive services.

Independent Practice Association (IPA)   Groups or networks of physicians in which physicians remain independent while contracting with HMOs.

Indirect compensation   That part of a compensation program which includes protection programs, pay for time away from work, and services.

Insurance company ratings   Nationally recognized independent rating companies like A.M. Best of Oldwick, Duff & Phelps of Chicago, Moody's of New York, and Standard & Poor's of New York rate insurance companies according to their performance and financial solvency.

Intrinsic compensation   Satisfaction that accompanies the successful performance of job responsibilities through participation in the policy-making process, job discretion, responsibility, and opportunities for staff development.

Managed health care   Approach to coordinating services around the patient and thereby producing a more efficient health care delivery system which also will be more cost-effective.

Mandatory fringe benefits   Benefits which are required by law and constitute a direct cost to a school district. All states require districts to contribute to employee retirement, unemployment, and workers' compensation programs.

Medical Savings Accounts (MSA)   Established by the Health Insurance Portability and Accountability Act, this program is an attempt to manage the rising cost of health care. Under certain conditions employers can place the savings that are realized through establishing high medical deductibles into an employee savings account which can be supplemented by employee contributions in order to pay minor health care expenses.

Merit pay   Financial compensation in addition to a person's salary as a reward for above average job performance.

Negotiated agreements   A practice that is used by school districts that have difficulty in recruiting and hiring highly qualified administrators and teachers. Such districts are designing compensation packages that are tailored made to meet the employment demands of desirable candidates.

Out-of-network   If an employee, spouse, or dependent accesses the services of a physician or hospital that is not under contract to an HMO or a PPO network, the health care plan pays a smaller portion of the costs that result from receiving the services.

Point of Service (POS)   An HMO plan that permits a member to access health care services outside the HMO. However, the HMO plan usually imposes a high deductible for such services and will pay a much smaller portion of the cost after the deductible is reached.

Preferred Provider Organization (PPO)   Individual health care professionals, hospitals, health care organizations, or groups of health care organizations that provide services to employees, their spouses, or dependents at a discount.

Primary care physician   Health care professional who acts as a gatekeeper, making the referrals that are required by the managed care plan for the patient to receive health care services.

Salary and wage administration   The management of direct compensation, which includes compensation research and development, payroll management, position control, and salary determination.

Salary schedule   Method of calculating an individual teacher's salary based on either an incremental or an index schedule that credits seniority, number of graduate course hours, and academic degrees.

Service   Component of indirect compensation that provides a benefit to employees, such as a wellness program, tuition reimbursement, employee assistance program, and paid attendance at workshops or conventions.

Small Business Job Protection Act of 1996   Commonly referred to as the "Minimum Wage Law" because it increased the take-home wages of employees.

Social Security   The U.S. government's attempt to care for and protect the aged by ensuring them a minimum standard of living through a monthly allotment of money resulting from a trust fund that is transferred from one generation to the next.

Third party health care   A company hired by a school district to manage its health care program, including cost analysis, cost projection, case management, catastrophic case management, utilization review, and claims management.

Unemployment compensation   State laws that provide benefits to individuals who are without a job, if they comply with certain regulations.

Voluntary fringe benefits   Indirect compensation programs provided to employees by a board of education, usually in the form of insurance programs, time away from work, and services.

Workers' compensation   State programs that provide benefits to an individual injured or disabled because of a job-related activity.

Chapter 9: Collective Negotiations

Agency shop   Situation in a school district in which certain employees are not members of the union that is the bargaining agent for the bargaining unit to which they belong and, thus, are required to pay a fee to the union.

Arbitration   An impasse procedure by which a board of education and an employees' union agree to be bound by the decision of a third party in the bargaining process or in a grievance.

Bargaining power   The favorable balance of influence to compel the other party's agreement with a proposal or entire proposal package because of the consequences accompanying disagreement.

Bargaining process   At-the-table engagement of representatives from the board of education and an employees' union concerning salary, fringe benefits, and working conditions.

Bargaining unit   Those employees who are organized into a category by reason of the fact that they have a community of interest in order for them to be represented in collective negotiations.

Bargaining unit determination   Process of determining which employees have a community of interest so they can be organized into a category for the purposes of collective negotiations. Size of the group and effective administration are additional considerations.

Certification of bargaining agent   Designation by an authorized state agency or the board of education that a certain organization or union is representing a bargaining unit as its exclusive bargaining agent.

Collaborative bargaining   The entire process of negotiations that includes recognition and bargaining unit determination, the bargaining process, impasse procedures, and master agreement administration.

Community of interest   Designation that a certain group of employees share common skills, functions, levels of education, and working conditions.

Court injunction   Order from a court of jurisdiction to perform or to cease performance of an activity. A court order requiring a group of striking employees to return to work is an example of an injunction.

Dues checkoff   Deduction of membership dues from an employee's paycheck remitted to the union or organization.

Employee organization   Organization or union that represents employees in the collective negotiations process concerning salary, fringe benefits, and working conditions.

Exclusive representation   Designation that refers to an organization or union that is the exclusive representative of a bargaining unit. Such designation is usually given by a state agency or the board of education after a recognition procedure has been carried out.

Fact finding   An impasse procedure under which testimony from interested parties is taken, and information is gathered and analyzed, to formulate a recommendation for resolving a grievance or an impasse in the bargaining process.

Fair share fee   Usually the equivalent of dues proportioned to cover the service that is rendered by a union or organization in the collective negotiations process. This fee is paid by nonorganization or nonunion members because they are benefitting from the representation.

Federal Mediation and Conciliation Service (FMCS)   An independent agency of the federal government created by Congress in 1974 for the purpose of promoting labor–management peace. The agency is staffed by professional mediators.

Grievance procedures   Process for resolving an allegation by an employee or an employee organization or union that a school district or an administrator of the district misapplied, misinterpreted, or violated a provision of a master agreement.

Impasse   Formal designation by the representatives of the board of education and the representatives of the employees that agreement cannot be reached on an issue or issues in the at-the-table bargaining process. Initiates predetermined impasse procedures.

Labor–management relations committee   Committee composed of administrators and employees from a school district who meet on a regular basis in order to resolve concerns, problems, and issues related to working conditions.

Management rights   Those responsibilities that are endemic and necessary to the administration of a school district.

Master agreement   Provisions arising out of the collective negotiations process that have been approved by both the board of education and the employees and have been put into writing. The provisions set forth in the master agreement have the force of board policy.

Mediation   An impasse procedure whereby a third party meets together or separately with the representatives of the board of education and the employees in order to help them resolve an issue arising during collective negotiations or from a grievance. Mediation is always a voluntary measure.

National Labor Relations Board (NLRB)   Federal agency created by Congress in 1935 through enactment of the National Labor Relations Act, that has jurisdiction to conduct union representation elections and to apply this act against unfair labor practices in the private sector.

Recognition   Acceptance by the board of education of an organization or union as the authorized representative of certain employees for the purpose of collective negotiations.

Representation election   Recognition procedure that identifies an employee organization or union as the exclusive representative of a defined bargaining unit. The organization or union receiving a majority of the votes is the exclusive representative.

Scope of negotiations   The subject matter of collective negotiations, usually consisting of salary, fringe benefits, and working conditions. The scope is commonly a bargained issue.

Union   Organized employee group whose representatives meet with the representatives of the board of education for the purpose of collectively negotiating salaries, fringe benefits, and working conditions.

Union shop   Agreement between the board of education and a union whereby an employee is required to become a member of a bargain unit as a condition of employment and to remain a member during the term of the bargained agreement.

Win–win bargaining   Approach to collective negotiations having the goal of producing a nonadversarial climate that will allow both sides to form consensus on issues related to salary, fringe benefits, and working conditions.

Work stoppage   Commonly referred to as a strike; occurs when employees of a school district refuse to perform their responsibilities as a protest against the actions of the board of education, usually in relation to the collective negotiations process.

Chapter 10: Legal, Ethical, and Policy Issues in the Administration of Human Resources

Civil law   Law that is concerned with protecting the rights that exist between individuals, between an individual and a corporate entity, or between two corporate entities. Most of the litigation that arises out of human resources management concerns civil law.

Common law   Also called "case law" because it is derived from court decisions rather than from legislative acts. Past court decisions are considered to be binding on subsequent cases if the material facts are similar, which is the doctrine of precedent.

Constitutions   Bodies of precepts that provide the framework within which government carries out its duties. The federal and state constitutions contain provisions that secure the personal, property, and political rights of citizens, which is a concern in developing human resources processes and procedures.

Contract   An agreement between a school district and an employee that consists of an offer and acceptance, a competent person, consideration, legal subject matter, and proper form.

Criminal law   Concerned with protecting the rights of society and thus, local, state, and federal governments representing the people are responsible for prosecuting wrongs committed against society by individuals or corporate entities.

Errors and omissions liability insurance   Insurance that pays for the defense of an employee and actual damages arising out of a civil lawsuit.

Ethics   Human conduct norms that provide a guide for administrators in the practice of human resources management.

Lawsuit   A petition filed with an appropriate court of jurisdiction setting forth a cause of action.

Libel   Defamation committed through communicating false information in writing that brings hatred or ridicule on a person and produces some type of harm to him or her.

Policy   Guidelines setting forth the authority and general means of attaining the goals and objectives of a school district or a division, department, or other administrative component of a district.

Reasonable person concept   Criterion in liability litigation against which the actions of the defendant will be compared. The reasonable person is someone who possesses average intelligence; normal perception and memory; and the same level of skills, knowledge, experience, and physical characteristics as the defendant.

Role of attorney   An attorney's expertise centers around his or her ability to analyze the material facts in a case, research the statutes and precedents of other court cases, and set forth the position of the plaintiff or defendant in a reasonable manner.

Slander   Defamation committed through communicating false information by word of mouth that brings hatred or ridicule on a person and produces some type of harm to him or her.

Tort   A civil wrong, other than a breach of contract, committed against a person or a person's property. Libel and slander are types of torts committed against a person.

U.S. judicial system   A mixed system that utilizes principles of both civil and common law.

Index